The Beginning of
American Aid to
Southeast Asia

The Beginning of American Aid to Southeast Asia

The Griffin Mission of 1950

Edited with introductory chapters
by
Samuel P. Hayes
Foreign Policy Association

Heath Lexington Books
D.C. Heath and Company
Lexington, Massachusetts
Toronto   London

To A. M.

Table of Contents

List of Tables

Preface

This is an account of an economic aid mission with a frankly political purpose. Although not unprecedented, it is only in recent years that this instrument of diplomacy has really come into vogue.

In January, 1950, Secretary of State Dean Acheson announced a revised and updated American policy towards Asia, following an intensive review within the Truman Administration sparked by the Communist defeat of Chiang Kai-shek's forces on the Chinese mainland and the vigorous Republican charges of Democratic "neglect" of Asia. As one element in implementing this new approach, a United States Economic Survey Mission to Southeast Asia was rather hastily thrown together and dispatched to the area. Its task was to discuss needs for economic and technical aid and to recommend aid programs designed to demonstrate the genuine interest of the United States in the people of Southeast Asia and to help the governments there strengthen their economies and build popular support.

Chosen to head the Mission was Mr. R. Allen Griffin, a California publisher, a Republican, and a friend of Senator William F. Knowland, who was one of the strongest critics of the Administration's policies and performance in Asia. Mr. Griffin had also been, in 1948-9, deputy chief of the China Mission of the Economic Cooperation Administration. Mr. Griffin was accompanied by three continuing professional staff, who were supplemented in each country by three to five experts who joined the Mission temporarily.

The Mission set out at the end of February, visited MacArthur's headquarters in Tokyo briefly, and then spent from ten days to two weeks each in Indochina, Singapore and Malaya, Burma, Thailand and Indonesia. From each country it cabled home a recommended aid program for the following fifteen months. Totaling some $66 million, these recommendations formed the basis of aid programs promptly undertaken (except in Singapore and Malaya) by the Economic Cooperation Administration.

Within about a year, nearly $50,000,000 had been "obligated" (procurement authorizations issued, etc.) for this program; and more than $10,000,000 of supplies and services had arrived in these countries. More important than the actual amount of arrivals, in the official view, was the political impact resulting in these countries from the publicity given to the original agreements to undertake the aid programs and the announcements of the various projects approved.

The Mission's detailed reports on each country are reproduced here. They include analyses of the political, economic and financial situation, special problems, detailed aid recommendations and justifications for these. Resident members of United States diplomatic missions as well as Mission members contributed to these reports. The writing of some sections and the rewriting and editing of all fell to the author of the present account, who was deputy chief of the Mission.

These reports were classified "Confidential" until they were declassified in late 1967. Copies of the original reports are now available from the Historical Office of the Department of State by paying to have photo-copies made. The texts reproduced here are exactly the same as the originals, except for the elimination of certain duplications, the addition of a few footnotes, and occasional corrections or word changes to clarify meaning.

In 1969, individuals who had been officials in the other governments of Southeast Asia at the time were shown the reports and the accompanying chapters and were invited to prepare their own accounts of the Mission's visits to their countries. Accounts were prepared by M. Léon Pignon, then French High Commissioner in Indochina; by M. Dinh Quang Chieu, then an official of the Vietnamese government; and by U Hla Maung, then Secretary, Ministry of Finance and Revenue, Government of Burma. Each of these accounts is included here following the appropriate Mission report—that is, the first two following Report 1, and the third following Report 3. They balance somewhat the "American view" presented by the Mission and the author.

The author wishes to express his appreciation to Mr. R. Allen Griffin, chief of the United States Economic Survey Mission to Southeast Asia, for his leadership and continued interest; to Mr. William McAfee, a colleague on the Mission, for his help in facilitating this edited version of the Mission's reports; to the Historical Office of the Department of State, for making available files relating to the Mission; and to the Center for Cultural and Technical Interchange between East and West (The East-West Center) for providing the research grant and the facilities that made it possible to put these materials into shape for publication.

The Beginning of American Aid to Southeast Asia

I. An Overview

1

Establishment and Operations of the Griffin Mission

As 1950 began, United States relations with Asia were a shambles. On mainland China, the Communist defeat of America's war-time ally, the Nationalist Chinese government, was complete, and that government's successful retreat to Formosa was small comfort. President Truman announced on January 5 that the United States would "not provide military aid or advice to Chinese forces on Formosa," but domestic political forces would soon veto that decision, reflecting deep divisions among Americans in their attitudes towards China, divisions that would endure for decades. In February, the Chinese Communists concluded with the Soviet Union a military alliance directed against Japan and the United States. In Korea, the North was lost behind the "bamboo curtain" and the South was in economic distress and under the shaky political control of crusty old Syngman Rhee. The new nations of India and Pakistan desperately needed heavy economic aid, but the United States—already involved in a massive aid program in Europe—was not interested in a second Marshall Plan, for Asia. Burma, racked by internal dissension, was suspicious of all foreign powers, including the United States. And this suspicion proved well-founded when the CIA was later discovered aiding the remnants of Nationalist Chinese forces still roaming the Burma-China border areas. Malaya was torn by a Communist-led insurrection that required substantial British forces to contain; and Malaya, as a British protectorate, had little relations with the United States in any event. The Philippines, for decades the United States's boasted protégé, was suffering rampant inflation, governmental corruption and general mismanagement, and was consequently most ineffective in battling its Communist-led Hukbalahap guerrillas. In Indochina the United States had vacillated, making noises of sympathy for "self-determination" but putting its dollars behind the French, mainly through the generous Marshall Plan aid that, in addition to helping France rehabilitate its economy, enabled it to carry the burden of Indochinese government deficits while mounting a large military effort against the Viet Minh. The United States was helping the French hold on in Indochina, and the nationalists saw this clearly.

Japan, Thailand, and Indonesia brightened the picture somewhat. In Japan, land reform, trust-busting, and democratization under General Douglas MacArthur were building the foundation for the astounding burst of economic and political development that would soon regain for Japan a position as a major world power. In Thailand, the government's uncertainty about where to cast its lot was being resolved by Peking Radio's sharp attacks on Prime Minister Pibun; soon thereafter the government concluded that American power and values were

3

more attractive and impressive than those of either the Russian or the Chinese Communists, and came down solidly on the American side, recognizing Bao Dai in February. And in Indonesia, the United States had finally, after much temporizing, midwifed an independence that seemed to offer hope for genuine economic and political progress.

But, on balance, the American position in Asia was weak—weak in terms of military power (outside Japan, the Ryukyus, and the Philippines), in terms of political support, in terms of influence. Part of this weakness derived, moreover, from the United States being so closely identified with the European powers that had for so long dominated the area.[a] Nationalism was now the dominant political force in Asia, and the ardent nationalists in power or seeking power throughout Asia did not generally view the United States as a friend on whom they could count.

At the same time, Republicans in the Congress—led by Senator William F. Knowland and Representative Walter H. Judd—were berating the Democratic administration of President Harry S. Truman for having "lost" China and for devoting primary attention to resisting Communist expansionism in Europe while giving far too little attention to the dangers of Communist expansionism in Asia. Senator Joseph McCarthy was collecting "evidence" and was soon (February 11) to make his first charge that the State Department harbored many Communists.

The Administration's recognition that it must build closer relations with the surging nationalist forces in Asia, its anxiety lest the Communists seize control of these nationalist movements and bring about "other Chinas," and its sensitivity to Republic criticisms of ineptness and neglect, together brought action. In mid-1949, Secretary of State Dean Acheson had initiated a broad review and re-evaluation of United States policy towards China, with the assistance of a panel of consultants headed by Ambassador-at-large Philip C. Jessup. In early January, 1950, he discussed his conclusions with Senate and House committees, and then, on January 12, he appeared before the National Press Club and spoke on "Crisis in China—An Examination of United States Policy." In this speech, he analyzed the threat of Communist penetration and subversion in Asia and the measures that the United States was prepared to take, in certain conditions, to counter this threat.

First, with respect to military attack, he stated that, if an attack was made on nations outside the United States defense perimeter, "the initial reliance must be on the people attacked to resist it and then upon the commitments of the entire civilized world under the Charter of the United Nations."

---

[a]The United States was extremely concerned about Europe, of course. The Communist coup in Czechoslovakia had recently snuffed out democracy there. The Iron Curtain had fallen between Eastern and Western Europe, as Churchill so eloquently proclaimed in Fulton, Missouri. The State Department feared that any serious weakening of France and the Netherlands (as by loss of their colonies) could lead to upheaval and Communist successes at home. Only later did it become clear that "police actions" and military involvement in Asia weakened the Netherlands and France much more than a generous grant of independence to their colonies would have done.

But he felt that it was "a mistake" to become obsessed with military considerations when viewing Pacific and Far Eastern problems. He considered that very important problems arose "out of the susceptibility of many areas, and many countries in the Pacific area, to subversion and penetration. That cannot be stopped by military means."

This susceptibility, he said, came from inexperienced and poorly equipped governments, from serious economic problems, from great social upheaval complicated by Japanese occupation and Soviet propaganda. The United States was prepared to help ameliorate these conditions.

Acheson also stated, however, that especially in the Southern Pacific, where new nations existed, the United States could only help effectively where its assistance was "the missing component" in a situation that might otherwise be solved. The United States could not furnish all the components needed to solve the questions. It could not furnish determination, it could not furnish the will, and it could not furnish the loyalty of a people to its government. But if these components were present, then (and not always then) there was a good chance for American help to be effective.

In Southeast Asia, Acheson stated, "we are organizing the machinery through which we can make effective help possible." He said that the United States was prepared to help with techniques of administration, of agriculture and industry, and that we would do this where we were wanted and "where we have the missing component which, if put into the rest of the picture, will spell success."

This policy statement reflected two important elements of United States foreign policy. One was the containment of communism. The other was concern for the economic development of underdeveloped areas—an element given salience in the "Point Four" program proposed in President Truman's inaugural address of January 20, 1949. The elements were interrelated, of course. But many in the government stressed that the American commitment to aid development abroad would exist and would be maintained whether or not Communist expansionism continued to be an active threat.

The first step in implementing the new United States policy towards Asia was to send Ambassador Jessup on a tour of Asia, to review our Asian policies with our ambassadors, to express our support for Asian governments—mostly new ones—and to explain the new Administration's intentions with respect to the "Point Four" Program. Although the detailed plans for the Point Four Program had been sent to the Congress seven months earlier, there were still many in Asia (and elsewhere) who expected it to involve large grants of capital rather than simply technical assistance backed up by expanded flows of private investment and public lending through established channels. The State Department considered it essential to rebut this.[b]

---

[b]Although the State Department officers and other bureaucrats consistently attempted to deflate the idea of massive aid, it is interesting that President Truman told Prime Minister Clement Atlee, of the United Kingdom, in December 1950 that he "had been thinking about some kind of Marshall Plan for Southeast Asia." (Harry S. Truman, *Memoirs*, Volume II, *Years of Trial and Hope*, p. 401. Garden City, Doubleday, 1956.) Of course, this comment was made some six months after the outbreak of the Korean War had intensified American anxiety about Communist expanionism in Asia.

The second step was to send two economic aid missions to Asia, the Griffin Mission (to Southeast Asia) in the spring and the Bell Mission (to the Philippines) in the fall. A military aid mission (the Melby Mission) was planned before the Korean War broke out in June, and was sent shortly thereafter.

The third step was to get congressional approval of funds to implement the recommendations for economic and technical aid that the Griffin and Bell Missions were expected to make.

This particular account concerns the Griffin Mission, its objectives, operations, and recommendations. Before elaborating on these topics, however, it is important to indicate what funds were expected to be available to finance the programs of aid to be recommended.

Sources of Funds for Aid to Southeast Asia

Since early 1949, when President Truman had proposed the Point Four Program, an interdepartmental task force had been working on the detailed legislation, program, and budget to implement his proposal. The program was sent to Congress on June 24, 1949, with a presidential message. Hearings had begun before congressional committees in the early fall of 1949, but Congress had not yet (in early 1950) taken legislative action. Still, the Administration had high hopes that the program would be enacted, and there was tremendous interest around the world in what this new program of aid might mean for the less industrialized countries. In public comment on the Griffin Mission, the State Department and the United States diplomatic missions abroad emphasized the Point Four character of the Mission's interests and spoke of the possibility of Point Four funds becoming available (after congressional approval) to fund its recommendations.

Mention was also made, from time to time, of the availability of loan funds from the Export-Import Bank for long-term, bankable development projects. The Bank extended a $100 million credit to Indonesia in February, 1950; and additional credits in Southeast Asia were considered possible.

A third possible source of funding existed in a special provision that Congress had added to the Mutual Defense Assistance Act of 1949. Section 303 of that Act read in part:

In consideration of the concern of the United States in the present situation in China, there is hereby authorized to be appropriated to the President . . . the sum of $75,000,000, which may be expended to accomplish in that general area the policies and purposes declared in this Act . . . .

The phrase "in that general area" was explained at some length in the Senate-House Conference report on this legislation, as follows:

. . . the term "general area" may require explanation. This phrase is somewhat more restrictive than would be the phrase "the Far East." At the same time it is not intended that the phrase be interpreted as confining use of the funds to China proper. In view of the difficulty of defining in advance all of the contingencies which may develop in the unfolding situation in China, the members of the committee of conference attempted no greater precision than is contained in the term "general area." This term, however, is to be interpreted in relation to the phrase: "the concern of the United States in the present situation in China." The area envisaged is the area which bears immediately upon that situation, and which is borne upon immediately by that situation. It is consonant with the unusual flexibility in the authority given to the President by this provision that China and the other countries in that general area should be only generally designated in order that the scope of assistance might be largely determined through experience as needs arise.[c]

Thus, there already existed legal authority and funds for United States grant assistance "in the general area of China." Although authorized by military aid legislation, these particular funds were available for "any form of assistance which will conduce to realizing the 'policies and purposes' declared in the legislation," were available for confidential use by the President, and were not limited to the fiscal year 1950. Thus they could legally be used for economic or technical aid. While the Mission did not consider them its principal source of financing for the aid it would recommend, it did consider them to be potentially available for certain types of aid.

The main source of immediate funding that the Mission had in mind was the unobligated funds appropriated in 1948 for the China Aid Program. At that time, $275 million had been appropriated for economic aid in China, to be administered by the Economic Cooperation Administration during the year ending April 2, 1949. Because of the progressively deteriorating situation of the Nationalist Chinese government and the contracting opportunities for effective use of economic assistance in China, these funds had not been utilized as rapidly as originally envisioned, and the period during which they might be used had been extended to June 30, 1950. At the time of the Mission's departure for Asia, about $100 million of these funds remained unobligated. Secretary Acheson had earlier suggested to the Senate Foreign Relations Committee that use of these funds be extended through June 30, 1951 and that part of them be authorized for use in the "general area of China," paralleling the concept expressed in Section 303 of the Mutual Defense Assistance Act. On March 7, responding to senatorial suggestions that whatever economic aid was proposed for the Far East should be covered by a single piece of legislation, Acheson repeated his suggestion. The senators responded favorably, although legislation authorizing this action was not enacted until June 5, 1950.[1]

It was clear that the Mission could reasonably count on part of the unused China economic aid funds. (Part would also be needed in Formosa.) Moreover, it might identify projects suitable for financing by the Export-Import Bank. Some of the confidential military assistance fund of $75 million might also be drawn upon. And, if the Point Four Program was approved by Congress, as most expected it would be, then some of the funds appropriated for that program would become available.[d]

Consequently, while no instructions had been given to the Mission about the dimensions of the total aid it might recommend, it did have in mind a range of from $50 million to $100 million as a possible "order of magnitude." (This was still a long way from the "Marshall Plan for Asia" that some were advocating; and the State Department made it very clear that it had nothing like the latter in mind.)

Personnel of the Mission

The Griffin Mission was a small one. Heading it was Mr. R. Allen Griffin, editor

---

[d]*The New York Times*, Feb. 24, 1950, page 1:7 and ff. In addition, Charles Wolf, Jr., who was in ECA at the time, states that the Mission was aware of "the possibility of securing a transfer, for use in the 'general area of China,' of some of the ERP funds to be appropriated for fiscal year 1951." (Charles Wolf, Jr., *Foreign Aid: Theory and Practice in Southern Asia* [Princeton, N.J.: Princeton Univ. Press, 1960], p. 84 footnote.) While such a transfer was in fact authorized by legislation enacted in January, 1951, (see p. 48) and funds were so transferred soon thereafter, the author was not aware of this possibility when he served on the Mission and does not recall its having been discussed until the fall of 1950, when it became apparent that additional funds would also be needed for economic aid to the Philippines. Examination of the classified files of the State Department uncovered no memoranda or other documents to support Wolf's contention.

In fact, two months after the return of the Mission, Assistant Secretary of State Dean Rusk (then in charge of the Bureau of Far Eastern Affairs) approved a staff memorandum of June 30, 1950, which expressed concern about the availability of funds for these programs and recommended that additional financing be requested from Congress in the form of a deficiency appropriation. The memo made no mention of the possible transfer of ERP funds. The first mention of such a transfer appears in a State Department memo of November 7, 1950, stating that "Informal advice has been received from ECA that they are seriously considering a proposal whereby a transferability clause will be added to their legislation."

What Wolf may well have done is confuse the transferability idea, which came up in the fall of 1950, with the abortive attempt of State and ECA in early February to get supplementary funds from Congress under ERP for aid to Indochina. Immediately after the United States recognized Vietnam and the Kingdoms of Cambodia and Laos, on February 7, 1950, State and ECA obtained a legal opinion that aid could be extended to Indochina under the existing ECA bilateral agreement with France (thus avoiding the time-consuming process of negotiating new agreements), and proposed to the Budget Bureau that $15 million be sought from Congress as a supplemental appropriation ($5 million for 1949-50, and $10 million for 1950-51). This proposal was informally discussed with the French in Paris, but they objected to the smallness of the amount and to the idea of aid under the ECA bilateral agreement with France. They hoped that the United States would undertake a much bigger aid program for Southeast Asia, authorized and appropriated under separate legislation, along the lines of the earlier Greek-Turkish aid program. Obviously, this would not only provide much more money for the whole area (including Indochina); it would also involve a more dramatic and deeper commitment to the area, which the French of course hoped for (since the United States by then had endorsed the Bao Dai "solution"). The Budget Bureau turned down the State-ECA proposal, however, and Griffin and the Mission knew this before their departure from the United States.

and publisher of the *Monterey Peninsula Herald*, a resident of Pebble Beach, California, a Republican, and a friend of Senator Knowland. He had been a colonel in the Army and, in 1948-49, had served as deputy chief of the China Mission of the Economic Cooperation Administration. The President's commission gave him the personal rank of minister. The deputy chief (the author) was an economist with experience in teaching, business and government. He had served the Lend-Lease Administration (and successor agencies) in North Africa and Europe, had been for two years special assistant to Dr. Willard L. Thorp, Assistant Secretary of State for Economic Affairs, and in the latter capacity had served for the previous year as the executive secretary of the interdepartmental Advisory Committee on Technical Assistance which developed the detailed program, legislation, and budget for the Point Four Program. An officer from the Bureau of Far Eastern Affairs of the State Department, Mr. William McAfee; an engineer from J. G. White Engineering Company, Mr. Henry Tarring, Jr.; and two secretaries, Miss Eleanor Koontz and Miss Mary D. Randolph, of the Department of State, completed the permanent membership of the Mission. Mrs. Griffin also accompanied the Mission throughout, in a private capacity, and proved most helpful in reporting on the attitudes and interests of private groups.

The size and composition of the Mission varied from country to country, as its permanent core was augmented by representatives of various government departments and agencies. Although recruited hurriedly from Washington, from foreign posts, and from other missions already traveling abroad, the professional quality of these temporary members was high. Their identities and the countries where they worked with the Mission are listed below:

Dr. Robert Blum, Chief, Dependent Overseas Territories Division, Economic Cooperation Administration Mission to France (Indochina)

Mr. Edward T. Dickinson, Jr., Director, Program Coordination Division, Economic Cooperation Administration (Indochina, Singapore-Malaya)

Col. Russell G. Duff, Chief, Far Eastern Branch, Intelligence Division, Department of the Army (Indochina, Singapore-Malaya, Burma)

Mr. Paul V. Kepner, Extension Service, Department of Agriculture (Thailand)

Dr. Howard M. Kline, Chief, Technical Missions Branch, Office of International Health Relations, U.S. Public Health Service (Burma, Thailand, Indonesia)

Mr. Alexander Lipsman, Treasury Department Attaché, U.S. Embassy, Manila (Indochina, Indonesia)

Dr. Ross E. Moore, Chief, Technical Collaboration Branch, Office of Foreign Agricultural Relations, Department of Agriculture (Burma, Thailand, Indonesia)

Dr. Albert H. Moseman, Agricultural Research Administration, Department of Agriculture (Thailand)

Dr. Raymond T. Moyer, Chief of Mission, Economic Cooperation Administration Mission to China, and Commissioner, Joint Commission on Rural Reconstruction, China (Indochina)

Mr. Walter Walkinshaw, Point IV Program Operations Staff, Department of State (Burma, Thailand)

Capt. Frederick B. Warder, Head, Far Eastern, Western, and Pacific Branch, Division of International Affairs, Office of the Chief of Naval Operations, Department of the Navy

The country-by-country variation in the composition of the Mission is summarized in Table 1-1.

Table 1-1

Composition of Mission, by Country Visited

	Number of Representatives (excluding secretaries) in:				
Department or Agency	Indochina	Malaya and Singapore	Burma	Thailand	Indonesia
Chief of Mission	1	1	1	1	1
Dept. of State	2	2	3	3	2
Economic Cooperation Administration	4[a]	1	1[a]	1[a]	1[a]
Dept. of the Army	1	1	1	–	–
Dept. of the Navy	1	1	1	–	–
Dept. of Agriculture	–	–	1	3	1
Treasury Dept.	1	–	–	–	1
Public Health Service	–	–	1	1	1
Total (excl. Secretaries)	10	6	9	9	7

[a]During four of the five country visits, Mr. Tarring, whose engineering firm held a contract for assistance in China, financed by ECA, participated as a regular member of the Mission. Although appointed temporarily as a consultant to the Department of State, his role was more that of an ECA representative, and he is accordingly so listed here.

An interesting sidelight on the workings of bureaucracy is afforded by the military representation during part of the Mission's work. During the Washington planning for the Mission, the negotiations with Mr. Griffin, the first cables to the embassies, and the recruitment of the Mission, there had been no indication of any intention to attach military personnel to it. The whole idea had been to make this a strictly economic mission, partly to avoid giving offense to the neutralist nations it was to visit, partly to keep its discussions focused (and to avoid public relations difficulties) in all countries, and partly because there was already in prospect a military aid mission to the same area, to be sent out later. Thus it was a surprise to all members, and especially to the chief of mission, when at its departure in San Francisco it was suddenly joined by an Army colonel and a Navy captain, properly accredited as members of the Mission. In Indochina (where the Viet Minh were battling the French and Bao Dai's government, and where there was already a functioning United States military advisory group) and in Singapore and Malaya (where a separate Communist-led revolt was in full swing) there were important military factors to consider in planning possible aid projects, and the military representatives participated in discussing these. In Burma, it became apparent that their contribution was over-balanced by the suspicions their presence engendered in the host government, and Mr. Griffin cabled the Department of State requesting termination of their participation in the Mission. They left the Mission in the middle of its visit to Burma.

Although prolonged discussion had been going on within the Administration about the problem of United States relations with Asia and what might be done about them, the Mission was rather rapidly thrown together. It was first recommended in a January 19, 1950, memorandum to Secretary of State Acheson from Assistant Secretary (for the Far East) W. Walton Butterworth. Within a month most members had been recruited. Those in the United States traveled separately to San Francisco. Some who arrived a day early took part in an extended briefing on Southeast Asia at Stanford University arranged for them by Dr. Eugene Staley. The high quality of the briefing is indicated by listing the other briefers as well:

Dr. Merrill K. Bennett, Executive Director, Food Research Institute and Professor of Economic Geography
Dr. Claude A. Buss, Professor of History
Dr. Harold H. Fisher, Chairman, Hoover Institute and Library
Dr. Ernest R. Hilgard, Professor of Psychology and Education
Dr. George H. Kerr, Lecturer in History
Dr. Felix M. Keesing, Professor of Anthropology; U.S. Representative on South Pacific Commission
Dr. C. Easton Rothwell, Vice Chairman, Hoover Institute and Library
Dr. Anthony E. Sokol, Professor of Asiatic and Slavic Studies
Dr. Vernon D. Wickizer, Economist and Professor, Food Research Institute
Dr. Mary Clabaugh Wright, Curator, Chinese Collections, Hoover Institute and Library.

Mr. Griffin's commission from the President had not yet arrived, however, as the departure time approached. According to some reports, it had been delayed by the President's lack of enthusiasm about the selection of a Republican for this assignment. Only some last minute negotiations with Washington made Mr. Griffin willing to proceed on February 27, as planned. His designation as minister was signed by the President the next day, and Mr. Griffin took the oath of office in Tokyo on March 3, at the General Headquarters of the Supreme Commander for the Allied Powers (SCAP).

Just prior to the Mission's arrival in Tokyo, a special United States mission had arrived there after touring South and Southeast Asia to ascertain the prospects of increasing the volume of trade between the countries in that area and Japan. This mission had been headed by Mr. Robert W. West, Deputy to the Undersecretary of the Army, and Mr. Stanley Andrews, director of the Office of Foreign Agricultural Relations, Department of Agriculture. Mr. West, along with Major General W.F. Marquat (Chief, Economic and Scientific Section, SCAP), and several engineering and technical experts at SCAP, met with the Griffin Mission on March 3 to discuss the possible use in Southeast Asia of Japanese technicians in cottage industries, farming, and fishing; and the possible sale of Japanese agricultural tools, fishing boats, and capital goods for development projects in Southeast Asia. At SCAP, Mr. Griffin also met with General of the Army Douglas MacArthur, and the Mission was briefed on Southeast Asia, and particularly on Vietnam, by Major General Charles A. Willoughby, Chief of Intelligence. (General Willoughby told the Mission that Vietnam was the strategic key to Southeast Asia, and that the principal problem in Vietnam was the reestablishment of law and order. He showed little appreciation of the economic, political, and psychological factors involved.)

The Mission's Task

The State Department's thinking about the Mission's task is well stated in an internal memorandum of February 7, 1950, prepared by Dr. Merrill C. Gay. It read in part as follows:

To recapitulate, the Mission should seek to find justified projects suitable for financing under Section 303 which will have immediate political significance, lay the groundwork for an anticipated Point Four program of unknown dimensions, give special attention to placing it in its proper perspective in order to avoid later disillusionment, counsel local authorities on how best to prepare for it, and brief our own representatives on the Department's current Point Four thinking. Finally, the Mission should investigate to the fullest extent possible in the time available the possible regional aspects and prospects of the Point Four program including the need for a regional organization, having in mind particularly the possibilities of developing an expanded trade between the countries visited and Japan.

In letters sent in March to the United States ambassadors in Burma and Indonesia, Mr. Griffin stated that the Mission's recommendations would in general fall into two categories:

1. Emergency or urgent economic needs that the host government desired we

support as fully as possible within our means. These would be projects affecting considerable numbers of people and having a desirable political effect, strengthening existing governments and indicating sincere American interest in the welfare of the peoples of Southeast Asia. (Funds for this category would come from Section 303 of the Mutual Defense Assistance Act and possibly from China Aid funds if Congress authorized their use for the "general area" of China.)

2. Point Four possibilities—here also emphasizing proposals that might result in aid being applied in the most critical areas and with the earliest effective results. (Funds were anticipated under the proposed Point Four legislation, not yet enacted by Congress.)

As is apparent from the above, the Mission was going to have to ride two somewhat incompatible horses. The first was a fire horse, bringing "trouble-shooting" aid to help combat immediate Communist pressures. In a sense, this was the ECA horse. ECA was already identified with the Cold War in many minds. And ECA was also identified mainly with its European participants, toward whom many Southeast Asians were suspicious and antagonistic. Especially in Burma and Indonesia, this horse would have to tread lightly.

The second was a plow horse, concerned with long run development of a people-centered, relatively non-political character that appealed greatly to neutralists and allies alike. (It wasn't really non-political; but its political objectives were long-run, not tied to current international maneuvering.)

It was expected that desirable short-term political results would be produced both by the performance of the fire horse, and by United States willingness to bring the two horses to help the countries of Southeast Asia. But the Mission recognized, as Mrs. Wright had forewarned it during the briefing at Stanford University, that the plow horse—long-run development of production—might result in more unrest rather than less, as it brought uncomfortable changes and gave people the small surplus of time and energy, together with some education, that made possible increased participation in political (and revolutionary) activity.

It was going to be difficult to ride the fire horse and the plow horse together; and even to ride them separately in the different countries visited by the Mission. For example, in an airgram from Rangoon on May 31, 1950, some two months after the Mission had left there, the American ambassador recommended that publicity about the proposed aid program in Burma stress its positive Point Four aspects, not its anti-Communist aspects, because Burma wanted "neutrality" and not to be drawn into a "power struggle." For the same reason, he recommended that public statements not couple aid to Burma with aid to Indochina.

After the Mission had returned to Washington and thought about its public posture, it restated the objectives that it had had in mind in its visits in Southeast Asia. In the preface to each of its five country reports, it stated that its task was to study the needs of (Southeast Asia) for emergency economic and technical assistance which would—

1. Quickly strengthen and expand the economic life of the area and improve the conditions under which its people lived;
2. Strengthen national governments in the area by helping them rehabilitate and develop the productive resources of the area and by helping them provide improved services to their people; and
3. Demonstrate concretely the genuine interest of the United States in the welfare of the people of Southeast Asia.

No ceilings were established in advance on the amount that could be recommended for any one kind of assistance, or for total assistance to any country, or to the whole region. Proposals were judged in terms of (a) the immediacy and kind of effect likely to be obtained; and (b) limits on the amount and kind of assistance each country could promptly absorb.

Certain additional guide-lines were important in the Mission's thinking. First, since actual fighting was going on in Vietnam, Malaya, and Burma, and there was considerable insecurity also in Cambodia, Laos, and Indonesia, proposed projects were examined in terms of the security of the areas where they would be carried out and in terms of the direct or indirect military values they might have. For example, a Washington-hatched proposal to send field workers to a thousand villages was quickly determined to be impractical. On the other hand, it was judged that physical rehabilitation of newly "pacified" areas in North Vietnam would provide direct support to the military effort there; and assistance in telecommunications, airports, and road and bridge repair would similarly have military as well as economic value.

In line with this thinking, emphasis was given to "quick impact" projects, where the people would quickly perceive that their government (and the United States) was interested in their welfare and already doing something about it. To the extent that this built popular support of regimes in power, this too would have military as well as political value. In general, the Mission's recommendations for immediate aid stressed such short-term results rather than long-term development. But it also recommended assistance for some long-term rehabilitation and development, on the principle that visible evidence of any new undertakings would have important morale effects.

Second, while United States assistance might strengthen government administrative services or educational or health institutions, or might break economic bottlenecks and thus release local energies, in fact the principal reliance for governmental and economic strengthening in all these countries would have to be on themselves. As in the European Recovery Program, external aid might play a key role in getting things started or moving again, but it could only be marginal.

Third, an important and related objective of the Mission was to place the Point Four program "in its proper perspective in order to avoid later disillusionment," as the Gay memorandum had put it. This had been a principal objective also of the earlier Jessup mission; and it was urged on the Mission by the political adviser at SCAP during its short stay in Tokyo. There were still those in Asia who looked for a great "Marshall Plan for Asia."[e] The Mission knew that there wouldn't be that kind of money for aid in Southeast Asia, and it doubted that that kind of money could in any event be wisely and productively used there. The "absorptive capacity" of the area was believed to be severely limited.

Fourth, the Mission was concerned mainly with the kinds of projects for which grant assistance was appropriate. Bankable projects might be considered by the Export-Import Bank or the International Bank for Reconstruction and Development. There was at that time a strong aversion in the Executive Branch and in Congress to any concept of "fuzzy" or "soft" loans. Grant assistance and bankable loans were the approved forms of aid. And the Mission was primarily concerned with the former.

The Mission's recommendations were to be for aid to be supplied during the roughly fifteen months ending June 30, 1951. Therefore, because the visit of the Mission to each country was so brief, and because its members could hardly be specialists in all of the kinds of projects presented, many proposed projects—and particularly the longer-range ones—were simply "put on ice" for later consideration by the continuing economic missions or staffs that it recommended be set up in each country, or for study by the Export-Import Bank (as in Indonesia).

The Mission's Schedule and Method of Operation

The Mission left San Francisco on February 27, 1950, and arrived in Tokyo on March 2. After four days there, it flew directly to Saigon, arriving there on March 6. Its schedule thereafter was as follows:

Saigon (with visits to Dalat, Hanoi, and Phnom Penh)	March 6-16
Singapore, Kuala Lumpur	March 16-23
Rangoon	March 23-April 4
Bangkok	April 4-12
Djakarta (with visits to Bogor and Bandung)	April 12-22

The Mission returned via Paris, where it reviewed its findings with Ambassador Averell Harriman, at that time the special representative in Europe of the Economic Cooperation Administration. Mr. Griffin returned to Washington by air. The rest of the Mission returned by ship to the United States, reaching Washington in early May.

As soon as the dispatch of a survey mission had been determined upon in Washington, communications had been sent by the Department of State to the

---

[e]See footnote b, on p. 5.

United States diplomatic establishments in the countries to be visited, indicating the scope of the Mission's responsibilities and the information which it would need to obtain. On the basis of these communications the diplomatic establishments informed the governments of the countries to be visited about the purpose of the Mission. On arrival in a country, the Mission was briefed by appropriate members of the United States post there, and at all important conferences members of the Mission were accompanied by representatives of the post most familiar with the problems under consideration. At the most important conferences the ambassador or the officer-in-charge accompanied Mr. Griffin. For a majority of the conferences the Mission divided itself into working groups on agriculture, industry, public health, education, and finance. To each group the post attached an officer familiar with the needs of the country in that field.

Members of the Mission discussed with representatives of the various countries the formulation of an aid program, including projects which these countries wished to undertake and in which United States assistance could be of significance. In view of the advance notice which the governments had received, they had in general, prior to the arrival of the Mission, prepared certain requests. (These are listed in the appendixes to the separate country reports.) On receipt of these requests, members of the Mission and of the diplomatic post analyzed them, and at subsequent meetings with representatives of the host government they reviewed the requests and made suggestions as to the feasibility of the projects proposed. Thus the final recommendations to Washington were based on requests from the various governments as to their needs, and on an evaluation of these requests by United States personnel assigned abroad and by the members of the Mission.

In addition to its official contacts, the Mission met where possible with American reporters, business men, missionaries, and other private American citizens; and with groups of private citizens of the countries visited. These meetings were most useful in broadening the range of views and information obtained.

In order to dramatize its recommendations and stimulate prompt action in Washington, the Mission sent a long (20 to 30 page) cable from each country it visited, detailing its findings, recommendations, and rationale. Each cable concluded with the phrase "Ambassador concurs."

The Mission's Reports

As summarized in the next chapter, the Mission analyzed the political, economic, and financial situation in each country, and recommended the initiation of a United States economic and technical aid program in each. Its recommendations totalled $66,093,000 for the five areas visited, for the period of roughly fifteen months from the date of the visit through the 1950-51 fiscal year. It also recommended the setting up of a continuing economic and technical aid mission or staff in each country (except Malaya and Singapore), and it recommended expanded facilities for the United States Information Service to permit publicizing United States aid activities and the expansion of English language teaching and other USIS activities.

The reports of the Mission were a team product. In general, the United States diplomatic mission provided analyses of the general political, economic, and financial situation and problems in each country.[f] The members of the survey mission wrote up the program recommendations with supporting justification. Because the specialized competencies of the different diplomatic missions varied a good deal, however, and because the composition of the survey mission differed from country to country, there were exceptions to this general division of labor. Also, because of the illness of the industry adviser on the Mission, detailed recommendations and justifications for aid to power, transportation, roads, telecommunications, and industry in Burma, Thailand, and Indonesia were never completed in a form comparable to the other sections of the printed reports. The various materials prepared were edited and rewritten by the author, and organized according to a standard outline into the five reports of the Mission. Much of this work was done during the homeward journey from Europe, aboard ship. In Washington, the manuscript was duplicated, and was given limited circulation to the interested government departments and agencies.

---

[f]The political analysis and appraisal provided by each diplomatic mission reflected the recent, intensive exchange of views at the meeting of United States ambassadors and ministers in Asia, held at Bangkok in early February, 1950. This meeting had been co-chaired by Ambassador Jessup and Assistant Secretary Butterworth.

2

The Significance of Southeast Asia and the Mission's Response

Basic to the Mission's whole activity and approach was an appreciation of the political, economic, and military significance of Southeast Asia. This underlay the sending of the Mission—as well as the sending of the subsequent Bell Mission (to the Philippines) and the Melby Mission, which was concerned with military aid for the area. This appreciation of the significance of the area was prominent in the discussions with the American diplomatic missions in each country visited.

Political Interests of the United States

The United States had important political interests in Southeast Asia. It had suffered a major set-back when the Communists defeated the Nationalist Chinese forces on the Chinese mainland, and it knew about the Communist decision in 1948, at meetings in Calcutta, to enter into a revolutionary phase of activity in Southeast Asia. The Communists had tried a revolution in Indonesia (in 1948), only to be suppressed. Communists were deeply involved in revolutions underway in Burma, Malaya, the Philippines, and Vietnam. The United States sought friends and allies among these new nations to join it in opposing the further expansion of communism. But it recognized that many intellectual, political, and military leaders were inclined to "sit on the fence" until it was clearer whether or not communism was the "wave of the future."

The United States wanted more than simply the containment of communism in Southeast Asia. It wanted free intercourse with the nations there—economic, cultural, and political. It wanted influence. And it realized that only by identifying itself more closely than in the past with the dynamic forces of nationalism could it hope to attain free intercourse and significant influence.

After the collapse of the Nationalist Government on the Chinese mainland, the United States felt that it had to move quickly to expand its diplomatic listening posts in Southeast Asia and to demonstrate its own interest in the area. It was eager to relate its interests to theirs, to bolster the existing governments, and to help them prevent the growth of Communist influence—and perhaps eventual Communist take-overs—in their own countries.

And these governments needed bolstering. They were politically fragile, in financial distress, and militarily weak. The United States feared that some might succumb to growing internal Communist pressures reinforced by the example of Communist success in China.

As the colonial powers had withdrawn from—or had been pushed out of—the

19

area, the character of the governments that succeeded them had come very much into question. The peoples in the area had had little recent experience in self-government (except for Thailand). They felt little identification with their national governments, and they had carried on little discussion and reached little consensus about the kind of government they should have. There were few experienced political leaders and public administrators, and little in the way of political structures to relate government to the people. Governments were ineffective and weak in most of these countries.

There were positive elements too, of course. In each country there were small elites who had studied, argued, and even fought about these matters for years, sometimes in jail, sometimes in guerrilla camps, sometimes in exile—and sometimes in the universities, the press, and in parliamentary bodies. But those who had well-developed political ideas were relatively few and highly fragmented. Socialists, liberal democrats, religious leaders, hereditary rulers, traditionalists, military leaders, Communists of various persuasions, put forward their proposals and tried to win enough power to put them into effect. It was in this heterogeneous and fluid situation that the United States saw danger and promise.

The interest of the United States was felt to be in stable, self-reliant, responsible and responsive governments, democratic, representative, committed to peace and to serving their people. The United States officially supported self-determination, but it was also keenly aware of the continuing economic, political and military interests of the United Kingdom, France, and the Netherlands, and it was reluctant to be a party to efforts to reduce their influence. It was happiest with governments friendly to the United States (and subsequently sought them as allies in the Southeast Asia Treaty Organization— SEATO) and with governments which shared its perception of the threat of aggressive communism and were opposed to it. It recognized, however, that some of these governments wanted to avoid international entanglements while they rebuilt and developed their own nations. Moreover, some of them were not strong enough to be neutral, much less to be anti-Communist, without outside help. Thus, the United States was willing—though somewhat slow—to help even those governments that chose a neutral path.

The United States had another kind of political interest in the area. Jolted by the "loss" of China, it had faced up slowly and reluctantly to the realization that new forces were stirring in Asia, that colonialism would no longer work, and that, if it wished to have some influence in the area, it would have to lean to the side of the nationalists, if not fully throwing in its lot with them. The latter it was of course reluctant to do, since it felt its interests lay even more importantly in Europe, where it was engaged in a massive economic recovery program (the Marshall Plan), in substantial military aid and in the development of a new military alliance (NATO) designed to block any military push by the USSR westward into Europe. Thus, the United States had an interest in developing new modes of cooperation between the former colonial peoples and their former colonial masters. It wanted to avoid their turning to isolation from the West, their continuing economic stagnation, and the possibility that they might join forces with the Communist bloc. Instead, it advocated partnership with the West, whether bilateral, through regional organizations, or through the United Nations. With this partnership could come the economic and technical resources necessary for economic development.

The United States hoped that it could help make the way of partnership a successful one. Thus, it accepted the new cooperative relationship between France and "The Associated States of Indochina" established in the March 8, 1949, Agreements. It backed the "Bao Dai Solution" in Vietnam. It supported the British role in Malaya and Singapore. And, having played a major role in the 1949 negotiations for Indonesian independence, it favored the continuation of a large role for the Dutch in the economic and financial life of Indonesia. In each case, it sought to maintain and promote a relationship that was seen as mutually beneficial. Success in these new relationships was viewed as providing a model that might be followed in other areas where independence had newly come or where (as in Africa) it might soon come.

In summary, the United States felt then, as it does today, that it had a political interest in the character of the governments that developed in the area, in their effectiveness in governing, and in their relationships with each other, with the former colonial powers, with the United States, with the rest of the non-Communist world, and with Communist countries.

Economic Interests of the United States

Prior to World War II, Southeast Asia had been a great producer and exporter of rice, tin, petroleum, coal, and various tropical agricultural and forestry products, such as rubber, copra, oil palm products, kapok, cinchona bark (for quinine), pepper, teak, agave, etc. The rice was important for the food-deficit countries in Asia, such as Japan, Ceylon, and India-Pakistan; the petroleum was widely used in Asia; and the coal, rubber, tin and other products provided important raw materials for the industrialized countries of the Northern Hemisphere. During World War II, moreover, some of these products were recognized as "strategic commodities" and, even after controls on their use were ended, they were stockpiled by the United States against the possibility of shortages in the event of some future conflict. Although the development of substitutes (e.g., synthetic rubber), of technological "stretch-out" (e.g., tin), and of alternative sources of supply were eventually to reduce Northern dependence on Southeast Asian production, in 1950 the continuing and increased availability of these commodities on open world markets constituted an important economic interest of the United States.

Beyond commodity availability alone was their importance in the great triangular pattern of international trade involving primarily the United States, Western Europe, and Southeast Asia. At a time when Western Europe was struggling to rehabilitate its industry and agriculture and to close the yawning "dollar gap" that Marshall Plan aid was temporarily bridging, Southeast Asia was very important to Europe as a source of raw materials that could be purchased for currencies other than dollars, as a market for its European industrial products, and as a big earner of the much-needed dollars that tended to flow from Asia to Europe either to purchase these industrial products or as profits, interest, repatriation of capital, or personal remittances. Moreover, France, the Netherlands, and the United Kingdom all had major investments in the area at the time, and their earnings on these investments were large. Although France and the Netherlands, at least, may have spent more trying to hold on to their overseas territories in Southeast Asia than they gained from their investments there, it is clear that—given these political decisions—the trade of Western Europe with, and its dollar earnings from, Southeast Asia resulted in the Marshall Plan costing the United States less, and perhaps terminating earlier, than would have been the case if this trade and these earnings had been denied the free world. So the United States had an important financial interest, as well as a commodity interest, in the economic recovery and progress of Southeast Asia and in open economic access thereto by the non-Communist nations of the world.

The United States had an additional, specific interest in the nations of the area as promising trade partners for Japan. Then still occupied by the United States, Japan required heavy American economic aid to rebuild its industry and rehabilitate its economy. If it could sell its services and capital goods in Southeast Asia, and if it could buy rice, coal and raw materials cheaply there, its dependence on American aid would be lessened.

This theme had been stressed to the Griffin Mission in Washington by the undersecretary of the army (Tracy S. Voorhees). It was reiterated when the Mission visited Tokyo and was briefed by Voorhees's deputy and by officers and civilian experts at SCAP. The refrain was, "Why not make each dollar do the work of two?" First, a dollar used to buy Japanese goods or services for Southeast Asia would help the latter area. Second, it would reduce the dollars needed to purchase United States commodities for Japan.

More general, and more long-run in nature, was the economic interest of the United States in the development of all the less industrialized countries, an interest underlying the Point Four program proposed by President Truman in his inaugural address on January 20, 1949. This program was based on political and humanitarian considerations too, but economic interest was an important factor. This interest derived from the recognition that prosperous neighbors are the most profitable neighbors; that international trade and investment grow as potential economic partners develop higher levels of production and consumption. The industrialized nations could make their own way to economic expansion (after rehabilitation from wartime destruction and disruption). But the less industrialized nations needed technical and capital assistance from external sources to achieve economic growth. The United States was willing to help, and to join with other industrialized nations in such help. Here, then, was the third element in the economic interest of the United States in Southeast Asia.

Military Interests of the United States

Finally, the United States had a military interest in the area, an interest shared with the United Kingdom, France, Australia, New Zealand, and, to a lesser extent, with the Netherlands and Portugal. Although Singapore was still an important naval base, the defeat of colonial forces by the Japanese in World War II, and the subsequent defeat of the Japanese, had left a great power vacuum in the whole arc of Asia, from South Korea around through Southeast and South Asia to Afghanistan. The substantial French forces in Indochina had their hands full battling the Viet Minh. The small British forces in Malaya were similarly occupied with the insurrection there. Only the United States had major military forces in being in the area, available to meet aggression should it appear. In the spring of 1950, it wasn't at all clear where or when aggression in Asia might take place. But, following the Communist success on the Chinese mainland, many feared that further Communist advances were imminent.

In Southeast Asia, there was much speculation that the Chinese Communists might undertake a military adventure southwards. In Indochina, the betting was that the Chinese would *not* invade Vietnam to help the Viet Minh defeat the French. The long early history of a thousand years of conflict with and subjugation by China, together with the recent looting by the Nationalist Chinese who occupied Vietnam in 1945, had left such strong feelings of antagonism that it was believed that another Chinese invasion might drive the nationalist members of the Viet Minh into the arms of the French and their Vietnamese allies, uniting them all against the invaders. But the Chinese interest in seeing the French defeated was recognized as great, and Chinese assistance—short of manpower—was already being given to the Viet Minh.

Much was made of the probable interest of the Chinese Communists in the great (and potentially much greater) exportable surpluses of rice available in Southern Vietnam, Thailand, and Burma; the tin and rubber of Malaya and Indonesia; and the petroleum of Indonesia and Burma. Whether these rich resources would be sought by a Chinese military invasion, or by agreements negotiated with friendly governments in the area, was a question. In either event, it was clear that the Chinese Communists would seek to reduce and eventually eliminate Western military power, political influence, and economic ties in the area, and to replace them by Chinese influence and economic involvement, if not military power.

Even if no overt military agression from Communist China was anticipated, however, Communist attempts to achieve these goals were already being made by subversion and indirect aggression. This was most obvious in Vietnam, Malaya, and the Philippines, where active insurrection was going on and where much of the revolutionary leadership was Communist. Communists were rebelling in Burma, too. And Indonesia had already had its Communist rebellion, put down by the Indonesians themselves at Madiun, in 1948. In Southeast Asia in early 1950, Thailand was the only nation which had experienced no significant Communist revolutionary activity.

Wherever conflict might break out in Asia, and whatever the source of the conflict, the military forces of the United States and its allies might be called into action. For rapid movement, they required ready access to the sea and air routes running through Southeast Asia. This highlights another aspect of the military, as well as the economic, significance of the area. The major air routes east and west (and south to Australia) ran through Singapore, Bangkok, Rangoon, and Djakarta. And the major sea routes between the Pacific and Indian Oceans ran through the Malacca Straits and, alternatively, the Sunda Straits. For military aircraft and naval vessels, as for commercial planes and ships, it was of great importance for the United States and other nations that these routes be kept open. This military and economic significance of the area's transportation routes was the final element of national interest considered by the Mission in its work.

Conditions Existing in Southeast Asia

Given the political, economic and military interests of the United States in Southeast Asia, what were the conditions there that called for action to serve these interests; and what kinds of action by the United States were feasible and promised results worth the effort? The Mission identified a number of temporary conditions for which short-run measures seemed suitable, and a number of more basic conditions needing long-run attention. For some of these, only action by the national government itself seemed appropriate. Others could be attacked with the help of the United States, but were outside the Mission's exclusive concern for economic and technical aid. And some seemed suitable for United States economic and technical assistance, in cooperative programs to be undertaken with national governments.

Insecurity

Of prime importance in the area, and hopefully short-run in duration, was the widespread civil disorder. This was partly simple banditry, but more often it was revolutionary in nature. Communists were in active rebellion everywhere but in Thailand and Indonesia. (They were active in the Philippines, too, but the Mission did not visit there.) In Indochina, another—and perhaps more important—revolutionary element was nationalism, expressed in a fierce desire to drive the French out. Religious and separatist rebellions were going on in Burma and Indonesia (supported in the latter area by remnants of Dutch and Dutch-trained military forces). In Northeast Thailand there were both nationalist Vietnamese refugees and disaffected Thais. In Northern Burma, refugee elements of Nationalist Chinese forces were making occasional forays across the border into China proper. And bandits, smugglers, and soldiers (and officers) living by their weapons showed up throughout the region.

This was obviously a very serious barrier to economic recovery and development, as it disrupted and blocked economic activity of many kinds in many areas, but the Mission could find few ways of helping overcome it directly. To some extent, the Mission took this situation into account in its program recommendations, as in recommending communications equipment for Malaya. And it was keenly aware that the heavy expenditures required of local governments for their campaigns to reestablish peace and order made budgeting for economic rehabilitation and development most difficult. But generally the Mission simply had to take this situation as a "given," something that the national governments would have to work on, but not suitable for much aid of the kind an economic and technical aid mission could provide.

Reduced Production

Throughout the area, production was much below prewar levels. The general civil disorder was partly responsible, as it not only blocked production in some areas and some industries but also prevented the movement of the primary commodities produced, as well as the movement of fertilizers, tools, spare parts, and the manufactured and imported consumer goods that provided the incentives for much agricultural production. Agricultural and health services were also greatly reduced. Severe undernourishment was rare, as most of the area was agricultural and normally produced food surpluses, and farmers traditionally provide for their own needs before marketing their crops. But the cities faced periodic food shortages (and hoarding and high prices). Exports were affected even more severely than actual production, and reduced foreign exchange earnings made for seriously adverse balances of payments and forced great reductions in imports. Because the governments normally obtained much of their revenue from charges imposed on exports and from tariffs on imports, their income was drastically reduced.

Inflation and Balance of Payments

Heavy government spending on military and police activity, coupled with lower government incomes, meant greatly unbalanced budgets in Indochina, Burma, and to some extent in Malaya and Indonesia. Inflationary pressures were building up in these nations, although they had been effectively contained in Thailand. With inflation came the familiar byproducts: hoarding, price and currency controls, import licensing, rationing, black markets, smuggling (which further reduced government revenues), flight of capital, greater opportunities for corruption in government services and controls, and so on. In general, the Mission did not attempt to work out large commodity aid programs to counter inflation or to correct adverse balances-of-payments. It viewed (too optimistically, to be sure) the inflation and its causes as temporary phenomena that could be cured in the fairly near future by monetary and fiscal measures combined with reestablishment of peace and order. It did not want to recommend large commodity aid that would take the pressure off the national governments to "put their own houses in order." Moreover, the United States was already deeply involved in a large commodity aid program in Europe through the Marshall Plan, and an additional massive aid program would have had rough sailing in Congress. The dimensions of aid that could be immediately supplied, without being subjected to the grinding of the congressional mill, were already known. Such aid would support enough rehabilitation and development projects to make a beginning and to demonstrate United States interest in the area. That would fulfill the principal purposes of the Mission.

Impact of Communist Success in China

Finally, a factor viewed as requiring urgent attention was the political and psychological impact of the recent Communist victory in mainland China. Those in the area who were committed Communists would certainly be much encouraged by this victory, and likely to press harder to exert influence in the governments, societies, and economies of the region. Those who were "independent" non-Communist groups or governments, or those who were anti-Communist, would be weakened in their influence and would feel pressure to "accommodate" to this great new power that had appeared on the near horizon.

A complicating factor in this situation was the presence in all countries of the area of large numbers of overseas Chinese, often dominating local trade and money lending. Most of these would presumably be pleased by the prospect of a reawakened, newly unified, potentially powerful China. And those among them (believed to be the great majority) who were not committed Communists still necessarily had to face the fact that their relatives, friends, and business interests on mainland China were now under Communist control. Thus their opposition to Chinese Communist activities in their own countries would be lessened; they might well be pressured into giving financial and other support to local Communist groups and to mainland Chinese organizations; and their support of non-Communist or anti-Communist organizations and governments in the countries of their residence would inevitably be weakened.

The effect of the Communist success on the Chinese mainland in encouraging and strengthening Communist elements throughout the area, at the same time discouraging and weakening neutralist and anti-Communist elements, was prominent in all the Mission's discussions. Recently oversimplified and often derided as the "domino theory," this appreciation of enhanced Communist appeal and threat played a real part in the Mission's thinking and recommendations. Both Vietnam and Malaya, where revolutionary activity was most intense and where it most clearly involved Communist leadership, were considered of special interest to the United States (and other nations of the non-Communist world) because a Communist victory in either was believed highly likely to heighten further the Communist pressures on other governments in the area.

Whether these other governments would bend before this pressure or would strengthen their resistance to it might well depend on the nature and credibility of United States offers to help. But power could not be ignored. And Chinese Communist power was growing at a time when Western power in the area seemed on the wane.

In addition to the problems considered relatively short-run in nature, and the urgent problem of countering the recent surge of Chinese Communist prestige and potential threat, the Mission identified a number of long-range problems generally characterizing the area. These related primarily to national unification and political development; the perpetuation of colonialism; social integration (especially the role of the overseas Chinese); and economic rehabilitation and development.

National Disunity and the Weakness of Governments

The withdrawal of the colonial powers from government, partial in some of these countries and practically complete in others, exposed the weaknesses that the colonial governments had produced—or had at the least permitted to endure. One weakness was that many individuals felt a primary loyalty to local and regional authorities, not to national governments. This was not significant in Thailand, and only of minor importance in Indonesia, where it had been the Dutch who had promoted the short-lived federal political system that overestimated the strength of regional loyalties. In Burma, however, the Karens and the backward populations of the Shan and Kachin states felt little attachment to the Burmese government. In Malaya, the local sultans were more important to most people than were the Federation authorities in Kuala Lumpur. And in Vietnam, the Tonkinese, Annamese, and Cochin Chinese had different traditions, histories, and loyalties. One of the first needs in most of these countries was to establish a strong sense of national identity, and to bring local governments, regional military units, and economic enterprises under the firm control of the central governments. The Mission saw its recommendations in education, agricultural and health services, transportation, telecommunications, and development planning as helping to meet this need. The better services the government could supply to its people, the stronger its authority; and the firmer its hand on the economy of the nation, the better known and the more respected it would be.

Continued Colonial Influence

Although colonial power had been much reduced during and after World War II, it was still important in the area. Its contributions had been many, in maintaining peace and order, establishing government services in public health, agriculture, and education, building and maintaining an excellent system of transportation, and developing important economic enterprises and the financial and commercial services necessary for a large international trade. While sympathetic to the demands of nationalism, the United States hoped that the positive benefits of colonial interest would not be lost to the area. Hence its willingness to try to help make the March 8 Agreements succeed in Vietnam, involving the collaboration of Vietnam, Cambodia, and Laos with France in the newly constructed "French Union." Hence also its reluctance to undertake any aid program that might have undercut British influence in Malaya and Singapore, as evidenced by the fact that the Mission's recommendation of modest aid for Malaya was not approved in Washington.

But the continuation of colonial interest and power, even at reduced levels, and even with the positive benefits it brought, was unacceptable to the ardent nationalists and therefore a source of friction and damage. This was most obvious in Vietnam, where many of the country's leaders refused to accept the March 8 Agreements. On the other side, the French officials, acting under the Agreements, sought to retain a preferred position for French advisers and culture. They raised difficulties about the United States providing technical assistance advisers. They also wanted all economic (and military) aid to be supplied through quadripartite bodies, on which they had a voice, rather than directly to the three separate local governments. And those French who continued as advisers to the local governments dragged their heels whenever matters of American economic or military aid were concerned. They even made difficulties when United Nations aid (for example, from UNICEF) was offered. In military "pacification" affairs, the French were in full control, and other activities had to be subordinated to those. And finally, French financial institutions and investment interests were extremely important. This perpetuation of a colonial relationship in the political, military, and economic realms was galling to many Vietnamese, both those on the government side and those with the Viet Minh, and was a major barrier to the effectiveness of the American economic and technical aid program.

Similar colonial influences were important in other countries in the region. In Malaya and Singapore, as in Brunei, North Borneo, and Sarawak, the British wielded comparable power but with a lighter hand and without provoking anything like the same nationalist reaction. While some Malays agitated for greater control over their affairs, the Communist-led (and predominantly Chinese) revolutionary activity in Malaya had little claim to being inspired by nationalism and never developed wide popular support. Still, British influence remained strong enough for the United States to hold off providing aid there.

As for Indonesia, there was for a brief time an almost fictional entity called the "Netherlands-Indonesian Union." It played no significant part in the affairs of the area. Colonial influences showed up in the early political structure of Indonesia, however, when the Dutch promoted the establishment of a number of rather autonomous states federated in the Republic of the United States of Indonesia (RUSI). Popular reaction against these Dutch-sponsored state governments, and against private Dutch military adventures (e.g., the Westerling

Affair), resulted in the separate parts being quickly incorporated into the unitary state of the Republic of Indonesia. However, elements in East Indonesia, with support from military units formerly controlled by the Dutch (including some Dutch officers), were still fighting a delaying action at the time of the Mission's visit to Indonesia. And the Dutch had refused to transfer sovereignty over Western New Guinea (called West Irian by the Indonesians), at the time of the granting of independence to Indonesia on December 27, 1949. A good many Dutchmen remained in the Indonesian government as technical advisers or on the faculties of the University of Indonesia. Unfortunately, they found it difficult to accept their new role, and some obstructed as much as they helped. On their part, many of the Indonesians were reacting to colonialism, as they saw it, when they looked suspiciously at Western private and governmental initiatives, and when they insisted on their own "independent foreign policy," which should be influenced by no other nation. Nevertheless, for some years the great financial, investment, and trading interests of the Dutch in Indonesia remained practically untouched. While there was little discussion of this during the Mission's visit (and many of the Indonesians then in official positions recognized the important role that the Dutch had played in building up the economy and could play in maintaining it), this situation did come to loom ever larger in the eyes of ardent nationalists, who were highly critical of the extent to which the Dutch had "milked the Indonesian cow" by means of their economic involvement there. Later on, of course, Dutch intransigeance with respect to the final disposition of West Irian was used by the Indonesians as a reason for expropriating most of the immense Dutch investments in the area.

Burma, which had become independent only in 1947, and Thailand, which had been independent for hundreds of years, were both relatively free of colonial influence. They had few foreign advisers, and relatively little foreign investment. In Burma, there remained a good deal of the British tradition in government and education. There was also great suspicion of Western intentions—a kind of negative vestige of colonialism. In Thailand, there was little evidence of Western colonial influence except, perhaps, for the government's willingness to give more attention to the possibility of danger from Communist China than they might in their hearts have thought was likely.

Thus, the perpetuation of colonial influence in Southeast Asia, whatever its actual and potential benefits, produced reactions that were generally harmful to economic development. Political agitation and overt revolution were direct results. And even where these were not present, the behavior of the "colonial types" often impeded rather than helped the changes and new projects that were essential for progress. The Mission saw this as a long-term problem, requiring new attitudes and new relationships. In private trade and investment, and in the provision of expert personnel in government and education, it hoped that accommodations on both sides would permit fully constructive relationships. All it could do directly was to offer the United States as an alternative source of advice, technical assistance, opportunity for technical training abroad, and modest amounts of economic assistance. By reducing dependence on the former sources of such assistance, it could encourage greater independence. And perhaps competition would improve the quality of such assistance from all sources.

Lack of Social Integration

The third general, long-term problem faced by the Mission was a lack of social integration in these countries. This was related to both the foregoing factors—being partly a result of colonial administration and partly a cause of weak national identity. In Vietnam, society was split along religious lines, with most of the Catholics in the North and mostly Buddhists (of various kinds) in the South; along ethnic and linguistic lines, with important minorities in the mountains—some of them very primitive; along political lines, with pro-French loyalists, anti-French nationalists, perhaps a majority "sitting on the fence," and with Communists and a number of powerful religious sects, like the Cao Dai, having political power and private armies; along racial lines, with a large minority of Chinese; and along economic lines, with the French planters, commercial class, and bureaucrats, rich Vietnamese landlords (especially in the South), and many poverty-stricken tenant farmers, plantation workers, and urban proletariat.

In Malaya, the Malays barely outnumbered the Chinese. Even then they were a minority of the total population, which included a good many Indians. Singapore was predominantly Chinese. Burma had Chinese too, but its more important minorities were ethnic-linguistic groups in the Shan and Kachin States, where they had a good deal of autonomy, and the Karens, who were not concentrated enough to have their own state, but who wanted one just the same. In Thailand and Indonesia, the principal minorities were Chinese, but Indonesia also had important Catholic groups, mostly in East Indonesia, and Hindus, on Bali. It also had a good many Eurasians, the offspring of Dutch and Indonesian parents, now unwelcome both in Indonesia and in Holland.

Throughout, the principal social integration problem had to do with the Chinese, often referred to as the "overseas Chinese." Their motherland still considered them her citizens, and a great many of them so considered themselves. Most had come—or their parents or grandparents had come—overseas to make their fortunes and then to return home to live out their old age. Only in Malaya and Thailand did they play an active role in political life. Most retained close ties with family, friends, and business interests in China, and their annual remittances home were large. Some had, however, transferred their allegiance to their country of residence. They planned to stay there, and sought citizenship when it was offered. But they weren't always welcome as citizens, and they had many personal rebuffs. For the overseas Chinese were able, energetic, with a keen sense for money and a willingness to work very long hours. They came to dominate the internal commerce and money lending of most of Southeast Asia. And their popularity suffered as a result. The people of other races who could not compete with them, and those who felt that the Chinese dealt with them too harshly, if not actually unfairly, developed a sense of grievance against them.

Moreover, many Chinese felt their own culture was superior, or at least preferable, to local cultures; and were extremely clannish, living close to each other and working and playing together. This didn't help their popularity, either. The consequence was that the Chinese minorities in these countries consituted a large, undigested mass, successful, with great economic influence, and unpopular.

Moreover, particularly after the Communist success on the Chinese mainland, and after the visible celebration of this event in many Chinese communities in Southeast Asia, the governments of these nations, and the neighbors of the Chinese themselves, began to suspect their loyalty. This exacerbated the already difficult relations between the Chinese minorities and the majority population groups in these countries.

While the Mission recognized this widespread problem, there was little it felt it could do about it, and little that the national governments asked it to do. It did recommend minor assistance in Singapore and Malaya, designed to help reduce the pro-Communist orientation of teaching in the Chinese language schools. But even this modest proposal was vetoed in Washington (on the grounds that the British had the primary responsibility for that area). The Mission's general position was that, by helping general economic rehabilitation and development, the situation of all elements in the population would be improved, and in this atmosphere of general progress and prosperity, problems of social integration would at least be a little easier to solve.

Economic Disruption and Stagnation

The long-range problem which the Mission was prepared to attack most directly, and which was important in all of these countries, was their need for economic rehabilitation and development. The destruction and disruption caused by the Japanese conquest and occupation of the area, by the Allied reconquest, and by the various revolutions for independence or other purposes that occurred in all of these countries but Thailand, left factories, mines, plantations, hospitals and schools run down or destroyed, bridges out, highways and railroads deteriorated, ports clogged and their equipment unusable, airports damaged. It left exhausted the stocks of petroleum products, spare parts, raw materials, building supplies, bicycles, farm tools, agricultural chemicals, medicines, and consumer goods necessary to keep the productive machine functioning efficiently and people working regularly. And, by isolating the area from its normal access to the scientific developments of the West, it produced a kind of technological stagnation. Production and distribution were reduced to levels far below those obtaining before World War II.

There was, in addition, a great and pervasive shortage of the skilled, experienced manpower needed in government, education, and industry. Partly because they had been colonized at an early stage of development, and the colonial masters had tended to monopolize the desirable jobs in government, industry, mining, and plantation agriculture; and partly perhaps because cultural factors posed a barrier to the development of indigenous entrepreneurs and public administrators, few nationals in Southeast Asia had developed as technicians and managers. During the war, the occupation, and the ensuing revolutions, many planters and entrepreneurs—mostly Europeans—had been killed or driven away. Many colonial government officials were now assigned elsewhere, or took early retirement. Other Europeans left voluntarily, not feeling comfortable with the new order of things, or not satisfied with the financial rewards. Perhaps the greatest failure of the colonial period had been in not attempting to develop skilled and enterprising leadership among the nationals of the area. This failure was now starkly exposed, as the European elites withdrew and essentially decapitated the government, industry, and education. The first task of the new governments was to find and train a whole new class of skilled leaders and managers, numbering tens of thousands. This task was especially difficult because the war and revolutions had interrupted the education of just those young nationals who might now be prime prospects for appointment. While their training was going on, the government needed the temporary services of foreign technical advisers. Yet they were suspicious of all foreign advisers, and the ones with whom they could work most readily, in terms of language and established work practices, were advisers from the countries of which they had formerly been colonies. For reasons mentioned above, this relationship was generally unsatisfactory.

Closely related to the skilled manpower problem was the technological backwardness of the area. Its own research had been seriously curtailed for nearly ten years. It had been cut off from (and rarely able to utilize even when not cut off) dramatic war-time technological developments (such as the use of DDT to control malarial mosquitoes). Moreover, each country had a long tradition of dependence on the intellectual and technological traditions of its metropole. Indonesians, for example, knew of American, British, and French science, in general, only through the Netherlands. In Indochina, the French attempted to perpetuate this kind of cultural monopoly through the March 8 Agreements. Burma and Malaya had British cultural and technological contacts but practically none with the United States. The long history of this round-about channeling of science and technology had produced a parochialism that itself accounted for at least part of the technological backwardness of the area.

Finally, the investment necessary to maintain and develop the plantations, mines, factories, irrigation works, transportation, and power had been severely curtailed since the start of World War II, and its flow had not been resumed at anything like normal levels because of the widespread insecurity and the general uncertainty about the policies of certain of the new governments. Both the Burmese and the Indonesian governments were strongly socialist in economic orientation, and their attitude toward new investment by foreigners was very much in question. The future of Indochina was too uncertain to attract private investment there. Failure to resume a substantial flow of capital into the private enterprises of the areas presaged even further declines in production in the future; and the governments themselves had little in the way of funds they could spare for investment in the roads, ports, railroads, power systems, irrigation works, and other public enterprises.

Thus, the great economic needs of the area were (1) to get production and distribution (and exports) back to normal levels, helping in this way to balance government budgets and to end inflation; (2) to find and train skilled manpower for leadership and management, as well as for teaching and the technical professions; (3) to gain access to the modern technology developed in all countries; and (4) to reinstate the flow of private and public capital from domestic and foreign sources into all kinds of investment uses, this of course necessitating the reestablishment of peace and order.

Attitudes of Southeast Asian Governments

These, then, were the problems the Mission found. How eager were the governments of Southeast Asia to take advantage of the willingness of the United States to help them attack some of these problems, by undertaking cooperative programs of economic and technical aid?

In general, there was ambivalence toward the United States. There was appreciation of the ideas and ideals of America's own revolt against colonialism. In Indonesia, for example, quotations from the American Declaration of Independence were daubed on many walls. There was appreciation of the American goals of equal opportunity, personal freedom, and individual dignity. There was appreciation of the American action in granting independence to the Philippines. Where important American private investment had taken place (primarily in Indonesia), there was appreciation of the fair treatment of workers, the substantial taxes paid, and the heavy contribution made to foreign exchange earnings. And there was respect for the American power that had helped defeat Nazi Germany and then had finally turned back the Japanese.

At the same time, there was suspicion of the long-run intentions of the United States. Did it simply wish to establish a favorable climate for American private investment? Did it wish to replace the French, the Dutch, and the British with its own economic colonialism (an idea zealously fostered by some of the Europeans still remaining)? Did it wish to line up allies on its side in the Cold War? Would the acceptance of economic aid, and especially of American technical advisers, interfere with the national governments' freedom to determine their own "independent" foreign policies, or their own particular combinations of socialism and free enterprise? One of the most widely stated desires of these countries was for more opportunity to learn English. Partly, this was a reaction against the blinders imposed by their colonial governments' emphasis on French and Dutch, and showed an appreciation of the usefulness of the English language in international life—cultural, technological, business, diplomatic. But partly it showed a keen interest in learning to communicate with—and getting to understand—the Americans. Understanding would be necessary whether America represented a threat or an opportunity.

The dominant political force in Southeast Asia at the time was nationalism.[1] Already stirring in the area before World War II, it had been greatly heightened by the spectacle of Japan's victory over the Western colonial powers and occupation of most of Southeast Asia. During the occupation, puppet governments had been established and led to believe that they would receive genuine independence after the war.

When the war ended, political and intellectual leaders, in and out of government, were dominated by the desire to throw off the political control and influence of the West. They went further and sought to reduce or eliminate Western economic investments and influence. And many of them attacked Western "cultural imperialism" and tried to limit the extent of Western cultural influences, language, music, movies, and so on.

While much of this was emotional and negative, there were important positive components too. There was pride in their own accomplishments. There was a recrudescence of national literature, music, painting, science. There was development and adaptation of the languages of the area. And there was independence of thought and action in national policy.

For example, Indonesia stressed that it was not a "neutralist" nation in the sense of disregard for what was going on in the world; its foreign policy was positive and "independent"; its decisions were based on what was good for Indonesia, not on what policies other nations followed or urged it to follow. Many nationalists saw clearly that their ability to make and carry out their own national decisions, in domestic and foreign affairs, depended on their building strong societies and economies, governed effectively and having broad popular support.

Still, the negative content of nationalism was much stronger than the positive, and it adversely affected the reception of the Mission and the atmosphere of the planning of aid projects. While directed mainly at the French, the British, and the Dutch, it affected relations with the Americans too, because the United States had once had possessions in the area (and still occupied Japan and the Ryukyus, and administered the Trust Territory of the Pacific); because American economic and military interests might tempt the United States to establish new forms of control; and because the United States was now closely identified with the former colonial powers in their joint attempt, through the Marshall Plan and NATO, to contain Communism.

Secretary Acheson's March 15 speech at the Commonwealth Club in San Francisco, in which he specifically applied the Truman Doctrine to Southeast Asia, sharpened the perception that the Cold War had priority in the foreign policy of the United States. But Asians did not perceive Communism to be nearly as threatening a force as colonialism. This was vividly illustrated by a scene the Mission encountered at a small town about twenty miles from Hanoi. On an arch across the street, a large banner was displayed for its benefit, reading "Communism, No! Colonialism, Never!"

And what about Southeast Asian attitudes toward trade with Japan, something dear to the heart of the United States Army and SCAP? These countries were quite willing to sell to Japan, although of course they preferred to earn dollars wherever possible. Even on the selling side, however, there was one cautionary note. Malaya and Singapore were serious food deficit areas and were accustomed to buying their rice nearby. They felt it important to have an assured supply of rice at a "reasonable price." On their behalf, the British high commissioner for Southeast Asia, Sir Malcolm MacDonald, expressed concern that SCAP might buy too much rice for Japan and force up the market price in the area.

On the buying side, there was much reluctance. The idea of using Japanese technicians in development projects was discussed by the Mission in each country, but most diplomatically, and with uniformly negative response. The Japanese had occupied their countries too recently, and had behaved too badly, to be forgiven so quickly. Perhaps later, but not then.

Even inanimate goods suffered from this understandable attitude. In Indochina and Indonesia there was grudging agreement that Japan was the logical source of supply for certain products. A million dollar order for small tools was envisioned in the discussions in Indochina, and a $600,000 order for small fishing boats and motors for Indonesia. But elsewhere, the less the Japanese were in the picture, the better.

Aid Recommended by the Mission

While they were ambivalent, all the governments of the area officially welcomed the Mission, prepared reports and proposals for it to consider on its arrival, and readily agreed to enter into the rather complex relationship of bilateral economic and technical aid. The principal kinds of assistance recommended by the Mission, based on the proposals made by the governments and discussed during the Mission's visits, are outlined in Table 2-1.

Although the Mission drew heavily on the Economic Cooperation Administration for aid experience and personnel, the kind of assistance recommended was very different from that supplied to Europe under the Marshall Plan, which the ECA administered. Commodity assistance as such played a very small part. Project assistance, involving the provision of equipment, technical supplies, technical advisers, and training in the United States, was the predominant form of aid. Of the total aid recommended, some $6,570,000 (about 10%) was intended to cover the costs of bringing about 275 technical advisers to four of these countries (not to Indochina) and the cost of contracts with engineering firms to provide economic and engineering advice (in Burma and Indonesia). An additional $1,530,000 was proposed to cover the costs of sending some 330 nationals to the United States for specialized training.

Although the Point Four program had not yet been approved by Congress, the aid recommended by the Mission was essentially of the kinds envisioned in

Table 2-1

Fields and Amounts of Assistance Recommended

Field of Assistance	Cost of Recommended Assistance	Percentage of Total
Agriculture, forestry, fisheries, land preparation, reclamation, irrigation	$23,153,000	35%
Power, transportation, roads, telecommunications, industry, development planning	17,472,000	26
Public health, sanitation, medicine, medical education	15,820,000	24
Education, including English language training and sports	5,223,000	8
Increased contact between national leaders and U.S. leaders	200,000	—
Commodities	4,225,000	6
Total	$66,093,000	100%

that program (a small interdepartmental staff had, during the period following the president's January, 1949, announcement, developed the detailed Point Four plans submitted to Congress). It might therefore be said that this program of aid really launched the Point Four program, in terms of actual country programming and provision of assistance. In recognition of this fact, the aid programs initiated by the Mission in Burma and Indonesia were subsequently (in 1952) turned over to the Point Four administrative agency, the Technical Cooperation Administration, to be administered as part of the general Point Four program. In Indochina, where military aid was very important, where much of the economic aid recommended had byproduct military value, and where commodity assistance later grew greatly in importance, administration of the program remained with the Mutual Security Agency (successor to the Economic Cooperation Administration). The program in Thailand was similarly administered by ECA and then MSA.

Certain differences among the country programs recommended by the Mission are apparent in Table 2-2.

As will be noted, the aid recommended for Malaya and Singapore was very modest, the principal items having been $3.2 million for radio equipment and $1

Table 2-2

Aid Recommended for Individual Countries

Cost of Recommended Assistance ($1000)

Field of Assistance	Indochina	Malaya & Singapore	Burma	Thailand	Indonesia	Total
Agriculture, forestry, fisheries, land preparation, reclamation, irrigation	$ 9,150		$ 4,168	$ 2,830	$ 7,005	$23,153
Power, transportation, roads, tele-communications, industry, development planning	5,100	4,200	2,390	4,532	1,250	17,472
Public health, sanitation, medicine, medical education	6,000		2,255	3,065	4,500	15,820
Education, including English language training and sports	750[a]	300	1,815	993	1,365	5,223
Increased contacts between national leaders and U.S. leaders			200			200
Commodities	2,500		1,400		325	4,225
Total	$23,500	$4,500	$12,228	$11,420	$14,445	$66,093

[a]Includes $250,000 for trainees to be sent to the United States. Their fields of training were not specified. For other countries, the cost of trainees was included in the total cost of the functional field in which they were to be trained.

million for heavy earth-moving equipment, both of types not available in the United Kingdom, and both to be used in the security effort. In addition, $300,000 was recommended for technical advisers, translators, and teachers to help reorient the pro-Communist materials and teaching in the Chinese language schools. These recommendations were not approved in Washington, however.

In Indochina, no real education program was proposed. The $750,000 recommended for "education" covered some fifty grants for training in the United States and $500,000 for expanded USIS activities, including English language classes and materials, additional USIS offices and equipment, and sports equipment and training. Nor was there any provision for American technical advisers. Both facts reflect the influence of the preferred position of French advisers and culture established by history (and language), by the March 8 Agreements, by the influence of the French already on the scene, and by the reluctance of the United States to undermine the cooperative relationship between France and the Associated States of Indochina that it hoped would be successful.

In both Burma and Indonesia, it was recommended that an engineering firm be employed under contract to provide economic and engineering advice, to help in national development planning, and to help execute major industrial projects. For this purpose, $1.25 million was included in the "Power, etc." category, for each of these countries. In Indonesia, no other funds were recommended in this category, because the United States had just recently (February, 1950) extended a $100 million credit through the Export-Import Bank, to be mainly available for industrial projects. With this financing available, it did not seem appropriate for the Mission to recommend grant aid for such projects.

Expectations of the Mission

The Mission had been charged to study the needs of the area for "emergency" economic and technical assistance that would "quickly" expand economic life, strengthen governments and demonstrate American interest.[a]

In light of subsequent experience, this charge to the Mission has been characterized as overoptimistic, on the grounds (1) that economic expansion, even if quickly achieved, may not have the political results desired; and (2) that external assistance alone cannot produce rapid economic expansion in under-developed countries because—much more than in Europe—various noneconomic factors are important determinants of the level of economic life and may be little affected by external aid. These factors include political, social, manpower, security, institutional, and attitudinal elements.

As to the second point, part of the economic problem found by the Mission was the need for repair, rehabilitation, and recovery of previous productive capacity, rather than development of new productive capacity. In Burma, for

---

[a]See above, page 12-13.

example, real gross national product in 1949-50 was only 58% of the prewar level.[2] In Indonesia, export production in 1949 was only 69% of prewar; cereal production was 87%; and even a year later, in 1950, sea fishery production was only 20% and lumber production 66% of prewar levels.[3]

A similar situation existed in Vietnam. This did parallel, in part, the European recovery problem. External aid can have much quicker and more dramatic economic results in such circumstances than when directed primarily to long-run economic development.

As to the first point, the Mission did, of course, expect that desirable political effects would be achieved. But it expected these to result from the very fact of its visits to these countries, its recommendations for aid, the aid agreements signed, the beginning of arrivals of aid, and the wide publicity given to all of these actions. Such political effects would obviously happen more quickly and be more noticeable than the longer-run political effects of the expansion of economic life brought about by the aid.

A second kind of criticism subsequently made was that the Mission expected unrealistically large results from aid of the types and amounts recommended. For example, in discussing the Mission's recommendations, Wolf writes that "Aid—heavily weighted by technical services—was viewed as likely to have a catalytic effect on the internal efforts of recipients Southeast Asian countries that would make small amounts of aid extremely productive and large amounts unnecessary."[4]

Wolf also, on the same page, which is wholly concerned with Southeast Asia, states, "As Secretary Acheson later described the programs: 'We provide only a small part of the resources required—but that small part has the effect of a catalyst in making the whole effort of the country succeed.'" It is correct that Secretary Acheson made this statement later, but not that he was referring to these Southeast Asia programs. He was referring to the Point Four program in general, as is made clear by reference to the original House Hearings quoted by Wolf.

The Mission's reports do not substantiate Wolf's assertion about overly optimistic expectations. It is of course correct that the Mission was influenced by the analysis underlying the Point Four program, which stressed the importance of improving technology. And some officials in Washington had described the potential impact (over many years, to be sure) of the Point Four program in rather glowing terms (partly, at least, vindicated in recent years by such dramatic discoveries as "miracle rice" and "miracle wheat"). But the Mission itself neither predicted dramatic increases in production as the result of the aid it recommended nor did it refuse to consider larger amounts of aid on the grounds that the aid already recommended would have such substantial results that additional aid would be "unnecessary." No ceilings on amounts of aid to be recommended had been set in advance.

The fact that larger amounts of aid were not recommended by the Mission was primarily a result of the limited "absorptive capacity" of the countries visited: i.e., the limited number of projects that appeared feasible to undertake promptly, and the limited number of skilled persons to organize and run them, whether aid was provided on a project or a program basis.

Publicizing American Aid

The Mission was keenly aware of the desirability of producing the maximum political impact obtainable through economic and technical aid. By publicizing the agreements to provide aid, and by getting some of the recommended activities under way as quickly as possible and publicizing them, it hoped to demonstrate the constructive interest of the United States in the area and to counter suspicions of a new American colonialism. By controlling the character of information activities, it hoped to temper the exaggerated expectations of some. And it hoped that the governments of these countries would gain popular support by promptly undertaking development activities benefiting their people, and by demonstrating their ability to get foreign assistance for their countries.

This factor was important in the Mission's selection of activities to recommend. It sought wherever possible to find "impact" projects, which would reach many people and impress them favorably. Examples were rural rehabilitation, mobile health clinics, and sports equipment. And this factor also caused the Mission to recommend support for increased USIS activities. It was aware that some of these governments, even if they had effective information services (which they didn't), might be reluctant to hurt French feelings, or British or Dutch feelings, by publicizing American aid. Expanded USIS activities, tailored to the needs and sensitivities of each area, coupled with a substantial influx of technical advisers who would make contact with many people at the "working" level, and reinforced by a substantial flow of trainees sent to the United States for a year or two (and in Burma by an exchange of "leaders"), were felt to be needed and would hopefully be effective in building an understanding in depth of American purposes, values, characteristics, and working methods.

Organizing for Aid

Finally, the Mission recommended certain organizational arrangements for carrying out the proposed aid. Aware of the unusual success of the Joint Commission on Rural Reconstruction in China, it proposed that joint commissions, or joint agencies in particular fields, be set up wherever possible. Under the chairmanship of a national of the country, such a mechanism would draw on the skills and insights of local experts, would reduce the frictions of cross-cultural cooperation, and would maximize mutual understanding and common interest.

The Mission recommended that United States economic aid in Indochina be administered by an economic mission paralleling the Economic Cooperation Administration missions in Europe, China, and Korea, separate from but closely integrated with the diplomatic and USIS missions. This recommendation was made at least partly because the Mission (and some of the diplomatic staff in Saigon) wanted such a mission to be able to work directly with the local governments, and it was not clear that this would be possible if the economic mission were to be completely merged into the diplomatic mission.

On the other hand, in Burma the Mission recommended that a minimal aid mission be set up, under a "Coordinator of Economic Cooperation Activities,... not a Chief of Economic Mission," and that the technical advisers brought in should work in Burmese government offices and agencies, having as little as possible to do, officially and socially, with embassy personnel.

In both Thailand and Indonesia, the need for a small economic aid mission was recognized, but again the title "Coordinator of Economic Activities" found favor. In both countries, the American ambassador felt strongly that the economic aid mission should be directly responsible to him, and should work in the closest cooperation with the embassy. The Mission therefore recommended this arrangement.

The Partnership of Diplomacy and Aid

While the emphasis throughout these reports and this summary is on the findings and recommendations of the Mission itself, it should be stressed that this was in all senses an integrated effort by the various departments and agencies of the United States government. The Mission was jointly staffed by personnel of the State Department, the Economic Cooperation Administration, and other government departments; its purposes, mode of operation, and the nature of its recommendations had been thoroughly discussed and agreed upon by all interested parties before its departure from the United States. The American diplomatic mission in each country had been fully informed about these matters ahead of time and initiated the discussions with the local governments that made it possible for the latter to prepare studies and aid requests prior to the Mission's arrival; and all recommendations made by the Mission were discussed with the chief of diplomatic mission (or chargé) in each country and had his concurrence. This was a United States effort to use economic and technical aid to bolster up an area in which it had important political, economic, and military interests. Subsequent history revealed a different pattern of implementation and results in each of the countries visited. But the goals sought and the means proposed were very much the same in each.

Implementation of the Mission's Recommendations

Time was of the essence in early 1950. The Griffin Mission had been hastily organized and spent no more than two weeks in any of the countries it visited. Its recommendations were cabled home at the end of each visit so that the Administration would have concrete plans to discuss at the congressional hearings then going on, and so that a beginning could be made on personnel recruitment and on procurement of supplies without waiting for the Mission to complete its visits and return home. Great importance was placed on the political impact that would come from early evidence that aid from the United States was on the way.

Extraordinary measures were taken in Washington to provide this evidence. Medical supplies originally purchased for other use in the Far East and en route there were diverted to Indochina. Public Health Service personnel were detailed to Saigon. Some of these supplies and personnel actually arrived (airlifted by the Department of Defense) in Vietnam before the end of July, 1950.

Funding the Program

But the question of congressional authorization for aid to Southeast Asia had not been settled by the time the Mission returned to Washington in early May. The President was, of course, free to use his confidential $75 million fund, appropriated under the Mutual Defense Assistance Act, for any kind of assistance he felt justified, in any country in the "general area" of China. On May 1 he made $750,000 of this fund available to ECA to launch the medical and health program in Indochina.[a] But the Administration was reluctant to tap this fund further. And Congress had not yet enacted the Foreign Assistance Act of 1950, which was to authorize the use of part of the original China Aid funds in the "general area of China." However, in March committees of both the House and the Senate had approved such use, and their Conference Report of May 19 ironed out minor differences between them. It reserved $40 million of these funds for use in China (including Formosa) "so long as the President deems

---

[a] It has been reported that this fund was also used to finance the setting up of the ECA mission in Saigon (see William Adams Brown and Redvers Opie, *American Foreign Assistance* [Washington: Brookings, 1953], p. 408). The records do not substantiate this, referring only to an emergency health program and procurement of medical commodities.

it practical" to use them there; $8 million for disaster relief in China;[b] and $6 million for educating Chinese students in the United States. The Conference agreed that the remaining approximately $40 million of these funds would be available for use "in the general area of China." In addition, some part of the $40 million reserved for Formosa might become available for use in Southeast Asia if the President concluded that it was not practical to use it all in Formosa.

With this assurance, the Economic Cooperation Administration, which had been designated on May 19 as the administering agency for economic and technical aid in Southeast Asia, went ahead with recruitment of the personnel it would need in Washington and overseas. For much of the new programs, of course, it would be necessary for specialized personnel to reach the countries involved and there work out more detailed plans and specifications than the Mission had had the time or the expertness to provide. On May 26, the ECA announced that it had already set up a United States Special Technical and Economic Mission (STEM) in Saigon and it was organizing missions for Burma, Thailand, and Indonesia. It also announced that it had set up a Far East Program Division to administer the program (along with aid to Formosa) and had appointed Mr. Harlan Cleveland as acting director of this division.

On June 5, Congress enacted and the President immediately signed the Foreign Economic Assistance Act of 1950 (Public Law 535, 81st Congress, 2d Session). Title II of this Act, cited as the China Area Aid Act of 1950, confirmed the agreements reached in the Conference Report of May 19. It authorized use of the unobligated funds originally appropriated (in 1948) for economic aid to China, "for carrying out . . . economic assistance in any place in China and in the general area of China which the President deems to be not under Communist control. . . ." The effect of this legislation was to free about $40 million immediately for use in the "general area of China" (i.e., in Southeast Asia). Title IV, cited as the Act for International Development, authorized the appropriation of $35 million for Point Four technical assistance to all "economically underdeveloped countries" ($27 million was appropriated for this purpose on September 6, 1950). The latter program was to be administered by a new organization, the Technical Cooperation Administration (TCA), set up by and within the Department of State and succeeding the temporary Technical Cooperation Division already in operation there.

Administrative Arrangements

While ECA had gone ahead in May to set up a field mission in Saigon, following the pattern of its Marshall Plan missions in Europe (administratively independent of the United States diplomatic mission, with direct communication to ECA

---

[b]This provision arose from widespread concern about reports of a severe famine on mainland China, and was intended to provide financing for relief shipments to be distributed by private agencies if permitted to operate there.

headquarters, etc.), and had established a headquarters division to backstop all its Far Eastern programs, a new element entered the picture with the passage of the Act for International Development, authorizing Point Four assistance to underdeveloped nations everywhere. Shouldn't administration of these Southeast Asia programs now be transferred to TCA?

Much of the assistance recommended by the Griffin Mission was of a Point Four character, directed to long-run development rather than to economic rehabilitation and recovery, and much of it was project rather than program aid. Moreover, available "general area" funds were limited to $40 million (part of which would be needed in the Philippines, where the Bell Mission was working out the details of an aid program), and the staff concerned with Southeast Asia hoped to supplement these funds with Point Four funds—even though the latter were very limited in 1950-51. Finally, TCA was a "permanent" agency while ECA was temporary; and the TCA staff wanted to start administering programs for which they would presumably be later responsible.

The bureaucratic jockeying over administration of these programs pitted unequal forces against each other. On the one hand, ECA had a going operation in Washington and in Asia; a good deal of prior experience in Southeast Asia;[c] field personnel (suddenly made available when the North Korean invasion forced ECA out of South Korea); tested administrative and legal procedures already in effect; draft bilateral agreements; more funds ($40 million for "the general area of China" versus $27 million for all underdeveloped countries); and strong support on Capitol Hill. TCA had a skeleton headquarters force and no personnel in the field, more restrictive clearance procedures, smaller funds, and weak support on the Hill.[d] The State Department also had, in its Office of Educational Exchange, experience in administration of educational and leader exchanges under the Smith-Mundt and Fulbright Acts. But over-balancing this was State's bureaucratic conservatism. For example, the "country desk officers" were appalled at the thought of technical and economic missions comprising eighty to a hundred persons per country. And the staff in State's Bureau of International Organization Affairs were insistent that the new activities be meshed with and not compete with the UN activities in Southeast Asia. The drive to "get on with the job" was likely to be weaker in this atmosphere than in the action-oriented ECA.

In congressional committee hearings, ECA representatives had pointed out that ECA operated on the basis of total country programs, rather than "project-by-project" (intended to be a somewhat invidious reference to TCA program planning), and that the proposed programs in Indochina and, to a lesser

---

[c]The ECA Mission to France had given intensive attention to French financial and economic relations with Indochina, in working on France's need for ECA aid; and ECA had made $101 million of commodity assistance available to The Netherlands for the Netherlands East Indies before Indonesia gained its independence. In fact, a team of ECA officials made a detailed study of the use of counterpart funds in Indonesia during a two-month stay in early 1950.

[d]At one stage in the legislative process, the Point Four Program had been made possible by a single vote in the Senate!

extent, in Burma included commodities to maintain levels of consumption and of raw materials to get production going again. This was a type of assistance well established in the European Recovery Program. In actual fact, the programs recommended by the Griffin Mission and undertaken by ECA were largely "project-by-project"; the Mission's recommendations had included only 11% for commodity supply in Indochina and Burma; and the goal of total country programming was not approached except in Vietnam. Still, the "general area of China" provision in the Foreign Assistance Act of 1950 authorized the continued use of funds originally appropriated for use under the provisions of the Economic Cooperation Act (of 1948, as amended). Moreover, if the program had been transferred to TCA, this would surely have slowed down operations in which speed was considered essential.

The conclusion of protracted discussions and negotiations in the summer and fall of 1950 was an ECA-State agreement of November 16, under which ECA was to administer projects in agriculture, industry, public health, relief and rehabilitation and housing; and State under Point Four was to handle projects in education, vocational training, assistance to teacher-training institutions and universities (except regular USIS-type projects), and scientific projects. Other projects, such as those in the field of public administration, were to be agreed upon one by one. And a "technical cooperation officer" would be assigned to each diplomatic mission to handle the projects under State's responsibility, and also to handle relations with UN agencies providing technical assistance to the country.

By the spring of 1951, it had become apparent that this division of functions was impractical. The two programs were then merged under ECA.[e]

In October, 1950, Mr. Griffin, who had returned to his California newspaper in June, was invited back to ECA and was appointed director of the Far East Program Division, in charge of the economic aid program in Formosa (and subsequently the Philippines), in addition to the four programs in Southeast Asia (for some time, aid to the three Associated States of Indochina was handled as a joint program, through the ECA mission in Saigon). The idea—at first quite seriously considered—that a regional office be set up in Asia (in some ways paralleling the ECA office of the special representative in Europe) had been abandoned.

Departing from the Mission's recommendations that full-scale, separate economic missions *not* be set up in Burma, Thailand, and Indonesia, the ECA drew on its European experience, where independence of action had been judged essential for prompt and vigorous aid activities, and set up a United States Special Technical and Economic Mission (STEM) in Rangoon and Bangkok by the end of September, and later in Djakarta (in addition to the STEM set up in Saigon in May). Each STEM was headed by a chief of mission who, according to

---

[e]On July 1, 1952, under new legislation (The Mutual Security Act of 1951) administration of economic aid in those countries (Burma and Indonesia) not receiving both economic and military aid was transferred to TCA.

the ECA legislation, ranked "immediately after the chief of the United States diplomatic mission in the country." While of course subject to the political decisions of the chief of diplomatic mission, in his position as the principal representative of the United States, each STEM had a good deal of operational freedom. The STEMs negotiated directly with "technical" ministers (industry, finance, economics, health, planning, education, etc.) of the countries and sent their own communications to Washington, with copies to the Chief of diplomatic mission but without his right of veto.

A first task in each country was to negotiate a bilateral economic and technical cooperation agreement. As an international agreement, this was the principal responsibility of the chief of diplomatic mission. Agreements were signed with Burma on September 13, with Thailand on September 19, and with Indonesia on October 16. Because the political authorities in the Associated States of Indochina were both inexperienced and also deeply involved in the further negotiations with France then going on in Pau, the United States agreed to accept from these States "letters of intent" to negotiate agreements, and these letters were received during the autumn. The agreements themselves were not signed until the following September (Vietnam, Sept. 7; Cambodia, Sept. 8; and Laos, Sept. 9, 1951).

A special problem was faced in Indochina, of course. The French wanted all economic aid to be funneled through a quadripartite body of which they would be an official member. The three local governments wanted to deal separately with the United States, to receive economic aid directly, and to administer economic rehabilitation and development projects themselves. If this was "foreign affairs," they were obligated by the March 8 Agreements to subordinate themselves to the French. If this was a domestic economic program, they had no such obligation.

The United States was, of course, trying to make the "Bao Dai solution" in Vietnam a success. To this end, it was important to strengthen Bao Dai by treating directly with his government and having him get the public credit for aid obtained and projects accomplished. This was not an anti-French attitude, though it was viewed as such by many of the French officials. It was in a sense pro-French, because only if Bao Dai gained public confidence as an independent force could the French possibly maintain what was already a waning influence in Vietnam.

The United States decided to treat directly with the governments of Vietnam, Cambodia, and Laos concerning all project aid, leaving to them to decide how much and what kind of consultation with the French they wanted to carry on. Letters of intent were received from and eventually agreements were signed with these governments individually. Economic project aid was supplied directly to them, not through a quadripartite body. The United States did, however, meet with a quadripartite body to plan the dimensions and composition, and to control the distribution, of the "commercial import program" used to counter inflation and to generate local currency for budgetary support of the three local governments. French private concerns and banks were also, of course, deeply involved in supplying and financing commercial imports, and the French government had a responsibility for economic and financial conditions.

Record of the First Year

By July 1, 1951, the end of the fifteen month period used for the Griffin Mission's recommendations, a remarkable record had been achieved. Bilateral agreements or letters of intent to execute such agreements had been signed. Country missions had been organized with thirty-one staff in Indochina, twenty-six in Burma, twenty-six in Thailand, and sixteen in Indonesia. These were exclusive of technical experts provided as part of the assistance program. And nearly $50 million of aid commodities and services had arrived or were "in the pipeline" (procurement authorizations signed or personnel commitments made).

The role of the Griffin Mission should not be overstated. Its recommendations were useful in outlining the general nature and size of the aid programs needed. But it had neither the expertise nor the time in each country to develop detailed lists and specifications for the commodities (or experts) to be supplied. The first task of the resident missions (the STEMs) was to develop such detailed lists and specifications so procurement could go forward. The Griffin Mission's task was to make a beginning and provide momentum.

ECA had started off the period with a small allocation of $750,000 of Mutual Defense Assistance Program funds, and on June 5 had obtained authority to use about $40 million of China Aid funds in "the general area of China." During the period, a new program in the Philippines was also undertaken by ECA, and this had to be financed from the same China Aid funds. Recognizing that additional funds would be needed for the area, the ECA appealed to Congress, which in January, 1951, authorized the transfer of up to 3% of the European Recovery funds for use in the Far East.[1] Under this law, ECA transferred $75,414,000 for use in China and in that general area during the first six months of 1951. In this way, it was able to provide $50 million to the Philippines, $98 million to Formosa, and nearly $50 million to Indochina, Burma, Thailand and Indonesia between June 5, 1950 and June 30, 1951. Its progress in committing the funds for specific uses in the latter four countries is shown in Table 3-1.

As all familiar with foreign aid know, the normal elapsed time between agreement on supplies and their arrival abroad is from one to three years (depending on availability in stock and the time needed to manufacture items not in stock). The normal elapsed time for personnel is two years (needed for recruitment; completing other commitments, as in teaching; language and other training, etc.). When starting a new program, the "pipeline" must be filled before goods and services can arrive in quantity. This was especially difficult to do in 1950-51, as the outbreak of the Korean War on June 25, 1950, caused critical shortages of many commodities. Yet, against the $66 million originally recommended (of which the $4.5 million recommended for Malaya and

Table 3-1

Authorizations for Aid in Southeast Asia, by Recipient Country,
by Quarter: June 5, 1950 through June 30, 1951

(Thousands of dollars)

Country	June 5-Sept. 30, 1950	Oct.-Dec. 1950	Jan.-Mar. 1951	Apr.-June 1951	Total
Indochina	$1,911	$ 5,014	$ 6,454	$ 9,094	$22,473
Burma	—	2,914	3,428	4,058	10,400
Thailand	373	2,608	2,809	3,086	8,876
Indonesia	659	3,756	1,629	1,929	7,973
Total	$2,943	$14,292	$14,320	$18,167	$49,722

Source: 13th Quarterly Report to Congress of the Economic Cooperation Administration, for the quarter ended June 30, 1951, p. 71.

Singapore was vetoed in Washington), nearly $50 million had been obligated within fifteen months, and more than $10 million worth of supplies and services were estimated to have arrived in the countries themselves. Table 3-2 shows a summary of the program as of July 1, 1951.

Only in Indonesia was the record disappointing. There, difficulties in recruiting mission personnel and technical assistance experts (both groups being required for preparation of detailed specifications for procurement) and Indonesian slowness in drafting and presenting projects, together resulted in deliveries to Indonesia by July 1, 1951, being only 3% of obligations, whereas this figure was 19% for Indochina, 27% for Thailand and 32% for Burma.

Indonesia had received other aid, of course. Drawing on the $100 million Export-Import Bank credit of February, 1950, about $70 million had been allocated to specific projects by June 30, 1951. Because of the production delays in procuring industrial equipment, however, no deliveries had yet been received. Against the $101 million of commodity assistance provided to Indonesia through the Netherlands, under the European Recovery Program (obligated before Indonesia became independent at the end of 1949), about half had arrived in fiscal year 1949 and the other half in fiscal year 1950. Indonesia had also received a credit of $63.6 million from the United States with which to buy surplus American military equipment and supplies.[2]

Thailand also received other economic aid. In the summer of 1950, the International Bank for Reconstruction and Development agreed to make three

Table 3-2

Status of Fiscal Year 1951 Program Funds, as of July 1, 1951

Country	Original Mission Recommendation	Obligations	Estimated Value of Total Arrivals (Including arrivals not yet reported as expenditures)
Indochina	$23,500,000	$21,828,000	$ 4,212,900
Burma	12,228,000	10,774,000	3,498,065
Thailand	11,420,000	8,876,000	2,429,710
Indonesia	14,445,000	7,973,000	241,038
Total	$61,593,000	$49,451,000	$10,381,713

Note: Figures for obligations and estimated arrivals from *Hearings on the Mutual Security Act of 1951* (S. 1762) before the Committee on Foreign Relations and the Committee on Armed Services, United States Senate, 82nd Congress, 1st session, pp. 554-555. The reasons for the minor discrepancies in the "obligations" column of this table and the "authorizations" total of the preceding table, for Indochina and Burma, are not known by the author.

loans to Thailand, totaling $25.4 million, for port, railway, and irrigation projects. ECA agreed to assist some of these projects with aid of its own.

Point Four Nature of Southeast Asia Programs

Reference was made above to the essentially "Point Four" character of most of the economic aid recommended by the Mission. One measure of this appears in the proportion of aid obligations accounted for by "services" (technical assistance experts and training). Although technical experts typically take a long time to recruit, the special priority given to this program (and the availability of some experts from the aid program in Korea, who had been evacuated after the fighting there began in June, 1950) resulted in a good record in Thailand and a fair record in Burma. By June 30, 1951, some sixty-two experts were in Thailand and fifty-four in Burma. As Table 3-3 shows, total obligations as of July 1, 1951, included 9% for services for Thailand; 12% and 14% respectively for services in Indonesia and Burma, in both of which the total cost of a contract for an engineering advisory group was included; but only 1% for services for Indochina, where there was both strong French resistance and some nationalist

Table 3-3

Fiscal Year 1951 Program
Estimated Dollar Cost of Program, by Country and Major Cost Components

(In thousands of dollars)

Country	Total dollar cost of program (Obligations)	Cost of supplies and equipment	Cost of Services		
			Total	Technical assistance experts[a]	Trainees[b]
Indochina	21,828[c]	21,542	286	286	
Burma	10,774	9,928	1,476	1,458[d]	18
Thailand	8,876	8,054	822	765	57
Indonesia	7,973	7,055	918	907[d]	11
Total	49,451	45,949	3,502	3,416	86

[a]Experts sent to country, but not administrative personnel of missions. Cost shown represents actual dollar obligations.

[b]Persons brought from country for training. Cost shown represents actual dollar obligations.

[c]Includes $34,000 Mutual Defense Assistance Program funds used for salaries and other dollar expenses of initial group of technicians sent to inaugurate health programs.

[d]Includes total cost of contract with United States engineering firm.

Source: *Hearings on the Mutual Security Act of 1951* (S. 1962) before the Committee on Foreign Relations and the Committee on Armed Services, U.S. Senate, 82nd Congress, 1st Session, p. 570.

resistance to bringing in advisers and sending persons to the United States for training. Of course, language also was a major obstacle in Indochina, and not an inconsiderable one in Indonesia.

The Point Four character of this aid is shown even more clearly in Tables 3-4 through 3-7, where the amounts authorized for each kind of activity in each country are given. It is notable that only in Indochina is the category "Maintenance of essential supply" important. There it accounts for about half of all expenditures authorized. In Burma it accounts for about a quarter. This category is similar to the commodity aid given for balance-of-payments and anti-inflation purposes under the European Recovery Program. The other aid (except for "Emergency relief," limited to Indochina) is all project-related and generally comprises Point Four-type assistance for rehabilitation and long-run development.

Table 3-4

Associated States of Indochina: Authorizations by Type of Project, July 1, 1950-June 30, 1951

(Thousands of dollars)

Type of project	Total dollar cost
Grand Total	21,828[a]
Emergency relief	1,195
Public health	3,729
Training and research	106
Hospitals and health centers	1,432
Endemic disease control (malaria, trachoma, yaws, gastro-intestinal, etc.)	1,281
Village sanitation	178
Village first aid	489
Medical and sanitary services (n.e.c.)	243
Agriculture, forestry, fisheries	1,619
Agriculture	1,250
Training and research	851
Irrigation and reclamation	319
Livestock production and disease control	80
Forestry	169
Fisheries	200
Transportation, power, other public works	3,316

[a]Includes $34,000 in fiscal year 1951 authorizations issued by ECA with Mutual Defense Assistance Program funds used for salaries and other dollar expenses of initial group of technicians sent to inaugurate health program. Also includes $66,000 in commodities for which exact destination was not specified at time of authorization, but now earmarked for the Associated States of Indochina. Excludes $711,000 authorized from fiscal year 1950 MDAP funds.

Table 3-4 (*continued*)

(Thousands of dollars)

Type of project	Total dollar cost
Transportation	2,758
Highways	2,037
Inland waterways	721
Housing and urban development	558
Handicraft and manufacturing, mining, other industry	—
General engineering advisory services	—
Education (mass education)	30
Public administration	334
Maintenance of essential supply	11,605
Requisites for production	8,815
Other essential civilian supplies	2,790

Source: 13th Quarterly Report to Congress of the Economic Cooperation Administration, for the quarter ended June 30, 1951, p. 141.

Table 3-5

Burma: Authorizations by Type of Project, July 1, 1950-June 30, 1951

(Thousands of dollars)

Type of project	Total dollar cost
Grand total	10,774[a]
Emergency relief	—
Public health	1,786
Teams for health education and disease control (malaria, smallpox, tuberculosis, etc.)	1,515
Hospitals and health centers	100
Vaccine production and other diagnostic facilities	20
Quarantine facilities and fumigation services	19
Training facilities (Rangoon Medical College)	132

[a]Includes $374,000 in commodities for which exact destination was not specified at the time of authorization, but now earmarked for Burma.

Table 3-5 (*continued*)   (Thousands of dollars)

Type of project	Total dollar cost
Agriculture, forestry, fisheries	1,243
Research, experimentation, extension, surveys	355
Seed improvement and distribution (rice and other)	279
Insect and rodent control	22
Livestock disease control	28
Agricultural extension	13
Research laboratory	10
Land and water classification	3
Rice storage	320
Irrigation and reclamation	310
Soil conservation	6
Irrigation	70
Flood control	234
Agricultural program—Frontier States	182
Agricultural improvement—Shan	99
Canning improvement—Shan	10
Animal production—Shan	73
Training and information (Agricultural College, Mandalay)	76
Transportation, power, other public works	3,616
Port rehabilitation	3,515
Inland waterways	15
Low-cost housing	86
Handicraft and manufacturing, mining, other industry (mining and technical services)	19
General Engineering advisory services	800
Education	648
Rehabilitation corps	24
Technical training and information	475
Educational facilities (Rangoon University)	149
Public administration (Union Bank of Burma)	32
Maintenance of essential supply	2,630
Requisites for production	2,413
Other essential civilian supplies	217

Source: 13th Quarterly Report to Congress of the Economic Cooperation Administration, for the quarter ended June 30, 1951, p. 139.

Table 3-6

Thailand: Authorizations by Type of Project, July 1, 1950-June 30, 1951

(Thousands of dollars)

Type of project	Total dollar cost
Grand total	8,876
Emergency relief	—
Public health	2,008
Teams for health education and disease control (malaria, filariasis, leprosy, trachoma, etc.)	732
Village sanitation (water purification, sewage, drainage, etc.)	182
Hospital maintenance and equipment	607
Biological and nutritional research	26
Medical research and training	211
Technical services, n.e.c.	250
Agriculture, forestry, fisheries	2,317
Agriculture	2,208
Research and training	906
Experimentation, demonstration, extension and soil surveys	305
Irrigation and reclamation	997
Fisheries	109
Transportation, power, other public works	3,932
Transportation	3,515
Road building and repair	1,381
Railroad maintenance and repair	965
Harbor development and administration	801
Electric power (for rural centers)	417
Handicraft and manufacturing, mining, other industry	619
Lignite and strategic metals development (tin, tungsten, etc.)	615
Geological survey	4

Table 3-6 (*continued*)

(Thousands of dollars)

Type of project	Total dollar cost
General engineering advisory services	–
Education	–
Public administration	–
Maintenance of essential supply	–

Source: 13th Quarterly Report to Congress of the Economic Cooperation Administration, for the quarter ended June 30, 1951, p. 144.

Table 3-7

Indonesian Republic: Authorizations by Type of Project, July 1, 1950-June 30, 1951

(Thousands of dollars)

Type of project	Total dollar cost
Grand total	7,973
Emergency relief	–
Public health	2,836
Malaria control	788
Maternal and child care	518
Village sanitation	11
Hospital and laboratory equipment and supplies, n.e.c.	1,121
Drugs (for government supply centers)	398
Agriculture, forestry, fisheries	2,548
Agriculture	580
Small farm rehabilitation	247
Livestock disease control	60
Plant disease control	88
Irrigation and drainage	71
Research	103
Training	11

Table 3-7 (*continued*)

(Thousands of dollars)

Type of project	Total dollar cost
Forestry	598
Hand tools	190
Sawmill equipment	408
Fisheries	1,370
Fishing boats and parts	1,127
Research	243
Transportation, power, other public works	—
Handicraft and manufacturing, mining, other industry	1,889
Handicraft and small industry rehabilitation	634
Rubber processing of smallholders' production	555
Canning	700
General engineering advisory services	700
Education	—
Public administration	—
Maintenance of essential supply	—

Source: 13th Quarterly Report to Congress of the Economic Cooperation Administration, for the quarter ended June 30, 1951, p. 142.

Summary

In summary, the Mission's cabled recommendations of March and April, 1950, were acted upon immediately. Authority and funds were obtained to make prompt procurement possible. The Far East Program Division of ECA was set up and staffed, and country missions were organized. Bilateral agreements were negotiated. Some procurement was initiated on the basis of the Mission's recommendations. Further procurement took place as soon as specialized personnel could be sent to each country and could do the detailed planning and provide the additional specifications needed. And shipment of supplies and movement of technical assistance experts and trainees began promptly.

The bureaucracy of a large nation is inclined to move slowly, especially where congressional approval for expenditures of new kinds or in new areas is involved. In this instance, the record shows that the bureaucracy could move rapidly, and did. An aid program for a new area was conceived and put into full operation

58

within an eighteen month period. Whether the credit should be given to the stimulus of Communist aggression in China and Korea; to the unusual degree of agreement between Congress and the Administration on doing at least this much for Asia; to the existence of a young, flexible, action-oriented government agency (ECA) with established procurement procedures; to particular individuals; or to a combination of all of these; the fact remains that prompt action was desired and prompt action took place. It is a history not likely to be often repeated.

II. The Reports:
The Mission's Work Through Its Own and Foreign Eyes

Needs for United States Economic and Technical Aid in Cambodia, Laos, and Vietnam [1950]

Summary

1. A major revolution is raging in Vietnam with substantial military forces engaged on both sides. The revolutionaries (Viet Minh) are led by Communists, but the majority are probably non-Communist. Their ardent nationalism and antagonism toward the French are so strong that they have accepted Communist leadership in their struggle to drive the French from the country and achieve complete independence for Vietnam. Apparently the majority of the population is sitting on the fence, while even the "pacified areas" are honeycombed with agents or sympathizers of the Viet Minh (Section I, A).

2. French military forces control the major population centers and lines of communication, but only a "political solution" is likely to bring an end to the conflict. If the majority of the Vietnamese can be convinced that the Bao Dai Government will be able to achieve real independence for Vietnam and provide a competent government for the country, the fence-sitters may declare for Bao Dai, and the non-Communist elements in the Viet Minh may withdraw their support from Ho Chi Minh and turn their nationalist fervor to constructive political and economic activity (Section I, A).

3. As a whole Indochina is still a food surplus area, although production of rice and corn is down somewhat from prewar levels as a result of wartime deterioration of facilities, civil strife, and the resultant interruption of communications (Section I, B).

4. Military expenditures are heavy (partly paid for directly by the French), and the various civil budgets are badly unbalanced, with the French making up the budget deficits. During 1949 the rise in living costs nearly came to a halt in Vietnam, following the application of direct controls, including import control, price controls, and a modest system of rationing (Section I, C).

5. Prewar exports of rice and corn to France and French colonies were very large and made an important contribution to France's balance of payments. These food surpluses might be of great importance to the food deficit areas of China (Section II, A).

6. Indochina is strategically important, for it provides a natural invasion route into the rice bowl of Southeast Asia should the Communists adopt this form

Report No. 1 of the United States Economic Survey Mission to Southeast Asia, prepared during and following the Mission's visits to Saigon, Dalat, Hanoi, and Phnom Penh, March 6-16, 1950; and first printed in Washington, May, 1950.

of aggression. Moreover, it has great political significance, because of its potential influence, should it fall to the Communists, on Thailand, Burma, Malaya, and perhaps Indonesia (Section II, B).

7. The overriding political problem of the day is the settlement of the revolution and the re-establishment of law and order (Section III, A).

8. The most urgent economic problems are rehabilitation of recently "pacified" rural areas, extension of medical and health services, rectification of import shortages, reconstruction and extension of telecommunication facilities, and the rehabilitation of industry. In the long run, there is need for more adequate and better balanced economic development (Section III, B).

9. France continues to provide most of the outside economic aid furnished Indochina (Section IV).

10. The aid which the United States has extended to France through the ECA is of major assistance to the French in carrying the present load in Indochina, but little U.S. aid has been given to Indochina directly (Section V).

11. A program of technical and economic aid estimated to cost $23,500,000 for the 15 months ending June 30, 1951, is recommended (Section VI).

12. The recommended program of rural rehabilitation (to cost $14,150,000) includes (Section VI, A):
    a) plowing service, repair and construction of irrigation facilities, well drilling, and the like;
    b) provision of medical and health facilities through dispensaries, clinics, and maternity centers;
    c) provision of agricultural supplies such as fertilizers, farm tools, seeds, and cattle vaccines; and
    d) the rehabilitation of dwellings.

13. Assistance is required in health and medical problems and in agriculture beyond that proposed in the preceding section (Section VI, B and C).

14. The factors most seriously limiting U.S. aid programs are
    a) the absence of law and order and the demands of the political and military effort on money and official time;
    b) the lack of experienced administrative and technical personnel;
    c) the antagonism of the Vietnamese toward the French; and,
    d) the opposition of the French to technical experts from countries other than France (Section VII).

15. To have the maximum effect on the international political situation, American aid should arrive quickly, should be well publicized, and should be distributed through the National Governments in order to build up the prestige of these Governments and to attract nationalists to Bao Dai. France, which has had long experience and which is currently pouring large sums of money into Indochina, has a responsible role to play in connection with any economic aid, but should not be given control nor allowed to insist on quadripartite arrangements unacceptable to the local governments (Section VIII).

16. In addition to the expanded USIS activities previously mentioned, there is

need for an expanded information and public relations activity to explain U.S. interest in Indochina, what it is undertaking, and why it is undertaking it. This will require not only delicate handling, but more handling, more people, and more equipment (Section IX).

17. U.S. economic and technical aid programs in Indochina must be directly administered under a single responsible Chief of Economic Mission. It is recommended that the ECA set up the field organization and appoint the Chief as its representative. If the local governments agree, joint bodies should be set up with U.S. representation in connection with the administration of aid programs (Section X).

I. The Current Situation

A. *Political Situation*

Indochina came progressively under French control as the result of French conquests beginning in 1858 over part of Cochinchina (South Vietnam), and continuing until the final acquisition of Laos from Thailand in 1893. (Two western provinces of Cambodia were added in 1907.) Five administrative units were established by the French, of which one (Cochinchina, the richest) was governed as a colony, and the other four (Tonkin, Annam, Cambodia, and Laos) nominally as protectorates, although under highly centralized direct French administration.

During the war, and especially during the period of full Japanese control in 1945, the already existing nationalism of Vietnam (by far the largest part of Indochina) received a tremendous impetus. Complete independence was declared for Vietnam in early 1945, under Japanese sponsorship, and, after the Japanese surrender, independence was reaffirmed under the leadership of Ho Chi Minh, a Moscow-trained Communist, who had attained great popular prestige by his effective leadership in the nationalist cause.

Vietnam was occupied by British and Chinese troops at the end of the war and its independence was not recognized by the French. By the end of 1946 French troops were able to relieve the British in Cochinchina, though they were opposed by the guerilla activity of nationalist rebels, which has continued to date. North of the sixteenth parallel, Chinese troops had permitted Ho Chi Minh's Government to operate, and it was this latter Government which signed an agreement permitting French forces to return to North Vietnam, in return for which the French Government recognized "the Vietnam Republic as a free State . . . forming part of . . . the French Union." As a result of disagreement over the interpretation of this agreement of March 6, 1946, hostilities broke out in Tonkin and Annam at the end of the year.

On March 8, 1949, the ex-Emperor of Annam, Bao Dai, signed an agreement with President Auriol whereby he would return to Vietnam as chief of state in exchange for certain French concessions, including the unification of Cochinchina, Annam, and Tonkin. This agreement and subsequent agreements with Cambodia and Laos recognized the three states as "associated states within the French Union" with full internal sovereignty and limited diplomatic representation. French citizens and citizens favored by treaty were to have extraterritorial privileges before the law, and French citizens were granted national treatment and preferences in other respects. Ultimate control over international defense and foreign policy rested with the French, and certain matters, including customs, treasury, immigration control, et cetera, were to be later determined by a joint conference of the three States and France.

The form of the government to be established in Vietnam is not yet decided, awaiting the action of a freely elected constituent assembly when established. Provisionally, Vietnam is headed by a "Chief of State", Bao Dai, formerly Emperor of Annam. The other two States are constitutional monarchies with popularly elected assemblies. The Cambodia National Assembly is currently dissolved. The powers and functions whose transfer is envisioned in the March 8 agreements are being progressively turned over to the governments of these three States.

These concessions have not been enough for Ho Chi Minh and for a substantial number of other Vietnamese leaders. Rebellion against the French, and against the Vietnamese cooperating with the French, has continued full-scale since December 1946 and has at one time or another touched most of Vietnam and spilled over the borders into Laos and Cambodia.

Today, the population of Vietnam is deeply divided, with substantial military forces engaged on both sides, with rebel (Viet Minh) guerrillas, agents and sympathizers honeycombing the whole country (including Saigon), and with large numbers of people, including many political leaders, sitting on the side lines refusing to commit themselves yet to either side. Complicating the picture is the Communist affiliation of Ho Chi Minh and some of his top leaders (including General Giap, his Chief of State), the impression made by Communist victories in China, and the beginning of support for the Viet Minh by Chinese across the border—a support taking the form of arms deliveries and the use of Chinese territory for escape, regrouping, rest, as a base of operations, and, reportedly, even the provision of strategic emplacements for artillery.

B. Economic Situation

Even today, people do not starve in Indochina, except in some areas of Tonkin province where there has long been a food deficit and where destruction, disruption of production, and interruption of imports from Cochinchina have seriously reduced food supplies. As a whole, Indochina is a food-surplus area; even with a civil conflict raging, people have enough to eat.

Production of rice is down somewhat from previous levels. In Tonkin, this results from wartime deterioration or destruction of villages, farmhouses, and many productive facilities, either during the fighting or as part of the Viet Minh "scorched-earth" policy. It also results from the fact that substantial areas are still in Viet Minh hands or are currently fields of combat. In Cochinchina, the other big rice-growing area, production is apparently high, although some falling off has undoubtedly occurred as the result of transportation barriers, which prevent the rice from moving out and therefore prevent the earning of money with which consumer goods can be purchased.

It is this transportation problem that affects export surpluses most. The rice normally moves out of the producing areas in barges drawn along the network of canals to the mills near Saigon. Because it was feared that the money obtained by selling the rice produced in the great plains of the Transbassac region would go to support the Viet Minh, which is quite active in that region, the French have enforced a blockade against the movement of Transbassac rice. The consequence has been that far less Cochinchina rice has been marketed than usual, and there is therefore almost none for export.

Corn production is down and exports almost stopped, for the higher corn country is generally in Viet Minh hands, or at least outside the area of effective police protection. The phosphate and metal mines are in Viet Minh hands. The coal mines are gradually being rehabilitated, but do not yet produce enough for domestic consumption. Some rubber plantations have been destroyed, but others are producing as virtual armed camps, and rubber exports are running at the rate of some 40,000 tons a year. Potential rubber production is estimated as approximately 115,000 tons per year.

C. Financial Situation and Counterpart Prospects

The military and political situation in Indochina dominates financial developments. Conditions of security have not been established; French military expenditures are heavy; and Indochinese budgets, local and national, are sharply unbalanced. This has resulted in an expansion of purchasing power to an amount which, despite substantial net transfers and payments abroad (see below under Currency Issue), could not be absorbed by the supply of goods and services available in Indochina without increased prices.

Prices were rising steeply until about July of 1949, and, although they have since leveled off, inflationary pressures are still strong and are likely to increase during the coming months, in part because Government expenditures, including those associated with U.S. aid programs, will no doubt have to be financed by inflationary means. Moreover, measures have been put into effect strictly limiting the flight of capital to France. This movement of capital had been somewhat deflationary in effect.

1. **Public Finance.** Independent fiscal operations are conducted in Indochina at various levels of Government. North, Central, and South Vietnam each administers its own tax and expenditure system, and the National Government of Vietnam now does likewise. Prior to the revolution, separate budgets

were maintained by 56 provincial governments—20 in the south, 26 in the north and 10 in the center—and some 3,000 villages and municipalities. Today a large number of village and municipal budgets do not exist insofar as the Governments of France and Vietnam are concerned, because the Viet Minh controls the areas concerned. Each of the States of Cambodia and Laos has a national budget and, as well, budgets applicable to lower levels of Government.

These budgets are established and administered by single political entities, each of which derives some revenue from the area under its jurisdiction, but depends also on subsidies from the central budget, solely under French jurisdiction and control, and applying to the Associated States of Indochina.

The major share of the deficits in the budgets of Indochina is financed by the French Government. A part is financed by the Indochinese Treasury, which obtains funds from the Bank of Indochina under French Government guarantees. The Treasury's debt to the Bank of Indochina at the end of 1949 was approximately Ps (piasters) 4 billion, or the equivalent of U.S. $200 million (at the official rate of exchange of U.S. $1 to Ps 20).

In 1949, ordinary expenditures of the tri-State budget, which appears to be larger than the sum of all other civil budgets in Indochina, are estimated at nearly Ps 1,900 million, while ordinary revenues from current sources are estimated at about Ps 1,600 million.

Nearly one-third of ordinary expenditures of the tri-State budget, or Ps 620 million, was devoted to the maintenance of peace and order, of which Ps 120 million went to repay the Indochinese Treasury for outlays on peace and order incurred in 1945-46. Government services, amounting to Ps 465 million, accounted for one-fourth of ordinary expenditures and the balance was devoted principally to the maintenance of public structures, roads, and to costs of administration.

About 90 percent of current, ordinary, revenues was derived from customs duties and excise taxes, receipts from the former amounting to more than Ps 800 million and receipts from the latter to almost Ps 450 million.

Ordinary expenditures of the tri-State budget for the whole of 1950 have not yet been budgeted, according to the French, pending discussions to be held at the Interstate Conference. However, in respect to the first quarter of 1950, the ordinary portion of the budget is in balance at an annual rate of Ps 1,380 million with all revenue derived from current sources. This rate is smaller than actual annual expenditures in 1949, and the decrease is largely due to the transfer of governmental functions to the three Associated States.

The extraordinary section of the tri-State budget shows expenditures of Ps 1,400 million during the fiscal year 1950 (July 1, 1949 to June 30, 1950), chiefly for the purpose of rehabilitating public property, including railway rolling stock, buildings, and roads. Extraordinary expenditures are entirely deficit-financed.

2. **Balance of Payments.** The most significant inflationary pressure is

generated by virtue of the inflationary financing of the military effort against the Viet Minh. In 1949, total piaster outlays by France (purchased from the Bank of Indochina), primarily for military purposes, amounted to some Ps 5.3 billion (U.S. $265 million at the present rate of exchange), distributed as follows:

	Billion Piasters	Equivalent to Million Dollars
French Army	Ps 2.9	$145
Partisan Troops	0.9	45
Tri-State Extraordinary Budget	0.9	45
Local Budgets (for peace and order)	0.6	30
Total	Ps 5.3	$265

These expenditures are decisive for the Indochinese balance of payments, and were sufficient in 1949 to offset the current account deficit with the franc zone, in respect to which the invisible deficit and the trade deficit each amounted to more than Ps 2 billion. Balance-of-payments deficits with non-franc currency areas were financed by France in an amount equivalent to approximately U.S. $20 million in 1949, of which $8 million went to the dollar area, $6 million to the sterling area, and $5 million to all other areas.

In the foreseeable future, there is little prospect that Indochina's international accounts can be restored to their prewar balance. Over the last three years the trade deficit has steadily increased, rising from Ps 501 million in 1947 to Ps 1,190 million in 1948. In 1949, with imports valued at Ps 4,000 million and exports at Ps 1,100 million, the deficit rose to Ps 2,900 million, or the equivalent of U.S. $145 million.

Foreign Trade of Indochina
(million piasters)

Year	Imports	Exports	Deficit
1947	967	466	501
1948	2,360	1,172	1,188
1949	3,946	1,129	2,817

The volume of exports during 1947-49 was much less than in previous years; in 1948 their volume was 40 percent of 1938 and in 1949 (rate of first 10 months) 29 percent of 1938. On the other hand, the increased value of imports has been matched by an increase in their volume, from 117 percent in 1948 (using 1938 as a base of 100) to 154 percent in 1949 (rate of first 10 months).

3. **Bank Credit**. The inflationary effects of deficit financing and French military expenditures have been reinforced by the extension of private credit. Commercial banks in Indochina during 1947 extended new credits amounting to approximately Ps 100 million; the net increase in new credit during 1948 amounted to Ps 250 million, and, in 1949 to Ps 265 million.

4. **Currency Issue**. The large volume of funds created by the governmental authorities and the banks was very substantially extinguished through the purchase of piasters by the Bank of Indochina in exchange for funds which covered net payments and transfers abroad. In 1949 such net payments and transfers amounted to Ps 5.4 billion. Accordingly, during the year, the currency issue of the Bank of Indochina increased by only Ps 560 million. But during the first two months of 1950 the currency issue rose by Ps 653 million, from Ps 3,843 million on December 31, 1949, to Ps 4,496 million on February 28, 1950. Heavy drawings on the Bank of Indochina by the Indochinese Treasury—for military expenditures—were mainly responsible for this sharp increase.

5. **Direct Controls**. Some effort has been made to restrain the rise in prices by the application of direct control. All imports which require the expenditure of non-franc foreign exchange are subject to price control. All imports from France and other parts of the French Union which require an import license are likewise subject to price control. From France, import licenses are needed for a small number of commodities, including nonferrous metals, chemical products, flour, milk, and a few other items. From other parts of the French Union, the most important commodity for which an import license is needed is sugar. Domestically produced commodities are also subject to price control, notably rice, coal, salt, cement, meat, coffee, copra, and soap. In addition the French have introduced a modest system of rationing and allocations.

However, enforcement and operation of control regulations is not effective, especially in view of the highly unfavorable political conditions existing in Vietnam.

6. **Cost of Living**. During 1949 the rise in living costs nearly came to a halt in Vietnam. A major factor countering the inflationary pressure was the substantial increase in the volume of imports. Another factor believed to be important was the backing up of rice stocks resulting from the French blockade of rice movements from the interior to the ports, a blockade imposed to prevent the collection of tolls by the Viet Minh. The cost-of-living situation is less unfavorable in the south than in the north, where, even before the revolution, rice was not produced in exportable quantities. Transport and communications throughout Vietnam are hindered by security conditions, and rice does not move in adequate amounts from the south to the north.

7. **Financial Aspects of an Aid Program**. It is doubtful that the inflationary

effects of a substantial addition to public expenditures needed to carry out an aid program could be materially offset by

a) reducing other governmental outlays for civil and military purposes;
b) increasing tax, customs, and other tax-type revenues;
c) borrowing from the public; or,
d) restrictions on the expansion of commercial bank credit.

The military and political situation dominates the level of governmental outlays, and a possible improvement in the utilization of public funds would play only a minor role in determining the level of such outlays. If all government departments are transferred to Vietnam during 1950, an additional burden will be put upon public expenditures, since the Vietnamese, without sufficient experience, will be undertaking new and difficult responsibilities. If France retains the Government Departments or unduly delays their transfer, opposition to French rule will be intensified, and military expenditures in particular may well be larger than in 1949. It is taken for granted that military expenditures will, if anything, increase in the future—because of Chinese aid to the Viet Minh, perhaps in response to our aid program, and because of increased support for the rebels if negotiations at the Interstate Conference do not bring results acceptable to the moderate nationalists.

Any significant enlargement of tax and tax-type revenues would need to come from custom duties and excises, and possibly some worthwhile sum might be derived from the fiscal monopolies. Present high levels of money income to Indochina would permit rate and duty increases at existing prices, but this involves knotty considerations. It seems unlikely that the French or the Vietnamese would be willing to chance a disturbance in the current cost-of-living situation. If prices recommence their upward movement in 1950, excise revenues will increase, while receipts from customs duties will remain dependent upon the foreign value of imports. The economic situation in France permitting, the French would no doubt prefer a higher level of Indochinese imports to raising customs duties, especially as American aid would make the former course relatively feasible.

An enlargement of revenues from better tax and customs administration, particularly tax enforcement, is a possibility, but not one to be counted on. A reform program would require the exposure of prominent figures, both in official positions and in private life; but widespread corruption at all levels of government and business makes it difficult to find an initial force for reform. Also necessary to a reform program is widespread acceptance of, and loyalty to, the Government in power, a situation not existing in Indochina.

A capital market has not been developed in Indochina. If it were proposed to sell Government securities, the effort would have to be directed toward banks, particularly the powerful Bank of Indochina, and a relatively small group of wealthy Indochinese, since the unequal distribution of wealth and income does not allow the accumulation of savings by the bulk of the population. Under the best of circumstances it would be difficult to sell securities in the absence of forceful measures, legislative or otherwise, and the task is even more formidable when the financial institutions concerned are almost wholly owned by foreigners.

The possibilities of imposing restrictions on bank credit need further examination, but it is not likely, in any event, that much can be accomplished. Bank credit in Indochina is extended largely to finance foreign trade and real estate construction, with some credit for export rehabilitation activities. The main aim would be to restrict credit for financing unessential imports so that funds already in existence would be used to buy these imports. On the assumption that the authorities are empowered to impose selective credit controls, restrictions would encounter stout opposition from the powerful French importing syndicates in Indochina.

In view of the above, it would be desirable—as an anti-inflationary measure—to sell aid supplies to the fullest possible extent, bearing in mind, however, that sales prices need to be fixed at levels which do not defeat the political objectives of the aid program.

This raises the question of the sources from which to derive sums of local currency which are needed in addition to the sales proceeds of aid supplies. If the additional sums needed are large, they cannot, in all likelihood, be obtained by a possible improvement in the use of public funds; or by an enlargement of tax, customs, and other tax-type revenues; or by borrowing from the public.

Insofar as public credit is concerned, a new bank of issue, primarily to replace the privately owned Bank of Indochina as the note issuing authority, is to be established when the Interstate Conference is held, as provided by the terms of the March 8 agreement. The conference was supposed to be held in March 1950, but has been delayed. The issues to be resolved, in respect to several matters, are extremely difficult, and the conference, if held, may lead to a further deterioration in the political situation. In any case, the French are opposed to vesting the new bank with broad powers, notwithstanding the desires of the Vietnam Government, and its potential ability to extend credit must be regarded with some reservation.

It is an open question whether existing and potential cash balances held by the Vietnam Government are large enough to supply, in whole or in part, the local currency to support economic or technical-aid programs, since the relevant information was not supplied to the Mission. In this connection, the French claim that the Vietnam Government has resources which it is not willing to use, or which could be used for more worthwhile purposes. At a minimum, this implies that the matter of cash balances is a bone of contention between the two parties.

On balance, it appears that the most likely source of local currency funds will be the French Government, unless aid is made available to Vietnam without active French participation. In this event the Vietnamese would have a powerful political incentive to supply the local currency needed, whatever sacrifice is involved, and conceivably might drastically reduce public outlays for other purposes.

Cambodia and Laos supplied practically no worthwhile information of a financial character to the Mission. Both countries claimed their national budgets were unbalanced and that the deficits were covered by France. Local currency needed for aid programs carried out in these two countries will undoubtedly have to be supplied by France.

II. Economic and Political Significance of Indochina

A. *Economic*

Indochina is normally one of the three major rice-exporting countries (with Thailand and Burma) of Southeast Asia's "rice bowl." Its great exports, reaching 1,762,000 metric tons of rice and paddy in 1936, have normally gone to feed the rice-eating areas of the world under French control, for its rice has cost too much to compete readily in free markets, at least before the war.

These rice exports were important to the consuming areas; they were important to France, which might otherwise have had to find sterling or dollars (as at present) to purchase the needed rice; and they might be of great importance to the food-deficit areas of China—a fact that can hardly be ignored in the light of China's desperate need for food today, and in the expansionist, imperialist nature of the communism that has already engulfed China.

Before the war, Indochina also produced much corn, which went primarily to France for fodder (exports reached 557,000 metric tons in 1936). It produced coal (1,725,000 metric tons exported in 1936). It produced rubber (57,900 metric tons exported in 1938). And it exported some tin, iron, salt, zinc, cement, tea, and dried fish.

Although not a major earner of foreign exchange before the war, Indochina was helpful to France in producing substantial quantities of goods for which France would otherwise have had to expend foreign exchange. Its economic revival as a saver or as an earner of foreign exchange would contribute substantially to that better balance in world trade which ERP and other U.S. and international economic programs are intended to help achieve.

B. *Political*

Indochina is politically important in several ways. First, it is a former colonial area in which a new pattern of cooperation between East and West is being attempted. The success of this effort will markedly affect Western prestige and Western influence in the whole of Southeast Asia. In the Philippines, in Indonesia, in Burma, less Western economic or political control remains than is envisioned by the March 8 agreements in Indochina. If these agreements can be implemented in cooperation with a united people in each of the three Indochinese countries, much mutual advantage can be gained by both parties, and the possibilities of increasing world cooperation in voluntary association of both Eastern and Western countries will be enhanced. On the other hand, if French influence is increasingly opposed and if the result of attempts to compromise is a widespread revulsion against the West, Vietnam, Cambodia, and Laos may draw away from association with Western countries and may seek the will-o'-the-wisp of "neutral" isolation, or may be drawn into a power bloc that intentionally sabotages genuine international cooperation.

Second, Indochina provides a natural invasion route into the ricebowl of Southeast Asia, if the Communists in China adopt this form of external aggression. In centuries past, invasions have come down the coast from China. Cochinchina itself is one of the great food-surplus producing areas, and control of its surpluses might appeal mightily to the famine-stricken Chinese. Moreover a Communist-controlled Indochina would have a potent impact on the development of Communist influence and power in Thailand, Burma, Malaya, and perhaps in Indonesia, even if no overt invasion of those areas occurred.

Political developments in Indochina, therefore, may help or hinder greatly the eventual development of a truly United Nations organization, and they will certainly affect the future orientation of the other States of Southeast Asia.

III. Dominant Political and Economic Problems

A. Political Problems

The over-riding political problem of the day, and the problem that must be solved before any substantial economic recovery or development can take place, is the conflict raging in Vietnam and touching Cambodia and Laos as well.

1. **The Bases of the Conflict.** Indochina faces a world in turmoil, has a powerful and potentially unfriendly neighbor, and yet is fettered by its legacy from the past.

Vietnam, Cambodia, and Laos look far back in history to their independently developed cultures and traditions and want again to live lives independent of each other, despite the advantages that would derive from common or at least coordinated economic and financial policies, and probably also from coordinated political policies.

The French in Indochina look back to a history of colonial administration in which they take great pride, and during which the economic resources of the area were substantially developed, public health was greatly improved, education of an "elite" was encouraged, and the three countries drew real benefits from economic and political integration. There is a natural desire on the part of the French not to see these advances wiped out by an extremist, unrealistic nationalism and by hastily conceived economic and political policies.

The Vietnamese, Cambodians, and Laotians look back on French control with a jaundiced eye, understating its contributions and magnifying its political and economic restrictions. Fired by an intense nationalism that so far is primarily negative, a reaction against control, they naturally tend to give less than enough attention to planning and carrying out positive, constructive policies.

Finally, the fairly recent past has also narrowed the possibilities of mutual adjustment, for the virulent disease of communism has infected some of the most effective and popular leaders in Indochina, a country where there are too few leaders who are either effective or popular.

The French have a large stake in prestige, in investments, and in their responsibility to the peoples with whom they have long worked. They are understandably reluctant to pull out until the three governments are going concerns, able to carry their full burden both domestically and internationally. The Vietnamese want the French to leave as soon as possible, and feel that everywhere, including the military field, responsibility is being transferred much too slowly. The Communist-led rebels (who include many non-Communists) take the same view but much more violently and uncompromisingly. Besides their extreme and impetuous nationalism, of course, the rebels are more and more committed to the inflexible Communist line.

Among all three groups, deeply felt emotions have been so exacerbated that reason and mutual accommodation have been unable to play anything like their proper part. These fetters from the past, made up of old ideals and dreams and now heavily encrusted with emotion, greatly hinder the working out by all non-Communist groups of what, to an outside observer, might be a thoroughly fair and reasonable solution.

2. **The Solution Being Attempted in Vietnam.** (Because Vietnam is by far the largest of the three States and because the three elements that must be reconciled are most irreconcilable in Vietnam, the following discussion pertains only to that country.)

French policy has been to find and support those responsible and respected leaders among the Vietnamese whose nationalism (ardent among all) was not so unreasoning as to make impossible an evolutionary adjustment to "independence within the French Union." The French sincerely believe that Vietnam will derive important advantages from its association with the other countries within the French Union and that the strength of the whole Union will thereby also be enhanced.

Bao Dai, formerly Emperor of Annam (one of the three parts of modern Vietnam), and now called "Chief of State of Vietnam," believes that the status negotiated with the French and spelled out in the March 8 agreements will be beneficial to Vietnam. He is supported by a number of respected and able Vietnamese leaders and by a substantial part of the population.

He is not, however, a French "puppet," although he is regarded as such by many Vietnamese and other Asiatics since his vigorous protests to the French have never been made publicly, and since he has failed to elicit from the French firm promises of future concessions. Where French aid and cooperation will help Vietnam, Bao Dai seeks it. Where he believes that the French are not acting in the best interests of Vietnam or are not acting fast enough to turn over the reins of agreed authority, he is quick to protest vigorously. The continuous popular pressure resulting from the more extreme nationalist demands of the Viet Minh, the widespread antagonism to and suspicion of the French, and the continuing need to win over the fence-sitters by evidence that he is able to forward Vietnam's independence and interests, combine to push Bao Dai and his government into continual efforts to wring more and faster concessions from the French. That complete freedom of action is not achieved by him does not at all mean that he is subservient to French demands. Quite the contrary, he is making continual demands of the French.

On the other hand, Bao Dai sees in Ho Chi Minh a rival leader, who has been and still is personally immensely popular and yet who is Moscow-trained, apparently a devoted Communist, relying on a clique of avowed Communists, and heading a "government" that has been recognized by Moscow and by Communist China as the "legitimate" Government of Vietnam.

The possibility of compromising with such a group, without losing effective control to them, is very small; and their control of the country would mean a foreign domination, and a vicious and unremitting kind of domination, that would be worse than any of which the French were ever accused and certainly far worse than any of the French controls envisioned under the March 8 agreement. Some of the "fence-sitters" have stated that the reason they do not commit themselves to Bao Dai is that they wish Vietnam to receive a status comparable to that of India, Pakistan, and Indonesia; others are still waiting it out, not because they want Ho Chi Minh to win, but because they are afraid of having been against him if he does win. They also fear immediate reprisal and even assassination from Viet Minh agents, who they believe are everywhere. It is no wonder that Bao Dai welcomes French military aid in quelling the rebellion of such a group.

The Viet Minh is strong, well led, well organized, well armed. It receives aid from China and from sympathizers all over Indochina. It receives indirect aid by virtue of the very fact that many personally unsympathetic Vietnamese are afraid to commit themselves to support Bao Dai, for fear of what may happen to them either now or after a possible Viet Minh victory.

Bao Dai's military and police forces are growing. They are being armed and trained by the French, and are being given more and more responsibility, both for policing and for front-line action. They are not yet strong enough, however, to stand up to the Viet Minh alone. It is only honest to say that, today, however general would be Bao Dai's support in a fair and secret election, his government could not last long if French troops withdrew from the country.

Besides nationalism and Moscow communism, there is another force influencing the situation in Indochina. This is Chinese communism.

According to previous estimates there are between 600,000 and 1,000,000 Chinese in Indochina. They are hardworking, aggressive, competent, shrewd. They dominate much of the business in the country. Some 200,000 to 300,000 of them live in Cholon, the twin city of Saigon.

Although they live and work in Indochina, few of the Chinese minority feel any deep loyalty to the country. They owe allegiance to friends, family, and business associates, many of whom are in China. Unlike similar groups in Thailand and Malaya, they have never been active in the political life of the country. Moreover, Communist doctrine and practices are presumably a threat to their business interests. Nevertheless, pressures may be exerted on them from Communist China and through Communist organizers to make them a potential subversive force. It would be very surprising if the Chinese minority now supported the government of Bao Dai.

There is always present, moreover, the unlikely possibility of outright invasion from the north. Long-standing antipathy exists between Chinese and Vietnamese, and the Vietnamese hold bitter memories of the looting by Chinese Nationalist troops in 1945 when they occupied all of Tonkin and parts of Laos and Annam down to the sixteenth parallel, after the Japanese surrender. Such an invasion would undoubtedly go far toward uniting the people of Vietnam in opposition to any group that was allied with the invader. On the other hand, inasmuch as the Chinese Communists are probably well aware of the antipathy that exists towards China and the fear of Chinese imperialism, they may well maintain an officially correct attitude and hold out prospects of friendly relations as an additional drawing card for Ho. This policy would not prevent the Chinese Communists from continuing to supply Ho with material and some technical assistance.

In the meantime, however, the presence of a strong, modern French Army near the northern border gives many Vietnamese a feeling of security against at least one danger. This is clearly recognized by Bao Dai and by the other leaders who support his policy of working for Vietnam with, not against, the French.

The situation boils down to this:

a) The French are gradually turning over much responsibility to Bao Dai and his Government, but retain certain powers as French Union powers. Prominent among these powers is military defense of the area against internal and external aggression;

b) The Viet Minh wants the French out completely, wants no part of the French Union, and wants to control the country for communism (and probably calculates correctly that only the French are now strong enough to deny Ho Chi Minh this control);

c) Bao Dai wants as much authority for a Vietnamese Government as possible, but knows the country would be lost to Communist control if the French Union now withdrew its military support. He supports the March 8 agreements, but will undoubtedly continue to press for an evolutionary interpretation of those agreements, as fast as he believes the Vietnamese can themselves maintain law and order in the country, and administer its affairs.

In this situation, the balance can only be shifted and a solution achieved by

a) Military suppression of the Viet Minh, by the Vietnamese so far as possible, and backed up by the French so far as militarily necessary. This is apparently feasible only in the accessible areas that contain the majority of the population, food production, and industry; or

b) Convincing enough fence-sitters and enough of the non-Communist nationalists in the Viet Minh that Bao Dai can and will promote Vietnamese national interests, as fast and as far as is feasible, given Vietnamese military and political effectiveness. This "political solution" is the one for which both Bao Dai and the top-level French are striving.

B. Economic Problems

Indochina's economic problems are partly short-run, resulting from the deterioration, destruction, and disruption brought about by the war and the recent civil turmoil, and partly long-run, based on inadequate or unbalanced economic development. Some of the short-run economic problems are also military or political problems in the sense that solving them would contribute to the solution of the military and political problems outlined above.

1. **Rural Rehabilitation.** The most urgent short-run problem is the rehabilitation of farmsteads and villages in the Tonkin delta area. The war with Japan and the recent fighting with Viet Minh forces, especially when the latter withdrew and scorched the earth behind them, have resulted in an enormous amount of destruction of homes, water buffaloes, farm equipment, and water and electricity supply systems. Many of the inhabitants of affected regions fled to escape from the disorders and they return to take up former occupations when the area is pacified. Those who remained and those who fled have both suffered serious losses from which they now are attempting to recover; but they are lacking many of the essentials of recovery. Aid is needed both for rehabilitation of public services (health supplies and medical facilities, water

supply, electricity supply, repair of roads, irrigation ditches and dikes), and to start the farmers producing again (preparation of the land for cultivation, housing materials and services, fertilizer, farm tools, seeds, animal vaccines, repair of rice mills).

2. **Health Services.** Quite apart from the special rehabilitation needs of areas recently pacified, there are also general needs for better health and medical supplies and services throughout Vietnam, Cambodia, and Laos. Wartime destruction and neglect of hospitals, clinics and training institutions, and limitations on imports of certain supplies and equipment, because of foreign exchange shortages, have resulted in a deterioration of the health and medical services now available in those three countries. Moreover, the three local governments are now beginning to undertake the responsibility for operating a considerable proportion of the health services of these countries, services formerly provided by the French. They see the need not only to regain prewar levels of service, but to provide more and better service. Malaria is prevalent in upland areas and other diseases are common outside of the major cities. Infant mortality is high. Although a health program is essentially long-term in nature, an immediate start on it would have beneficial political effects. Mobile units and temporary clinics would bring emergency aid to many neglected areas, and the experience gained during this first period would be invaluable in developing a long-range program in the health field.

3. **Import shortages.** Certain fields of reconstruction and economic activity are held back by shortages of imported commodities. This is particularly true of the cottage textile industry (short of cotton yarn and raw silk), of power and transportation (short of petroleum products), and of reconstruction of housing, bridges, and public buildings (short of galvanized sheeting and steel reinforcing bars).

The supplies of these commodities have been limited by the shortage of foreign exchange, despite French assistance on the franc trade deficit and ECA assistance to the French Union as a whole on the dollar trade deficit. Encouragement to production and reconstruction is particularly important now, when both unemployment and a lack of consumer goods and housing are severe.

Supply and distribution of moderate quantities of such products would give an immediate impulse to production and construction.

4. **Telecommunications.** One of the particularly critical economic problems of the area is the reconstruction and extension of its telecommunications. This is important on political and military, as well as economic, grounds. Outside the major cities, telephone and telegraph wires, all above ground, have generally been cut. Radio is the only practicable means of telecommunication. Radio facilities are, however, quite inadequate.

Radio communication facilities among major towns are heavily overloaded, and messages are consequently often delayed. No rapid communication at all is available to most small towns and villages. The people there get their news by rumor or by mail. They have relatively little way of knowing what their government is doing for them, or, in fact, who is in control of the government. They do not learn quickly or fully about the successive transfers of control from the French to the local governments.

Their inability to get information is matched by their inability to make their views known to the government. For them to feel any sense of identity with the government, to experience any participation on which their loyalty may base itself, they must be able to communicate more easily with the major centers of political activity.

Similarly, the government is unable to spread information about its own or the Viet Minh's current or impending military activity, or to get prompt news of rebel attacks on isolated villages.

Improved radio communication among the major towns, and between the towns and villages, would benefit commerce and travel greatly. It would also assist the governments of the three countries to keep in touch with much more of the population, broadcasting information and news, and getting back in turn quick reports of local political and economic conditions. Its military value, in keeping track of rebel movements and speeding aid to beleaguered villages, would alone justify a substantial expenditure in this field.

5. **Rehabilitation of Transportation and Industry.** Two important bottlenecks in the economic life of Indochina result from the destruction of bridges (highway and railroad), small craft, and port equipment. Imported materials and equipment are needed to rehabilitate these key elements in the transportation system. Foreign trade would be facilitated thereby, but internal trade and travel would be helped even more, and there would also result some military benefit.

Power and light facilities in most areas have deteriorated or been partly destroyed during the last 10 years. Shortages of power and light constitute barriers to industrial activity and also affect military security.

Certain mines (especially the phosphate mines in Tonkin and the Laotian coal mine near Vientiane) need rehabilitation or development so that they can supply minerals urgently needed within Indochina. A small amount of money and effort quickly applied to these mines could have an important and prompt economic effect.

6. **Knowledge of English.** An urgent economic-political problem in Indochina is posed by the almost complete ignorance of English by any non-French personnel other than top government officials. This is an important handicap in many technical fields, in trade and tourism, and in government. It severely limits the possibility of non-French speaking technical experts doing their most productive work in connection with aid programs, and it means that very few Indochinese students can profit from study in the United States,

England, Canada, etc. Moreover, it prevents the development of better acquaintance with and understanding of Westerners other than Frenchmen. Familiarity with the English-speaking world, its history, government, attitudes, business, technology, etc., might make a real difference in the attitudes of Indochinese toward the possibilities of mutually beneficial cooperation with the West.

There is today a great enthusiasm for English in Indochina. No store has a French-English dictionary in stock; English books and magazines are snapped up, what few can be imported. And the few English classes that are offered, such as those given in Saigon at the Seventh Day Adventist Mission, are jampacked and have long waiting lists. Provision of English teachers and teaching materials would be one of the most effective ways of stimulating economic development and the growth of internationalism in Indochina.

IV. Aid Currently Being Extended to Indochina from Sources Other than the U.S.

Since Vietnam, Laos, and Cambodia are now recognized as Associated States within the French Union, since France has important economic interests there, and since the French have long trained and provided technicians and advisers, as well as administrators, for the various governmental services in Indochina, it is only to be expected that France would still be providing much economic and technical aid to these three countries. Some 1,200 Vietnamese and 100 Cambodian students, for example, are reported to be now studying in France.

As Government functions are transferred from the High Commissariat (French) to the Government services of the local state governments, substantial numbers of French personnel ordinarily are also transferred—sometimes as advisers, often in line positions. The future need for foreign advisers is clearly anticipated in the March 8 agreement with Vietnam, and the similar agreements with each of the other two governments, which specifies that:

The Vietnam government will apply, in the first place, to subjects of the French Union every time it needs counsellors, technicians or experts in public services and establishments or in enterprises having a public character concerned with the defense of the French Union.

The priority granted to subjects of the French Union will only cease in case the French Government is unable to supply the personnel required.

Of course, these advisers are to be paid by the Vietnam Government, so it may be somewhat misleading to consider them as one form of technical "asssistance."

On the other hand, France is currently meeting the major share of the budgetary deficits of the three local governments (contributing about $30 million to these individual budgets in 1949), is financing the tri-State extraordinary budget (to the extent of $45 million in 1949), is providing substantial dollars, with ECA aid, to cover certain imports from dollar areas, is supporting the piaster at an artificially high rate vis-à-vis the franc, and is spending some $410 million on national troops and on its own military effort in the area.

This is clearly important economic aid by France. How much of it could continue if ECA were not in turn aiding France is another question.

The United Nations and the specialized agencies are not providing any economic or technical assistance to Vietnam, Laos, or Cambodia, except for a fellowship granted by the United Nations which is enabling a Chief of Section of the Ministry of Finance of Cambodia to study forestry in Canada this year. It is true that France offered in the March 8 agreements "to put forward and to support the candidacy of (Vietnam, Cambodia, Laos) when the latter conform(s) with the general conditions set out by the Charter of the United Nations for admission to that organization"; and that associate membership has already been arranged in the Economic Commission for Asia and the Far East (ECAFE), and the three Governments have been admitted to membership in the World Health Organization. On the other hand, the priority reserved for French technicians, noted above, may operate to limit any assistance the United Nations and specialized agencies might otherwise be prepared to extend. Even the offer of the United Nations International Children's Emergency Fund (UNICEF) to provide $457,900 for a child-feeding and anti-tuberculosis vaccination campaign in Indochina has apparently not been taken advantage of.

V. Aid Currently Extended by the United States

Practically no American governmental aid of any sort is now reaching Indochina directly. It is true that some ECA aid is provided indirectly through the French Union program, but the United States gets no public credit for this and has no local representatives to see that it is used wisely. Moreover, ECA aid indirectly helps France finance the military and other governmental expenditures she is now making in Indochina, but the United States gets no local credit for this and presumably wants none. No other U.S. Government aid is supplied to Indochina. Cambodia is itself paying the expenses of three students who are studying corn hybridization in the United States.

There are a few U.S.-supported private religious missions that are active in Indochina, supplying medical and educational services. These include the Seventh Day Adventists and the Christian and Missionary Alliance. The American Foundation for Overseas Blind has provided Braille publications and equipment, and the World Student Service Fund has provided certain textbooks for colleges and faculties in Vietnam. There were six Vietnamese students studying in the United States in 1948-49, but it is not known under what sponsorship.

VI. Recommendations for Emergency Aid

Summary of Program Recommendations

1. Rural rehabilitation
   a) Medical supplies and equipment including mobile units, buildings for clinics, water purification equipment, educational supplies $6,000,000
   b) Engineering units for 20 centers, including tractors with equipment for land preparation, irrigation ditch repair, and earth moving equipment for dike and canal operations   3,500,000
   c) Agricultural supplies including fertilizers, seeds, farm tools   3,050,000
   d) Rice mills   2,000,000
   e) Short-term reconstruction of roads   1,000,000
   f) Technical equipment, publications, training aids for use in implementing aid projects   600,000

                                          $16,150,000 $16,150,000

2. Commodities, including cotton, cotton yarn, reinforcing steel, galvanized sheeting, raw silk and POL   2,500,000

3. Telecommunications—rehabilitation and extension of present system   1,000,000

4. Trainees to U.S. (50 at $5,000 each)   250,000

5. Power, light, and engineering projects for mines, ports, bridges, etc.   3,100,000

6. Funds to supplement present USIS activities   500,000

                          Total $23,500,000

A. *Rural Rehabilitation and Agricultural Improvement*

1. **General Objectives.** This program is designed to follow in a pacified area as soon after the conclusion of military operations as conditions permit, to help the rural people re-establish themselves and carry on their accustomed

occupations. It aims principally at helping them to meet their immediate problems of living and to build up production to a high level. It is foreseen that complete recovery from the damaged conditions now existing in many areas will require five to ten years. The soundest form of aid under such a situation would consist of assistance to measures which help the people re-establish production with the expectation that, out of the returns of production, they themselves will gradually find the means of acquiring the many things now needed.

2. **Locations Where Operations Should be Undertaken.** The present disturbed conditions in the countryside, now prevailing over a considerable part of Vietnam, Cambodia, and Laos, greatly limit the extent to which the proposed program can be successfully operated. Furthermore, from a political point of view it is more important that such a program be established in some areas than in others. Taking these two factors into consideration, it is recommended that the initial operations be undertaken in accessible portions of the Tonkin Delta, with a few centers in pacified portions of Cochinchina if conditions permit. It is recommended that, subsequently, the program be introduced into other areas as quickly as they are pacified and provision can be made to do so.

3. **Types of Activity**

   a) *Engineering.* Plowing service, with mechanized equipment, as a pilot operation undertaken in 20 centers, where war has caused a serious shortage of draft animals and farmers find it difficult to bring land back into cultivation.

   The repair and construction of irrigation facilities, possibly road repair, well drilling and other types of activity, making use of mechanized equipment largely available for the above operations.

   b) *Health.* Dispensary and maternity services through local clinics formerly existing in these areas, which need to be rebuilt and strengthened.

   Mobile clinics; hospital service in hospitals located in principal centers, existing before the war, which need to be rebuilt and strengthened; health and sanitation education.

   c) *Agricultural Supplies.* Ammonium phosphate fertilizer: 5,000 tons for delivery to meet needs of the rice crop transplanted in June and July, largely in the Tonkin Delta but also in Cochinchina; 15,000 tons for rice crops planted the following winter and early summer.

   Farm tools and equipment; hand tools and simple implements, some of them of improved types, to be procured in Japan for immediate use before local production is available, and for demonstration; assistance to local blacksmiths, supplying iron and simple blacksmith equipment, to assist them in getting back into the production of tools commonly used and understood.

Seeds; vegetable seeds to be imported, to meet shortages as found to exist in areas being rehabilitated. Improved seeds of field crops, as rice, will be obtained largely from local sources.

Vaccines for the control of rinderpest of cattle and other animal diseases, which can be produced by the Pasteur Institute in Indochina.

d) *Rehabilitation of Dwellings.* Piaster loans to purchase the most essential timbers for simple structures. Hauling or leveling services (performed by engineering unit).

4. Organization Recommendations

a) Responsibility for carrying out the specific projects developed under each of the above four categories should be assumed by the appropriate government agency, or by a private agency, such as the Pasteur Institute, where it excels and has facilities.

b) Over-all responsibility for coordinating the different categories of activities in this program, and for providing the administrative and executive staff in field centers, should be assigned by the government to an appropriate agency which would take steps to see that this coordination and administration is effectively provided for.

c) In the field, the program should be carried out through centers established in the principal city of each province, and through subcenters in each of its subdivisions, of which there usually are between three and five.

d) The programming of United States aid to specific projects in this program should be the responsibility of a mixed Commission, in general based on the pattern developed by the Joint Commission on Rural Reconstruction in China. This Commission should operate under an agreement with the United States economic mission, which agreement defines its area of responsibilities and relations to the economic mission. Attached to this mixed Commission should be a corps of specialists—Indochinese, French, and Americans—who would advise the Commission on projects, supervise the use of United States aid, and give technical assistance to sponsoring agencies.

e) In order to gain from this program the greatest possible political benefit, it should be carried out under some appropriate name, preferably including some well-conceived catch phrase which could readily be publicized (suggestion: "People's Recovery Aid Program"). It should be publicized by a substantial effort in information and training aids, through such media as posters, comic books, leaflets, film strips, radio, and motion pictures.

5. Justification.
The need for reconstruction of areas devastated by fighting is described in Section III, B, 1, above. Aid in rural rehabilitation will increase stability within recently pacified areas and lessen the difficulty in keeping order. At the same time, news of improved conditions on the Vietnam side will filter over the lines, possibly making the population less cooperative with the Viet Minh forces and more eager to get on the Vietnam side.

Perhaps most important of all, a substantial program bringing effective assistance to those who need it should increase the prestige of the Bao Dai Government and gain for it the adherence of patriots who are aware of the country's problems and wish to align themselves on the side that does something about them. These reasons justify efforts to push this program on the largest feasible scale, progressively into as many areas as permitted by conditions.

Aid in carrying out a program of rural rehabilitation in recently pacified areas has been requested in a general letter to the U.S. Economic Survey Mission from the Vietnamese Secretary of State for Agriculture, written at the request of His Majesty Bao Dai; but no specific plan for this program, containing recommendations for assistance, has yet been received. The proposals here presented are based on discussions and information obtained in Indochina, and on experience with the rural reconstruction program of the Joint Commission on Rural Reconstruction in China. Before any program can be undertaken in Indochina, agreement on its general outlines must first be secured. Then, it will be necessary to define specifically the localities within the general area of the Tonkin delta and Cochinchina where operations can first begin; and agreement must be sought with the French military authorities as to when their responsibilities for rehabilitation cease, and when these responsibilities are taken up by the civilian administration under Bao Dai.

Obviously, for success, a program of this sort will require a great deal of imagination, patience, determination, and energy. It is not to be expected that the most effective program possible will be hit upon in all its details at the beginning. Six months or more may be required for the Commission to think through its problems and devise the most effective ways of meeting them. With determination, however, it should be possible to overcome difficulties and establish a program which not only will be useful in solving this immediate problem of rehabilitation but also may assist the newly established government services of these countries to develop an action program designed to help the mass of the people.

In connection with this program it is believed that a careful study of the experience of the Joint Commission on Rural Reconstruction in China will offer useful suggestions.

The selection of representatives to serve on the Commission is a matter of the utmost importance. The American member should be French-speaking, have a wide knowledge of rural programs, be interested in the objectives of the program, and prepared to work cooperatively with other nationals for its success. Some resistance may be encountered to the idea of having an American serve on this Commission. It probably will be found true that the French will have the best judgment and the soundest suggestions in a large number of cases. However the Chief of the U.S. Economic Mission should have his own representative on this Commission to advise him on appropriate action, as well as to bring to the work of the Commission another viewpoint and the contributions which the right kind of American might make.

The suggested list of activities does not include action by the Government on social problems such as land reform, arrangements to eliminate usurious rates of interest, and action which lessens the harmful effects of the monopolistic control on rice marketing now held by Chinese merchants. The present does not appear to be an appropriate time for the newly established government to attempt action on such matters but they will eventually require action if living standards of a considerable proportion of the peasants in Indochina are to be appreciably raised. A rural program will be greatly strengthened by the addition of effective action along these lines.

B. Health (in Addition to the Rural Rehabilitation Program)

1. **General Objectives.** The Governments of Vietnam, Cambodia, and Laos are now beginning to undertake responsibility for operating a considerable proportion of the health services of these countries, including hospitals, clinics, and training institutions. It is recommended that aid be given, supplementing what is available from other sources, to provide the medical supplies and equipment to the extent needed for the operation of these services during the period contemplated in the present aid program. If available, it is recommended that piasters be allotted to help with the rebuilding and furnishing of certain of the required structures, destroyed during the war, especially for structures needed to provide trained personnel and services in the rural rehabilitation program. If needed, the use of appropriated (dollar) funds for materials and furnishings that have to be obtained from abroad also is recommended.

2. **Justification.** Requests from each of the three States of Vietnam, Cambodia, and Laos place high priority on assistance in meeting health problems. An appreciation of health services was developed under the French regime, when medical work on different levels, including training, was established. Many of the facilities then established were destroyed during the war with Japan or subsequently. These Governments now are anxious for assistance to rebuild hospitals and training centers and the services of the Government through which these programs are carried out. However, assistance to this program, which is essentially long range in nature, has a deeper justification of extreme importance. This justification applies at least equally to the development of agriculture. Communism now derives its principal following on the issue of nationalism. Economic distress at the present time is mentioned in Communist propaganda, but it is secondary. Nevertheless, the need for rural reform programs is urgent, as was apparent in the Mission's trips in the rural areas in the Tonkin Delta and in the countryside around Saigon. Farmers in Vietnam are living in unjustified poverty and distress only in part because of the present disturbed conditions. Some of this distress arises from a lack of attention to health problems. Related to it are the existing conditions of

agriculture. A great deal of improvement can be brought about through development of irrigation, control of animal diseases, distribution of improved seeds, and the use of commercial fertilizers. The current poverty, however, is also due to usurious interest rates, monopolistic control of rice marketing by Chinese merchants, and high land rentals. In the conditions created by this situation there exists an issue of which the Communists may some day decide to take advantage, if it happens that the present issue of nationalism has less popular appeal. If the Bao Dai Government, on the other hand, seizes the initiative in this matter and establishes itself as the government of rural reform it will possess a tremendous advantage that would be useful now and possibly still more useful later. Although long range, therefore, assistance to the development of an effective government program and services in both the fields of agriculture and health could have a very important short range effect. It should not be overlooked, furthermore, that the year immediately ahead will be formative in these Governments, and aid given at this time could help mold these essential services more quickly and directly along lines that would be soundest and most useful in the future.

3. **Comments**. The Chief of the U.S. Economic Mission should secure for his staff a high caliber public health specialist with experience qualifying him to advise in a situation such as now found in Indochina. As in other categories, funds should not be committed to any program of aid until the outlines of that program and the type of assistance required are agreed upon. Undue haste in this matter may lose an opportunity to insure that the aid is used for the most useful purposes possible and to help influence the development of government services along sound lines.

C. Agriculture (in Addition to the Rural Rehabilitation Program)

1. **General Objectives**. The Governments of Vietnam, Cambodia, and Laos have assumed or shortly will assume responsibility for operating the government services in agriculture of these countries. This will include the operation of experiment stations, research laboratories, field extension services, and training centers. Many of the structures used in this program were destroyed or damaged during the war, and equipment has been lost or destroyed. It is recommended that substantial assistance be given toward the supply of technical equipment, supplies, and reference material needed for the rehabilitation of these services during the period of United States aid. If available, it is recommended that piasters be provided to assist in the re-establishment of essential structures, particularly of institutions or establishments which supply information, material (such as vaccines), or trained personnel required for the operation of the rural rehabilitation program.

2. Justification. Statements justifying expenditure for health program and services, made under the preceding heading, apply equally here.

D. Procurement Recommended for Rural Rehabilitation, Health, and Agricultural Improvement Programs

To assist in carrying out the above three types of programs, the following categories of equipment and supplies are recommended for procurement, using appropriated (dollar) funds. It is recommended, however, that no procurement be initiated until general outlines of the programs into which they fit have been agreed upon between the Chief of the U.S. Economic Mission and authorized representatives of the other governments concerned, and until agreement also has been reached on the kind and quantity of material to be procured. The amounts recommended are approximate total amounts required, based on present information. It should be understood that changes in the amounts may be necessary subsequently, arising out of changes in the situation, new information, and discussions with the other governments concerned.

1. Medical and sanitation supplies and equipment, (including mobile units, educational supplies, building supplies) $6,000,000

2. 20 engineering units, for pilot operations (including tractors with attachments and parts, for land preparation, $2,000,000; and earth moving equipment for irrigation ditch repair, dike operations, and canals, $1,500,000)   3,500,000

3. Agricultural supplies (20,000 tons ammonium phosphate, $2,000,000; farm tools, largely from Japan, $1,000,000; vegetable seeds, $50,000)   3,050,000

4. Rice mills   2,000,000

5. Short-term reconstruction of roads   1,000,000

6. Technical equipment and supplies, and publications and training aids   600,000

Total $16,150,000

1. Medical and Sanitation Supplies and Equipment ($6,000,000)

   a) *Justification.* This item covers assistance to Vietnam, Cambodia, and Laos. It includes medical and sanitation supplies for hospitals, clinics, and training centers; equipment required for the same institutions; supplies and equipment needed in the rural rehabilitation program, including vehicles and equipment for mobile clinics; materials and furnishings procured abroad for use in rehabilitating buildings. In a program for the people this item appears to deserve very high priority. It was mentioned prominently in every request received. It will bring direct and immediate benefit. Properly applied for purposes of agreed programs it will aid the newly formed governments to build up programs and services to support them, thereby increasing their prestige and strength.

b) *Comments*. An exact list of the supplies and equipment required for these purposes has not yet been compiled. The compilation of this list, based on programs in which it is agreed they shall be used, should constitute one of the first tasks of the Mission after it is established.

2. Engineering Units ($3,500,000)

a) *Justification*. A pilot operation made up of 20 units of mechanized equipment is recommended. The equipment will be mainly of two general categories: equipment to prepare land for planting; and equipment for the moving of earth, in the repair of irrigation systems, the building of dikes and the like. The purpose of this program is not to introduce mechanization in the cultivation of rice. It is an emergency measure, designed to meet the present shortage of animal power in Vietnam. No feasible way is seen to replace the water buffaloes needed on farms, and the use of mechanized equipment appears, after study, to be an effective measure that can be employed for the purposes indicated. Since a substantial amount of land is out of cultivation and public works are in disrepair, it is expected that the use of these units will contribute significantly toward the rehabilitation of these areas. At the same time their use will serve to dramatize this rural program and call attention to aid that is being given. Items of equipment suggested include, for each center: 5 tractors; 5 sets of disc plows; 5 disc harrows; 1 Martin ditcher; 2 wagons; 1 leveler; and spare parts. The estimated cost includes the cost of POL.

b) *Comments*. Careful attention to the selection of the proper types and sizes of tractors used is essential, to insure that they are suited to the conditions under which they will be used. In the Tonkin area it appears likely that several types of tractors would be best in one center, from the Cub or Farmall type to larger types of about 44 horsepower. Experience in the operation and repair of these types of mechanized equipment does not now exist generally; and a complete organization to handle the project will be required. Some technical assistance in developing the necessary personnel and maintenance facilities can be supplied by private farm equipment companies established in the area. It is envisaged that the sets of equipment will be distributed among the subcenters of the Province in spots most needed. One of the duties of the person in charge of each unit should be to study needs and opportunities and provide for the fullest possible use of the equipment in services which achieve the desired object. These services might include the plowing and harrowing of land; the repair and construction of irrigation laterals and small canals; the hauling of building materials, fertilizers, etc.; and the grading or leveling of building sites and agricultural land. It probably will be found desirable to begin with the operation of not above 5 or 10 of the units, adding others as needed and possible, until the total number is in operation.

3. Agricultural Supplies ($3,050,000)

a) *Justification and Comment. Fertilizers ($2,000,000).* Farmers in parts of Tonkin and Cochinchina are to some extent familiar with the use of superphosphate, originally from the phosphate rock mined in Tonkin. Indications are, however, that nitrogen may contribute even more to an increase of yields; so ammonium phosphate would appear to form nearly the ideal fertilizer for this region, especially since it will leave no acid residue in the soil. This opinion is strengthened by results obtained in Kwangsi Province of China, to the north, where soil conditions are similar. Soils will almost certainly respond well to its application, though experimental data have not been presented. Farmers in both Tonkin and Cochinchina spoke of the need of fertilizers, and the average rice yields of Indochina are only about one-third the average yields of Japan. Since this type of fertilizer is new, a certain amount of demonstration may be needed; and therefore it is recommended that only 5,000 of the 20,000 tons be brought in for the rice crop which is transplanted in June and July. Studies will be required to determine the proportions which should go to Tonkin and to Cochinchina. Since haste will be necessary if procurement is to be effected in time to arrive by June, it is suggested that agreement on this item be sought by the Mission and procurement initiated at the earliest possible moment.

Farm Tools ($1,000,000). The need for attention to the supply of farm tools and implements arises out of the shortage created as the result of destruction and loss during the war, especially in Tonkin. Hand tools and farm implements are usually made by blacksmiths, found in many places throughout the countryside. A part of the amount requested is to be used for the purpose of iron and steel and for simple smithy equipment needed to get these blacksmiths back into operation. A larger part is intended for use in purchasing in Japan a selected list of tools and implements believed to be suitable for use in Indochina, for immediate distribution. It is suggested that the first order be limited in quantity but include a rather wide selection of types of the following: shovels; rakes; grubbing hoes; weeding hoes; hand-propelled paddy weeders; plows for paddy fields; pedal-driven threshing machines; small power-driven rice huskers; and small power-driven rice polishers. Reference is made to a catalog prepared by the "Japan Export Advancement Association of

Agricultural Machinery and Implements," of which a copy has been left in the American Legation, Saigon. In selecting the individual items to be imported, farmers in parts of the country where they are to be used should be consulted, not officials in Saigon or Hanoi.

Seeds ($50,000). Improved varieties of rice have been developed in experiment stations of Indochina and are available for distribution. They should be sought and used, if possible, to distribute to farmers lacking seed of this crop. Vegetable seeds, on the other hand, often are difficult to supply from local sources. Furthermore, a number of varieties obtainable abroad have been found to be suitable for use in countries like Indochina. It is recommended, therefore, that appropriate varieties be imported in quantities that can be absorbed. Action to procure seeds, however, should be preceded by a careful investigation of types and varieties most likely to be useful, and of quantities likely to be absorbed.

4. **Rice Mills.** Rice is the principal crop of Indochina. The agricultural economy, therefore, depends largely on the production and processing of this product. Owing to the lack of maintenance, war damage, and antiquity the rice mills of Indochina cannot produce to capacity nor can they maintain the quality desirable for export. The mills are in the main over 40 years old. This results in a very high percentage of broken rice which brings a substantially lower price on the world market. At present the mills have sufficient capacity to mill the rice that is currently flowing into Saigon-Cholon, but should the blockade on rice movements from the Transbassac region, currently enforced by the French, be lifted in the future, the mills would not be able to handle the rice production.

Practically all rice mills are located in or near the Saigon-Cholon area. This necessitates the transportation of large tonnages of paddy to that area and in many instances the reshipment of paddy husks back to the rural areas. With the construction of new rice mills studies should be conducted to determine the feasibility of locating the rice mills at concentration points in the rice-producing areas rather than adding to the concentration in and around the Saigon-Cholon area.

The specific requirements for the rehabilitation of the rice mills were not developed owing to the shortness of time available. However, it is estimated that the capacity for and the quality of products can be greatly increased with the expenditure of $2,000,000 for rehabilitation of existing mills. It is recommended, therefore, that this sum be earmarked for rehabilitation and construction of rice mills.

5. **Road Reconstruction.** Throughout Indochina during the period of occupation by the Japanese the roads were permitted to go without repair, and the scorched earth activities of the Viet Minh have resulted in a badly deteriorated road system. Equipment and materials for the repair of roads and bridges are not available. From both the economic and security

standpoints, as regions are pacified, it is extremely necessary that communications be resumed with these areas. To provide contact by road, basic materials and equipment for road repair and reconstruction must be provided. Requests were received for equipment and material to establish five district maintenance shops, each of which would be fully equipped with modern equipment. In the long-term plan when the country is pacified, these maintenance shops would be necessary for proper maintenance operations. However at present it would be most difficult to maintain proper security for five scattered shops. Any large stock of materials or concentration of equipment would undoubtedly be a target for Viet Minh guerrilla activities. Therefore it is deemed advisable that only such equipment and material that is found to be the minimum requirement and that can be used effectively should be provided at this time.

It is felt that labor should be used to the greatest extent possible and should be supplemented by equipment only where large operations are necessary. As areas are pacified, large numbers of people return to their homes, and work on highways would give them a means of livelihood until crops could be planted and harvested.

Requests received involved major repair to and reconstruction of 17,000 kilometers of highways, of which 800 kilometers are listed as being of first importance. In an emergency program it is not felt that time or funds should be spent in construction of modern highways, but roads and highways should be repaired only to the extent necessary to assure communication with outlying areas. Studies should be conducted by the mission to Indochina to determine which roads should be repaired and to what extent. Also they should determine the minimum equipment necessary to accomplish this end.

It is felt that $1,000,000 should be sufficient for procurement of equipment and materials for a 15 months' period ending July 1, 1951, if work is restricted to emergency repairs. It is recommended that this sum be made available for this purpose.

6. **Technical Equipment; Publications, and Training Aids ($600,000).** Technical equipment, supplies, and publications would be used for institutions and establishments of the government playing significant parts in the program and services of the government in agriculture. Health programs and services can secure such supplies and equipment out of funds requested as a separate item for the health program. Equipment and supplies for training aids would be used largely in field educational activities promoting projects in the program. They might include paper and other supplies and equipment for the preparation and reproducing of pamphlets, and equipment to make film strips, filmstrip projectors, and motion picture projectors.

E. Industry, Power, and Transportation

In considering the immediate industrial program for Indochina the following factors must first be taken into consideration (a) security of area; (b) the long-term and short-term requirements; (c) speed with which facilities can become effective; (d) economic need for facilities; and (e) ability to provide facilities locally.

Primary consideration must be given to certain fields of industrial enterprise that form the backbone of an industrial economy. These are generally considered to be (a) power; (b) communications; and (c) fuel. In addition thereto, the primary products of the country under consideration should be studied and the specified facilities for handling and processing these products should be given consideration. In Indochina the economy is largely based on agriculture—92 percent of the population is engaged therein. The principal products are rice, rubber, and corn. There is normally an important surplus of each of these, which surplus is exported into the world market. In the case of Indochina it is necessary to add to the three primary classifications of industries a study of the facilities for processing these three products.

Extraordinary requirements of Indochina also must be considered. These result mainly from the destruction of homes, farm implements, and farm beasts of burden by the "scorched earth" policy of the Viet Minh. As areas are pacified, the restoration of these facilities is of the greatest importance. This matter has been considered in the agriculture section of this report and therefore will not be considered as part of the industrial program.

Currently, a struggle is being fought between the Vietnamese and the French relative to the form the economy of Indochina will take in the future. The Vietnamese would like to change from an agricultural to an industrial economy. The French feel that the economy should remain primarily agricultural. There are numerous unexplored and undeveloped natural resources such as zinc, gold, iron, magnesia, phosphates, and sulphur. However, for the purposes of immediate aid neither the long-run question of agricultural vs. industrial development nor the opening up of these natural resources has been considered. Long-term economic and engineering studies are necessary to determine the feasibility of the various plants. Consideration might be given to providing technical assistance to conduct studies, but no capital expenditures should be made for this purpose at this time.

For purposes of immediate aid to Indochina only those things that will tend to stabilize the existing economy and indicate to the people that the Government can do more for their welfare than can the Viet Minh have been considered.

Power. In all of Indochina there is an installed generating capacity of 76,500 kilowatts. Of this total 58,300 kilowatts are installed in the three cities of Saigon, Hanoi, and Haiphong. There are numerous independent small power plants scattered throughout the country that provide power for lighting purposes in the small villages. These small plants have been destroyed or are in a badly deteriorated condition at best.

It is recommended, therefore, that fifty 100-horsepower mobile Diesel electric generators, 3 phase, 210/120 volts, 50 cycle be provided. It is proposed to place these units in pacified areas in order that lighting can be provided as people return to their homes. These plants also will provide sufficient power for temporary pumping of water. As permanent power plants are rehabilitated, the mobile power plant can be moved to another newly pacified area. The estimated cost of these units totals $755,000.

It is further recommended that two Diesel power plants of 2,500 kilowatt capacity each, together with all necessary transformer and switching equipment, be supplied for installation in two of the larger industrial areas, such as Saigon, Hanoi, Haiphong, or Cantho. The location of these units should be determined at the time of their arrival in Indochina. The security situation at the time of the writing of this report is not sufficiently stable to make a firm recommendation as to location. However, 5,000 kilowatts of electric power can be used to advantage in any of the above-mentioned cities. These two units are estimated to cost $670,000.

Requests were received for power installations greatly exceeding the capacities recommended above. These requests in the main are economically justified. However, owing to the insecurity of the area and due to the limitations of funds available, it was felt inadvisable to recommend their installation at this time.

Bridges. Throughout Indochina the "scorched earth" policy of the Viet Minh has resulted in the destruction of many bridges along the highways, thus making entire areas inaccessible. To establish communications with these areas most expeditiously it is recommended that 2,000 linear feet of "Bailey Bridge" be furnished. As permanent bridges are repaired or replaced, the Bailey Bridge can be disassembled and moved to newly pacified areas. The cost of 2,000 linear feet of Bailey Bridge designed for a 16-ton loading is being investigated.

The detailed justification of the balance of the proposed industrial and transportation expenditures has not yet been prepared because of illness of the officer of the Mission responsible for this portion. The over-all estimate of $3,100,000 for expenditures for power, light, engineering projects, etc., is therefore subject to revision.

F. Fifty Trainees to the United States ($250,000)

There is an intense interest among young Indochinese in visiting the United States and in studying there. Moreover, trained Indochinese are needed in every field except, perhaps, law and medicine (and there is certainly a shortage of medical personnel everywhere outside of Saigon). Provision of trainee grants would be one of the most effective ways of demonstrating genuine United States interest in the Indochinese people, and would at the same time give them a feeling of belonging to a world far wider than (and in many ways different from) the French Union. The propaganda value of selection for education in the United States would be very great, and hundreds would be influenced by each trainee so privileged.

G. Supplemental USIS Activities ($500,000)

English classes should be established by the USIS in Saigon, Hanoi, Phnom Penh, and perhaps elsewhere in Indochina, to meet the wide demand to learn English. Training would be directed especially to students and officials likely to study in the United States (or other English-speaking countries) and those working with Americans on joint-aid programs in Indochina, but should reach as wide a public as possible.

Such classes should employ modern high-speed methods of instruction, as developed during the war.

Additional USIS offices should be set up in Indochina, more materials on United States culture and technology should be available (especially through filmstrips and other audio-visual techniques), and a large program of translation and distribution of technical pamphlets into Vietnamese, Cambodian, and Laotian should be undertaken.

Finally, the USIS should be provided with American sports equipment for distribution to town and village schools and playgrounds throughout Indochina. This should include basketball equipment and replacement supplies of balls, as well as soccer and softball equipment. Training programs for village sports leaders could and should also be set up in Indochina. Distribution of sports equipment and training in its use would reach youths throughout the three countries, and would be a rapid and inexpensive way of showing United States interest.

VII. Factors Limiting the Amount, Speed, or Kind of Aid Programs that are Feasible

The dominant element in planning any aid program in Indochina is the degree of law and order obtaining in areas of projected operations. Reasonable security for aid personnel obtains in Hanoi, Haiphong, Vientiane, Hue, Tourane, Phnom Penh, and Saigon, and in smaller towns in certain pacified or unaffected areas (the latter mainly in Laos and Cambodia). Relatively limited rural areas in Vietnam, primarily in the Red River delta in Tonkin, can be considered safe for aid operations. The general insecurity of most of Vietnam places very severe limitations on the extent of aid operations that can be undertaken, and is the reason why French and Vietnamese officials alike declare that the most effective economic aid that can be furnished Indochina is military aid.

As a corollary, the economic aid supplied should have a military utility also, wherever possible. For this reason, emphasis in the aid recommendations made above has been given to rural rehabilitation and health activities that help stabilize recently pacified areas, to telecommunications, to power and light, to roads and bridges, and to propaganda activities, all of which would bring important support to military operations.

The Vietnamese, Cambodian, and Laotian Governments are very short of experienced, trained, administrative and technical personnel, particularly personnel who speak English. Although the French saw that an elite group was well educated, this group was not given responsible administrative posts and thus not made ready for self-government. This will be a major limitation on aid programs, for effective operations require responsible direction as well as local technical personnel to work with, and to learn from, foreign aid personnel.

This would not be so serious a limitation if the Vietnamese, particularly, were not so eager to launch out on their own, without depending on French personnel for advice or execution. The French have many able and experienced personnel in Indochina, and could carry a larger load than the Vietnamese want to put on them. The natural Vietnamese desire for "independence" thus raises a barrier to the economic and technical development needed to become ready for independence.

The attitude of uncooperativeness is not limited to the Vietnamese, however. On the other side, the French have admittedly done too little and done it too late in training Vietnamese for responsible positions, and then turning over to them real responsibilities. Even now, while official policy tries to accelerate this process, Frenchmen on the "working level" are loath to let go, and so slow the process up.

Moreover, the French have fought hard against the "penetration" by other Western influences that might weaken the French position even though contributing importantly to Indochinese development. Thus, American, and presumably other, business concerns have found it almost impossible to get established and do business in Indochina.

This attitude comes out very explicitly in the March 8 agreement with Vietnam, in section IV, which reserves priority to France in furnishing experts and advisers (quoted above, in section IV of this report); in section V, which specifies that French law will be applied in civil and commercial cases wherever a Frenchman is involved; in section VI, which reserves a privileged place for the French language in Vietnamese institutions and provides for other special relationships with France in cultural affairs; and in section VII, which establishes full national treatment for French business interests in Vietnam, in addition to the applicability of French law.

The first provision mentioned, concerning priority for French experts, obviously sets up a major barrier to any United States economic or technical assistance program, especially if this agreement is interpreted narrowly. Two questions arise here. First, is an American who helps expedite or distribute American economic aid to be considered an "expert adviser?" He is likely to have some expertness, to be sure, but he is not present in connection with the regular functioning of the local government, and obviously does not replace any expert obtained to advise or participate in such normal functions. It is believed that the French authorities will not consider such United States "aid experts" to be barred by the March 8 agreements, but will on the contrary welcome their participation in economic aid programs in the area.

The second question has to do with American experts provided independently of economic aid or supply programs, and performing advisory, demonstration, or training services either within the local governments or under their auspices. These are, it should be noted, expert personnel whose salaries are being paid by the United States. They are therefore additional to, and do not replace, any French experts employed by the local governments. It is not believed that the March 8 agreements were meant to exclude the possibility of such additional non-French experts, but the question is apparently currently under consideration by the French authorities and the officials of the three local governments. The Vietnamese officials realize their obligations under this section of the March 8 agreement, although of course pressing for a liberal interpretation. In any case, the agreement does not limit foreign technical training in any way, and the Vietnamese are eager to take advantage of American training facilities.

Many of the above considerations apply to the possibility of United Nations and specialized agency personnel being assigned as technical experts to advise the Governments of Vietnam, Cambodia, and Laos. When these three Governments become, on May 17, 1950, full members of the World Health Organization, they automatically become eligible for technical assistance from the United Nations and from all of the specialized agencies. A liberal interpretation by the French of section IV of the March 8 agreements would clear the way for substantial multilateral technical assistance programs, but a restictive interpretation of this section could cut these three countries off from all expert advice, although not from training grants, under the technical assistance programs of the United Nations and its affiliated bodies.

The existence in Vietnam of a rebel "government," recognized by the USSR and its satellites (including Communist China) as well as by Yugoslavia, might cause some complications in such programs. Aid to "French-controlled" territories could be carried on in any case. Unless one of the specialized agencies admits the rebel Viet Minh "Government" to membership, which is highly unlikely, no proposals are likely to be made to provide UN technical assistance to the Viet Minh. A proposal of the latter sort, if made, would in all likelihood be strenuously opposed by the French Government, as happened when the UNICEF in 1948 and 1949 split a tentative allocation of $457,900 for use in Indochina between the "French-controlled" areas ($305,300) and the Viet Minh areas ($152,600). (These funds were to have been used for child feeding and anti-tuberculosis vaccinations with BCG vaccine.) Although the French Government has requested that such aid be provided for areas in Indochina under its control, no implementing action has been taken by UNICEF because of unsettled conditions. No implementing action can be taken on the Viet Minh allocation until a request is received from the Viet Minh "Government" and an agreement reached by that "Government" with the Fund. The French Government has announced that, as a member of the Executive Board of UNICEF, it would protest any implementation of the Viet Minh allocation.

VIII. Special Considerations Affecting
the Provision of Aid to Indochina

To have the maximum effect on the internal political situation in Vietnam, American aid should arrive quickly, should be distributed through the Vietnamese themselves, and should be widely and effectively publicized as aid made possible by direct U.S.-Vietnam arrangements. On the other hand, continual attention must be given to retaining the benefit of French experience and competence in a mutually beneficial cooperative endeavor.

A. The Need for Prompt Action

So much interest has been stimulated by U.S. recognition of Vietnam, Cambodia, and Laos, by the visit of the U.S. Navy, and by the discussions with the U.S. Economic Survey Mission, that failure to follow through promptly with concrete action, even if minor, would bring about a great let-down. An issue has already been made by the Vietnamese, Cambodians, and Laotians of their capacity and intention to state their own needs for economic aid, without French intervention, particularly from Paris, and of their intense desire to receive and distribute economic aid by themselves, also without French intervention. If their statements of needs and assertions of independence are not quickly given substance, there will have been a considerable tempest about nothing, with loss of potential influence both for the local governments and for the United States.

B. The Case for Direct Aid

There are two very important aims to be served by direct U.S.-Vietnam relationships on economic aid. In the first place, it would make possible the avoidance of any control, or even appearance of control, by the French. In the second place, it would build up the prestige and authority of Bao Dai—not simply as an independent agent working directly with the United States (although this would be significant) but also as head of an effective Government interested in the welfare of the people themselves, and able and ready to take actions to help them.

C. Letting the People Know

It is not Bao Dai's Government that needs to be impressed by the fact of United States economic aid, or by the directness of such aid. The Government is composed of men who are already committed. It is among the fence-sitters and the great unconvinced portion of people that new strength must be sought, by demonstrating the genuine interest of the United States in the economic and political development of the three countries. Economic aid will therefore have relatively little impact on the political situation unless it is widely and effectively publicized. This may mean opening up new channels of communication, such as village radios, where inadequate channels now exist. It may mean adapting audio-visual techniques to the special needs of Indochina. And it may mean a substantial increase in the total cost of United States aid. It is, however, a *sine qua non* of any economic program that is intended to have both an economic and a political effect.

D. French Responsibilities in Connection with Economic Aid

France has been for some time, and is at present, pouring large sums of money into Indochina, to support the large-scale military effort there, to cover the budget deficits of the three local governments, to cover the balance of payments deficit of the area, and to pay for those central administrative functions (other than military) that remain the responsibility of the High Commissioner. Quite apart from the military operation, French financial support has been absolutely necessary to keep the three local governments afloat.

In the last analysis, of course, the French financial contribution to the area has been made possible by ECA aid to France, and the balance-of-payments deficit of the area has been taken into account in calculating France's need for ECA aid. The United States is therefore already indirectly aiding Indochina. On the other hand, so long as Indochina remains part of the franc area (its piaster is already supported by France at an unrealistically high rate vis-à-vis the franc), so long as the three countries use a common currency and continue their customs union, and so long as France contributes heavily to the costs of government in the area, there will be financial questions of common interest to all three countries that cannot be settled without French participation nor, in fact, without French leadership. Direct or indirect, as United States aid may be, France will have to continue to aid, and will therefore have a right and a duty to participate in discussions of problems affecting the need for her contribution. Carrying out these French responsibilities will continue to require a central commissariat with administrative authority in Indochina.

Moreover, certain economic activities are of such immediate importance to all three countries, and also to France, that they are administered by a quadripartite organization (for example, the rice board). There are other fields in which the economies of the three countries are interdependent, such as transportation and meat supply, from Cambodia and Laos to Vietnam, but where no quadripartite planning or administration now goes on.

Finally there are fields, such as power, where future development may require joint planning if not administration.

This is recognized in the March 8 agreements, section VII of which reads in part as follows:

H.M. the Emperor of Vietnam, believing that, in the economic and financial field, he has common interests with the sovereigns of Cambodia and Laos, on the one hand, and with the French Union, on the other, and that it might be profitable to the Vietnamese nation that these interests be harmonized with a view to the prosperity of all, recognizes that joint organizations might well be formed for the purpose of studying and harmonizing these interests, and getting action under way.

In order to reach agreement on the composition, scope, and powers of such joint organizations, it is intended shortly to call a quadripartite conference, to be concerned particularly with the communications services, immigration control, customs and external commercial relations, treasury, and plans for reconstruction and modernizing of agricultural and industrial equipment.

The French consider that the need for unified direction in these several areas, based on the requirements of administrative efficiency, or on the countries' financial or economic interdependence, argues strongly for central direction and control over the economies of the three countries. They therefore propose that additional quadripartite entities be created to carry out this function. The three local governments minimize the importance of quadripartite action, and wish to avoid it wherever possible. Not only is there suspicion of and antipathy towards the French, but there is also considerable mutual suspicion among the three countries. The resolution of this question will significantly affect the amount and kind of American technical and economic aid requested, the manner of distribution of economic aid, and the status and functions of technical experts provided.

IX. Information Activities Supporting the Aid Program

Provision is made in the aid recommendations presented above, for certain USIS activities (trainees, English classes, translation program, sports equipment) that will have particularly significant propaganda value in addition to their justification on economic or educational grounds. Provision is also made for battery-operated village radio receiving sets. Moreover, certain of the aid programs, such as rural rehabilitation, health, and agriculture, will require training aids and information materials to be successful, and provision of the necessary funds has therefore been recommended above.

There is need also, however, for expanded information and public relations activities to explain United States interest in Indochina; what it is undertaking to do through its aid program, and why it is taking on this task. This is a peculiarly difficult task in Indochina, where the greatest care must be taken to show that the United States is helping the Indochinese live their own lives and yet is not derogating legitimate French interests and manifest French contributions, to show keen United States interest and yet not suggest a greater commitment than the United States is prepared to undertake, to support anti-Communist leaders and yet not be tarred with the charge of simply buying allies in the cold war (allies who would be or perhaps already are, in the front line of a hot war), to be more pro-French than the Vietnamese and yet not pro-colonialism, to push the French towards liberal and constructive actions and yet not be misinterpreted as wanting to replace them.

This requires delicate handling. It also requires more handling—more people, more office, more equipment, more materials, more funds. It means more activity in Indochina, and more in Washington. A first step, of course, is immediate initiation of Voice of America broadcasts in Vietnamese. Beyond this, however, substantially increased funds should be provided to expand all USIS activities in Indochina in time to take full advantage of the arrival of United States economic and technical aid.

X. Organization for Field Administration of Aid Program

The economic and technical aid program recommended for Indochina totals $23,500,000 for the 15 months ending June 30, 1951 (which presumably means in practice for 12 or 13 months). This is the largest program recommended for any country in Southeast Asia. It is also the program likely to draw on the greatest variety of authorized funds (as ECA is authorized to aid Indochina, including as it does three members of the French Union); and it is without question the program most deeply involved in complex and fundamental political considerations.

For these reasons, it is of the utmost importance that all United States economic and technical aid programs in Indochina be directly administered under a single responsible Chief of Economic Mission (CECOM) and that there be the closest integration of the direction of United States economic and technical activities with the direction of United States diplomatic and information activities.

It is recommended that ECA set up the field organization and appoint CECOM as its representative, recognizing of course that CECOM must also derive authorities under section 303 of MDAA, Point Four, and possibly other legislation.

CECOM should work particularly closely with the United States diplomatic mission in Indochina, in establishing general objectives and policies, appraising the political impact of existing or projected aid activities, and initiating, modifying or terminating programs where required by political considerations.

It is recommended that, if the local governments agree, joint bodies be set up, with United States representation, in connection with the administration of aid programs. The top United States representative in any such joint body should be responsible to CECOM.

In view of the provisions of the March 8 agreements reserving priority to France in the furnishing of expert advisers, it is anticipated that most American aid personnel in Indochina will be there in connection with the administration (preferable under a joint commission) of aid programs involving the distribution of aid supplies. Such personnel would therefore be responsible for their detailed operations directly to joint commissions or to CECOM. In any case, CECOM would have responsibility for the success of aid programs and for the satisfactory performance of all United States aid personnel.

It is recommended that consideration be given to freeing CECOM (and Embassy officers) from administrative detail by establishing a Joint Administrative Staff (as in Korea) to handle all housekeeping functions both for the legation and for the economic mission.

Appendix

1. The Mission arrived in Saigon at 1:15 p.m., March 6, 1950, and remained in Indochina until 11:30 a.m., March 16, 1950.
2. The Mission during its stay in Indochina was composed of the following persons:

Department of State

The Honorable R. Allen Griffin, Chief of Mission, with the personal rank of Minister.
Samuel P. Hayes, Jr., Deputy Chief of Mission and Adviser.
Henry Tarring, Jr., (March 10-20), J.G. White Engineering Company, Consultant to the Dept. of State, Adviser.
William McAfee, Adviser
Eleanor L. Koontz, Secretary
Mary D. Randolph, Secretary

Economic Cooperation Administration

Edward T. Dickinson, Jr. (Washington Office), Adviser
Raymond T. Moyer (Joint Commission on Rural Reconstruction, Formosa), Adviser
Robert Blum (Paris Office), Adviser

Department of the Treasury

Alexander Lipsman (March 6-18), Adviser

Department of Defense

Russell G. Duff, Colonel, USA, Adviser
Frederick B. Warder (March 11-16), Captain, USN, Adviser

3. The following formal conferences were held during the visit of the Mission to Indochina:

   a) Conference with the High Commissioner of France in Indochina, His Excellency, Léon Pignon, March 6, 4 p.m.
   b) Conference with the Prime Minister of Vietnam, His Excellency, Nguyen-Phan-Long, March 6, 4:45 p.m.
   c) Conference with the Commander in Chief of French Armed Forces in the Far East, Gen. Marcel Carpentier, March 6, 5:30 p.m.
   d) Conference with the Governor of South Vietnam, Governor Tran-Van-Huu, March 6, 6:15 p.m.
   e) Orientation conference with members of the United States Legation staff March 7, 8:15 a.m.
   f) Conference with High Commissioner and advisers, March 7, 10:15 a.m.
   g) Conference with officials of the Cambodian Government, March 8, 8:30 a.m.
   h) Conference with officials of the Laotian Government, March 8, 11:30 a.m.
   i) Conference with United States press representatives, March 9, 2:15 p.m.
   j) Conference with Vietnam officials, March 9, 5:00 p.m.
   k) Round table discussion with officials of France, Vietnam, Cambodia, Laos, March 10, 8:00 a.m.
   l) Conference with ex-Emperor Bao Dai, Dalat, March 10, 11:00 a.m.
   m) Round table discussion with French and Vietnam officials, March 11, 8:30 a.m.
   n) Hanoi Conferences—During the visit to Hanoi, conferences were held with the Governor of North Vietnam, with many provincial and local government officials, and with General Allesandri, Commander of Forces in North Vietnam, and members of his staff and subordinate commands.
   o) Audience with the King of Cambodia, Phnom Penh, March 14, 5:30 p.m.
   p) Conference at High Commissioner's with officials of France, Vietnam, Cambodia, Laos, March 15, 5:00 p.m.

4. A list of certain of the persons with whom the Mission conferred in Indochina follows (names not listed necessarily in order of rank):

U.S. Legation

Edmund A. Gullion, Chargé d'Affaires

H. Francis Cunningham, Jr.
Stephen H. McClintic
John T. Getz
T.J. Duffield
Mr. Glazer
John Donnell

French Officials

A. Civilian Officials
   Léon Pignon, High Commissioner of France in Indochina
   Marc Biron, Director of High Commissioner's Staff
   Jean Bourgoin, Adviser on Planning, Director of Public Works
   F. Camboulive, Chief Inspector of Technical Education
   Albert Charton, Adviser on Education
   Robert Davee, General Secretary of Economic Committee
   Dr. P. Dorolle, Assistant Adviser on Public Health
   Robert Jean Dufour, Adviser on Social Problems
   Roger Robert du Gardier, Diplomatic Adviser, Minister Plenipotentiary
   Robert du Pasquier, Director of Agriculture and Cattle Breeding
   Paul Gannay, Inspector General of Bank of Indochina
   Gerard E. Huet, Director of Rice Bureau
   Rene LeDoux, Representative of French Ministry of Finance
   Arthur Longeaux, Adviser on Public Works and Means of Communication
   Romain V.J. Penavaire, Economic Adviser
   Pierre Perrier, Director of French Security Service
   Mr. Savourey, Director of Electric Power Company
   Rene Schneyder, Assistant to Adviser on Planning
   C.H. Bonfils
   George Mazot
   M. Cambouline, Inspector of Technical Education

B. Military and Naval Officers
   Gen. Marcel Carpentier, Commander in Chief of French Armed Forces in the
      Far East.
   Gen. Marcel Alessandri, Commander of Forces in North Vietnam
   Gen. Charles Chanson, Commander of Forces in South Vietnam
   Vice Admiral Paul Ortoli, Commander of Naval Forces in Far East
   Surgeon Gen. A.H. Robert, Adviser on Public Health

Vietnamese Officials

H.M. Bao Dai, Chief of State
Nguyen Phan Long, Prime Minister (until May 7)

104

Duong Tan Tai, Minister of Finance (in Long's Cabinet as well as Cabinet formed May 7)
Le Tan Nam, Counselor to Minister of Interior
Le Van Hoach, Chief of Caodaist Party in South Vietnam
Le Van Ngo, Secretary of State for Labor and Social Progress
Nguyen Huu Tri, Governor of North Vietnam
Nguyen Van Xuan, Prominent Political and Military Figure
Tran Van Chi, Secretary of State for Agriculture
Tran Van Don, Prefect of Saigon-Cholon Area
Tran Van Huu, Governor of South Vietnam (became Prime Minister May 7)
Le Quang Huy, Minister of Public Works (Minister of Communications in new Cabinet)
Vuong Quang Nhuong, Minister of Education (same position in new Cabinet)
Hoang Cung, Undersecretary of State for Commerce (Minister of Economy in Cabinet formed May 7)
Nghien Van Tri, Councillor to H.M. Bao Dai
Huynh Van Diem, Public Works Engineer
Dinh Quang Chieu, Electrical Engineer
Tran Van Meo, Engineer and Member South Vietnam Assembly
Nguyen Dan, Journalist
Nguyen Van Dinh, Adviser to Vietnam Delegation to ECAFE
Le Van Ho, Lawyer
Nguyen Duy Doc
Ly Cong Trinh
Tran Van Thi, President of Syndicate of Vietnamese Importers and Exporters
Vu Tian Huan, Chief of Cholon Province
(In addition to the above, many working-level officials were met.)

Cambodian Officials

H.M. Norodom Sihanouk, King of Cambodia
Yem Sambaur, Prime Minister (until April 30)
Huot Sam Ath, Department Chief, Ministry of Agriculture
Lam Keu, Assistant Chief of Veterinary Service
Neal Phleng, Minister of Public Health (Head of Group which conferred with Mission)
Tieu Long Nek, Representative of Cambodian Government to High Commissioner of France in Saigon
Hem Chiamreun, Water Service and Wildlife

Laotian Officials

Ngon Sanaikone, Representative of Laotian Government to High Commissioner of France

Outhong Souvannavong, Minister of Foreign Affairs, Education and Information
Tiao Souvannaphouma, Minister of Public Works and Planning (Head of group
  which conferred with Mission)

Others

Frank S. Gibbs, Minister of Great Britain, Saigon
Arthur G. Trevor Wilson, H.B.M. Consul, Hanoi
M. Marchal, Curator of Angkor

American Press Representatives in Saigon

Mr. Christopher
Mr. Fielder
Carl Mydans
Seymour Topping
Robert Miller
Mr. Mathew

5. During the visit in Indochina members of the Mission made two trips in
   addition to the visit to Dalat, present residence of H.M. Bao Dai, and the
   short visits to the countryside in the area of Saigon. On March 11, Mr.
   Griffin, Mr. Dickinson, and Dr. Moyer flew to Hanoi accompanied by Mr.
   Gullion. During the two days spent in the Hanoi Area, members of the
   Mission had the opportunity to observe firsthand the devastation resulting
   from fighting there, to visit areas recently retaken from forces of the Viet
   Minh, and to confer with French and Vietnam officials. On March 14 and 15,
   Mr. Griffin, Mr. Hayes, Mr. Dickinson, Mr. Blum and others visited Anghor
   Wat, Siem Reap and Phnom Penh. In the latter city, they were received in
   formal audience by King Norodom Sihanouk.
6. There follows a list of the most important documents submitted by the
   various Governments in Indochina (in cataloging the documents the letters F,
   C, L, and V, were used to indicate the Government from which the document
   came).

Documents Submitted by the French

a) Rapport sur les Modalités de l'Aide Américaine a l'Indochine, le 5 mars 1950
   (Memorandum on Ways and Means of American Assistance to Indochina
   March 5, 1950)
b) Annexes to the Above Listed Document, Submitted Under one Cover as
   Follows:

(1) Note sur le niveau de vie de la population indochinoise. Prepared by J. Royer of National Statistical Bureau. (Memorandum on the Standard of Living of the Population of Indochina), March 4, 1950.

(2) Note sur la construction immobilière (Saigon-Cholon et Phnom-Penh, 1946-1949) prepared by Mr. Denoueix of Brossard et Maupin Company. (Memorandum on Building Construction (Saigon-Cholon and Phnom-Penh, 1946-1949), March 4, 1950).

(3) Note sur les condition propres à relever les rendements dans la culture du riz. Prepared by G. Huet, Director of Rice Bureau. (Memorandum on the Conditions necessary to increase production of rice), January 25, 1950.

(4) Note sur L'Asie de Sud-Est, pivot stratégique du Continent Asiatique—Rôle de l'Indochine. Prepared by M. Dugardier, Diplomatic Adviser to the High Commissioner. (Memorandum on South East Asia, Strategic Keystone of the Asiatic Continent—The Place of Indochina), January 4, 1950.

(5) Note sur l'approvisionnement du marché indochinois en produits d'importation. Prepared by Office of Foreign Trade, Saigon, (Memorandum on Supplying the Indochinese Market with Imported Products), March 5, 1950.

(6) Note sur le concours accordé au Vietnam pour la constitution de son armée. Prepared by Financial Adviser to the High Commissioner. (Memorandum on the Assistance Given to Vietnam in the Formation of its Army), February 3, 1950.

(7) Note au sujet des possibilités d'intervention financière des États Unis en Indochine. Prepared by Adviser on Planning to High Commissioner. (Memorandum Concerning the Possibilities of Financial Intervention by the U.S.A. in Indochina), January 20, 1950.

(8) Note sur les travaux projetés d'hydraulique agricole et d'exploitation rizicole. Prepared by Adviser on Planning. (Memorandum on Contemplated Projects of Rural Irrigation and Rice Cultivation)

(9) Note sur les besoins de l'Indochine en matériel aéronautique. Prepared by Director of Civil Aeronautics. (Memorandum on the Needs of Indochina as Regards Aviation Equipment)

(10) Note sur le crédit agricole. Prepared by Adviser on Planning. (Memorandum on Rural Credit)

(11) Note sur l'élaboration des programmes d'importation de l'Indochine. Prepared by Office of Foreign Trade, Saigon. (Memorandum on the Preparation of Import Programs for Indochina)

(12) Note sur l'éventualité d'une aide des Etats-Unis d'Amérique en Matière Sanitaire. Prepared by Surgeon General Robert, Adviser on Public Health. (Memorandum on the Possibility of Assistance on the Part of the U.S.A. in the Field of Public Health)

c) Note complémentaire (addition à la Note Francaise du 5 mars 1950)

(Supplementary Memorandum (addendum to French Memorandum of March 5, 1950))

d) Programme D'Avenir

(1) Port de Vatchay (Port of Vatchay)
(2) Terrain d'Aviation (Airfield, Camranh)
(3) Port de Banghai (Port of Banghai)
(4) Centrale de Hongay (Hongay Electric Works)
(5) Aménagement des Terrains d'Aviation (Maintenance of Airfields)
(6) Routes du Laos (Laos Highways)
(7) Travaux d'hydraulique agricole (Agricultural Hydraulic Works)

e) Aide Immédiate (Immediate Assistance)

(1) Aide Économique Américaine (American Economic Aid)
(2) A List of Heavy Equipment Required to Make the Big Works in Indochina.

f) Reconstruction et Développement du Port de Saigon (Reconstruction and Development of the Port of Saigon)
g) Projet de Répartition des 50 groupes Electrogènes Diesel de 100 HP Triphase 210v/120v 50 cycles (Project for the Distribution of 50 Groups of Diesel Generators)
h) Premier Rapport de la Sous-Commission de Modernisation de l'Indochine (First Report of the Subcommittee for the Development of Indochina)
i) Fonds Nécessaires à l'Institution du Crédit Populaire au Vietnam (Funds Necessary to Establish People's Bank)
j) Plan d'Organisation Pour 5 Ans (Public Health)
k) The Franco-Vietnamese Agreement of March 8, 1949
l) Justification of Equipment Necessary for Fluvial Navigation
m) La Coopération Agricole en Indochine (Agricultural Cooperation in Indochina)

Documents Submitted by the Government of Vietnam

a) Projet de Mechanisation de la Rizi culture (Project for Mechanizing Cultivation of Rice)
b) Letter to Mr. Griffin from Ministry of Agriculture, March 10, 1950
c) Brief Statement of Agricultural Problem and Proposed Solution
d) Réforme Agraire (Agrarian Reform)
e) Organisation de l'Agriculture dans le Cadre Provincial (Organization of Agriculture Within the Provincial Sphere)
f) Institut des Recherches Agronomiques et Pastorales (Institute of Agronomical and Rural Research)

g) Note Verbale Relative à l'Aide Économique Américaine en ce qui concerne les Besoins de l'Administration des Eaux et des Forêts du Vietnam (Verbal Note concerning American Economic Aid Relative to Vietnamese Water and Forestry Administration)

h) Fonds Nécessaires à l'Institution du Crédit Populaire au Vietnam (Funds Necessary to Establish People's Bank)

i) Étude Sur Les Besoins du Vietnam en Matière Sanitaire (Study on Sanitation Needs in Vietnam)

j) Le Ministre des Travaux Publics (The Ministry of Public Works)

k) Liste des Besoins (Travaux Publics) (List of Public Works Needs)

l) Programme de Rééquipement et de Reconstruction en 1950 (Travaux Publics) (Program of Reequipment and Reconstruction in 1950 (Public Works)

m) Énergie Électrique (Electric Power)

n) Replacement throughout the Country of Roads and Bridges

o) Remises en État des Routes du Vietnam (Road Repairs in Vietnam)

p) Situation Générale des Aérodromes du Vietnam (General Condition of Airports in Vietnam)

q) Recapitulation Travaux Publics, Communications et Reconstruction (Resumé on Public Works, Communications, and Reconstruction)

r) Note April 1, 1950 sur l'Aide Technique que les États-Unis Envisagent d'Apporter au Vietnam (Secretariat d'État au Commerce et à l'Industrie) (Note Concerning Technical Aid Which the U.S. Plans to Contribute to Vietnam)

s) Letter of March 14 Enclosing Examples of Public Works Requirements and General Summaries

Documents Submitted by the Government of Cambodia

a) Procès-verbal de la séance du Conseil des Ministres tenue la Vendredi 25 Novembre 1949, sous la présidence de S.E. Yem Sambaur. (Minutes of Proceedings of the Cabinet, held on Friday, November 25, 1949, with H.E. Yem Sambaur presiding)

b) Rapport sur la réunion spéciale des Chauvaykhet et du gouverner de la ville de Phnom-Penh, le 2 fevrier 1950. (Report on the special meeting of the Provincial Governors and the Governor of the City of Phnom Penh, February 2, 1950)

c) Letter from Prime Minister and Minister of Foreign Affairs Yem Sambaur, Phnom Penh, February 27, 1950, No. 8 AFE/X concerning Cambodian needs for military assistance

d) Note sur la Situation Générale de Cambodge (Memorandum on General Situation in Cambodia) Prepared by Tieu Long Nek, former Minister, Delegate of H.M. The King of Cambodia, February 9, 1950

e) État des besoins en effectif, armement, moyens de transport et de communications de la ville de Phnom Penh et des provinces du royaume (non compris le secteur autonome) (List of needs in manpower, arms, means of transportation and of communication of the City of Phnom Penh and the provinces of the Kingdom (not including the autonomous sector).)

Documents Submitted by the Government of Laos

a) Note on American Aid to the Kingdom of Laos, March 13, 1950
b) Budgetary Expenses of Laos.

5

Vietnam, Cambodia, and Laos and the Griffin Mission

Léon Pignon

This article will cover briefly the following topics:

I. The political and military situation in Vietnam, Cambodia and Laos at the time of the visit of the Griffin Mission to Indochina.
II. The attitude of the French authorities toward the proposal to provide American economic and technical assistance to the Associated States of Indochina.

I. The Political and Military Situation in Indochina

The political and military situation in Indochina, at the time of the arrival of the Griffin Mission, in March 1950, was reasonably satisfactory, everything considered. But there were, at the same time, very serious misgivings about the effects that the victory of the Communists in China would have on the chances of success of the plans, both short and long term, of the responsible authorities in Indochina. Let us examine more concretely and in some detail the situation in each of the Associated States.

1. Political and Military Situation in Vietnam

It was clear—and it had always been clear—that settling the problem of Vietnam would lead to a settlement of the much less serious and less critical problems of Cambodia and Laos. For this reason, a more detailed discussion of the political and military situation in Vietnam will be presented first.

This name—Vietnam—had reappeared, after a century of disuse, about a year before the Griffin Mission arrived in Saigon. The new State, re-unified under this old, symbolic name, had been recognized as independent by France on March 8, 1949. The chief of state was the former sovereign of Annam and Tonkin, Emperor Bao Dai, who had been forced to abdicate in September 1945 by the revolutionaries organized into the party, or more exactly, the revolutionary "front," commonly given the abbreviated name, the "Vietminh."

Mr. Pignon was French High Commissioner in Indochina at the time of the Mission's visit. His article was translated by the editor.

All the nationalists, moderate or extreme, considered the reunification of Vietnam as absolutely indispensable. For them, it was even more important than independence, to which French public opinion was resigned (on condition that an agreement on fairly close association with the French Union continued in effect). The legal obstacles to reunification—including the fact that Cochinchina was, under the terms of the French Constitution, actually French territory and its inhabitants French citizens—were cleverly utilized by influential members of the Cochinchinese bourgeoisie, who constituted a very active pressure group, to influence French public opinion and certain politicians or political parties in France. Opposition to reunification appeared clearly during the debates of the territorial assembly of Cochinchina, elected for the express purpose of deciding whether to relinquish the status of a French territory and to unite with Annam and Tonkin. The decision to do so was reached with much difficulty.

A second question remained, fraught with much more uncertainty: how would the Vietnamese react to the ex-sovereign as chief of the new State? Bao Dai had not been chosen by an elected assembly, nor had he been the object of popular demand. Supported by a small group attached to the concept of the monarchy or to him personally, his reappearance on the political scene was the result of long and careful negotiations between, on the one side, the French Government, but, on the Vietnamese side, Bao Dai alone. The situation was even more peculiar in that France, following the old principle that "the Republic does not make Kings," did not itself want to restore the ex-sovereign to his throne, and yet on the other hand could not, for overriding political reasons, simply ask him to undertake a vague mission of exploration or of mediation, which he could not have accepted anyway. To have him assume right away the functions of Chief of State, in a country whose political organization had not been determined and which, in addition, was divided and ravaged by a cruel war was to take a chance, but a chance for which good arguments could be presented. Bao Dai was the only person of international stature who could be presented as a credible alternative to Ho Chi Minh. His nationalism had been clearly demonstrated while he was still on the throne. He had for a while cooperated with Ho Chi Minh, who had shown him unusual respect, which indicated the importance that the Communist leader still attributed to the dispossessed sovereign. What the French politician and philosopher, Jean Jaurès, had called "the secular charm of the monarchy" weighed heavily in his favor in the central provinces of Annam, and even in Tonkin among the older people. In Cochinchina, which was not at all monarchist, he was at least no stranger: he had married, and his marriage had flattered local opinion at the time, a young Cochinchinese known for her beauty, her charm and the dignity of her life, belonging to the best Catholic bourgeoisie. In Cochinchina as elsewhere, and even doubtless more than elsewhere, there were many—probably a majority—of uncommitted families—"fence-sitters"—ready to give their support to a moderate nationalist who could combine peace with independence and at the same time enjoy the friendly protection of non-Communist powers. For these families there would be time, after quiet had returned, to decide about the monarchist or republican form of government, and about the federal or unitary structure of Vietnam.

In Annam, only part of the territory had, in the course of a series of actions, been taken back from the domination of the Vietminh. The areas liberated were the three southernmost provinces; the central provinces around the old capital, Hue, from the Faifo River to the south of the land of Dong-Hoi, as well as nearly the whole of the plateaus where the Moi's lived. The situation was good in the southern provinces, except for persistent insecurity in the forest area bordering Cochinchina; also good in the central provinces, although with some deterioration north of Hue; and very good on the plateaus, where a policy of autonomy for the mountain tribes, much debated by the Vietnamese, met with great success. In Tonkin, a series of successful actions, together with political activity in the name of His Majesty Bao Dai undertaken among the numerous Catholics in the southern provinces, had freed the delta from the regular Vietminh forces, and a certain measure of calm permitted some administrative and economic reorganization. The ethnic minorities, with the exception of certain groups of Thos, had rallied to France or had never deserted her.

It was about at the time that the Griffin Mission arrived in Saigon that the Vietminh—it was later admitted—felt most uncertain of success. But it was also the time when they put together in the "liberated territories" of north Tonkin, in contact and in liaison with the Chinese Communists who had at last appeared on the border, the forces for the next offensive, comprising large and well trained units, with high morale and superior equipment. The French authorities knew of the danger, but did not fully appreciate the fighting strength of an army which could not be considered modern in Western eyes, since it still lacked airplanes.

2. Political and Military Situation in Cambodia

In March 1950, both the political and the military situations in Cambodia seemed somewhat worse than they had been the previous year.

The Cambodian Government, and at the top King Norodom Sihanouk himself, were not very pleased by an independence copied from the one designed for Vietnam. In particular, the restrictions on its sovereignty relating to the legal and tax status of certain aliens—the French of course, but, especially because of their number, the Vietnamese and Chinese too—irked the Cambodians a good deal, but the basic reason for their misgivings vis-à-vis the new regime which had been set up in Indochina derived from the creation of a Great Vietnam by the reunification of Tonkin, Annam, and Cochinchina. Cochinchina had been conquered by the French from the Vietnamese, who themselves had previously seized from Cambodia, in the relatively recent past, the provinces of the Transbassac, where an important Khmer minority still lived. Although the French had not restored to Cambodia the Transbassac, where the Vietnamese were rapidly becoming a majority of the population, at least its administration had been impartial, and the mouths of the Mekong and Bassac Rivers, outlets to the sea which were vital for Cambodia, had remained in friendly hands. To the irredentism of the most active nationalist Khmers was added the unspoken anguish of the realists. In the absence of special guarantees which, in any event, would have quickly lost their credibility, they finally were led to want to take upon themselves, in complete freedom, the responsibility for the destiny of Cambodia. The disaffection just mentioned was not itself very serious and did not seriously prejudice the traditionally good relations between the French and the Cambodians, but nonetheless it limited the freedom of action of the French authorities in their policy towards Vietnam.

The few rebels of pure Cambodian race called "Issarak Khmers" were not themselves a danger, but in certain provinces they kept the situation at a level of insecurity which was used to advantage by the much more dangerous Vietnamese infiltrators under Vietminh command. The French and their Allies lacked the military resources that would have easily overcome at that time the still feeble enemy outposts that were to turn out to be serious danger spots in the years that followed.

3. Political and Military Situation in Laos

Because of its shape and terrain, Laos is difficult to govern and impossible to defend. The most responsible Laotians were aware of this, and despite the existence of fairly strong nationalistic feelings were not eager to obtain their independence before peace and stability returned to South Asia, and in particular to the former French Indo-China. One might even say that independence was imposed on them against their will. Since 1893 they had enjoyed a protection which had shielded them from the raids and depredations of the Siamese and Chinese. Moreover, in this poor and isolated land, without colonists, the French administrative hand had been very light and had operated primarily through the traditional authorities, the king, the princes and the aristocratic families, generally easy-going and close to the people. Thus, it might be said that independence was an ideological objective whose realization could have been delayed, rather than a strongly felt need. This was particularly true of the Lao population, a branch of the Thai race inhabiting the Mekong valley. It was not exactly the same for the primitive mountain peoples, supposedly of pre-Malayan stock, who lived in the mountains and on the plateaus, and whom the Laotians disdainfully called "Khas" (savages).

Thus, while at no time in the association of France and Laos did the protecting power carry out the slightest act of repression against the peaceful and friendly Lao people, it was necessary to undertake several minor operations against certain groups of unruly Khas in the southern plateaus. The Vietminh were to make good use of the resentments of the minorities against the dominant ethnic Laos whose administration, after the departure of the French officials and military personnel, showed itself to be oppressive and contemptuous and at the same time less confident of its strength than their Western predecessors had been. The latter, secure in their strength, had been impartial and tolerant in handling the details of daily life.

Moreover, the Vietminh found among certain members of the Laotian elite some who, bitter at not themselves gaining power, helped the Vietminh penetrate the society and find protection; at the same time that different mountain tribes provided guides and some troops.

The threat which was soon to preoccupy everyone was limited, in the spring of 1950, to a small number of mountain districts, strategically well placed. Nonetheless it was expected that the tiny rebellion in Laos would be quickly subdued if the large Vietminh revolution should end in failure.

II. Attitude of the French Authorities Toward American Aid in Indochina

The attitude of the French Government in Paris was practically indistinguishable from that of the French officials in Saigon.

Only a search through the archives would make it possible to recapture the exact content of the instructions sent by the French Government to the High Commissioner in Saigon. Memory indicates that they were succinct and favorable to American assistance; and that they in essence relied on the judgment of this high official not to undertake, in the course of the exploratory negotiations of the Griffin Mission, any commitments contrary to French policy.

It will be useful to outline such of the fundamental points of French policy in Indochina as might be contested with the arrival of the Griffin Mission and with the subsequent developments in American aid.

a) France was determined to retain control of the foreign relations of the Associated States. This determination had always been an essential element in the negotiations with the States and had, perhaps, been the source of the most serious difficulties. The author of this chapter remembers having heard Ho Chi Minh declare, "You want to prevent us from having any friends." Likewise, he remembers having very often quoted, in his reports to Paris, a section from a speech where Pandit Nehru listed the essential attributes of independence. The Indian statesman wrote that a country, newly arrived on the international stage through its acquisition of independence, could, by agreement, accept temporary abridgements, even very important ones, of its independence, as in national defense, to avoid temporarily expenditures that would be too costly for a developing nation. On the other hand (said Nehru), a nation must absolutely retain control of its own foreign policy, as this would guarantee it eventual recourse against any abuse by the other party to the agreement: this control could be obtained at minimum cost by diplomatic representation in the major capitals of the world and by membership in the United Nations.

Whether they had read the words of Pandit Nehru or not, the Asian partners of France were convinced that control of their own foreign affairs was an absolute imperative.

A narrow interpretation of the French Union, as defined in Title VIII of the Constitution of 1946, and the fear of anticolonialist pressures, particularly from the United States, explain without justifying the restrictive position taken by France, a position, however, which was very quickly modified. In its desire to assure the success of His Majesty Bao Dai, France went to great lengths to make plain the new status of Vietnam. As a result, Vietnam very quickly was granted complete freedom to accept the establishment of foreign legations, and was permitted to name representatives in the national capitals not excluded by the French-Vietnamese accords, with only the formality of a short and easy negotiation.

b) France had decided in March 1945 to adopt a federalist solution for the institutional problems which faced Indochina after its liberation (from the Japanese). Although this federalist approach had not been officially spelled out since its original appearance in the famous declaration of March 23, 1945, it was still the touchstone for all questions despite great changes and, most importantly, despite the recognition after March 1949 of the right to independence of each of the three countries grouped together in the Federation.

Very simply, France had decided in 1945 to grant a very large measure of control over internal affairs to each of the states which were members of the Indochinese Federation, at the same time reserving to the federal authorities, under the higher control of France within the French Union, complete authority in such areas as foreign trade, foreign financial dealings (which implied control of customs, and of receipts therefrom) and national defense, as well as the possibility of frequent intervention in other areas. Foreign affairs, at least important matters, remained the responsibility of France, within the limits, too rigidly defined, of the French Union.

The agreement of March 6, 1946, with the Democratic Republic of Vietnam, in spite of the haste with which it had been drafted, provides an example of what internal autonomy, more or less reflecting France's conception of federalism, might have been like.

These federal prerogatives were in fact the occasion, if not the basic cause, of the first bloody confrontation between the French and the Vietminh (the incidents at Haiphong of November 20, 1946, which arose out of a dispute over customs regulations).

Despite the weakening already indicated (the grants of independence to the three Associated States), the federalist doctrine was very much alive in the spring of 1950 and was still to be important in the negotiations at Pau in the summer of 1950 which brought together France, Vietnam, Cambodia, and Laos under the chairmanship of a renowned political leader, Mr. Albert Sarraut. The principal purpose of the Pau Conference was to define the federal relationships which should, in the general interest, obtain among the states henceforward recognized as independent. However, it is not the purpose of this chapter to discuss the federalist doctrine, its advantages for the financial and economic plans for rehabilitation and development, or its unrealistic character as regards the political situation.

It is enough to point out, after having very briefly defined it, that it was on everyone's mind at the time when the Griffin Mission began its work.

The Laotians, recognizing the poverty and weakness of their country, were the only ones who opposed the ending of the financial and economic aid provided under the federal scheme. This was indispensable to them. They also opposed, perhaps even more strongly, the ending of the French role as arbiters. France's other partners, by contrast, hoped for the immediate loosening and early dissolution of all federal ties. It is significant that the Cambodians date their independence from 1953, not 1949.

The Frenchmen in the administration, on the other hand, were, with the exception of the senior political staff of the High Commission, and the High Commissioner himself, imbued with the federalist doctrine, some of them because of what it is convenient to call a "colonialist" attitude, and others—more numerous—who in good faith considered this a more efficient and economical way of doing things. The French in the private sector were also very widely in favor of the federal idea, which seemed to them to assure them of good management of public affairs and to protect their activities and their interests.

It may be appropriate to mention here the influence which the French experience in Indochina had on their later decisions concerning the federations of French West Africa and of French Equatorial Africa. The French in Africa were wise enough to accept the break-up of these federations, even though these were sensible economic and financial structures, in order not to deny the separatist desires (stronger than the objective facts) and also in order to take into account the attitude that characterized all the political leaders, which made them prefer to be "first in their villages rather than second in Rome."

The factors that have been discussed above explain the frame of mind of the French officials whom Mr. Griffin and his associates met in Saigon and elsewhere in Indochina in the spring of 1950.

The French authorities, aware of their short-run and long-run problems, were pleased by the interest in Southeast Asia shown by the United States, and in addition to the economic and technical aid which itself was most valuable to the three countries, were very eager for military aid, mainly supplies and equipment, which was necessary as much for the French Army as for the new Indochinese armies which were beginning to be developed.

Of course, to placate public opinion, the French were eager to maintain the appearance of federalism by insisting that some of the meetings with the Griffin Mission include all five parties (three Indochinese States, France, United States). But they were willing to make many accommodations provided that they could remain privileged intermediaries with the American mission, both because of their experience and responsibilities in Indochina and because of the long-standing Franco-American friendship. If there was some apprehension about the direct involvement of a new partner in the Indochinese game, especially a very powerful partner, there was also a very keen desire for assistance that each day appeared to be more necessary.

What was important to them was not so much to be present for all phases of the bilateral negotiations as to be kept completely informed about them. They were principally worried about the fate of their cultural and educational activities and interests. Defending the primacy of the French language and culture was to become a predominant concern in the course of the years and the disappointments that followed.

The Cambodians and Laotians, in spite of their different attitudes towards federalism noted above, were both of them correct and courteous partners.

By contrast, the Vietnamese were involved in many incidents. The President of the Council at that time, M. Nguyen Phan Long, had as his political axiom "Play Washington off against France." In this way he sought to wring from France the maximum of concessions, in order to show the Vietnamese nationalists that a clever diplomat could, without blood-shed, gain more than the armed struggle of the Vietminh had gained over a long period.

He therefore insisted that the meetings and negotiations having to do with Vietnam should be attended only by Vietnamese and Americans, without Cambodians or Laotians, and of course without the French.

As unpleasant and as unjustified as these incidents were, their effect was only to irritate the French officials, by their effect on public opinion. They did not have, at least in the opinion of this author, any bearing on the work of the Griffin Mission, primarily because of the tact and understanding of the members of that Mission.

Paris, March 14, 1969

6

Beginning of United States Economic and Technical Aid in Vietnam

Dinh Quang Chieu

During most of the Second World War, Indochina was still under French administration in spite of the occupation of the region by Japanese Armed Forces. The head of its federal government was still a *Gouverneur Général* appointed by the Marshal Pétain régime. But in early 1945 the Japanese took full control of the administration and declared Vietnam independent (implicitly under Japanese influence). This was too late for any political benefit to the Vietnamese, since signs of the approaching Japanese defeat became so evident that nobody could reasonably believe in an independence conferred only by a vanishing Power.

The situation was no better after the Japanese surrender to the Allied Forces, when it was clear that the French did not recognize independence for Vietnam and that British and Chinese troops were going to occupy the country. Contradictory reports added to the confusion, and a great many people concluded that the prospect for complete independence was none too promising. However, many still hoped that, somehow, colonial domination would no longer be tolerated in this region and, if complete independence was not possible in the immediate future, a temporary solution would be adopted which would be satisfactory, at least to moderate nationalists.

But after the occupation of the country by Nationalist Chinese troops in the North and by British Forces in the South, soon followed by the French Expeditionary Forces, people were led to revise their former appraisal of the situation. Many nationalists joined the Vietminh to combat the French Expeditionary troops. Loyalist pro-French individuals and profiteers remained in the cities enjoying the relative security provided by the French. Soon a local assembly and a provisional Government of Cochinchina were formed in an attempt to detach the territory of this former French Colony from the grasp of the Communist North.

In the North, after the departure of Nationalist Chinese Troops arranged between the French and the Chinese governments, the battle between the French and the Vietminh resulted in the occupation of the main cities by the French, and the Vietminh continued the fight by means of guerilla warfare. From the North to the South throughout the whole country the opposition to the French was led by the Vietminh, with its nationalist elements entirely under the control of the Communists.

M. Chieu was an official of the Government of Vietnam at the time of the Mission's visit.

119

During this troubled period from 1945 to 1950, very few people had a clear idea of United States intentions and goals as regards the fate of this country. Some felt deceived by the apparent lack of expression of United States interest, and others thought they sensed some arrangement already made between France and the United States concerning the future of Indochina.

Then, under the pressure of events, came the March 8th, 1949, Agreements between France and the three States of Vietnam, Cambodia and Laos, initiating a new form of political relationship among these States. The three territories known as Tonkin, Annam, and Cochinchina became Vietnam, an Associated State within the French Union, with Bao Dai, the former Emperor of Annam, as Chief of State. This was a French move towards a limited independence for Vietnam: giving it internal autonomy while finance, diplomacy, foreign trade and defense remained under the supreme control of the French. Although this was an appreciable improvement in the political status of these French possessions and protectorates, it was satisfactory only to those who remained loyal to France, and a little less to some moderate nationalists who chose to accept this intermediate solution, which they considered as a temporary stage on the way to complete independence. But ardent nationalists opposed the new regime by passive resistance or fighting.

The Communist-led Vietminh continued the guerilla war against the new government, as against any government which was not under their control. Many patriots who had cherished the illusion of the possibility of recovering complete independence by fighting in the Communist ranks then finally admitted their mistake and courageously turned away from the Vietminh to join the newly established regime. Political leaders, intellectuals, and technicians returned from abroad to support or collaborate with the new government, reinforcing the administration inherited from preceding regimes. Bao Dai also received support from an appreciable part of the population, which looked to him as their hope for peace and security, and which considered the limited independence within the French Union acceptable under the prevailing political conditions. In fact the unification of the three regions (Tonkin, Annam, and Cochinchina) into Vietnam was a political success to the credit of Bao Dai regime as against the separatist movement in Cochinchina that was kept alive by some politicians.

Internal autonomy carried the burden of setting up a new administration from top to bottom. Fortunately, the basic administrative machine was already established, with some trained and experienced cadres inherited from the French administration. A difficult task was to instill in these cadres a sense of command and responsibility. The entire activity of the government was focused on the internal organization of the country, and it was obviously beyond its capability to bear at the same time the burden of external responsibilities such as defense, diplomacy, finance, etc.

Being an Associated State in the French Union, Vietnam's foreign relations were handled by France. The Vietnamese military and police forces were growing steadily but were still unable to fight the Communist guerilla war alone. If the French had not taken the major part of this military responsibility, there would have been no alternative but to call for the aid of other friendly powers, and no doubt the United States would soon have been directly involved in this region. Few people knew whether the United States had been consulted on the March 8 Agreement, but it was thought generally that, since France was among the Allied Powers participating in the Marshall Plan and receiving American support in the anti-Communist fight, this Franco-Vietnamese political settlement had already been discussed with and been approved by the United States.

The loss of continental China to the Chinese Communists intensified the fear of Communist expansion in Southeast Asia. Vietnam was the most exposed target on a natural invasion route south. Undoubtedly it was the most important bastion for the security of the area and, should it fall to the Communists, they would not be long in taking control in the rest of the region: Thailand, Burma, Malaya, and perhaps Indonesia. More support was then expected from the free world in a common effort to contain the Communist threat. The visit of the Griffin Mission was therefore not a surprise and, although its purpose was said to be economic and technical aid only, the general feeling was to attach importance to this visit and to consider it as the first step to a deeper American involvement in the area.

In fact, the task of the Griffin Mission was to collect sufficient information for a rapid evaluation of the current situation and to propose a short term aid program aimed to have the maximum effect on the political situation in the area.

Concerned departments of the Government of Vietnam were instructed to prepare the necessary reports and documents. The Vietnamese request for aid was confined to public works, agriculture, public health, power supply ... French reports covered the broader aspects such as the standard of living of the population, military assistance, the supply of imported goods, more specific requests for aviation equipment, public health, rural irrigation. Although the time allowed for preparing these reports was short, it was thought that the Mission received sufficient information to work out its recommendations for an emergency aid program.

At the time of the Mission's visit to Vietnam the situation was not as dark as one might have expected. Vietnam was a food surplus area, except in the North, where food deficits were periodic and where the situation worsened with the interruption of rice imports from the South due to the guerilla war. In spite of the war and restrictions on rice movements, the rice production in the South was still sufficient to maintain some exports of rice. The production of rubber, reduced to a slight extent by rebel sabotage in the plantations, still accounted for a large part of Vietnamese exports. Foreign trade and payment deficits were, however, covered by the French, who also had to cover the deficit of the Vietnamese budget. On the other hand, the local expenditures of the French Expeditionary Forces were heavy and steadily growing. All this resulted in strong inflationary pressures and in an appreciable increase of purchasing power, not balanced by a sufficient expansion of the supply of goods and services. Prices were rapidly rising and controls were established in an attempt to curb them; a system of rationing and allocations was introduced for some consumer goods and food products, but it was limited in range and time due to its adverse political and economic effects.

Efforts were made to increase government revenues, notably by raising taxes and increasing imports (the taxes on which were an important source of government revenue). France, which received substantial aid from the United States, was in a position to cover the Vietnamese deficit of payment. It was also known that the American aid to France was of prime importance to the French in carrying their military and economic burden in Vietnam, and this was in fact an indirect aid of the United States to Vietnam.

Considering the above facts, the recommendation of the Mission for an emergency aid program was consistent with a realistic policy which consisted of:

1. improving the conditions of living
2. helping government to rehabilitate and develop the productive resources and improve its services to its people
3. demonstrating the genuine interest of the United States in this area
4. strengthening the economy

The largest part of the proposed program was devoted to rural rehabilitation, with the rest covering some raw materials, semi-finished products, petroleum products, telecommunication system, power, mines, training and expansion of the English language training and other activities of the USIS. There was a real need for the reconstruction of the rural area, which had been devastated by the fighting and guerilla destruction. In the newly pacified regions rural rehabilitation was of great importance in gaining the support of the rural population for the government. Inhabitants of these regions (particularly the Red River delta and the Mekong River delta) suffered heavy losses from which they were courageously attempting to recover. Lacking the essentials, they needed emergency aid. Public services were to be rehabilitated (hospitals, roads, water supply, electricity supply, irrigation and dike protection systems). Home reconstruction, farm equipment replacement, seeds and fertilizer supplies were also of great importance. Long term loans were also to be extended to these inhabitants by a governmental organization; otherwise they would have to borrow money from usurers.

The destruction of hospitals and medical facilities had resulted in a serious deterioration of the health services. The Vietnamese government, to which the responsibility of operating these services was gradually transferred by the French, desired better health services. Although the complete rehabilitation of health services was a long term program, it was obvious that immediate supply and operation of mobile clinics in the most affected areas would speed up an improvement in health and would have the most beneficial effects on the political situation. Furthermore, government health organizations would gain valuable experience at limited cost in the operation of these units, instead of handling more ambitious long-term programs.

The roads, railroads, and communication systems were heavily damaged, mostly by guerilla activities. From the economic, military, and security standpoints, communications between the central authorities and the newly pacified areas were essential and justified the requests for equipment, materials and funds for the reconstruction of the transportation and communication systems. This also was a long term program, requiring substantial funds and numerous experienced personnel. It was therefore advisable to start an emergency program limited to the reconstruction of systems of first importance, particularly in the newly controlled areas.

Although the emergency aid recommended by the Griffin Mission was limited in amount and goals, it was considered as the materialization of the expectations and the hopes of many people that the Communist threat would sooner or later lead the United States to a direct involvement in this area, and right-minded people would have no valid reason to oppose it if its purpose was clearly explained and widely proclaimed. In fact a great many Vietnamese found in this expression of interest by the United States, and its implication of a future direct involvement, a possibility of accelerating the recovery of complete independence for their country. They had in mind not a rivalry between the French and the Americans but, on the contrary, a closer cooperation between the two powers for a more efficient fight against the common enemy and a more realistic evaluation of the political situation. In addition, there were unfortunately but inevitably anti-French feelings among a few nationalists, as well as the antagonism of some French who were not willing or able to look towards the future. Unrealistic nationalism and obsolete colonialism still existed, but not at a level that would endanger or impede progress towards a satisfactory political settlement. But this antagonism was one of the factors that seriously limited the aid program.

The French, who had a long experience in the administration of Vietnam, and who were spending large amounts of money there, were understandably inclined to claim the major role in any economic aid and wanted direct control of this aid, or at least its handling by quadripartite organizations. Direct control by the French was obviously out of the question: it would have adverse effects on the political situation. Finally a compromise agreement was arranged: while the portion of the aid called "direct aid" or "project aid" was actually handled by the government of each of the Associated States, the other part of the aid, called "commercial import program" or "commodities import program," with its purpose of generating local currency counterpart funds, was administered by a quadripartite organization known as "Commission provisoire d'importation de l'Aide Commercialisée." This committee was created, under an arrangement between the three Associated States, the United States, and France, to handle the distribution of the "commercial aid." Its central office was in Saigon, and it was composed of four members and the ECA representative: one delegate from each of the Associated States, the representative of the French High Commissioner, and the Controller of the ECA Mission. The part of the ECA observer was of great importance: he transmitted the import program as proposed by the Committee to the ECA Administration for approval and commitment of the necessary funds (Procurement Authorizations), advised the Committee on ECA regulations and controlled the use of the Commercial Import Program. The French representative also had an important role in coordination and liaison. Since France was financing most of the imports to the three Associated States, the Commercial Aid Program established by the Committee had to be kept in line with the general import program. The financing of the Commercial Import Program was carried out through a special procedure involving the Committee, the Crédit National (France), the French Treasury, the French American Banking Corporation, and ECA in Washington. Although five parties were concerned in the policy making and the operation of this Committee, there were no significant problems which it was unable to solve by itself without recourse to higher authorities. Fortunately, the Committee, in its discussions and proceedings, confined itself to economic and financial matters, where political considerations were not generally important. It is noteworthy that the delegates to this Committee had in general, during the approximately five years of its existence, an uncommon sense of cooperation. This was of great importance for the smooth operation of the quadripartite organization.

The Direct Aid was handled through arrangements between ECA and each of the three Associated States, although this was contrary to the French conception of external aid to the Associated States. These States desired direct contact with the United States in the planning and handling of the economic and technical aid without intervention of the French. But France was still financing the largest part of the war effort and was covering the budget deficits and the balance of payments deficits of the three Associated States; and the French had to consider the need for coordination of the interdependent economies of the three countries. They wanted direction and control at least by quadripartite organizations if not by the French themselves. The Bao Dai government recognized the need for joint planning in the economic and financial field, in order to harmonize the interests of all concerned parties, as well as the need for joint organizations, particularly in the fields of communications, customs, finance, foreign trade, treasury, reconstruction, industrial development . . . But the government of each Associated State attempted to minimize the quadripartite concept and to avoid such organizations wherever possible. These factors had adverse effects on the provision of United States aid to Indochina.

Other obstacles were also encountered in the planning and the implementation of the aid. For example, insufficient knowledge of English at top levels of administration and an almost complete ignorance of this language at working levels were a serious problem and limited the productivity of the non-French speaking American personnel. But many Vietnamese were eager to learn English and, with the organization of accelerated courses in English, the problem of language became minor.

Under the March 8 Agreements, whenever technical advisers were needed, Vietnam had to grant priority to French Union subjects unless France was unable to supply the required personnel. In Indochina, the French personnel in technical and economic fields were sufficient to meet the demand from the governments of the Associated States. However, in the field of United States aid, with its special procedures, the French should have been more cooperative by adopting more flexibility in their interpretation of the March 8 Agreements in the field of technical assistance. A fair cooperation from the beginning would have accelerated the implementation of American aid and might have made it of greater value. It must be pointed out that, fortunately, these restrictions were practically and progressively relaxed as time went on, with more mutual understanding and a realistic evaluation of the facts.

The Vietnamese personnel were not well prepared to undertake their new responsibilities. The French had not devoted sufficient efforts to the training of these personnel, and, on the other hand, they were not allowed sufficient time to prepare themselves for their new tasks.

In the field of general business, the French were protected against the penetration of foreign influences by special privileges arising from the application of the March 8 Agreements:

1. French law was applied in civil and commercial cases wherever French individuals or entities were involved;
2. French business interests were given all the benefits and privileges of national business concerns;
3. French language and culture had a privileged position.

As a matter of fact, at that time, few foreign businesses other than French and Chinese showed much interest in the area. American business, in particular, was not interested as yet in Vietnam, except in certain fields where it was already represented by French subsidiaries or French firms dealing in international commercial and banking activities. The preferential treatment allowed to French interests was therefore not a serious obstacle to the establishment of American business interests in Vietnam.

In consideration of the above factors and the prospect of United States aid to Indochina, the recommendation of the Griffin Mission for a specially appointed ECA Mission to administer economic and technical aid was fully justified. It was obvious that, without such an organization, the planning and the implementation of this aid would have been delayed and jeopardized by lack of coordination and by delays in and complexity of communications through diplomatic channels. Furthermore, the creation of national counterparts of ECA Mission personnel at almost every working level in each of the Associated States helped establish direct contacts which were an important factor in implementing the aid. Without them, there would have been greater difficulty in utilizing the available aid.

During the first years of operation, American aid encountered some obstacles, such as language problems, lack of qualified local personnel, complexity of the aid procedures . . . but with the rapid training and adaptation of the local staff appointed to help in the administration of aid, the operations gradually became easier and more effective. At the end of the first fiscal year, an encouraging record was achieved, although the American personnel appointed to Indochina totaled only about thirty persons. Compared with the number of persons now in the Mission (more than 2000 civilian officers of United States origin working with Aid-Vietnam), it was really quite efficient. The present situation is, however, completely different, as it is influenced by military, political, and economic aspects of aid and the direct involvement of the United States in Vietnam.

Whatever may be thought about the goal of United States aid and its effectiveness in this region, it now appears evident that, without the intervention of the United States, the attempt of the Allied Powers to defend the entirety of Indochina against Communist aggression would have been disastrous. Not only Indochina but also all the rest of Southeast Asia would have now come under Communist control.

However, during the first years of American aid to Indochina, the Allied Powers interested in this region were not entirely favorable: the intentions of the United States were not fully understood. While the United States supported a reasonable nationalism and the self-determination of the colonial people, it was also aware of the interests of the former colonial Powers in this area, and it was inclined to avoid any appearance of wanting to reduce or counter their continuing influence or whatever remained of their interests. This delicate position indeed backed up the ultranationalists' feeling that the United States was not a friendly country on which they could count in their resolute fight against the colonial Powers.

On the other side some French were inclined to view the expression of interest of the United States towards Indochina as an attempt to replace French influence. In any event, after the Geneva Conference in 1954, with the partition of Vietnam and with more than one million refugees from the North to be settled in the South, the aid of friendly countries appeared as necessary as ever. Fortunately, United States aid was already in operation and running as well as possible. It was only a matter of increasing and adapting the aid to meet the new needs. If this aid had been started only after the 1954 Geneva Conference, it would have been too late for the survival of South Vietnam. From this viewpoint, one may consider that the decision of the United States to send the Griffin Mission to this region and the recommendations of this Mission were of the greatest importance and among the most significant events of history.

Saigon, September 8, 1969

7

Needs for United States Economic and Technical Aid in the Colony of Singapore and the Federation of Malaya [1950]

Summary

1. In the Crown Colony of Singapore and the Federation of Malaya almost half of the population is Chinese. A campaign of violence is currently being conducted by some 3,000 to 5,000 Communist-led and predominantly Chinese terrorists, designed to drive Europeans away and to disrupt the government and economic activities of the area (Section I).
2. The Federation of Malaya in 1949 produced 45 percent of the world's production of natural rubber, 34 percent of world tin production, and substantial quantities of coconuts, copra, coconut oil, palm oil, palm kernels, and pineapples. Thus Malaya is the largest net dollar earner in the whole sterling area. Economic deterioration in Malaya would adversely affect the United Kingdom, as well as all countries dependent on its exports. Should Malaya fall to the Communists, Burma, Thailand, and Indonesia would face greatly increased Communist pressure (Section II, *a*).
3. The immediate economic problem is how to keep production of rubber and tin going in the face of terrorist activities; longer range problems involve the future production of tin and rubber, for the present insecurity prevents tin prospecting and also discourages the large outlay required for planting new rubber trees.

   The resettlement of Chinese squatter communities, at present living in outlying areas, or the construction of roads to open up such areas, is an immediate need, for such communities now form the life line of the Communist terrorists. Enlargement and reorientation of Chinese education is also needed.

   Suppression of the Communist campaign of violence is the key to the solution of all other problems (Section III).
4. The overwhelming portion of outside aid has come from the United Kingdom, which has made large amounts of financial aid available, as well as important military assistance (Section IV).
5. It is recommended that emergency aid estimated to cost $4,500,000 be made available (Section V). The recommended aid comprises:

Report No. 2 of the United States Economic Survey Mission to Southeast Asia, prepared during and following the Mission's visits to Singapore, Johore Bahru, and Kuala Lumpur, March 16-23, 1950; and first printed in Washington, May, 1950.

a) \$3,200,000 for radio equipment, with one U.S. radio engineer to advise on detailed specifications (Section V, b).
b) \$1,000,000 for heavy earth-moving equipment including bulldozers, rock crushers, side dump trucks, etc., with one U.S. engineer to advise on detailed specifications (Section V, c).
c) \$300,000 to revise texts at present in use in Chinese language schools and to train more teachers for Chinese primary schools (Section V, d).

6. It is recommended that limited additional long-term assistance be provided for research on scrub typhus, for plant breeding, the Technical College in Kuala Lumpur, the University of Malaya and technical schools in Malaya, the medical school of the University of Malaya, and that limited technical assistance be provided to Singapore in industrial development, building research, modernization of machines, radio repair training, and manufacture of vaccines (Section VI).
7. It is neither necessary nor appropriate for the United States to undertake a large aid program in view of the British responsibility for the area and the Commonwealth interest therein (Section VII).
8. It is recommended that an officer be attached to the Consulate in Kuala Lumpur or the Consulate General in Singapore to coordinate aid activities under the policy direction of the chief diplomatic officer (Section VIII).

I. The Current Situation

Singapore, a Crown Colony of the United Kingdom, is a small island with a teeming city of a million people, of whom 80 percent are Chinese. It has a thriving port and some industry, particularly the smelting of tin ore from Malaya, Thailand, Burma, and other countries.

There is law and order in Singapore and life and trade go on unmolested. The Malayan Communist Party was small in 1948 when it was outlawed and went underground. Acts of violence with political motivation are rare, although some grenades have recently been thrown on the island. On the other hand, it is reported that substantial sums of "protection money" are collected from merchants and real-estate owners in Singapore to support the Communist terrorist bands on the mainland.

The people of Singapore are prosperous and busy and seem to care little about local political affairs, although the Government of Singapore has been trying to encourage wider political participation. As in other overseas Chinese communities, however, there is a deep underlying loyalty to China, as evidenced by the large sums of money contributed to the Chinese Government to support the war against Japan. It is too early to see what effect this loyalty to mother country will have in the new circumstance of Communist domination of China. Understandably, a feeling of uncertainty pervades the island, and business, though flourishing, shows little inclination to expand its investment there. There is even some evidence of flight of capital.

The Federation of Malaya includes nine Malay States and the former Straits Settlements of Penang and Malacca. It is a British Protectorate, with sovereignty in the States resting nominally with the sultans. The British retain exclusive control of defense and foreign relations, and final appeals in all court cases rest with the Privy Council in London. Through a system of British advisers resident in the states, Britain directs all affairs except the Moslem religion (generally subscribed to by Malays) and Malay customs.

Malaya lives primarily on its rubber and tin, a continuing production of which, at adequate prices, is essential to its economic functioning. The chief item of consumption is rice, of which only a third of normal needs is produced domestically.

Malaya has a plural society: less than one-half are Malays, who comprise the peasant farmers and most civil service officials. Nearly as many are Chinese, who dominate trade and who provide much of the wage-earning labor on the plantations and in the mines. The remaining 10 percent of the wage earners are Indians. Less than one percent are Europeans, who manage the plantations and hold most of the top civil service posts.

Law and order do not obtain in Malaya. Although neither nationalism nor economic distress provides an important grievance in the area, there is rebellion of a sinister and effective character. Some 3,000 to 5,000 bandit terrorists, Communist-led and predominantly Chinese, are organized in uniformed and apparently coordinated groups. Their purpose is partly an exciting life with personal gain (banditry has a long history in Malaya), but, much more, a deliberate effort to drive Europeans out of Malaya, and to disrupt the government and the functioning of the major productive enterprises upon which the economy of the country depends.

Important British forces, aided by local military units, civil police, and volunteer organizations, have been mobilized to protect the area's people and productive enterprises and to suppress terrorist activity. This effort has not yet been successful. Terrorist activity has recently increased in the face of increased suppression operations. Many rubber plantations cannot be adequately protected, tin prospecting has had to come to an end, and all the villages and towns except Kuala Lumpur are subject to attack at any time. Travel through the country must be in convoy, and even then is dangerous.

Current production of rubber and tin has not yet been seriously affected, but the continuation and development of these and other industries is threatened by the continuing terrorist activity. Moreover, the presence of effective guerilla forces, frankly Communist in orientation, means that Malaya (with its large Chinese population) is a peculiarly inviting target for expanded Communist aggression, either from within or from without.

II. Economic and Political Significance
of Singapore and Malaya

a) Economically, the Federation of Malaya is of great importance as the world's leading producer of rubber and tin. It is also an important supplier of copra and palm oil. All four products are high on the U.S. strategic commodity list.

In 1949, rubber production was 671,503 tons, or about 45 percent of the world's production of natural rubber and about 35 percent of the world's 1949 production of natural plus synthetic rubber. Exports of rubber in 1949 totaled 899,000 tons, of which 265,000 tons went to the United States, 234,000 tons to sterling area countries (primarily to the United Kingdom), 387,000 tons to OEEC countries (including the United Kingdom), 86,000 tons to the Union of Soviet Socialist Republics and satellites (including China), and minor quantities to other countries. Exports in 1950 are following this same general pattern.

Without Malaya's rubber, supplies would be short in many markets of the world, prices of rubber goods would rise and production costs would also rise as marginal, high-cost production was drawn upon and as the United States and other countries came to depend more heavily on production of synthetic rubber, which for many purposes is less suitable than natural rubber.

In 1949, tin ore production was 54,910 tons, about 34 percent of the world's production in that year. This was somewhat below the 1936-40 annual average of 63,500 tons.

In 1948, tin metal production from the smelters at Singapore and Penang was 50,000 long tons, as against 127,000 in 1940.[a] In 1949, tin metal production reached 62,677 tons. As before the war, Malaya was the world's largest producer of tin metal, accounting for some 37 percent of world production.

Exports of tin metal in 1948 totaled 47,215 long tons, and were valued at the equivalent of $100,800,451. In 1949, exports totaled 54,783 long tons, valued at the equivalent of $116,782,000. The United States took 62 percent of Malaya's tin exports (by value) in 1948 and 80 percent in 1949.

Without Malaya's tin, the world would be markedly short of the amounts critically needed for essential purposes, both civilian and military. There is no satisfactory substitute for tin.

Malaya also produces and exports substantial quantities of coconuts, copra, coconut oil, palm oil, palm kernels, and pineapples.

Total 1948 exports of Singapore and the Federation of Malaya were valued at the equivalent of U.S. $810,644,118, and 1949 exports at the equivalent of U.S. $723,035,000. Exports to the United States were valued at U.S. $215,426,831 in 1948, and U.S. $182,809,000 in 1949. The area is the largest net dollar earner in the whole sterling area.

Malaya's exports, especially of rubber and tin, to dollar markets are of critical importance in the effort to achieve a balance of payments between the sterling area and the dollar area. Without these dollar earnings, the United

---

[a]After the war, the tin ore bought by the United States from Thailand was smelted in the Texas City smelter. Before the war it was smelted in Singapore or Penang and purchased by the United States as tin metal.

Kingdom would have to depend much more heavily than at present on financial aid from the United States or face a noticeable reduction in its already austere standard of living.

Malaya's imports, which come primarily from the United Kingdom, provide important markets for sterling area production, helping the United Kingdom maintain its arduously achieved over-all balance of payments. Economic deterioration in Malaya, resulting either from terrorist activities or from a decline in world demand and prices for its chief exports, would adversely affect the United Kingdom both in its over-all balance of payments and in its dollar earnings.

As a market, Malaya absorbs large quantities of rice, sugar, cigarettes, cotton piece goods, and many other products that contribute to the relatively high standard of living enjoyed by Malayans. The time will surely come again, perhaps soon, when its thriving market for rice, textiles, and other products will be highly important for the maintenance of prosperity elsewhere.

All this would be lost if Malayan rubber and tin production were halted and its economic life disrupted, as organized Communist terrorist gangs are now attempting to do.

b) Politically, the Federation of Malaya is under the protection of the United Kingdom, which controls its government and administers its finances, defense forces, and foreign affairs. Local leaders already play an important part in its government, however, and are being aided and encouraged to take on broader responsibilities.

Because Chinese residents already outnumber the Malays (if Singapore and the Federation are considered a single unit), and may shortly outnumber the Malays in the Federation of Malaya itself, the political significance of the area is apparent. If Communist China engages in a cold or a hot war with the United Kingdom, the loyalties of resident Chinese will be put to a severe test. Moreover, if there should ever be an attack on the Malays by Communists from China, or if the Communist terrorists already attacking the country from within ever achieve substantial strength, the whole Malayan social structure might be torn apart. If Malaya were ever Communist-controlled, there would result greatly increased Communist pressures on Burma, Thailand, Indonesia. On the other hand, political stability with orderly political and economic development within the Federation would be a real force for stability and democratic development in neighboring areas.

c) Singapore has a special economic and military significance as a great trading port, tin smelter, substantial earner of foreign exchange, contributor to the economic development of the Federation of Malaya, and as a major military base. Any Communist control of the Federation would quickly threaten Singapore. It is highly unlikely that Communist control would develop first in Singapore.

d) The United States, in common with the rest of the non-Communist world, therefore has an important stake in the peace and in the economic health and development of Singapore and the Federation of Malaya and in their political development within the democratic traditions of the United Kingdom and toward their eventual goal of responsible self-government.

III. Dominant Economic and Political Problems

a) The major short-term economic problem today confronting the Federation of Malaya is how to keep its rubber and tin in production in the face of constant terrorist attacks by organized Communist gangs (and apparently by other bandits also) without long-term assurances of political stability in Malaya and profitable prices for tin and rubber. Also present is the problem of how to insure future production by resuming tin prospecting (now physically impossible) and by replanting great areas of over-age rubber trees with high-yielding strains. Tin prospecting (and even some current tin production) can be resumed only when civil law and order again reign. Rubber planting requires both civil stability and large amounts of capital. The latter is unlikely to be forth-coming in adequate amounts until there is a marked lessening not only of internal Communist aggression but also of the threat of potential aggression from China.

b) The presence of numerous Chinese squatter colonies in outlying regions constitutes an important obstacle to effective suppression of terrorist activities and is therefore an urgent political problem as well as a social one. These squatter colonies constitute the supply lines for the Communist terrorists. They comprise families unable to find work in the towns or tillable land near the villages. They take up semijungle land, usually far from villages, and eke out a bare subsistence by growing rice, vegetables, poultry, and hogs (which the Malays will not raise).

Because of their distance from villages and the lack of adequate roads to these squatter colonies, it is usually impractical for the civil police either to protect the people in the colonies from terrorist raids and intimidation or to control the support (in money, food, information, rest and recreation, and recruits) they frequently give to the terrorists.

One of the most urgent problems of the area, therefore, is the resettlement of these people on cleared land within the ability of the police to protect and the building of roads to such colonies as are now resettled, so that police protection and control can more easily reach them.

c) A third urgent problem is increasing and improving educational opportunities for the Chinese, especially in villages and rural areas.[b] Only about one-third of Chinese children in the 6 to 11 age group are at present in school. In the cities, the financial support of the relatively prosperous Chinese business classes has insured reasonably adequate standards in the Chinese schools, and many have therefore qualified for government grants (available to private

---

[b]The British are undertaking an expanded educational program for the Malays, whose literacy rate is lower than that of the Chinese.

schools meeting specified standards). In small villages and rural areas (and of course in squatter colonies), very few schools are available, and those are very poorly staffed and equipped. Of the 240,000 students in Chinese language schools, most are in urban schools.

There is therefore the problem of providing many more rural schools for Chinese students, which means recruiting many more teachers. Money can be found to equip schools and pay teachers, if the teachers can be found.

There is a second, and even more serious, aspect of this problem. It concerns the orientation of the teaching now going on in Chinese schools. The texts used reflect the attitude of many Chinese—that China is their real home and deserves their loyalties. (China does not recognize the right of any Chinese, or child of a Chinese, to renounce his Chinese citizenship.) The teachers have nearly all come from China or studied there, and are particularly pro-China and not pro-Malaya in outlook. Moreover, the spontaneous committees of Chinese that help arrange private financial support of Chinese schools exert an important control over teaching policies through the very fact that their financial support is vitally necessary.

Together, texts, teachers, and committees combine to build a strong orientation of Chinese students toward China (although 94 percent of them are Malaya-born). More than this, the Communist sympathies of many teachers and the coming of Communist control in China infect students with a pro-Communist as well as a pro-Chinese bias.

New textbooks, new teachers (and more of them), and a well-defined pro-Malayan educational policy are therefore needed if the Chinese are ever to become integrated into the Malayan social structure and bulwark it, rather than split it. This would be welcomed by many of the Chinese themselves, for it would demonstrate that the government was really interested in them as well as in the Malays. Moreover, it would help the Chinese to carry out their declared intention of becoming citizens of Malaya, with all the rights and duties thereby entailed.

d) A fourth urgent problem is the improvement and extension of roads, particularly in jungle areas. At present, pursuit of terrorists is badly hampered by poorly engineered roads in some areas (where ambushes take place from over-hanging banks when vehicles slow up in climbing steep grades), and by complete lack of roads, particularly feeders and transverse roads connecting main highways, in other areas. Development of additional roads would help suppress the terrorists, would facilitate resettlement of squatter settlements, and would contribute to long-term economic development.

e) In the long run, the Federation needs continuing economic development on which to base a rising standard of living. It needs to expand its rice production and to keep rice production costs low, for this is the major element in the Malayan cost of living. It needs to diversify its production both for home consumption and for export. It needs to modernize its rubber production and to reduce the costs of this production to meet the competition of more efficient producers in other areas, particularly Indonesia. It needs to train more of its own engineers and doctors and to develop a much larger body of governmental and business administrators from among the resident population. It needs to amalgamate the separate elements in its social structure, bringing all races into all occupations, instead of allowing the Chinese to provide most of the businessmen, the Chinese and the Indians most of the mining and plantation labor, and the Malays most of the civil servants and a great part of the farming peasantry. It needs to make wage-earning, business and even government more attractive to Malays; and it needs Chinese and Indians in its civil service. Finally it needs to develop an awareness by large parts of its population, including many Chinese, of its identity as a nation, deserving of their loyalty and support as responsible participants in a functioning democratic process.

f) Nationalism is neither strong nor militant in Malaya. In the past the general conditions accompanying the existence of a plural society and the general absence of strong grievances against the governing power tended to preclude strong nationalistic impulses. The Chinese prospered economically more than they could in their homeland, while the Malays were content with their agricultural pursuits and British paternalism. The large resident Chinese community generally feels strong loyalty to China, from which many of them have recently come, which is nearby, and with which they have many family and business ties. The effective denial of federal citizenship to most Chinese residents under the provisions of the constitution and their virtual exclusion from civil service positions probably reinforce this attitude.

The presence of a large Chinese community precludes any strong Malay demands for near-term independence and forces the Malays to rely on British support. The Malays in the past have displayed little taste for business or government, and little sense of national identity. They look for religious leadership to the sultans of the Malay States, who have exclusive control over Islamic matters and Malay customs. They can quite effectively make their views known, however, if the government proposes actions they consider contrary to their interests. They are beginning to participate more widely in political activity and in time may develop an adequate base for self-government. Despite their traditional antipathy toward the Chinese, there are signs of some likely concessions by the Malays to Chinese desires for an improved political status. Proposals for more lenient citizenship qualifications for Chinese have been put forth by the Communities Liaison Committee, a government-inspired group made up of prominent representatives of racial groups.

The most influential political group is the United Malays National Organization (UMNO), a right-wing organization of Malays favoring collaboration with the British in a policy of gradualism on the ground that the Malays are not yet prepared for self-government. Moreover, the presence of the large Chinese community, which controls the retail trade and much other business, would pose major problems for an independent nation. It, at present, precludes any strong Malay demands for independence and in effect forces the

Malays to rely for support on the British, whom they have no desire to see leave at any time in the foreseeable future.

Among the other political groups, none are of very great importance, for the Malays participate little in political activity, and the Chinese and Indians have had little opportunity to do so. The Malayan Chinese Association claims a membership of 100,000 and supports the British in their anti-terrorist operations. The Malayan Indian Congress, though small, relatively ineffective, and suffering from internal dissension with respect to orientation toward India or toward Malaya, would favor more immediate self-government for Malaya. The small Malay Nationalist Party, a left-wing group whose president has been under arrest since 1948 for conspiring with the Malayan Communist Party, advocates fairly near-term national independence.

g) Shortage of funds, accentuated by the cost of anti-terrorist operations, both limits the availability of local funds for various development purposes and constitutes a drain on U.K. resources. Despite U.K. financial assistance in the form of grants and loans since 1945 totaling over £ 100 million (including grants of £ 8 million toward the cost of the emergency alone), a series of deficit budgets has reduced the Federation of Malaya's accumulated surplus balance from some £ 28 million in April 1946 to about £ 6 million at the beginning of 1950. In addition, expenditure amounting to about £ 15.5 million has been financed by the issue of public loans. Revenue at present levels is scarcely sufficient to meet normal recurrent expenditure even if special expenditure on the emergency is omitted. The continuation of terrorist activities limits the possibility of increasing local revenues by discouraging investment for long-term development; by preventing the extension of health, education, and other social services to wide rural areas; and by retarding replanting of large rubber areas and tin prospecting activities. It is possible that unless the situation in Malaya improves rapidly, funds from U.K. and Malayan sources combined will be insufficient for both the extra emergency requirements and an even modest implementation of economic development plans. Prerequisite to both short- and long-term economic and political development is the reestablishment of civil law and order in the country. Banditry has a long tradition in the Federation. At the end of the war there were in private hands large quantities of arms, some provided by the allies for the wartime resistance movement (which was led by Communists, predominantly Chinese), and some left by the Japanese when they surrendered in 1945. Banditry immediately became a problem, but at first it was not terrorist in nature or political in orientation. It apparently appealed to young men as an easy and exciting life, far better than a humdrum job in the paddy fields or as a clerk, especially for those who had participated in the wartime resistance.

In June of 1948, however, following a Communist Conference held in Calcutta in February, 1948, at which orders to take direct action in Southeast Asia were issued and coordination was initiated, the complexion of banditry in Malaya changed. Armed gangs sought out European managers of rubber estates and tin mining operations, Chinese Kuomintang sympathizers, and labor contractors, and murdered them in cold blood. This was the beginning of a systematic campaign to wipe out the European elements that directed the major economic industries of the country, and thus to disrupt its economy and hopefully its government.

Terrorist gangs, composed of the former bandits and the newly militant Communists (who had attempted to work above ground in trade unions and political activities prior to that time) appeared, many in uniform, with three-starred caps. Their camps were used as centers for intensive political indoctrination. Their organization and leadership improved, and they gradually acquired better weapons, apparently smuggled in along the coast. They operated more to disrupt the economy than for personal gain, although they demanded tribute from individuals and villages to support their activities. They demanded that villagers, especially in the Chinese squatter areas, provide them with information, money, and supplies. They razed uncooperative villages and murdered informers. They did not voice grievances of an economic or social character, but frankly aimed at eliminating Western influence in the country.

Large military and civil police forces, both British and Malay, are presently engaged in protecting villages, rubber estates, and tin mining operations, and in attacks on terrorist gangs wherever they can be tracked down. Although believed to number only between 3,000 and 5,000, the terrorists find such protection in the jungle and extract such information and supplies (and some recruits) from the villages that relatively little progress against them has been made. In fact, since the announcement at the first of the year that March would be anti-bandit month, with many volunteers sought to supplement the regular police forces, terrorist attacks have been stepped up. At present, the situation seems to be getting worse, not better.

IV. Economic Aid Already Being Planned for or Given to Malaya

(a) Sources other than the U.S.

The United Kingdom has already provided very large sums for the post-war rehabilitation and development of Malayans, for governmental and social services, and for bandit suppression there.

The U.K. Government bore the cost of the administration of Malaya from the time of its liberation in September 1945 until the reestablishment of civil government in April 1946. The net total of expenditure during this period is known to have been in excess of £ 7 million, much of which was capital expenditure on rehabilitation works. Apart from the above the United Kingdom Government has made or promised the following specific contributions:

	Total financial assistance already sanctioned £ million	Amount spent up to Mar. 31, 1950 £ million
Colonial Development Corporation and London loans	20.7	8.4
Colonial Welfare and Development grants	7.5	0.8
War damage grants & loans	40.3	....
Army expenditure	36.0	21.8
Direct grant towards internal security costs	8.0	5.0
Total	£ 112.5	£ 36.0

It should be emphasized that the above figures refer to government expenditure only and ignore capital expenditure on rehabilitation or development from non-government sources, the amount of which is very large but not readily ascertainable.

It is anticipated that the Commonwealth Plan of Aid to Southeast Asia (called the "Spender Plan")[c] to be discussed at the Sydney conference in May, may make certain recommendations for economic and technical aid to Malaya by Commonwealth countries.

The United Nations International Children's Emergency Fund (UNICEF) has approved the expenditure of $104,200 in Malaya for 13 fellowships (2 for 6 months, 4 for 1 year, 7 for 2 years) for study abroad of maternal and child health and maternal and child welfare (total, $51,980); equipment, books, etc., for the Nurses Training School at Penang, which is being enlarged (total, $20,220); and four instructors for 1 year apiece at this school (total, $32,000).

UNICEF has also approved the expenditure of $27,850 for Singapore, to cover 4 one-year fellowships in rural health, municipal health work, assistance to handicapped children, and social welfare ($17,850); and to pay for a technical consultant in the care of handicapped children ($10,000).

In addition, UNICEF has approved the expenditure of $20,600 for Brunei, for two public health nurses, some teaching supplies and equipment, and 25,000 pounds of dried skim milk; and $49,000 for Sarawak, for three nursing instructors, teaching supplies and equipment, one fellowship in child welfare, and $10,000 worth of dried whole milk, included in $49,000 total.

Certain British missionary societies provide educational services in the area.

---

[c]This Plan was finally adopted at a Conference held in Colombo, Ceylon, in October, 1950, and has since been known as the "Colombo Plan" [Ed.].

(b) From U.S. sources

There are two U.S. Army doctors now studying scrub typhus in Malaya. They have done very valuable research there in establishing effective cures and vaccines for scrub typhus and are now studying the prevention of the disease by controlling the insects that transmit it. This research is of importance not only for Malaya, but for other countries as well, including the United States (where Rocky-Mountain fever control can use the same methods).

The Interdepartmental Committee on Scientific and Cultural Cooperation (SCC) of the U.S. government has allocated, but not yet obligated, funds for two Malayan nationals to start training in 1950 in U.S. crop-production methods.

The U.S.-U.K. Fulbright Agreement makes possible the exchange of scholars and professors between the United States and Malaya and Singapore, but no U.S. grantees have yet been approved for assignment to Singapore or Malaya, and the dollar costs of study in the United States prevent residents of Malaya or Singapore from requesting the travel assistance (in sterling) available from Fulbright funds.

The Economic Cooperation Administration (ECA) has approved the sending of 30 geological and 30 geodetic experts to survey various U.K. colonial areas (including Malaya) at a dollar cost of $1,500,000 and an estimated sterling cost of £ 460,000.

It should perhaps also be noted that the heavy contributions to Malaya made by the United Kingdom (mentioned above) would have been much more difficult to finance and might have had to be materially reduced, if the United States had not made great loans and grants to the United Kingdom. These may therefore in part be considered indirect contributions to Malaya by the United States.

Finally, at least four private religious groups in the United States have been providing aid in the form of books and equipment, relief supplies, and medical and educational services.

V. Recommendations for Immediate Aid

Summary	Dollars	Number of Personnel
1. Radio police network, radio stations, patrol cars and jungle squad equipment.	$3,200,000	1
2. Road building and earth-moving equipment.	$1,000,000	1
3. Education	300,000	20 to 30
Total	$4,500,000	22 to 32

All of the following recommendations are based on requests made by the British authorities in Singapore and the Federation of Malaya.

a) As the elimination of terrorist activities is the all-important prerequisite to both economic recovery and long-term economic and political development, and as purely economic aid would have little effect without such elimination and in wide areas would be unsafe to carry on, it is evident that the most urgent short-term economic aid should be of kinds that would support the police and military effort.

Military aid was not within the scope of the mission; but economic aid to the civil police can be thoroughly justified on both economic and political grounds. At present, the efficiency of bandit suppression is markedly affected by the lack of almost any radio-communication facilities for the civil police. Ambushes occur; isolated police stations are attacked; but word does not reach reinforcements until hours or even days later. Bandit suppression is also hampered by the lack of heavy earth-moving equipment (made only in the United States) with which to build jungle roads and airstrips and to prepare areas for the resettlement of Chinese squatter groups in communities that might be properly protected and subject to reasonable controls.

It is therefore recommended that the United States undertake to provide certain radio equipment and heavy earth-moving equipment for civil use in the Federation of Malaya.

b) The estimated cost of the radio equipment recommended is \$3,200,000. This would include 500 light portable two-way radio sets for jungle squads. The portable equipment available from the United Kingdom is reported to be 40 percent heavier than that used by the U.S. Army and therefore would hamper unduly the mobility of jungle squads.

It would also include 1,500 two-way radio sets for patrol cars and for isolated police stations. It would also include a substantial supply of spare parts, equipment and supplies for maintenance and repair shops, jeeps with repair tools, generators for the larger sets, and a battery-charging plant for the small sets.

The radio network made possible by this equipment would greatly increase the efficiency of the police by allowing them to bring up reinforcements immediately to points attacked by terrorists. Telephone wires, if any, are always cut before an attack begins. If this equipment were available, it would no longer be possible for the whole complement of 21 police in an isolated station to be wiped out in a 6-hour battle without word reaching reinforcing units until hours after the last man was killed. With such equipment, jungle squads could track down bandits with greater mobility and effectiveness, knowing that reinforcements would quickly arrive if they met gangs too large to handle.

As a school for radio operators is now turning out numbers of graduates in Malaya, the British believe there would probably be enough operating personnel to handle these sets. On the other hand, a number of maintenance men should accompany the equipment and stay for two years, training a local maintenance staff.

Although it is recommended that the $3,200,000 required for radio equipment be earmarked right away from any available funds, its procurement could not be effectively planned at a distance. It is recommended that a highly competent radio engineer, familiar with radio communication in tropical jungles, be sent immediately to Malaya to examine thoroughly into detailed needs and to advise on the specific U.S. equipment that would meet those needs. Such a survey should not require more than two months and, if initiated promptly, should permit procurement of equipment to begin before June 30. The technician sent should be prepared to examine and advise on military radio installations also, on request, and to advise on integration of the civil and military radio networks.

c) It is estimated that the heavy earth-moving equipment recommended, together with certain accompanying personnel, would cost about $1,000,000. This would include bull-dozers, rock crushers, side-dump trucks, etc. The type of heavy equipment needed is manufactured only in the U.S.

Provision of this equipment would make possible the construction of jungle airstrips and new roads into the jungle for the primary purpose of suppressing the terrorists. The equipment would also be used in clearing areas and building roads to facilitate resettlement of squatter colonies. It would also be used to improve certain sections of existing roads that are particularly subject to ambush or otherwise likely to hamper fast movement of civil police and military forces. Although use of this equipment would be limited to short-term, high-priority construction aiding the suppression of terrorist activities, it is obvious that improved communication facilities would make a substantial contribution to long-term development after the end of terrorist activity. It should be added that a long-term road-development program for Malaya has been submitted to ECA for financing. This does not duplicate the above project.

As in the case of the radio equipment, it is recommended that a highly competent highway engineer, conversant with the construction of jungle roads and airstrips and with land clearance in jungle areas, be sent to Malaya to advise on the exact types of equipment needed in the light of United States availabilities.

d) The third recommendation for immediate action concerns aid to Malaya in training more teachers for Chinese primary schools and in revising textbooks used in these schools.

Teacher training would be undertaken by one or more new schools established for this purpose. Teachers for these teacher-training schools are needed. They should be trained in educational methods and able to speak South Chinese dialects, especially Cantonese. Such teachers are not available from U.K. sources and it is recommended that they be recruited in the United States, perhaps from among missionary educators returned from China and perhaps from among Chinese born in America.

Related to this is the need to revise primary textbooks, and it is recommended that personnel be recruited in the United States for this purpose also. Such personnel should be familiar with text-book preparation, should know South Chinese dialects, and would undertake to replace the pro-Chinese and pro-Communist content of existing textbooks with pro-Malayan content, consistent with that of the textbooks being used in other language schools (especially Malay and English) in Malaya.

It is estimated that from 20 to 30 personnel would be needed for these two purposes, at a cost of some $300,000 (in U.S. dollars), which should be earmarked at once. A stipend in local currency would be paid by the Government of Malaya, which would help cover local expenses.

It is recommended that recruitment, on a preliminary basis, be started for the personnel above described. It is also recommended that two such educators, one familiar with teacher training and one familiar with text-book preparation, be recruited and dispatched immediately to Malaya to develop plans for the two operations envisaged. Such a planning survey should not take longer than two months, and the funds to support the operations could then be committed.

It is further recommended that some private educational organization or institution be invited to undertake a contract to provide the services above described, to recruit the required personnel, and to be responsible for the professional competence of the result. The contract for these services should be let before June 30.

e) Finally, it should not be overlooked that an important short-term political impact can be obtained simply by the action of *initiating* longer-term projects. Although the economic or social effects of such projects might not be felt for years, an immediate psychological and political effect would result from such clear evidence (1) that the Government (and the United States) were interested in the welfare of the people themselves; and (2) that the Government (and the United States) believed in the future of the country, in its return to peaceful and prosperous conditions, and in its long-run contribution to world peace and prosperity.

For this reason, the long-term projects discussed below should not be ignored or deferred during initiation of short-term projects. Action should be started on the former as well as the latter.

VI. Recommendations for Long-Term Technical Assistance

Most of Malaya's long-run development projects either have little need of U.S. governmental aid or are susceptible to little external assistance. When terrorist activities are suppressed, investment capital can be expected to come forward from private sources to finance replanting of rubber areas, extension of tin exploration, and development of other export products, such as pineapples, bauxite, iron ore, timber, palm oil, fish and fish products, and cocoa. Further development of roads, ports, railroads, water control, power, telecommunications, government aids to agriculture, health, education and other social services require substantial expenditure of local currency, not dollars, plus equipment generally available (with some exceptions) in the sterling area. But unless the emergency situation improves rapidly, local currency for such development may not be available.

Moreover, it is particularly in such long-run development projects that the United Kingdom is aiding Malaya (through the Colonial Welfare and Development Fund and the Colonial Development Corp.); and the Commonwealth Aid Plan (the Spender Plan) is expected to be of much more significance for long-run than for short-run projects.

There are certain fields, however, where technical assistance from the United States and United Nations can be of considerable importance. Because it will not be known how much and what kinds of technical assistance will be provided by the Commonwealth under the Spender Plan, precise recommendations for U.S. technical assistance cannot yet be made, except for item *a*) below. However, there are a number of fields where U.S. technical assistance is likely to be requested.

a) It is recommended that arrangements be made at once to continue the research on scrub typhus now carried on in Malaya by the U.S. Army scrub typhus team. Having established the efficacy of a cure and a vaccine for scrub typhus, this team is now investigating methods of preventing it by controlling the mites that transmit it to man. The results of this research are of great importance to other areas of the world, including the United States, whose Rocky Mountain fever is related to scrub typhus. The Army team will soon have to terminate its work and return home, unless arrangements are made to finance its continuing work, possibly under Point Four or Public Law 402 funds.

b) It is possible that aid will also be requested for the manufacture locally of the very expensive drugs needed to prevent and cure scrub typhus. One or two plant-breeding experts will be needed for the government agricultural research station. There is only one expert there now. These experts should be competent to develop and propagate high-yielding strains of rice and to help work out the distribution of improved seed to the Malay farmer. The formerly available fine strains of rice were lost during the war. Improved strains would be an effective way of increasing paddy production.

c) Additional technical staff is needed to build up the faculty of the newly established Technical College in Kuala Lumpur. There is a real shortage of technically trained Malays and Chinese, particularly outside of Singapore, and this college was started to remedy this lack. Adequate funds are available to the college and could be called upon to cover the local currency expenditures of personnel sent in from outside. The college has been unable to attract sufficient staff from within the sterling area.

d) Technical equipment, books, and periodicals are greatly needed for the technical schools of Malaya and for the University of Malaya (at Singapore and Johore Bahru). Adequate equipment and publications are lacking in the science laboratories, veterinary schools, forestry schools, technical schools at Kuala Lumpur and Singapore, and in the University.

e) Professional training, particularly in medicine and engineering, is inadequate to meet the need in Singapore and Malaya. Both private practice and the government service need more doctors and engineers. There is need to build up the capacity of the medical school of the University of Malaya, to start an engineering school at the University, and to make provision for sending more students abroad for advanced professional training; at present, students may be advised to change their vocational plans if these require study in hard-currency areas. Aid to the University of Malaya might be undertaken by a private U.S. educational institution, under a U.S. Government contract, if this would be the most effective way of mobilizing educational competence in the United States.

f) Singapore itself, though generally able to finance its own long-term development, needs technical assistance of the following kinds:

i) A general economic survey of industrial development possibilities, especially in the field of secondary industries.
ii) A building research institute to carry on research into construction materials, methods and equipment adapted to cheap tropical housing.
iii) Advice on the modernization of machinery and methods in quarrying and certain manufacturing industries.
iv) Training facilities for radio repair and service technicians.
v) Advice on the possibilities of manufacturing BCG vaccine on the island for use in anti-tuberculosis campaigns in Singapore and the Federation of Malaya.

VII. Local Factors Limiting the Magnitude of Effective Aid Activities in the Federation of Malaya

In view of the nature of the British responsibility in Malaya and the extensive aid the British are already providing, it would be neither necessary nor appropriate for the United States to undertake a large program of aid to the Federation.

In general, U.S. aid to the area should be limited to those fields where the necessary equipment or technicians cannot be obtained from the United Kingdom or elsewhere in the Commonwealth or where a special advantage would be obtained by securing aid from the United States.

The second major factor limiting the extent of feasible aid to Malaya is the condition of civil disturbance. American technicians would be able to work only in certain major towns and their environs and in a few specified rural areas, probably even there requiring special police protection. Similarly, only such U.S. equipment should be provided as could be adequately protected from damage by terrorists. The areas where operations would be possible may be different by the time aid arrives.

Finally, it appears that the British authorities in the area will prefer to get technical and economic aid through the Commonwealth Plan and through the United Nations and specialized agencies, only calling on the United States for assistance when these sources are believed unable to supply it.

These three factors have been taken into account in developing the recommendations made above.

VIII. Administration of U.S. Aid Programs

The urgent aid projects recommended above are of diverse character, and the operation of any one would have little bearing on the operation of the others. For this reason, it is not believed necessary to set up an integrated economic aid mission in Malaya with central responsibility for all economic aid activities.

Rather, it is recommended that there be attached to the Consulate in Kuala Lumpur, or to the Consulate General in Singapore, a single officer to work on all aid programs under the policy direction of the chief diplomatic officer. This aid officer would be the central and continuing point for official U.K. contacts with the Consulate on aid matters, would facilitate the work of all aid personnel, and would keep records of all aid furnished. He should maintain contact, through the diplomatic mission, with all sources of aid in the United States, with aid activities in other countries of Southeast Asia, with U.N. or other specialized agency personnel visiting Malaya making contact with the diplomatic mission, and with any regional U.S. office for economic aid that might eventually be established. This officer would help U.S. aid personnel sent to the area but would not have administrative responsibility over them. They would receive policy direction from the chief of the diplomatic mission and technical direction from their own agencies in Washington (or, if employed by a private agency, from that agency).

Appendix

1. The Mission arrived in Singapore at 4 p.m., March 16, 1950, and remained in Malaya until 10 a.m., March 23, 1950.
2. The Mission during its stay in Malaya was composed of the following persons:

Department of State

The Honorable R. Allen Griffin, Chief of Mission, with the personal rank of Minister

Samuel P. Hayes, Jr., Deputy Chief of Mission and Adviser
William McAfee, Adviser
Eleanor L. Koontz, Secretary
Mary D. Randolph, Secretary

Economic Cooperation Administration

Edward T. Dickinson, Jr. (March 16-21), Adviser

Department of Defense

Russell G. Duff, Colonel, USA, Adviser
Frederick B. Warder (March 21-23), Captain, USN, Adviser

Duncan Campbell, U.S. Labor Attache to the United States Missions in Indonesia, Malaya, and Thailand, attended certain of the conferences, as did John Sumner of the Economic Cooperation Administration, Indonesia.

3. The following formal conferences were held during the visit of the Mission in Malaya:

a) Orientation meeting with Consul General and staff, March 17, 9 a.m.
b) Conference with Commissioner General for Southeast Asia and his principal advisers, on general conditions in Southeast Asia and needs of the Federation of Malaya, March 17, 11:30 a.m.
c) Conference with the Australian Ambassador to France in connection with coordination of Commonwealth-United States aid in Southeast Asia, March 18, 9 a.m.
d) Conference with Commissioner General on aid to Burma and Indochina, March 18, 10 a.m.
e) Conference at Government House on aid to Singapore, March 18, 12 m.
f) Conference with advisers to Commissioner General on aid to Malaya, March 19, 10 a.m.
g) Conference at Kuala Lumpur with High Commissioner for the Federation of Malaya and his principal advisers, March 20, 11 a.m.
h) Conference at Kuala Lumpur with Chief Secretary, Federation of Malaya and advisers concerning security needs for Federation police, March 20, 3 p.m.
i) Conference with American businessmen and missionaries in Kuala Lumpur for general expression of views, March 20, 5 p.m.
j) Conference at Kuala Lumpur with Chief Secretary and advisers concerning education, March 21, 9 a.m.
k) Conference at Kuala Lumpur with representatives of the planting industry, March 21, 10:15 a.m.

l) Final coordinating conference with Commissioner General in Singapore, March 22, 10 a.m.

m)Conference with American business representatives in Singapore, March 22, 5:30 p.m.

4. A list of certain of the persons with whom members of the mission conferred follows:

United States Consulate General, Singapore

W.R. Langdon, Consul General
A. Bland Calder
John N. Hamlin
W. Henry Lawrence, Jr.
James J. Halsema
Lt. Comdr. W. Gordon Cornell, USN, Attaché
Lt. Col. Earl C. Stewart, USA, Attaché

United States Consulate, Kuala Lumpur

Richard A. Poole
Laurance Van B. Nichols
A.F. McLean
R.G.L. Wall
John Sumner (ECA in RUSI)
Duncan Campbell (Labor Attaché for RUSI, Malaya, Siam)

British Officials (not all in order of rank)

Rt. Hon. Malcolm MacDonald, Commissioner-General for the United Kingdom in Southeast Asia
J.C. Sterndale-Bennett, Deputy Commissioner General for the United Kingdom in SEA (Foreign Affairs)
A.D. York, Acting Commissioner-General for the United Kingdom in SEA (Colonial Affairs)
General Sir John Harding, Commander-in-Chief, Far East Land Forces
Frederick C. Benham, Economic Adviser to Commissioner-General
W.M. Clyde, Director of Economic Activities, Office of Commissioner-General
R. Mackworth Young, Foreign Office
D.J. Cheke, Political Head of Chancery
H.W. Nightingale, Secretary for Economic Affairs, Colony of Singapore

J.E. Pepper, Acting Financial Secretary, Colony of Singapore
Sir Patrick McKerron, Officer Administering the Government of Singapore
J.D.M. Smith, Acting Colonial Secretary, Colony of Singapore (Formerly Financial Secretary)
F. MacFadzean, Representative, Colonial Development Corporation
George V. Allen, Vice-Chancellor, University of Malaya
Sir Henry Gurney, High Commissioner for the Federation of Malaya
M.V. Del Tufo, Chief Secretary, Federation of Malaya
J.A.E. Morley, Acting Economic Secretary, Federation of Malaya
W.N. Gray, Commissioner of Police, Federation of Malaya
Brig. R.G. Collingwood, Chief of Staff, Malaya District
G. Edwards, Director of Public Works, Federation of Malaya
D.C. Watherson, Secretary of Defense, Federation of Malaya
Mr. Watson, radio expert from England
Major Short, Hq., Malaya District
M.R. Holgate, Director of Education, Federation of Malaya
E.D. Fleming, Secretary for Chinese Affairs, Federation of Malaya

Australian Ambassador to France

Sir Keith Officer

American Businessmen and Missionaries, Kuala Lumpur

Wm. Warren, Managing Director, Anglo-Oriental (Malaya) Ltd., Tin Mining Company
F. Stuart Miller, Acting Manager, Pacific Tin Consolidated Corporation
W.B. Caufield, Manager, James Millar & Co., Ltd. (Tractors)
Joseph H. Emery, Standard Vacuum Co., Ltd.
The Rev. Gunnar J. Teilman, Methodist Mission
Maj. Robert Traub, Head U.S. Army Scrub Typhus Team

Representatives of the Planting, Industry, Kuala Lumpur

H.H. Facer
Dato Thuraisingham
Khoo Teik Ei
Tuan Sheik Ahmad bin Shiek Mustapha
Inche Mohamed Salleh bin Hakem
J.S. Ferguson
J.R.W. Collett
G.M. Knocker
H.K. Dimoline

American Businessmen, Singapore

Winston B. Braxton, Carrier International Limited
Leon D. Britton, RKO Radio Pictures (Malaya), Incorporated
Michael E.G. Brown, Malayan Guttas Limited
Frank Chamers, Jr., Pan American Airways
H.R. Crawford, General Manager, Singer Sewing Machine Company
Meredith C. Dack, Firestone Tire & Rubber Company
W.W. Geddes, Standard Vacuum Oil Company
F.D. Harrison, Goodyear Orient Co., Limited
David A. Hegels, Coca Cola Export Limited
Thomas W. Hickey, Jr., Connel Bros. Company (Malaya), Limited
R.G. Hill, National City Bank
W.R. Johnson, Texas Company (China) Limited
T.J. Johnston, Eastman Kodak Company
Samuel E. Knowles, International Harvester
H.E. McFarland, Western Electric Company of Asia
Glen E. Parrott, Cotz Brothers and Company
D.F. Ross, Goodrich Company (SS) Limited
John E. Semmes, Isthmian Steamship Company
James K. Shafer, National Carbon (Eastern) Limited
L.S. Skoblin, Radio Corporation of Malaya
F.K. Spangler, American President Lines
Frederick L. Waterhouse, Fred Waterhouse Company Limited

5. On March 20-21 the following members of the Mission visited Kuala Lumpur, seat of government of the Federation of Malaya:

Department of State

R. Allen Griffin
Samuel P. Hayes, Jr.
William McAfee

Department of Defense

Russell G. Duff, Col., USA

During the visit to Kuala Lumpur all the members of the Mission were conducted on a tour through the Wardieburn Rubber Estate and through a tin dredge of the Pacific Tin Consolidated Corporation under escort. The members of the Mission were accompanied on these trips by Consul Richard A. Poole.

6. As indicated previously, the Consul General, Singapore, and members of his staff briefed the Mission the morning following its arrival. Subsequent conferences were held by members of the Mission with A. Bland Calder, senior economic officer; John N. Hamlin, senior political officer; and W. Henry Lawrence, Jr., officer in charge of U.S. Information Service. Members of the Consulate General staff participated in all the conferences held with British officials and were in constant touch with the Mission during its entire stay in Singapore.

7. A list of documents submitted by the Federation of Malaya and the Government of Singapore follows:

a) Memorandum F.S. 784150, prepared for the consideration of the Griffin Mission, the annexes to which provide details on the following subjects:

Chinese primary education
Police radio equipment
Police armored vehicles and jeeps
Marine transport for the police
Interpreters (Chinese speakers) for the police
Road construction plant Telecommunication equipment
Increase of electric power

This memorandum was forwarded under cover of a letter of March 28, 1950, from M.V. Del Tufo, Chief Secretary, Federation of Malaya, to Consul Richard A. Poole.

b) Draft Development Plan, Federation of Malaya. Kuala Lumpur, Government Printer, 1949. (No. 68 of 1949.)

c) Letters of March 24, 1950, from Mr. Morley to Mr. Poole relative to a proposal to send two Malayan agriculturalists to the United States under Point Four.

d) Statement on Foreign Policy by the Australian Minister for External Affairs, the Honorable P.C. Spender, K.C., March, 1950.

e) Speech delivered by the Commissioner-General to the United Malay Nationalist Organization on March 4, 1950.

f) Suggestions for Possible American Aid for the Colony of Singapore in connection with President Truman's Fourth Point.

g) The University of Malaya, Foundation Day.

h) University Education in Malaya.

i) Colonial Office Memorandum for the use of Mr. Griffin.

Needs for United States Economic and Technical Aid in Burma [1950]

Summary

1. Burma became independent on January 4, 1948. Today the Government's major backing comes from the Socialists, most of whom are definitely anti-Communist and are aware that Burma needs Western assistance in her development. Several unrelated insurrections are going on, the most important of which is the struggle of the Karens, a large minority group, for a relatively autonomous state within the Burmese Union (Section I).
2. Rice exports are now only a fourth of prewar exports, and industrial and communication facilities are either in disuse or in urgent need of rehabilitation. Burma's foreign trade is only a fraction of its prewar volume (Section II).
3. The Government's revenues have been declining in the face of rising demands for expenditures, and budget deficits are large and growing larger. Administrative and social services have been sharply cut (Section III).
4. Agricultural services offer the broadest field through which the Government can aid its people. Medical facilities were badly damaged in recent years and there is a great scarcity of trained medical personnel. Less than half of the Burmese children of school age are in school at any given time. Funds to maintain prewar medical and educational standards are not available. The lack of experienced personnel for technical and administrative posts constitutes a formidable barrier to effective government (Section IV).
5. The United Kingdom has loaned Burma since the war approximately £70 millions, and the Commonwealth has recently loaned Burma £6 million more. The United Nations has provided a small amount of technical assistance through UNICEF, WHO, ILO, and UNESCO (Section V).
6. Under the Fulbright agreement rupee funds equivalent to $200,000 can be expended each year to cover the costs of certain educational exchanges. The United States allotted $37,000 of Smith-Mundt funds for Burma during the fiscal year 1950 (Section VI).
7. A program of technical and economic aid estimated to cost $12,228,000 for the 15 months ending June 30, 1951, is proposed (Section VII). This would cover aid in the following categories:

Report No. 3 of the United States Economic Survey Mission to Southeast Asia, prepared during and following the Mission's visit to Rangoon, March 23-April 4, 1950; and first printed in Washington, May, 1950.

Agriculture	$4,168,000
Public Health	2,255,000
Education	1,815,000
Industry, Transport and Communications	1,140,000
Commodity Program	1,400,000
National Economic Development Planning	1,250,000
Increased Contact with Burmese Leaders	200,000

8. Among the factors seriously limiting the kind and extent of aid programs carried on in Burma are (1) the shortage of governmental personnel available to participate, (2) Burmese suspicions of Western motives, (3) the shortage of government funds to cover local currency expenses, (4) the extent of insurrectionist and bandit activities, and (5) the shortage of housing for United States personnel, particularly in Rangoon (Section VIII).
9. United States aid programs should not be carried on in association with the British or utilize British personnel. Moreover, reliance should not be placed on the British or the Commonwealth to carry the major portion of the aid Burma will need. However, too big a flow of United States aid might hurt the Government of Burma by suggesting that the Government had somehow sold out. There are, therefore, good reasons for encouraging the United Nations to do as much as it can for Burma (Section IX).
10. The aid program will only be effective in strengthening the Government of Burma if an energetic information program is carried on. Information activities should, however, particularly stress the role played by the Government of Burma (Section X).
11. Most of the United States Government technicians brought to Burma should work in the various divisions of the Burmese Government. There should be a single United States representative to negotiate projects, agreements, and provide general supervision of the program. It would be desirable to set up a joint body with the Government of Burma to discuss policies and direct certain aid activities (Section XI).

I. Current Political Situation

On January 4, 1948, Burma received its independence from the British and became a wholly independent republic called the Union of Burma. The Government that then assumed, and has since maintained, responsibility for the country was sponsored by a popular-front political organization, known as the Anti-Fascists People's Freedom League (AFPFL). The AFPFL was formed as an organ of the resistance movement during the Japanese occupation and emerged at the end of the war as the dominant political organization. It enjoyed wide popular support, and most of the other political organizations and service organizations were affiliated with it. However, the League soon began to weaken because of the struggle between Communist and non-Communist elements within the League for its control, the assassination of Aung San and other important League leaders, and the important issues for rallying popular support. It has now lost much of its former prestige; its membership and popular support have greatly declined; and only one major political organization, the Socialist Party, remains affiliated with it.

Despite the fact that the Socialists are so important a component of the AFPFL, they hold only three minor portfolios in the Cabinet. The Prime Minister, Thakin Nu, who, following the assassination of General Aung San, succeeded him as head of the AFPFL, is not a Socialist and neither is the Deputy Prime Minister, Defense and Home Minister, General Ne Win. These independent members of the Government are, however, in close contact with the Socialists, especially the Right Wing Socialists, with whom they cooperate closely and in the main harmoniously. Socialist influence in the Government is, therefore, much stronger than the small number of Socialist cabinet ministers would indicate, and Government policies are virtually identical with those advocated by the Right Wing Socialists.

The Government leaders and Right Wing Socialists, although strongly influenced by theoretical Marxism, are definitely anti-Communist and have become convinced that Burma's transformation into a socialist state, an objective to which they still subscribe, must come about gradually through democratic methods and procedures with such assistance as can be obtained from the Western democracies. This view, which represents a considerable modification of their earlier, more radical position, is the result of the hostile attitude of the Burma Communist Party, the failure of the hasty nationalization program, the Chinese Communist threat, and the example of India and Pakistan. But although Thakin Nu, Ne Win, and the Right Wing Socialists recognize that, without outside assistance, Burma's economy will continue to deteriorate and may eventuate in a complete disintegration of the country as a political entity, the Left Wing Socialists are still opposed to accepting aid from the Western democracies. The dissatisfaction of the Left Wing Socialists with the Government's present more moderate policy has created considerable tension between them and the Right Wing and may result in a party split. Anti-Westernism and suspicion that foreign aid may be accompanied by attempts at foreign domination in varying degrees are widespread, both in and outside the Socialist Party.

The problems that faced the Government when it came to power were formidable. The country's war-disrupted economy had been only partially restored. Because of a lack of qualified civil servants, the administrative structure was corrupt and inefficient. Bands of well-armed brigands preyed upon the populace. Worst of all there was no national unity and no recognition of the necessity of subordinating factional interest for the good of the nation as a whole. The ethnic minority groups were all distrustful of the Burmans, but the Karens were particularly dissatisfied because, in consequence of their being widely scattered, they had not been given an autonomous state of their own by the new constitution as had the Shans and Kachins. Nor was there any unity among the Burmans, who were divided into some half-dozen different political groups each more concerned with its own preeminence than with the welfare of the nation.

Less than 3 months after Burma received its independence, a Communist-led insurrection broke out. Later in the year other dissident elements, including some army units, also went into revolt. At about the same period the Karens renewed with increased vigor their demand for an autonomous state of large dimensions and began to show increasing defiance of governmental authority. Karen-Burman tension increased greatly as the year 1948 drew to a close, and in January 1949 the Karen National Union (the principal Karen political organization) together with its military arm launched a revolt with the object of gaining an autonomous or independent state. The Karen revolt was not coordinated with the Communist-led insurrection, and the Karens are, in general, strongly anti-Communist, but in some places there was local cooperation to a limited degree between Karen and Communist forces. The insurrectionary disorders have severely taxed the military and financial resources of the government. Large areas are still held by various insurgent groups, and effective administration is largely wanting even in areas nominally under government control.

At the time of writing the Government of Burma is opposed by the following insurgent groups, in order of importance:

1. The Karen National Defense Organization.
2. The White Flag Communists, a Stalinist group having contacts with the Communist parties of India and China, who follow the Cominform line in attacking the present Government as British puppets.
3. The White Band People's Volunteer Organization, consisting of the major part of the semi-military organization created by Aung San, whose opposition to the Government arises partly from their dislike of the Socialists and partly from their inability to adopt a peaceful mode of life after many years of guerrilla fighting and underground revolutionary activity.
4. The group of Army officers and men who mutinied in August 1948 and who, in various sections of Burma, notably Prome, have entered into alliances with other insurgent groups while maintaining their own internal organization.
5. The Red Flag Communists, a local independent non-Stalinist party strongly opposed to the Moscow-oriented White Flag Communists.
6. The Arakanese Moslems, who have long been hostile to the Burmese Buddhists of the area and whose depredations have increased as a result of the Government's preoccupation with other insurgents.
7. The "First Kachin Brigade," a local insurgent group operating in the Northern Shan States under a vigorous and aggressive leader, Naw Seng.

Although none of these groups is powerful enough to withstand the Government's forces in a pitched battle, the total effect of their guerrilla activities is to cripple the transport system and thus seriously affect the country's economic life.

The Government therefore faces the dual problem of curbing their power to disrupt Burma's economy and of carrying on a rehabilitation program which will repair the damage caused by the war and the insurrections and will convince the general population that the insurgents are acting against the country's best interests.

The principal factors influencing Burma's foreign relations are:

1. its belief that to side with either the Western democracies or the Soviet bloc would imperil its recently achieved independence and freedom of action.
2. its proximity with Communist China, with which it has a long, partially undefined and frequently disputed border and which could make good use of Burma's surplus rice.
3. its association, even after independence, with Great Britain and the Commonwealth, with whom it has strong economic ties, but whom it still suspects of imperialistic designs.
4. its need for foreign assistance on terms which will not, in its view, threaten its complete independence from foreign economic or political domination.

Burma's surplus rice is of great importance to the economies of Ceylon, Pakistan, and India and at present is also needed in Japan and other Asiatic countries. Its timber, oil, and minerals (many of them critically short in world supply) are currently being denied to the world by the unsettled internal situation. Geographically, Burma offers a pathway (through Kengtung state) from Southern Yunnan province to Thailand and Indochina. Its sparse population and good food-producing potential, as well as its strategic situation, make it an attractive goal for Chinese expansion, either overtly or by subversion, to neither of which processes could Burma hope, by itself, to offer any considerable defense.

II. Major Economic Problems

Two devastating military campaigns during World War II, followed by almost three years of widespread lawlessness and rebellion, have created a chaotic economic situation in Burma. Insurgent movements against the Government have severed vital transportation routes and have paralyzed large areas of the country's economy and accelerated the rate of economic deterioration.

Before the war, Burma was the largest exporter of rice in the world and was an important supplier of this commodity to South Asiatic countries. Climate, soil, and an adequate and cheap labor supply combined to favor the growing of rice and other essential agricultural products. British capital and technicians developed Burma's valuable mineral, petroleum, and timber resources, which found a ready and profitable world market. Adequate transportation was provided by the Burma Railways and by the Irrawaddy Flotilla Company, which operated a large inland water fleet on the Irrawaddy River. Burma suffered heavy devastation during the war. Some attempt was made at rehabilitation immediately after the British reoccupation of the country, and the newly established independent Burmese Government endeavored to continue these measures upon its assumption of control. However, the political instability that followed in the wake of independence and the lack of experienced personnel remaining in the government brought these programs to an abrupt halt. With the spread of disorder, cultivation was reduced, movement of goods impeded, and the economic pace slowed.

Rebel seizure of strategic areas in central and southern Burma halted virtually all land and river transport. The principal sections of the country were only accessible to each other by an expensive and limited air service. Rice production was so reduced that exports in 1950 are estimated at 25 percent of the prewar level;[a] only 830,000 tons of rice will probably be available for export during this year as compared with the prewar level of more than 3,000,000 tons.[b] The teak industry, once a large revenue-producing enterprise, has, for all practical purposes, closed down. Mining, another great prewar industry, has stopped except for small quantities of tin and tungsten which are being extracted from some of the mines on the Tenasserim Coast. Apart from small monthly shipments of petroleum from the Chauk fields to Mandalay, virtually no petroleum has recently been produced and refined in Burma, so that this important prewar export item now has to be imported. Burma's foreign trade has been reduced to a fraction of its prewar volume, and although, according to Government of Burma statistics, the country has maintained a favorable balance of trade for the last two years, this has been done by cutting down imports to an extent which has seriously affected national production.

III. Current Financial Problems

Burma's financial position has become increasingly critical. The Finance Minister in his Budget Address put the situation in these terms:

The distressing features of our national finance today are mounting expenditures and declining receipts. Had it not been for the rehabilitation contribu-

---

[a]Two other factors also strongly discouraged rice production: (1) During the war, the Japanese occupation had cut Burma off from her traditional export markets, which had taken about half of the annual rice crop prior to that time. During that period, therefore, there was no incentive to produce rice for export, and by 1945-6 the acreage under rice had declined to half that of 1938-9. (2) The internal price of rice was maintained unchanged after 1948, despite the sharp rises in prices of other goods. As a consequence, there was a reduced incentive to increase rice acreage again. See: Chapter 1 on "Burma", by U Tun Wai, in *Asian Economic Development*, ed. Cranley Onslow (New York: Praeger, 1965), pp. 3, 18 [Ed.].

[b]As the government monopoly of the export trade in rice has recently accounted for nearly one-quarter of total government revenues, the seriousness of low exports of rice is obvious.

tion of Rs. 149,000,000^c the budget deficit for the year 1948-49 would have been much bigger than it is now estimated. The drain on the finances of Burma have [*sic*] never been heavier before than it is this year. The strength of our economy has been severely tested and our preparedness to protect our prosperity has been challenged throughout the year.

The budget deficit for the financial year of 1948-49 was estimated at Rs. 74,397,000, or twice the deficit of Rs. 34,521,000 for the previous financial year, and had it not been for the fact that the Government was able to integrate the rehabilitation fund of Rs. 149,000,000 (which represented the profits of the operations of the State Agricultural Marketing Board, the State Timber Board, and the Union Bank of Burma) into the budget as current revenue, the deficit would have been at least Rs. 225,000,000.^{d}

The principal revenue short-fall appeared in the estimates for land taxes. Originally revenue from that source was estimated as Rs. 35,200,000, but this estimate had to be revised downward in February 1949 to Rs. 20,000,000 and at the end of the year to Rs. 5,000,000. Under the prevailing conditions of law and order and the confusion in land titles, this is probably one of the most difficult taxes to collect and it is unlikely that even the smaller estimate will be collected. The Customs duties also provided less revenue than the Government had originally anticipated. The original estimate under this head was Rs. 118,000,000, but with the continued shrinkage of Burma's foreign trade, customs revenues were reduced proportionately, and the figure in the final budget estimate was reduced to Rs. 80,000,000. Forest revenue estimates originally fixed at Rs. 17,800,000 were cut to Rs. 10,583,000, since work in most of the forests and the sawmills ceased during the early part of 1949. There were also corresponding decreases in revenues under the headings of excises, excise taxes, state lotteries, stamps, registration, irrigation, etc.

On the other hand, the Government was forced to increase its expenditures for policing operations and defense purposes. The allotment for policing operations was increased from Rs. 56,770,000 to Rs. 66,770,000, and for defense purposes from Rs. 94,953,000 to Rs. 115,000,000. To meet the costs of administration and the problem of correlating these costs with reduced revenues, the Government instituted economy measures and increased some forms of taxation. During January 1949 the Government cut the salaries of all public officials and employees, from the President of the Union of Burma down to the lowest grades, by 25 to 50 percent. Unessential items of expenditure were reduced to an almost irreducible minimum, and a 25 percent reduction was effected in the existing strength of all services except the defense and police forces. Even after effecting all these economies, the budget showed a deficit of almost 11 percent of the total value of the budget.

The budget for 1949-50, though heavier than the previous one, is still

^{c}Rs. [Rupees] 4.95 equals one United States dollar.

^{d}The 1948-49 budget provided for expenditures of Rs. 589,680,000 and revenue of Rs. 515,283,000.

unbalanced. The new budget calls for a total expenditure of Rs. 590,649,000, as against anticipated revenues of Rs. 573,577,000, with a resulting deficit of Rs. 17,072,000. Defense still accounts for the preponderant proportion of the government expenditure, and in the 1949-50 budget represents almost 40 percent of the total government expenses. General administration and social services on the other hand have been sharply cut, foreboding a further deterioration in the Government administrative arm and a further lowering of public service morale since Government employees have been caught in the vise of reduced pay and a rising cost of living. It is even questionable whether the Government can actually obtain the revenues which it is anticipating under the present budget. For example, Rs. 118,000,000 are expected from the operations of the State Agricultural Marketing Board from its monopoly of the purchase and sale of rice for export and the State Timber Board. Since the State Timber Board has actually been operating at a loss during the year and will probably continue to do so for some time to come, it is likely that a good part of this revenue will not be obtained. In addition, the Government hopes to derive Rs. 121,000,000 from customs revenues. This is an astonishingly high figure when compared with Rs. 80,000,000 for 1948-49, especially since the Government will probably earn less foreign exchange during the present fiscal year as a result of further cuts in its export trade and be forced to further curtail imports into the country.

At the end of the year the Government estimated its indebtedness at Rs. 940,000,000, consisting of a prewar debt of Rs. 481,400,000 to the Government of India, Rs. 371,300,000 to the United Kingdom on its postwar rehabilitation loan (of which half has already been waived), several million rupees to the United States under the Surplus Property Agreement, and an internal debt of Rs. 80,000,000. In addition, Burma agreed in March 1950 to a Commonwealth loan of £6,000,000, which would help cover its current budgetary deficit. The debts to India and the United Kingdom were not serviced during 1949, nor is it likely that any payment will be made upon them during the present year. With reference to these loans the current budget merely contains the statement that "provision for annuity of these liabilities . . . has been omitted as was done last year."

IV. Urgent Economic Problems

A. Agriculture

In considering Burma's needs for emergency aid, the following factors are paramount:

1. Burma is primarily an agricultural country. Her chief crop is rice. Rice brings in most of her foreign exchange and provides revenue for operating the Government.

2. Research and education in the fields of agriculture, and some services in the form of extension, were given to the farmers before the war. In the main, Burma's public services were directed by former members of the Indian Civil Service. At the time of the Japanese occupation, during the liberation, and during the unrest following the liberation, foreign technicians and administrators left the country, some of the physical plant of her educational and research institutions was destroyed, and practically all of the equipment of all of the schools and stations was destroyed. The Government of Burma is attempting to restore these institutions, notably the College of Agriculture and Experiment Station at Mandalay and the College of Veterinary Medicine and the laboratory for the production of vaccine and serums at Insein.

3. Most of the technical agricultural work and agricultural services to farmers has been in the field of production (primarily of rice), and little attention has been given to the organization of marketing services. In prewar years the Indians, and to a lesser extent the Chinese, provided the agricultural credit and purchased, milled, and exported the agricultural commodities.

4. During the development of Burma as a major rice exporter, the money-lenders and millers gradually acquired title to more than 60 percent of the rice-land in the central plain. Landlordism in Burma was as firmly established as anywhere else in the world. The landlords, most of whom were foreign, left the country during and after the occupation. Tenants are now operating a majority of the land as though it were their own. The land tenure situation is unsatisfactory because such a large proportion of it is extra-legal. Landlordism, however, is not now operating on a significant scale.

5. The professional agricultural people in Burma have great respect for the technical ability of the United States Department of Agriculture and a high regard for United States agricultural institutions. They wish to send agricultural leaders to observe our methods and institutions. They wish to send students to our colleges and universities. They would like to receive expert advice and counsel from American technicians working in Burma. They are, however, concerned lest the terms of reference of these advisers may permit United States political or economic domination. The Burmese have experienced colonialism and are now very suspicious of outside influence.

6. The investigational, educational, and extension work carried out in one part of Burma is not easily carried to other parts of the country, even in normal times. The Union is a grouping of states with various cultural and ethnological backgrounds and in many cases with considerable political autonomy.

7. The greatest need is to engender confidence in the people that their Government is intelligently interested in their welfare and is carrying out programs designed to meet their day-to-day problems. This could be done by increasing the number and competence of their technicians and administrators, by coordinating their investigational, educational, and extension work into integrated programs designed to solve real problems, and by directing the main effort to the villages. Training of personnel and assistance in program

planning can be initiated immediately. The carrying of public services to the villages is dependent upon the training of nationals with the proper orientation and upon the extent to which law and order can be established.

8. Burma's natural resources, including land, water, forests, and petroleum, coupled with the low population pressure, constitute conditions very favorable to rapid economic development and rising levels of living. Inexperience in administration, few and inadequately trained technical people, political immaturity, and social unrest are factors limiting economic development.

B. Problems Affecting Health and Medical Services

1. The loss of physical plant and equipment. Because Burma has undergone two series of bombings, occupation, and demolition-on-retreat by military forces and because there has been more than a year of sporadic dacoitism (banditry) and insurrection covering virtually the entire country, there has been destruction and confiscation of the basic buildings, equipment, and apparatus which are essential to carrying on even a minimum program for the prevention of disease and for the treatment of the sick. Many hospital buildings have been destroyed, and even those which have escaped outright destruction have been either badly damaged or stripped of their equipment and apparatus. The loss of buildings and apparatus which were formerly used for the production of smallpox, cholera, and rabies vaccines, and a variety of other prophylactic and therapeutic sera, has brought to a virtual standstill the prewar program of manufacturing most sera and vaccines. The vaccine depot at Meiktila was completely destroyed and both the Harcourt-Butler and Pasteur Institutes in Rangoon were stripped of libraries and equipment for the manufacture and storage of sera.

Although the Rangoon Medical College building was untouched, its library, museum, teaching materials and equipment, and the laboratory apparatus and chemicals essential to instruction in medicine were looted. For example, a prewar library of an estimated 20,000 books and periodicals, contained in specially designed cases to prevent deterioration during the wet season, has now been reduced to less than 1,200 books and periodicals, and there are only enough replacement cases to contain the present collection. The books and periodicals which remain are, for the most part, those of little value.

The ship fumigating and sterilizing equipment for the Port of Rangoon, at which the ships of all nations call, was also destroyed.

Although the Rangoon General Hospital building was undamaged and the hospital has been in continuous operation, some equipment was removed and some other equipment is largely worn out. The hospital, which was built in 1906, needs substantial quantities of new equipment in some departments, and three or four departments which were never separately organized should be created in order to improve the clinical teaching of medical students from the Rangoon Medical College.

2. Shortage of trained personnel in all departments. Before the war relatively few trained, experienced health and medical personnel were Burmese nationals. The majority of the technically trained and experienced staff in the civil hospitals, in the medical college, and in the country's public health units were either English, Indian, Anglo-Indian, or Anglo-Burmese. Many of these people left the country during the Japanese occupation. Relatively few of them returned, and a large percentage of those who did return have not stayed on but have gone back to either England or India or have taken up other work.

Although during the last two years the enrollment at the Rangoon Medical College has increased from 30 students to 130 students per class, the resulting increase in the number of doctors will not be felt until 1952-53 or thereafter. In 1948 the Government of Burma decreed that all those students who passed the Rangoon University examination for admission to the medical college should be admitted without any further selection or investigation of qualifications. This decision was not followed with any authorization for an increase in the staff or in the facilities and equipment for teaching the additional students. Hence, the standard of medical education, already lower than that in prewar Burma, was further depressed, and future students at this institution will necessarily receive a lowered quality of instruction and training.

In early 1950 the Government of Burma approved a substantial increase in the faculties of anatomy and physiology, and the World Health Organization has also made a grant of $10,000 to aid in building up the library. However, the new faculty positions can only be filled with great difficulty because of the acute shortage of teachers, and the WHO allocation will provide only a fraction of the total replacement needed for the library.

3. Pay and Morale in the Civil Service. When, in 1937, Burma was separated from India, virtually all government positions were transferred from the Indian Civil Service to the Burmese Civil Service. This transfer caused a substantial loss in retirement benefits, and the new salary scale was between 30 and 40 percent lower than that of the Indian Civil Service. Moreover, a 1949 pay cut of 15 percent even further depressed the already discouragingly low level for all government works, including those in health and medicine. Moreover, the Government has not made a sufficient appropriation to carry on the established health programs. This lack of professional opportunity, together with the loss of trained subordinates and the depressed wage scale, has resulted in a very serious deterioration in the morale of those employees who have remained. Lastly, the shortage of private practitioners has made the emoluments of private practice very great, and some members of the government health and medical service have resigned in order to take advantage of these opportunities.

4. Inadequate expenditures for health. The revenues of the Government of Burma for general purposes have fallen off very sharply because of inability to collect taxes. The great increase in military expenditures for the suppression of banditry and insurrection and the diversion of some funds to long-time economic development projects have left only a very small budget for all other government services. All health and medical services together receive only 1.5 percent of the current national budget. This allocation does not permit the operation of a health and medical program up to the level which existed before the war nor provide any opportunity to restore the war damage or go forward with further programs commensurate with the present needs of the country. For example, malaria is the greatest single cause of illness, but, despite the country's need of maximum productivity from its agricultural workers, the total number of malaria control units has been cut from ten to one.

Prior to the war and for a short time after the establishment of independence, local district governments also contributed to the operation of health programs, but civil and political disturbances have been so widespread that local taxes are not collected and local expenditures for health and many other public services have been virtually suspended.

Hence, the health needs of Burma are general needs for the personnel and equipment requisite to the re-establishment of preventive medical and health services and the strengthening of teaching facilities and resources with a view to providing better training for all health and medical services.

C. Education

It is estimated that approximately a third of the Burmese are literate. Although various private sources including Buddhist monastic schools and foreign-supported mission schools carry on considerable educational activity in Burma, the backbone of the educational system has been the state-supported public schools. There are, however, far too few schools to provide adequate educational opportunities, and it is considered likely that less than half of the Burmese children of school age are in school at any given time. Only a small number go as far as high school and a much smaller number get a college education, but from the small group of college-trained people has come a great proportion of the leaders of modern Burma. In a country such as Burma, which has but recently gained its independence, the shortage of an educated group from which leaders can be drawn is especially serious. The schools have provided, and will continue to provide, a practical means of reaching those on whom the future stability of Burma may in a significant degree depend.

Burma's public educational system comprises primary schools with grades 1 through 4, and post-primary schools with grades 5 through 9. Above this level there are state-supported technical schools and the University of Rangoon.

The schools of Burma still reveal the effects of the war and of the period of civil strife which has followed the achievement of independence. During the years since 1941 a considerable number of school buildings have been destroyed or damaged and not rebuilt. School equipment such as texts, library books, and laboratory apparatus has been lost or worn out and not replaced, and the relative economic position of the teacher has become poorer. Funds adequate to maintain prewar educational standards are not available. Examples of war damage within the Rangoon area are the University of Rangoon Library, which remains roofless on the campus, and the plant of the University Teachers Training College, which is still rubble. In the more recent period of civil strife, during which fighting has taken place in many villages throughout the country, a large number of primary and post-primary school buildings have been destroyed.

The Burmese Government is seriously concerned over the present status of the country's educational system. Efforts of the Ministry of Public Instruction to undertake remedial steps have been to a great extent frustrated by a lack of funds. Outside assistance in the educational field continues to be provided by foreign missions and through the Fulbright program, under which a group of Americans are now in Burma. It is evident, however, that there are great areas in which further outside assistance could render valuable services. Such assistance would have a short-range impact through direct immediate improvement in the educational facilities being offered in many schools.

D. Industry, Transportation, and Communications

Information on Burma's urgent needs in the fields of industry, transportation, and communications was developed by the Mission but, due to the illness of one of the Mission members, has not yet been prepared in a form suitable to this report. When the preparation of this material is compiled, it will be circulated as a supplement to this report.[e]

E. National Economic Development Planning

Same as D.

F. Commodity Program

Same as D.

G. Training in Public Administration

The lack of trained and experienced personnel in technical and administrative posts in the service of the Government of Burma constitutes a formidable barrier to effective government and to full utilization of Burma's resources for economic development and is a major limitation on the amount of technical

---

[e]This supplement was never completed, but detailed project planning proceded anyway. [Ed.]

assistance that can be absorbed by Burma. Burma achieved independence before adequate preparation of the necessary personnel had been made, since British authorities did not develop enough technical and administrative personnel among the resident population, at least for the responsible positions in government: the withdrawal of British and Indian personnel from these positions has inevitably brought about a great deterioration in the quality and effectiveness of governmental administration.

There is a very thin layer of highly trained and competent personnel, a fairly large group of personnel trained at the lower levels, and a big gap in between. Despite the century of British rule, most of the population and even a substantial number of responsible government officials are unable to speak or understand English. There are few governmental personnel who can spare the additional time required to work with foreign technicians and who, therefore, might be available as advisers or co-workers. Lack of officials who speak English still further limits the number who would be able to work with American or Commonwealth personnel who do not know Burmese. Similarly, there are relatively few persons in the government service who are at the same time adequately prepared in language and professional training to profit fully from advanced training in the United States or other foreign countries and able to be spared from their present tasks. Most of them are now terribly overworked, and if they left for training abroad, there would be no one to take their places.

The great need for training of present and additional governmental personnel in Burma, coupled with the shortage of people who might be effectively trained abroad, argues strongly for the setting up of training programs in public administration in Burma itself, as one of the most needed and potentially most fruitful kinds of technical cooperation.

V. Aid Provided or Planned from Sources Other than the United States

Despite, or because of, Britain's long rule over Burma, the Government of Burma is very reluctant to look to the United Kingdom for technical or financial aid. It is true that, by the terms of the agreements under which Burma achieved its independence, there is a British military and naval mission in Rangoon, but its advice is very little sought or taken. Moreover, the United Kingdom has loaned Burma since the war about £70 million for reconstruction and rehabilitation purposes, and has waived about one-half of this loan. The Burmese Government recently accepted a Commonwealth loan of £6 million to cover some of its current budget, although this was only agreed to after once being refused because the Burmans believed strings were attached to it. It is possible that additional aid will be forthcoming under the "Spender Plan" of Commonwealth aid to Southeast Asia,[f] but the United Kingdom is only one of several

---

[f]Known as the Colombo Plan after its establishment in October, 1950 [Ed.].

participants in this, as in the Commonwealth loan. There is a single Englishman (Furnivall) in a top advisory post in the government, but he is only an exception to the Burmans' very general and very deep suspicion of and antagonism towards the British.

The United Nations has provided a small amount of technical assistance to Burma, as follows:

A statistician was sent by the United Nations to advise the Burma Government (1949) and, when he had to leave on account of sickness, a replacement was sent (1950).

UNICEF has allocated $228,900 for Burma but has not yet approved any plans for operations there.

WHO made a brief survey of Burma's health needs (1949) and made a grant of $10,000, to help rebuild the medical library of the University of Rangoon.

ILO sent two missions to Burma (1947 and 1948) to help in the preparation of reports to be submitted at regional meetings of ILO.

The United Nations has granted a fellowship to an official of the Government of Burma to study resource development in the United States.

UNESCO has sent an expert to study Burma's needs for fundamental education, and is expected to comply with Burma's request for a mission to spend about a year in Burma (beginning October 1950, and costing about $60,000), to study and advise on fundamental education, compulsory primary education, secondary education, teacher-training, and educational finance and administration.

In January 1950, Burma requested WHO and FAO jointly to provide technical assistance to improve food production and health standards in malarial areas. This program would begin in September 1950; would comprise technical advice, experts, equipment and supplies; would begin with a 4-months' survey period, involving 8 experts and costing $336,000; and would continue for 5 years, with 44 experts throughout these 5 years (costing $500,000 per year). Action has not yet been taken on this request.

VI. Aid Provided or Planned from United States Sources

The United States signed a Fulbright agreement with Burma in 1947, establishing a rupee fund equivalent to $3,000,000, of which the equivalent of $200,000 can be expended each year to cover certain rupee costs involved in the exchange of students, research scholars, and professors attached to educational institutions. Under this agreement, the following exchanges have taken place during 1948 and 1949:

8 Burmese students to the United States.
3 research scholars to the United States.
35 grants to Burmese to study at the American Medical Center at Namkham.

9 U.S. professors to Burma.
1 secondary school teacher to Burma.
2 U.S. research scholars to Burma.
3 U.S. students to Burma.

The United States has allocated $37,000 of Smith-Mundt funds for Burma for the fiscal year 1950. Most of these funds are to provide dollar support for Fulbright exchanges. The 1950 program for both Fulbright and Smith-Mundt exchanges allows for 51 grants.

A number of private American religious missions provide agricultural, educational, and health services in Burma. These include the Church World Service, Seventh Day Adventist, and American Baptist Missions.

The Government of Burma recently employed a private American firm, Behre, Dolbear, & Co., of New York, to study existing geological data and make recommendations for expanded geological survey and exploration activities.

VII. Program Recommendations

The recommendations for economic and technical aid to Burma made by the Mission are summarized below. They are followed by detailed descriptions of individual projects.

A. Agriculture

Rice storage	$ 75,000
Provision of modern assembly storage facilities	350,000
Improvement of existing rice mills	765,000
Installation of two pilot rice mills	245,000
Rehabilitation of technical institutions	375,000
In-service training of Burmese in United States	80,000
Improvement of tools and mechanization	500,000
Earth-moving and pile-driving equipment	200,000
Fertilizers	78,000
Rural rehabilitation	1,500,000
	$ 4,168,000

B. Public Health

Replacement of war-lost equipment for production of vaccines	290,000
Ship-fumigating equipment and quarantine advisers	130,000
Rehabilitation of Rangoon Medical College and Rangoon General Hospital	435,000

Hospital and Nurse Training	250,000
Public Health Demonstration and Control Units	1,000,000
Trainees in Medical Services	150,000
	$ 2,255,000

C. Education

Scientific demonstration equipment	$	70,000
Re-equipping and staffing Government Technical Institute of Insein		90,000
Laboratory equipment, University of Rangoon		25,000
Athletic equipment and instructors		130,000
Manual training aids and instructors		200,000
Agricultural and industrial school—Kachin State		310,000
Mobile mass education project		200,000
Books, periodicals and library assistance		400,000
Technical pamphlets and translations		160,000
Training Program		100,000
Expansion of USIS film activities		30,000
Contingency fund		100,000
	$	1,815,000

D. Industry, Transport, and Communications

Final recommendations are not yet ready. Tentative proposals provide for an expenditure of	$ 1,140,000

E. Commodity Program

1,000 tons newsprint	$	150,000
4,000 bales cotton		1,250,000
	$	1,400,000

F. National Economic Development Planning

18 months private contract between Government of Burma and United States engineering firm	$ 1,250,000

G. Training in Public Administration

United Nations funds	....

H. Increased contact with Burmese leaders	$ 200,000
Total expenditure	$12,228,000g

A. Agriculture

1. Rice storage—$75,000. Storage losses of paddy and rice due to insects and rodents and to spoilage from the elements are significant but of an unknown quantity. Estimates run from 5 to 10 percent of which one-half would be preventable by proper storage and effective insect and rodent control. On the basis of these approximations, preventable losses would equal 200 to 400 thousand tons of rice. At present prices this amounts to a gross annual loss of from 10 million to 20 million dollars.

The SAMB (State Agricultural Marketing Board) is very sensitive to the problem of storage losses but has no trained men to analyze the problem nor to recommend and conduct a program of storage improvement and loss reduction.

It is recommended that a storage engineer and an entomologist be sent to Burma for a period of one year to train Burmese technicians in storage inspection, godown design and construction, and in insect and rodent control. With these specialists, there should be provided transportation equipment, control equipment, and sufficient supplies of insecticides and rodenticides to initiate demonstration programs.

Dollar Costs for Technical and Demonstration
Assistance in Improving Rice Storage

Two Technicians	$30,000
Cars	4,000
Equipment	10,000
Supplies	20,000
Miscellaneous	11,000
Total	$75,000

2. Provision of Modern Assembling Center Storage Facilities, 100 to 300-ton capacity—$350,000. The rice farmer stores paddy (rough rice) in large bamboo baskets (25- to 30-bushel capacity), taking it directly from the threshing floor. It is then moved by the farmer or by the middleman to assembling centers provided with makeshift godowns. From the assembling centers it moves to terminal or mill storage.

SAMB proposes to construct modern "assembling center" storage facilities to give modern service to the farmer. It is recommended that SAMB be aided in constructing 50 of such storage centers, which would demonstrate storage methods, would facilitate the formation of cooperatives, the management of

gIn addition, the cost of certain mine-sweeping should be included here, but could not be estimated by the Mission.

agricultural credit, the distribution of improved seed, tools and fertilizer, and would provide nuclei from which agricultural extension work would develop.

Dollar Costs for Construction of 50 Modern "Assembling Center" Godowns. 100- to 300-ton capacity

Godowns	$150,000
Equipment	75,000
Fumigator	2,000
Poisons	3,000
Personnel (5)	50,000
Freight 30%	70,000
Total	$350,000

3. Improvement of Existing Rice Mills–$765,000. Probably the greatest loss of rice takes place in the milling. Although no dependable data are available on milling losses, even on such factors as the present extraction rate or percent of brokens, the performance from mill to mill varies tremendously and the total milling losses for the industry are very great.

The SAMB is convinced that Burma must improve her rice milling if she is to regain her position in the trade. The SAMB has asked for 2 rice-milling engineers to survey existing mills, to develop a program for training mill operators, and to develop a program for improving the existing rice mills.

The rice mills have received no major repairs or replacements of parts and machinery since 1941. If milling efficiency is to be improved rapidly, material, as well as technical advice and training, is necessary.

It is recommended that an emergency project on existing mills be undertaken, having as its objectives, first, the reduction of milling losses in respect to quantity and quality and, second, efficiency as regards cost of operation. This project should include the provision of foreign rice-mill experts to train national experts in mill survey and the adjustment, repair, and installation of mill equipment. It should include also dollars (or other foreign exchange) to pay for repair and replacement parts for the rice mills. These parts would be sold to the private owners of these existing rice mills, thus generating a counterpart rupee fund that could be used to pay the local costs of this aid project or others.

Dollar Costs for Improving Existing Rice Mills

Technical personnel (2)	$ 25,000
Skilled millwrights (4)	40,000
Parts and equipment	700,000
Total	$765,000

4. Installation of two 60-ton Pilot Rice Mills for Investigation, Development of Processing Methods, and Training of Mill Operators–$245,000. SAMB has presented a request and cost estimates for four installations, each consisting of a 60-ton mill with four godowns, as follows:

Cost in Rs. for each Installation

Local	*Foreign*	*Total*
491,900	392,000	883,900

It is recommended that aid be given in installing two pilot mills in the two principal milling centers:

Total Dollar Costs of Two New Pilot Rice Mills

Personnel		
Technical (2)		$ 25,000
Mechanical (2)		20,000
Material		200,000
	Total	$245,000

5. Technical Education, Demonstration, Investigation—$375,000. The College of Agriculture and the Agricultural Station at Mandalay and the College of Veterinary Medicine and the laboratory for the production of vaccines and sera at Insein were well-equipped institutions. They have been successively occupied by the Japanese, the Western powers, then partly rehabilitated, then taken by insurgents. They are now in government hands and in operation, although far from their former state in respect to equipment. Both institutions are sorely needed for economic recovery and of utmost importance in rebuilding national confidence and hope. The rehabilitation of other institutions, such as the agricultural station at Pyinmana, recently reoccupied by Government forces, is urgently needed also.

Some foreign staff is needed immediately under emergency assistance and may be expanded and balanced later under Point Four.

Insein: Animal biologist with experience in the production of animal vaccines (Rinderpest), Anthraxpolorum, and others in quantity.

Mandalay: Farm machinery specialist—agricultural chemist (soils); entomologist—pathologist—extension man.

Shan and Kachin States: At least two extension men for vocational training and extension for each state.

For Farm Schools: At least one vocational education man.

It is recommended that material and technical aid be provided for these institutions as follows:

Dollar Costs of Aid to Agricultural and Veterinary Institutions

Equipment and Supplies		
Veterinary College and serum laboratory at Insein		$ 50,000
Agricultural College and Station at Mandalay		100,000
Agricultural Station and School, Taunggyi		35,000
Agricultural Station, Kachin State		25,000
Pyinmana and others		40,000
	Total	$250,000

Personnel (Nine altogether, for one year apiece)   125,000
                                        Grand Total $375,000

6. Fertilizer Demonstration Program—$78,000. Technical agencies of the Burmese Government have carried out fertilizer trials sufficient to demonstrate the response to ammonium phosphate on certain of the rice lands and on potatoes, and the response to ammonium sulphate on sugar cane. The officials in the Government believe, and the Mission concurs, that a fertilizer demonstration program will be one of the best means of bringing the benefits of technical aid to the rural people in the most rapid manner. The Ministry of Agriculture is prepared to initiate demonstrations of the use of ammonium phosphate on 10,000 acres of paddy land and 1,000 acres of potato land. The average application on paddy land would be approximately 100 pounds per acre and, on potato land, approximately 200 pounds per acre. They are also prepared to demonstrate the use of ammonium sulphate on 4,600 acres of sugar cane with approximately 200 pounds per acre. All of the sugar land and most of the paddy land proposed to be fertilized have been recently reoccupied by Government troops.

Dollar landed cost of ammonium phosphate and ammonium sulphate
per ton and total cost in Rangoon

400 tons, 20% ammonium sulphate @ $57	$22,800
600 tons, 16-20-0 ammonium sulphate @ $92	55,200
Total	$78,000

7. Flood Control—Equipment for Levee Construction, and Controlled Spills—$200,000. The Irrigation Department was well organized under British engineers. This Department was annually faced with the task of constructing a number of retirements. Retirements are auxiliary levees constructed behind existing embankments at points where the embankment system is threatened by undercutting of the river. The total construction of this type of work amounts to approximately 800 million cubic yards annually. This earthwork has to be done in the interval between the time when the crops are off the land and the beginning of the monsoon. Usually approximately 100 working days are available, which coincide with Burma's festive season, and thus many valuable days are usually lost. Before the war Indian labor was available for this type of work and the earthwork was done manually. Immediately after the war, most of the retirement work was done with earthmoving equipment. The Irrigation Department had at its disposal for this purpose four D-8 tractors, two D-4 tractors, two 12-cubic yard carryall scrapers, two 6-cubic yard scrapers, five tamping rollers, and 18 3-cubic yard dump trucks. This equipment has been lost in the insurrection.

The following equipment should be on the job in Burma by November 1: four 18-cubic yard self-propelled scraper units; four 20-horsepower pumping units, 8" diameter delivery, 10" suction, diesel-powered; six dump trucks of 2½-ton capacity.

Another great task of the Irrigation Department is to provide protection against flooding and silting in the Puiuntaza Plain. This plain is traversed by five hill streams that carry an abnormal quantity of sand and silt in suspension during the flood period. This heavy charge in suspension raises the stream beds as they reach the flatter slopes on the plain, and there is continual threat of break-through and new alignment of the streams. These break-throughs not only cut vital lines of communication but also result in uncontrolled flooding and the destruction of crops. Past experience of the engineering department has demonstrated that controlled flood spills are the best system for controlling floods of this nature. The controlled flood spills require a considerable amount of pile-driving work. The pile-driving often has to be carried out during the flood season in order that breaches may be controlled quickly. Equipment for controlled flood spills are, first: one air compressor mounted on wheels, capable of delivering 400 cubic feet of air per minute at 100 pounds pressure; one number 6 McKiernan-Terry double-acting, pile-driving head with 80 lineal feet of holes; four concrete mixers of 5 to 7.5 cubic feet capacity.

The estimated cost of this equipment needed for level construction and controlled spills is $200,000.

8. Farm Machinery and Small Hand Farm Tools—$500,000. Large tracts of land in Burma under single ownership and formerly farmed by tenants are now abandoned and grown to coarse grass and bush. Many of the landowners were Indians and returned to India at the time of the Japanese invasion and during the period of insurrection since the reoccupation by the Burmese. The problem here posed involves the reclamation of the land (which might best be done with power farm equipment); purchase of the land from landowners or by some other arrangement; organizing cooperatives, which is a popular and might be an effective move in Burma to win the support of the farm producers; and the colonizing of the land by owner-operators who would be members of these cooperatives.

This activity involves not only the acquiring of mechanical equipment, but also the training of nationals in its use and maintenance; the development of agronomic practices suited to mechanical cultivation; fitting of the land for irrigation; and the development of socio-economic institutions, such as the cooperatives above mentioned, which would permit of the use of the land by small owner-operators in an economic manner. The Government of Burma has some understanding of the problems involved here but is not equipped with technical people and program planners and managers to carry the work forward. The Government people have asserted their willingness to acquire the land and to make arrangements for getting it into the hands of owner-operators in a regularized manner.

Personnel needed are two agricultural engineers, both experienced in the application of farm machinery to the land, with one of them experienced in fitting lands for irrigation and the other with particular experience in rice production and processing; 2 skilled mechanic trainers; 1 skilled farm machinery operator trainer; 1 man with experience in agricultural production, credit, and marketing cooperatives; 1 agronomist; and 1 rural sociologist.

A limiting factor to agricultural production in Burma and one which would provide incentive to production is small-hand tools. These would include hoes, knives or machetes, axes, and harvesting sickles.

Both the farm machinery and the hand tools could be sold to individuals or to cooperatives for counterpart and would provide funds for financing the local costs associated with the agricultural machinery and other necessary agricultural projects.

The estimated dollar cost for these 8 technicians, the farm machinery, and the hand tools is $500,000.

9. Rural Rehabilitation–$1,500,000. The occupation of Burma by the Japanese, guerrilla activity during this occupation, and demolition during the expulsion of the Japanese by the Burmese and the British, followed by some years of insurgent action, have caused a great deal of destruction and loss of production in the rural areas of Burma. This destruction has included rural housing, damage to canals and bunds, the loss of livestock (it is still against the law to kill or slaughter any cattle for meat in Burma), loss of small tools and the inability to acquire small tools through the years, and the destruction of marketing facilities. The general objectives of the rural rehabilitation program should be to enter the pacified areas immediately with broad-scale rehabilitation activities to cover the fields of health, sanitation, housing, provision of mechanical or other means of plowing of the land, provisions of seed fertilizer, small tools, etc.

The rural rehabilitation recommendations for Indonesia in the Mission's Report No. 5, although applied to a different environment, and in many cases to a different degree of destruction, are nevertheless, within their general objectives, operating procedures, types of assistance to be given, and the methods for the carrying out of the work, applicable to Burma. Since this is treated extensively in the report on Indonesia, reference is made to that report for general guidance and justification for the Rural Rehabilitation Program here recommended.

At the time of the Mission's visit it was impossible to get into most of the area of Burma and to talk definitely and to see on the ground what would be required in rural rehabilitation and just what would be the distribution geographically, as well as the kinds of things which should be brought into the economy in order to bring about the most rapid advance in production and stability of the rural people. The Mission recommends that $1,500,000 be set aside for this general category of work.

B. Health

1. Rehabilitation of Harcourt-Butler Institute and Pasteur Institute–$290,000. The purchase of sufficient equipment to permit the resumption of the manufacture, storage and distribution of smallpox vaccine up to a three-year target of 5,000,000 doses per year is recommended, with the qualification that this should be undertaken only if the Government of Burma will engage enough public vaccinators to administer vaccinations at a rate which will permit the vaccination of the entire population in three years. Prior to the war, between 1,500,000 and 2,000,000 doses of smallpox vaccine were manufactured each year. Now, none is being manufactured in Burma, but about 300,000 doses per year are being purchased from India. A 5,000,000-dose annual production will permit the vaccination of a half million children each year during the first six months of life, and the vaccination of about 4,500,000 adults.

The Ministry of Health has agreed to ask for a redefinition of the existing law on re-vaccination. The present law requires vaccination within the first year of life and again at the age of 12 years. It is now planned to require re-vaccination every three years. At present there are at least 5,000 cases of smallpox each year, one-fourth of which are fatal. These deaths can be virtually eliminated if this program is successful.

The purchase of sufficient equipment to permit the resumption of the manufacture of cholera vaccine is recommended so that Burma can produce up to half a million doses annually for an indefinite period. Only an estimated 10 percent of the population have a safe and potable water supply and, as long as unclean and undependable water is used by 90 percent of the population, cholera is virtually certain to break out sporadically from time to time. Before the war the Government produced between 300,000 and 400,000 doses per year; they are now spending Rs. 50,000 per year to import cholera vaccine from India.

The Government of Burma has never produced plague vaccine, but in Burma there will always be a danger that plague vaccine will be needed. At the present time the Government is importing a half million doses of plague vaccine at an average cost of nearly Rs. 35,000 per year. Because it is believed that the production, storage, and distribution of plague vaccine up to half a million doses annually, at small extra cost, can be integrated with the production of smallpox and cholera vaccine, the purchase of the necessary equipment and apparatus is recommended.

Prior to the war the Pasteur Institute produced each year nearly 200,000 cc of anti-rabies serum for both preventive inoculation and treatment of persons suffering from injuries by rabid animals. There are no accurate figures of the incidence of rabies at the present time, but the Government is now importing approximately two-thirds of the prewar production at a cost of almost Rs. 20,000 per year. Professional opinion is that the incidence of rabies has increased since the war. The production of other sera and vaccines, such as anti-diphtheria, tetanus, dysentery, and TAB, has either been suspended entirely or reduced to a fraction of the prewar level and present-day needs. These vaccines and sera could be produced in reasonably adequate quantities with the purchase of the equipment recommended.

The Pasteur Institute also provides the only bacteriological services to hospitals (except Rangoon General Hospital), health centers, and private physicians in all Burma. Because of the limited equipment and apparatus remaining, this Institute is able to run only a few simple routine tests, principally serology. Histological, micro-biological and other tests which should be available in at least one diagnostic center for the country cannot now be performed. It is recommended that the services of the Pasteur Institute be built up to provide at least the essential diagnostic services, and that plans be considered in the near future for the establishment of a similar center to serve upper Burma.

It is recommended that one United States consultant familiar with vaccine production be provided in connection with the above program.

2. Ship-fumigating and sterilizing unit for the Port of Rangoon— $130,000. Rangoon is the largest and most important port in Burma and the largest rice port in the world. Plague has often been carried along with other cargo. The prewar fumigating and sterilizing unit was either carried off or destroyed, and uncertain hand methods are now being employed. It is recommended that a modern mobile barge-mounted fumigating unit be provided, at an estimated cost of $130,000. In addition, it is recommended that provision also be made for the necessary advice and guidance of at least two quarantine officers, including at least one physician and one engineer, to survey the needs of international health protection and to instruct the local staff in the use of a modern unit.

3. Rehabilitation of the Rangoon Medical College—$435,000 (for this and the next project together). The Rangoon Medical College is the only medical teaching institution in Burma, and it is urgently in need of both additional staff and equipment to permit it to reach and to exceed its prewar teaching standards. The most urgent needs for equipment, specimens, apparatus, and supplies are for the departments of anatomy, physiology, pathology, pharmacology, biochemistry, and physiotherapy, including visiting professors in four departments for one year each (pathology for two years) to reorganize the teaching and research program in conjunction with the local staff which is available.

Although the needs in all departments are urgent, it is recognized that the necessary faculty members cannot all be accommodated at one time. Priority should be given to pathology, pharmacology, biochemistry, and physiotherapy in that order. Those for anatomy and physiology could be deferred until the second or third year. Because all departments of the college are so urgently in need of both equipment and apparatus, it should be assumed that there are no teaching materials or laboratory facilities available. Visiting professors should be prepared to outfit their specific departments virtually *de novo*.

The sizeable prewar collection of anatomical and pathological specimens and of library books and periodicals was almost wholly destroyed or lost. Only a few specimens and about 1,200 volumes remain. The newer works of authority and the older established texts have been totally lost. Nearly all journals have been interrupted at 1935-38. The WHO grant of $10,000 will not complete the task of building a first-class reference collection in modern scientific medicine. Both library and museum facilities are needed most urgently, and an allocation of funds for this purpose is recommended.

4. Rehabilitation and improvement of the teaching facilities at Rangoon General Hospital. Although the actual needs of a modern medical teaching center would require either the complete renovation of the existing buildings and/or the construction of new buildings for several departments, such as outpatient, pathology laboratory, radiology, and special facilities for pediatrics, otorhinolaryngology, and physical therapy, the present recommendations are limited to the departments which are either in a state of utter disrepair or are nonexistent. It is recommended that there be provided to the Rangoon General Hospital:

1. A visiting professor or orthopedic surgeon with a full set of equipment and apparatus to supplement and replace the inadequate and worn-out equipment which now exists.
2. An adviser on blood banks and on dry plasma technique to organize a national blood bank and laboratory. There is none in the entire country at the present time. The need also includes the training of local staff in the collection, drying, processing, and storage of blood.
3. A prosthetics workshop director with full equipment to establish a facility for making prosthetic appliances and to train local staff in the technique and methods. At present there are no facilities for the manufacture or supply of artificial limbs or appliances in the country, despite the fact that the accident and injury rate to limbs is very high.

The estimated cost of rehabilitating the facilities of the Medical College and of the Hospital is $435,000 for one year.

5. Hospital and nurse training—$250,000. All hospitals in Burma except the few run by private physicians and by religious missions are under the jurisdiction of the Ministry of Health, and the civil surgeons of the Ministry therefore direct the entire curative medical program of the country. Burma does not have any school or facilities for training these civil surgeons in modern methods of hospital management or for training nurses and nurse teachers in improved techniques of nursing or nurse training. In the capital city of the Southern Shan States, Taunggyi, a new 100-bed addition to an older but still modern unit of 50 beds has recently been completed. This hospital center offers an ideal opportunity for demonstrating American methods of hospital management, nurse training, nurse teacher training, and the close relationship of preventive and curative medicine. The request of the Government of Burma, which it is recommended the United States Government fulfill, is for an experienced administrator of small hospitals, a supervisor of nurses, a public health officer, and not more than two nurse teachers, plus the necessary hospital equipment and teaching materials for a minimum period of three years. The American staff would be given full authority to operate the hospital as a medical care and teaching center primarily for training Burmese staff. It is recommended that $250,000 for one year be allocated to the staffing and partial equipment of this hospital and teaching center.

6. Public Health Demonstration and Control Units—$1,000,000. Because of the loss and dispersion of prewar health units and personnel, nearly all available funds and staff of the Ministry of Health are being devoted to curative medicine and hospitals. Public health and preventive medicine have been greatly retarded and are in need of immediate stimulation to regain even prewar levels and to bring the benefits of scientific preventive medicine particularly to those people who live outside the major population centers. Because the hospitals are located in the principal cities, only through a vigorous program in preventive medicine can improved health services be made available to rural people. Prior to the war the Rockefeller Foundation established and maintained for five years a public health demonstration unit in Hlegu; the whole unit was destroyed and the staff dispersed by the war. It is proposed to reestablish this center and to create still another center in northern Burma, to organize a venereal disease team in upper Burma to complement a proposed WHO unit in Rangoon, and to reestablish malaria control units as rapidly as circumstances will permit.

Although the ten anti-malaria units which were created immediately following independence have been disbanded and the staff either discharged or shifted to other work, a number of these units could be reconstituted in a rather short time and returned to malaria work if there were funds and equipment and if the civil disturbances in the country have been sufficiently quieted by that time. Malaria is the disease of first importance to health and to economic development, and the creation of malaria-control teams should have the highest priority.[h]

The majority of these anti-malaria units should be mobile in order to reach the maximum number of people in rural areas and small villages, and all units should be jointly staffed by American and Burmese personnel with the object of training local staff as rapidly as possible. All teams should be organized and equipped for at least a 2-year period. It is recommended that $1,000,000 be set aside for one year to organize and equip as many of these teams as can be adequately staffed and as political circumstances permit. The number of Americans needed for this program will depend on the rapidity with which the program can be implemented.

7. Long-Term United States Assistance Recommended for Trainees— $150,000. The needs of Burma for improved health and medical services are so great and so varied that any division into long-term and short-term assistance

---

[h]In this connection, it should be noted that Burma has requested technical assistance from WHO and FAO in a joint program to improve food production and health standards in malarial areas (see section V).

may be somewhat arbitrary. Long-term assistance is naturally dependent on the progress which is made with whatever short-term assistance is provided and this, in turn, will probably depend upon the rapidity with which Burmese personnel can be recruited and trained. These factors cannot be estimated with any accuracy at this time. However, the Government of Burma arranged their original requests in an order of priority which suggests a division between long- and short-term needs for technical assistance.

One of the most serious deficiencies in health organization and administration is the failure of the system for reporting births, deaths, and selected diseases. The lack of reasonably accurate figures on morbidity and mortality makes it difficult to estimate the magnitude of health problems or to measure progress. Accordingly, technical assistance in evaluating and improving the reporting system and in advising on health statistics should have an early priority, recognizing that any substantial improvement in the system and the resulting data will require long-term effort.

The Government of Burma requested a technical adviser (bacteriologist) for the Harcourt-Butler Institute (*a*) for consultation on the integration of plague vaccine manufacture with that for smallpox and cholera for an estimated period of 6 months, (*b*) for advice on strains, media, and methods of producing plague vaccine for an estimated 6 to 12 months, and (*c*) for the organization of a program of research in a number of problems which are peculiar to Southeast Asia.

The Government of Burma requested a technical adviser to work with the staff of the Pasteur Institute in consultation on methods and equipment and on the training of bacteriologists and technicians in the manufacture of sera and some therapeutic agents such as penicillin. This request is not immediate because of the lack of staff, buildings, and equipment, and should not be met for 2 to 5 years.

At first, one member, and later others, of a teaching staff to organize and conduct a graduate training program for public health physicians was also requested. The present supply of physicians trained in public health is very low, and present prospects are that medical graduates in the next few years will not be well trained in general and in preventive medicine in particular. Hence, although the need for special training facilities is acute at this time, the Government of Burma has not given this project a very high priority. This request may be expected to become pressing in perhaps three years.

Visiting professors of anatomy and physiology to supply deficiencies for the Rangoon Medical College have also been requested. These are not needed quite as urgently as the four professors requested immediately as part of the emergency program. However, American professors are needed and will be sought in the future for a variety of posts.

Although it is now contemplated that the Government of Burma will soon make a formal request for a joint WHO-FAO nutrition demonstration team, it is not clear that the request will be granted and, even if it is approved, the needs for dietary surveys, for nutrition education, and for research will remain unfulfilled. Almost nothing has been done in this field, and the needs for improved nutrition are very great in a diet largely based on rice.

Within not more than three years the Pasteur Institute will need the advice and assistance of a trained veterinarian experienced in the organization and management of animal farms for scientific purposes. At the present time their activities are at such a low ebb that they will not have need for such assistance until a separate animal farm is approved and plans prepared.

As a result of the present and prospective shortage of all types of trained people in public health and medical science, an estimated 30 trainees each year will be required at an estimate cost of $150,000 per year.

8. Local factors limiting the amount or speed of feasible aid to Burma

a) *Acute housing shortage.* The lack of living accommodations suitable to American personnel who have not formerly worked or lived in Burma requires careful staging of the assignment of such personnel. The necessity of finding satisfactory housing in advance is a slow and uncertain process and will be difficult even in Rangoon. This places a real limitation on those projects which call for new equipment and apparatus for whose effective use American advisers are needed. This includes the recommended orthopedic surgeon, prosthetics workshop director, pathologist, ship fumigating unit, and the blood bank and plasma adviser. On the other hand, those technical advisers who will work in the field will need to be provided with some special housing facilities, such as trailers, because of the complete absence of hotels or other suitable housing in the small towns and villages.

b) *Feasibility of field programs.* Although the political and military situation has recently improved somewhat, and although it is believed likely that it will continue to improve, the extent to which public health or any other kind of activities can be undertaken in the field depends largely upon the number of districts and villages which have been declared safe. The projects recommended here can operate with profit in areas which are now considered safe. It must, however, be recognized that insurgent bands, dacoits, and other lawless groups may make some of the most needy areas unsafe for men and materials for some time to come.

c) *Further planning needed.* Only one of the projects recommended here as urgent requires any further study before becoming operative; it involves the relationship of plague vaccine manufacture to the manufacture of smallpox and cholera vaccines. However, a skilled laboratory bacteriologist will be required to spend three to six months in Rangoon advising the Harcourt-Butler Institute on the overall design of a laboratory and the extent to which the several facilities can be integrated before it can be finally decided what kinds of equipment for the manufacture of plague will be feasible.

d) *Malaria control.* The Government of Burma emphasized in their discussions the urgent need for the resumption of malaria control, but they seemed unable to fix the number of malaria control units which could be put into the field at any given time. Hence, the present recommendations.

e) Supply of local personnel. The available public health and curative medical staff of the Ministry of Health are so few and are spread out so wide and thin that it is difficult to visualize how many people could be spared from their present assignment to undertake new programs. This applies to both fully and partially trained people and places a real limit on the speed at which the emergency program will be able to go forward. It is not possible at this time to give even a forecast of what this rate will be, but it must be left in the hands of whoever is placed in charge of the public health program because he will be better able to make a thorough and man-by-man inventory of the number and kinds of people who are available at once and those who can be made available soon through short intensive training.

C. Education

1. Scientific Demonstration Equipment for Post-primary Schools— $70,000. The dearth of scientific equipment in Burma has been most keenly felt during the period since the war, for the war itself greatly stimulated interest in the sciences. The students with whom the Mission talked seemed in general agreement that Burma's primary educational need was for more adequate equipment for scientific training. The administrative head of the University of Rangoon placed the re-equipping of research laboratories as the University's top priority request. It would appear that the Burmese student regards scientific training as both a key to significant personal work and a necessity if Burma, newly independent, is to progress as a nation.

The Government of Burma requested by memorandum scientific apparatus and equipment for post-primary schools in Burma. The equipment requested comprised basic laboratory equipment and supplies to permit demonstration experiments by teachers of introductory science courses. In the meeting held at the Ministry of Public Instruction at which the memorandum was given to the Mission, the Burmese officials present stressed the fact that it has been impossible since the end of the war to re-equip laboratories and replace scientific equipment necessary for the most rudimentary type of science training, except in a very limited number of schools. Members of the Mission who inspected schools in the Rangoon area, where schools are in general better equipped than elsewhere in Burma, observed first hand the great shortage of scientific apparatus, even in advanced institutions of learning.

As accurate an estimate as time would permit was made of the availability of teachers to utilize this equipment and of its suitability for the post-primary schools for which it is proposed. The inclusion of a minimum number of hours in science in the teacher-training courses and the general interest of Burma's students in science indicate that the amounts proposed can be utilized effectively. Americans familiar with Burma's schools either through teaching, through Fulbright work, or other experience believed the request reasonable and worthy of being filled. It may be noted that the request was for equipment for schools in Burma proper only. At the meeting during which the request was presented representatives of the frontier states were present, and it was agreed that in the distribution of any equipment which might be provided the interests of the frontier states would be considered.

It is the opinion of the Mission that the very real interest of the Ministry of Public Instruction in seeing that science equipment reaches Burmese students will make reasonably sure its rapid distribution and effective use.

2. Re-equipping and Staffing of Government Technical Institute, Insein—$90,000. As a further expression of its interest in technical education the Ministry of Public Instruction requested that $30,000 be made available to recondition and re-equip the Government Technical Institute at Insein, which offered below university level training for engineering students, and that four American instructors be provided. The school plant was damaged by the fighting during and since the war. The equipment request of the Ministry appears moderate and appropriate. If the four desired U.S. specialists could be found to assist in staffing this school, the re-equipping and staffing of it would represent a concise, self-contained American-assistance project whose impact would be immediate and significant. There is particular need in Burma for the skilled technician on the foreman's level. This is the kind of technician the Institute is designed to produce.

3. Laboratory Equipment for the University of Rangoon—$25,000. The final request for equipment of a scientific character came directly from the University of Rangoon. This report was not received until after the first recommendations had been cabled, so it represents an amount beyond the total specified therein. It provides for the equipping of the University's laboratories with certain scientific research equipment for graduate students at a total cost of approximately $25,000. In view of the deep interest of the Burmese students in science and the importance of this group in the present national life it is believed that this would be a justifiable investment of U.S. funds. In a sense this completes a scientific educational assistance program of considerable scope.

4. Athletic Equipment and Instructors for Primary and Post-primary Schools—$130,000. A further request by the Ministry of Public Instruction was for physical education equipment for primary and post-primary schools.

During the past year an American Fulbright professor has been working in Burma in the field of physical education and has had an enthusiastic response to his efforts. Prior to the war, certain of the larger schools were equipped with sports and games material which was effectively used. The success of the physical education program carried on by various mission colleges in Southeast Asia bears adequate testimony to the interest in such programs. Although not favoring a physical education aid program of the scope of the one requested by the Government of Burma, the Mission favors an allotment of funds which will permit the distribution of a significant amount of equipment in the primary and post-primary schools. It is felt that two physical education exchange teachers could provide useful service in this program. In this connection, the Mission discussed with Dr. Louis E. Alley, the present United States Fulbright professor in physical education, the possibility of getting the State University of Iowa, from which Dr. Alley comes, to take a continuing interest in providing United States physical education instructors to teach in Burma. Dr. Alley felt that the University might be interested in such a continuing bond. The Mission believes that such a direct tie-up would provide a very desirable continuity and direction to the program.

5. Manual Training Aids and Instructors–$200,000. A request for equipment for public schools included types of manual training aids, consisting primarily of tools for woodwork and carpentry.

Manual training has never been an integral part of the Burmese educational system. One of the characteristic attitudes of the student class is that an education frees one from the necessity of manual work of any type. The provision of manual training courses would not only enrich the curriculum for all students, particularly those whose academic training will be short, but might make a significant contribution through its influence on the attitudes of students toward manual work. As this is a new program for schools of Burma, it is believed that four American instructors should be sent to Burma to introduce the program through the two government teacher-training institutions. These instructors should likewise be made responsible for the selection of tools, equipment, and books to be provided by the United States.

6. Agricultural and Industrial School for Kachin State–$310,000. An additional project in the technical education field involves one previously informally requested by representatives of one of the frontier states and previously made the subject of a specific recommendation by the American Embassy, Rangoon, in a despatch of April 1949, in which the project was analyzed in detail and the specific amounts necessary to carry it through were estimated. This project involves an agricultural and industrial school for the Kachins, to be located at Myitkyina. During the war approximately 3,000 Kachins served with U.S. forces operating in North Burma in Kachin territory. Their thorough knowledge of the jungle, jungle-fighting abilities, and devotion to the duties they were performing for the U.S. forces enabled them to assist greatly Army forces there and to save many American lives. In some respects, therefore, this project may be considered a joint United States–Burma war-dead memorial. The U.S. Government should, in general, avoid proposing aid projects which might increase sectional feeling in Burma by providing aid for any particular racial group. However, by far the greatest portion of the aid proposed for all of Burma is being recommended for Burma proper, and one of the major medical projects is proposed for another frontier area, the Shan state.

If the project is approved by both the United States and the Government of Burma, whose concurrence remains to be obtained, it is believed that the Kachin state should be asked to make available the necessary land at Myitkyina, the capital and communications center of the state. Emphasis in teaching in the school should be on agriculture, the basic means of livelihood of most of the Kachins, and on such industrial arts as carpentry (using locally available materials), blacksmithing, general machine work, printing, weaving, and the like. The head of the school should be a Kachin, but there should be American instructors in agricultural subjects and in industrial arts.

Great care would have to be taken in setting up such a school to insure that financial responsibility for its continuance is assumed by the Government of Burma and the Kachin state, although continued provision by the United States of Fulbright professors would be useful and wise.

7. Mobile Mass Education Project—$200,000. A Government of Burma program for rural adult education directed at raising living standards through reducing illiteracy, improving health and sanitation conditions, and developing agriculture and cottage crafts has been underway since April 1949. A teacher training and demonstration center is operating in Rangoon, with 66 trainees, who are selected high-school graduates with aptitude for social service in rural areas. The course is for 6 months, and it is planned eventually to produce 140 trainees each year.

The first group of teachers is to be assigned this spring to twenty selected areas in the Pegu, Insein, and Hanthawaddy districts of Burma proper. The center in each of these areas has been selected so as to be within easy access of a group of villages. These will serve as centers both for the education of the villagers themselves and for the mobilizing and training of voluntary social workers to assist in expanding the work into the other villages, with heavy emphasis placed on encouraging the villagers to carry on the work themselves. As trained personnel and equipment become available, it is planned to extend this program to the other areas of Burma. Lack of materials and equipment now seriously impede the effectiveness of the program. Technical advisory personnel are needed to assist in the initial steps of the program. Both have been requested through the Mission by the Government of Burma.

It is proposed that two U.S. technicians, one in the organization and operation of adult and rural education programs and the other in the development of training aids, be assigned to work with the Mass Education Council (the government body responsible for the program). It is proposed also that limited funds ($50,000) be provided to assist in paying salaries of local personnel during this initial period of the program's operation.

Equipment proposed is the following ($150,000):

a) 5 mobile training units, equipped with projectors, radio, films and film slides, and public address system ($30,000).
b) 1 mobile water-borne training unit as above for use on canals and rivers ($20,000).
c) 21 radio receiving sets, one for each of the centers ($4,000).

d) Equipment for production of elementary films and visual materials, and costs of production and distribution, for use by the mobile units and in training centers ($96,000).

8. Books, Periodicals and Library Assistance—$400,000. Technical books and periodicals, and adequate facilities and management for those libraries which do exist, are seriously lacking in Burma. This is a result both of war damage and the absence of trained librarians.

The need for filling this gap is urgent. Evidence of this is seen in the heavy pressure on the USIS library in Rangoon—1,600 visitors daily—and the fact that the Government itself is constantly turning to the USIS for technical publications. No other accessible, organized library exists.

The central library of the University of Rangoon, once comprising some 40,000 volumes, was totally destroyed during the war. This University, with a student body of 4,000, now is carrying on with several small departmental libraries of around 100 volumes each and a central library which consists of a dilapidated collection of several thousand uncataloged odds and ends. In addition to this library, there are others in Rangoon, one in Mandalay, and several elsewhere in Burma which are in serious need of expansion of their technical collections. Further, small collections of books could usefully be made available to the teacher-training schools and to selected private organizations. It is proposed that funds be set aside for such stocking of libraries, to include both books and periodicals, and for necessary equipment (primarily card catalogs) which otherwise would not be available.

A prerequisite to any grants of books should be a reasonable assurance that they will be organized and utilized effectively, under the supervision of a trained librarian. It is proposed that a library technician be assigned, preferably to the Ministry of Education, to conduct a training course in library techniques and to advise on the organization and management of existing libraries. Simultaneously, training of a selected number of Burmese in the United States on library techniques should be carried on. This is provided for separately below under the project "Training." The U.S. technician would also survey library needs on the basis of which grants of books and equipment would be made.

It is recommended that all such grants should be clearly identified as a gift of the United States through labeling in the book itself. The collections might also be set aside as separate sections of the various libraries, where this would not interfere with their over-all organization.

9. Technical Pamphlets and Translations—$160,000. There is continuous and heavy demand for technical materials published in the United States, by Burmans anxious to find out how things are done in this country. The publications of the U.S. Government Printing Office, prepared by the various technical agencies of our government, are now being made available in limited quantities through the USIS. This does not nearly meet the demand. Yet these, and similar types of pamphlets published by United States private organizations, serve as an effective and inexpensive way for disseminating technical information among large numbers of people. It is the belief of the Mission that implementation of this project could provide an important factor in supplementing and backstopping the work done by U.S. technicians in their specialized fields, and in reaching large numbers of people throughout the entire country.

It is proposed that funds be provided for the purchase and free distribution of these publications in English (for the use of the considerable English-reading populace), and that selected pamphlets in all fields be edited as necessary and translated for distribution among the non-English reading population. To the greatest extent possible, translating and publishing facilities in Burma should be utilized.

10. Training—$100,000. Training of Burmans in the United States to supplement the work of the U.S. technicians assigned to Burma has been requested by the Government of Burma. These persons would be selected with a view to working with U.S. technicians in Burma, and carrying on the work of the technicians after their departure. Directly related to the education projects outlined above, trainees would be placed in post-primary school science teaching, physical education, vocational training, library management, audio-visual aids, adult and rural education, and general primary and post-primary school teaching methods. Funds are proposed to provide for 20-25 such trainees.

11. Expansion of USIS Film Activities—$30,000. The showing of U.S. films and film-strips by the USIS is currently being carried on under a schedule booked 6 months in advance. These showings provide one channel for reaching large numbers of people at all levels and constitute a vital part of any educational program. Funds are proposed to permit the assignment of an additional American, and added local personnel, to expand this activity.

Extensive use of audio-visual aids is provided for as a part of the Government of Burma's mobile mass-education project described previously (para. 7). Since such a channel does exist, the USIS favors its use in order to avoid having the United States accused of seeking means to spread its own propaganda. At the same time, however, it is felt the expansion of USIS film activities proposed above can make a vital indirect contribution to the overall mass education program.

12. Contingency Fund—$100,000. The long-run effectiveness of much of the assistance proposed in the various fields of this economic aid program can be enhanced by encouraging American professors and research scholars to work in Burma and Burmans to work and study in the United States. This applies to all fields which contribute to economic development, and not merely to education alone. Such exchange can be provided for under the Fulbright program, but full use of those funds is impossible without dollar support. It is proposed that funds be set aside to provide dollar support to Fulbright grants in those fields of study and teaching which clearly contribute to economic development.

In addition to the trainees and technicians specifically provided for in the education projects, it is anticipated that some additional personnel needs may develop in the course of the program. The proposed contingency fund provides a limited amount for meeting such additional needs.

D. Industry, Transportation, and Communications–$1,140,000[i]

To assist in alleviating shortages in river transportation equipment it is recommended that material be provided for six barges which will be built in Burma. Also as part of the communications rehabilitation program, it is recommended that corrugated iron siding, roofing, and other equipment be provided for the port of Rangoon and that pre-fabricated pontoon sections be furnished for use in jetty construction. In order to provide technical know-how in this field, it is proposed that technicians be provided on methods of applying towing power, maritime diesel operations, and in port operation and pilotage. It is also proposed that the service of one Navy mine sweeper be provided to clear the approaches of Rangoon and Moulmein harbors. Additional recommendations in this general category call for replacement parts for outlying thermal power stations, and radio sets for feeder service from outlying districts to central stations.

E. Commodity Program–$1,400,000

It is recommended that approximately 1,000 tons of newsprint be made available and that 4,000 bales of cotton be provided.

F. National Economic Development Planning–$1,250,000

To comply with the Government of Burma's request for the provision of top-level advisers for industrial planning and administration, it is recommended that the United States make available funds to cover an 18-month contract between the Government of Burma and a United States private engineering firm.

---

[i]Because of the illness of one of the Mission members, the detailed recommendations made for industry, transportation, and communications; commodity planning; and national economic development planning (sections *D-F* above) are not yet in a form suitable to this report. A supplement containing them will subsequently be circulated. The substance of the recommendations contained in the Mission's cabled reports from Rangoon for these sections is given in the above paragraphs. (Note: This supplement was not prepared, but a number of specific projects in these fields were planned and carried out. [Ed.])

G. Training in Public Administration

In view of the shortage in Burma of competent and experienced administrative personnel at all levels of government, training programs in public administration should be undertaken promptly.

The training program undertaken should include not only a full-time and rather formal curriculum in public administration, but also intensive 2- or 3-month training institutes and part-time afternoon or evening courses which could be taken by government civil servants. There should also be in-service training abroad for such civil servants or potential civil servants as could be spared.

In view of the experience in the United States, where business and public administration are often taught in the same institutions, and in view of the great shortage of non-Chinese businessmen in Burma, it is believed that consideration should be given to extending the coverage of such training programs as are established to include business administration as well as public administration.

If the United States itself were to set up training programs of this sort as part of its bilateral technical assistance program, there might arise suspicion that the curriculum would be unduly slanted in favor of the private capitalist economic philosophy or the cold war political urgency characterizing United States thinking. As the people of Burma are already extremely suspicious of Western (including United States) economic and political objectives in this region, the effectiveness of a training program of this sort might be considerably reduced if training were identified solely with the United States. For this reason, it is recommended that the United Nations should be encouraged to set up training programs in public and business administration in Burma.

H. Increased Contacts with Burmese Leaders—$200,000

The success of any contemplated aid program in Burma will depend to a large extent upon the rapport which is established between individual Burmese leaders and the Americans with whom they come into contact.

Present Burmese leaders are not well acquainted with either American culture or Americans. In spite of a wide diversity of personalities, almost all Burmese leaders share two common attributes; a socialistic political orientation and a long-standing dislike and suspicion of the British.

As a prosperous country, originally a British colony and characterized by little formality in personal relations, the United States appeals to the imagination of the Burmese leaders. This appeal can be successfully exploited if the Burmese leader can be convinced that the United States is interested in him as an individual and sympathetic to his country.

At present the political power in Burma rests within the loose grouping of the AFPFL, and more specifically, with about a dozen men who control the

Socialist Party. These men are primarily interested in labor and peasant organizations, cooperative movements, education, and the general economic development of the country along the lines of doctrinaire Socialist theory.

It is recommended that a number of influential Burmese leaders, not necessarily Government officials but politically important, be encouraged to visit the United States individually or in pairs for periods of time ranging from 1 to 3 months. These individuals would not necessarily qualify for grants under Smith-Mundt or Fulbright programs. Such visits would include consultation with the Departments of Agriculture and Commerce and with the Social Security Administration, field trips to inspect cooperative projects, meetings with labor leaders, and inspection of American business and education practices. The estimated cost of travel and other expenses for each of these leaders is $4,500. Consideration might be given to the possibility of including in this group one or two prominent Buddhist laymen who could *inter alia* visit and study the famous Buddhist collection in the Library of Congress.

It is also recommended that representative American leaders in fields of special interest to Burmese leaders be brought to Burma for similar discussion visits at an estimated cost of $4,500 each.

Inasmuch as Burmese leaders often have insufficient funds to enable them to attend American or international conferences, fairs, and exhibitions in their private capacities, it is recommended that funds be set aside to finance Burmese leader participation in conferences which would be of interest to them and consistent with our policies.

Publications, mostly books, in the fields of labor, agriculture, health, consumer cooperatives, industrial development, and American foreign policy and history should be purchased for presentation to Burmese leaders and institutions. Estimated cost is $15,000.

Through enlargement of existing USIS facilities, particularly in the audio-visual field, it would be possible to extend various facilities and aids to Burmese leaders on a loan basis for the use of their organizations. Implementation of this project should be centered in the hands of USIS, for which reason no estimate of the cost involved is being submitted herewith. (See paragraph 11, under C, Education.)

VIII. Factors Limiting Amount, Kind, or Speed of Economic and Technical Aid

In common with other Southeast Asian governments, the Government of Burma is extremely short of trained, mature, competent, practical administrators and technicians. This is a serious barrier to technical aid programs and to economic development projects, since the men are just not there to participate in them and run them. There are even too few with enough training and English to profit fully from training in the United States, and what few there are are desperately needed to carry on the government in Burma itself. Burma's governmental personnel is so meager that it cannot even afford to release some so that their competence can be increased.

Burmese officials and educated leaders are hypersensitive about any imagined infringement of their sovereignty, and extremely suspicious of Western motives in offering them aid. They are very reluctant to accept technical or policy advisers from the United Kingdom and will very carefully scrutinize any recommendations made by U.S. experts. For this reason, it will be even more important than usual to select extremely tactful, sensitive personnel for United States aid programs in Burma and not to rush large numbers of them into the country. Confidence in Americans will gradually develop, but it cannot at all be taken for granted (as it can in Thailand, for example), and undertaking aid programs without it would be futile.

Moreover, the Burmese are strongly opposed to making any commitment, or accepting any aid that implies a commitment, to line up with the Western powers in an anti-Communist camp. It may, for this reason, be necessary to avoid United States aid to certain projects that, desirable as they may be on economic grounds, may be interpreted as involving an anti-Communist motive. An example of such a project would be aid in the repair and development of airports in Burma, which might be misinterpreted as potential U.S. air bases.

A similar factor possibly limiting certain kinds of U.S. aid is the doctrinaire economic philosophy of many top Socialists (who refuse to serve in the Cabinet), whose Marxist beliefs are inconsistent with the present government's announced policies of attracting foreign private investment (although its regulations on prospecting and mining leases, intended to attract private capital, are still too burdensome to be attractive), and bringing in foreign technical advisers. U.S. advice that stresses private enterprise, or kinds of aid (such as guarantees to private U.S. investors, or technical advice on tax law) that only favor private foreign investment, might arouse so much opposition from non-government Socialist leaders that not only would that aid be opposed but the whole U.S. aid program might be thrown out at the same time. There are signs that the government is losing its rosy view of the advantages of government ownership, as it has had such unsatisfactory experience with government operation of the teak forests and the river transport system (both severely affected by the civil disturbances, of course), but it will be a long time before government officials really go all out for private enterprise, if they ever do.

Another characteristic of Burmese government officials, stemming doubtless from their experience, is a tendency to propose and study quite impractical schemes (such as changing the meter gauge on all their railroads). This, combined with their sensitivity and suspiciousness, may mean that an inordinate amount of the time of American experts will have to be spent in examining and tactfully deflating all sorts of premature schemes for mechanization and industrialization, when the same time and effort would pay far higher dividends if devoted to improving agricultural and health services. This will, of course, impede the work of U.S. experts as it already impedes the useful work of Burmese officials.

The budgetary stringency of the Burmese Government, which is already operating at an enormous deficit despite pay cuts for teachers and government officials, will also be a barrier to the undertaking of aid programs. It will be impossible for the Burmese Government to supply substantial local currency for aid programs, or to assign many Burmese civil servants to work on such programs, as government staffs have been so severely pared.

Development projects that involve substantial expenditures without an immediately increased flow of consumer goods would feed the already serious inflation in Burma and will have to be held to a minimum, regardless of the source of the funds to be invested in them. This will limit possible irrigation, road and railroad repair and building, hydroelectric power, and other development projects, at least until the present governmental budgetary deficits are much reduced.

In substantial areas of the country, it is still unsafe to undertake technical or economic aid projects. Formal rebellions and informal banditry are widespread across the waist of the country, in the south, and along the northern border of the Shan State. Insecurity will for some time to come be an important limiting factor on the amount and type of U.S. aid programs that can be carried on in Burma.

A final limiting factor applies primarily to U.S. personnel. Housing is almost completely unavailable, especially in Rangoon. It will be possible to house additional U.S. personnel at only a very slow rate, and even then the housing will rarely accommodate, or be suitable for, personnel with children. It is anticipated that this alone will be one of the most important limiting factors in the U.S. program of aid to Burma.

IX. Considerations Affecting Form or Channels of United States Aid

The United States itself is not free from Burmese suspicions that the real objective of any U.S. aid would be to bring Burma into an anti-Communist front. It is hardly conceivable to Asiatic minds that *any* aid would be given without strings somewhere attached. In fact, it is possible that too big and obvious a flow of U.S. aid would *hurt* the Burmese Government by convincing other political groups that the government had sold out. Because of hypersensitivity on this score, the greatest tact and skill will have to be employed to make it clear that the United States is interested in helping Burma become politically and economically strong enough to make its *own* decisions in the world. This will mean great caution in trying to maintain, for greater efficiency, any substantial U.S. control over aid activities. It will probably even mean that American aid personnel should refrain from categorical statements of their own opinions, or of U.S. policy, with regard to the menace of world communism. Reiteration of this theme might be interpreted as undue pressure on Burma, for the official U.S. position is already well known.

U.S. representatives should also be very tactful and restrained about criticizing the rather doctrinaire leftist Burma Government's state socialism plans. Not only would such criticism wound hypersensitive Burmese officials (who feel inadequate to their jobs anyway), but it would also be interpreted as doctrinaire capitalist penetration by the United States.

There are, therefore, good reasons for encouraging the United Nations to do as much as it can for Burma and for supporting its constructive activities there. Such activities will be of genuine help to Burma and deserve support on that score alone. They may find more ready acceptance and, therefore, be more effective than U.S. aid, as coming from an international organization. Moreover, U.S. support of U.N. activities will demonstrate to Burma the genuine U.S. interest in Burma's successful development and, by demonstrating that genuine good will, may make more convincing U.S. protestations of disinterested concern.

Finally, although several rebellions are now going on in Burma, government leaders look forward to the day when the country will again be united and peaceful and when they will be working again side-by-side with Karen and other rebellious leaders. They are trying to fight a civil war in such a way that it does not leave ineradicable wounds. Similarly, they are casting about for every kind of constructive activity that can be undertaken in "pacified" areas to make things easier for the people there, even though many of these people had most likely been supporting the rebel troops shortly before. A high priority should be given in all U.S. aid programs to activities that will demonstrate the conciliatory, common welfare spirit of present government leaders and that will help to heal the psychological as well as the physical wounds of civil war as quickly as possible.

X. Public Information Activities Supporting the United States Aid Program

Even more than in other Southeast Asian countries, public information activities in Burma should be tailored to local attitudes, sensitivities, and inexperience. Burmese officials have had only an academic experience with many governmental problems, and their theoretical approach is still heavily Marxist, although not Communist. They are likely to read into public information materials purposes and biases that fit the capitalist stereotype in their theoretical framework and to attribute to such materials a major importance as instruments of U.S. policy. They do not take for granted certain major assumptions of U.S. policy, and the information materials distributed in Burma should therefore be such as do not take these assumptions for granted—lest these materials be misinterpreted as pressure, or otherwise raise barriers that defeat their own ends. Information activities should also be discreet in amount and media, for similar reasons.

On the other hand, the economic, and particularly the technical, aid activities proposed for Burma will only be fully effective in getting broad participation, in strengthening the Government of Burma, and in showing U.S. interest in the real welfare of the people, if an energetic information program is carried on at the same time. Although few of the agricultural population participate actively in the political process, their participation is growing, and their support is sorely needed by the government, which does not have many sources of political support. This is particularly important in this period of civil disturbance, when popular support may mean a good deal for the success of government efforts to achieve a quick but liberal peace.

Literacy, even in rural areas, is reported to be quite high, and information materials may be effective either directly or through the village head men, monks, and teachers who provide the usual channels of communication between city and country.

Information activities, presumably through USIS, should stress the role played by the Government of Burma, so that it gets the major credit and benefit, and should play down the contribution of the United States (though not ignoring it) lest the sensitivities of government officials be wounded, or the apparent volume of U.S. aid convince the population that the government must have sold out and that the U.S. is taking over.

Indirect public relations activities, through substantial amounts of books, scientific equipment, and training aids and through trainee programs aimed at the potentially important student class, should therefore be stressed.

XI. Organization for Field Administration of Aid Programs in Burma

The program proposed for Burma involves approximately 80 U.S. technicians to work in Burma (from a few months to several years in each case), approximately 100 students and trainees to study and work in the United States, and about 12 million dollars worth of materials, supplies, equipment, etc. A program of these dimensions means a major task of general supervision, coordination, and such control over individual performance or distribution of materials as is required to insure the success of the program.

The sensitivity of Burmans to the idea that political considerations might be involved in economic or technical aid programs should be taken into account in deciding the form of the organization set up in Burma to administer these programs. Preferably, the economic and technical aid personnel should have offices in buildings physically separate from the U.S. Embassy; should have relatively little to do officially or socially with Embassy personnel; and should carry on their work on an obviously technical level—working with Burmese government officials who are also on the "working level."

Most of the U.S. technicians brought to Burma will work right in the various divisions of the Burmese Government under the direction of the heads of those divisions. The task of general supervision and coordination must, therefore, be performed without distorting the proper relationship of these U.S. technicians both to the department of the Government of Burma where they are assigned, and to the U.S. Government agency by which they are employed and which furnishes technical backstopping for them.

These experts should have their offices right in the departments where they are assigned to work. There should be the minimum possible supervision and control, and the minimum possible appearance of supervision and control by any U.S. representative *not* connected with a Burmese Government department.

There will, of course, have to be a single U.S. aid representative to negotiate project agreements, discuss general aid policies with the government and with the U.S. diplomatic mission, provide general supervision and evaluation of aid personnel and programs, and carry certain administrative responsibilities (payroll, office space, local employment, etc.). This official should be a Coordinator of Economic Cooperation Activities (CECA), however, not a Chief of Economic Mission. He should provide general policy guidance (in conformity with the political guidance of the American Embassy), and facilitate the work of American experts. He should not be responsible for day-to-day technical guidance of aid personnel for, even if he were competent to do so, such detailed supervision would arouse suspicion and resentment of Burmese officials, who would understandably wish to carry this responsibility themselves.

It would be desirable to set up a joint body with the Government of Burma to set policies for or actually direct certain aid activities, if this could be done without suggesting undesirable U.S. control. The Joint Commission on Rural Rehabilitation pattern in China, where 3 Chinese and 2 Americans constitute a Joint Commission, would be a possible model. On any such joint body, The CECA or his representative should represent the U.S., but Embassy representatives should not be on such a body.

If a private company, under a contract with the Government of Burma financed by the United States, provides advisers in national economic development planning or other fields, as recommended in Section F above, these advisers would not be responsible to any U.S. Government representative in Burma, but the chief of such a group should, of course, maintain informal contacts with CECA and occasionally also with the Embassy. Such contacts should not be frequent or formal, for such a group of advisers will be most effective only if both they and the Burmese officials recognize that their responsibility is directly to the Burmese Government, not to the U.S. Government.

On the other hand, the increased information and public relations activities undertaken as a part of or as a result of U.S. economic and technical aid programs should be administered by USIS, in the Embassy, not by CECA. In this way functional duplication would be avoided.

While the processing of persons exchanged under various programs (Fulbright, Smith-Mundt, Point Four, etc.) should be centralized and should continue to be performed by USIS, CECA and his staff would, of course, play an important role in recommending the number and kind of technical personnel to be exchanged, and should participate to the extent desired in their actual selection. CECA would also be the source of recommendations on the content of technical filmstrips and training aids, the selection of technical publications, and the choice of the areas where such training aids should be used and the libraries to receive such publications, since these would be integral parts of any technical assistance program. The physical handling of such materials should, if possible, continue to be done by USIS.

Appendix

1. The Mission arrived in Rangoon at 5:30 p.m., March 23, 1950, and remained in Burma until 9:00 a.m., April 4, 1950.
2. The Mission during its stay in Burma was composed of the following persons:

Department of State

    The Honorable R. Allen Griffin, Chief of Mission, with the
      personal rank of Minister
    Samuel P. Hayes, Jr., Deputy Chief of Mission and Adviser
    Henry Tarring, Jr., J.G. White Engineering Co., Consultant
      to the Department of State, Adviser
    Walter Walkinshaw (March 25-April 4), Adviser
    William McAfee, Adviser
    Eleanor L. Koontz, Secretary
    Mary A. Randolph, Secretary

Department of Agriculture

    Ross E. Moore (March 23-April 4), Adviser

Public Health Service

    Howard M. Kline (March 23-April 4), Adviser

Department of Defense

    Russell G. Duff (March 23-March 27), Colonel, USA, Adviser
    Frederick B. Warder (March 23-March 27), Captain, USN, Adviser

3. The following formal conferences were held during the visit of the Mission in Burma:

a) Orientation meeting with the Embassy staff, March 25, 8:15 a.m.
b) Preliminary meeting with Burmese Cabinet and other officials, March 25, 10:30 a.m.
c) Conference with representatives of the Ministry of Agriculture and Forests, March 28, 10:00 a.m.
d) Conference with representatives of the Ministry of Transport and Communications, March 28, 10:00 a.m.
e) Conference with representatives of the Ministry of Health, March 28, 10:00 a.m.
f) Conference with representatives of the Ministry of Agriculture and Forests, March 29, 10:00 a.m.
g) Conference with representatives of the Ministry of Industry and Mines, March 29, 10:00 a.m.
h) Conference with officials connected with the Ministry of National Planning, March 29, 10:00 a.m.
i) Conference with the five major Chambers of Commerce, March 30, 10:00 a.m.
j) Conference with Fulbright representatives, March 30, 2:30 p.m.
k) Conference with student leaders from Rangoon area, March 30, 5:00 p.m.
l) Conference with Burmese Cabinet and other officials, March 31, 10:00 a.m.
m)Conference with representatives of the government concerned with education problems, March 31, 2 p.m.
n) Conference with representatives of Frontier States, April 3, 10:00 a.m.

4. A list of certain of the persons interviewed by the Mission in Burma follows, order within lists not necessarily being in order of rank:

American Embassy Staff

Ambassador David M. Key
Counselor of Embassy Henry B. Day
Mr. H.D. Spivak
Mr. David Kline
Mr. L.M. Purnell
Mr. M.H. Noble
Major J. Sitterson, USA

Burmese Officials

The Honorable Sao Hkun Hkio, Foreign Minister
The Honorable U Tin, Minister for Finance
    and Revenue
The Honorable U Win, Minister for Rehabilitation

The Honorable U Kyaw Myint (Gale), Minister for
  Industry and Mines
The Honorable Bo Khin Maung Gale, Minister for
  Agriculture and Forests
The Honorable Mahn Win Maung, Minister for Transport
  and Communications
The Honorable U Tin (Myanaung), Minister of Health
U Hla Maung, Secretary, Ministry of Finance and Revenue
U Nyun, Secretary, Ministry of Commerce and Supply
U Aung Soe, Secretary, Ministry of Agriculture and Forests
U Kyaw Thein, Secretary, Ministry of Industry and Mines
U Ba Nyein, Deputy Secretary, Ministry of National Planning
Dr. Set, Chairman, State Timber Board
U Thet Su, Chairman, State Agricultural Marketing Board
U Aye Maung, Chief Engineer, Irrigation
U Khin, Director of Agriculture
Mr. Bhattacharjee, Director of Veterinary Services
U Hman, Chief Conservator of Forests
U Chit Pe, Deputy Secretary, Ministry of Agriculture and Forests
U Shwe Mra, Secretary, Ministry of Transport and Communications
U Tun Thwin, General Manager, Burma Railways
Mr. S.C. Liu, General Manager, Inland Water Transport
U Taw, General Manager, Union of Burma Airways
U Ba Choe, Director, Telecommunications
U Kyaw Tha, Chairman Port Commissioners
U Saw Iwin, Secretary, Ministry of Health
Dr. Tha Mya, Director, Medical and Public Health Services
Dr. G.L. Chowdhury, Superintendent, Rangoon General Hospital
Col. Min Sein, Principal, Rangoon Medical College
Dr. Ahad, Director, Pasteur Institute
Daw Khin Kyi
Naung Chin Kachin
Dr. S. Suvi, Assistant Director, Harcourt-Butler Institute
U Saw Tun, Deputy Director of Industries
Dr. A.N. Ghosh, Director, Metallurgical Research and Planning
U Pu, Mining Adviser, Ministry of Industry and Mines
Dr. Ba Thi, Officer-in-Charge, Geological Department
U Mya (Henzada), Vice-President of the National Planning Board
U Ka Si, Chief Secretary, Ministry of National Planning
U Kyin, Financial Commissioner (Commerce)
U San Lin, General Manager, Union Bank of Burma
Mr. J.S. Furnivall, Planning Adviser, Ministry of National Planning
Mr. K.W. Foster, Financial Commissioner (Land Revenue)
The Honorable Sima Duwa Sinwa Mabng, Minister for Kachin Affairs
The Honorable U Vam Thu Maung, Minister for China Affairs
Major Shan Lone, Secretary, Kachin Ministry

Burmese and Others Prominent in Politics or Industry

U Kyaw Nyein, Secretary-General of the Socialist Party, former
   Foreign Minister
Group-Captain P. Holroyd-Smith, Director of Civil Aviation
U Aung Than, owner of Air Burma
Thakin Lwin, President of TUCB
Thakin Tin, All-Burma Peasants Union
U Tha Tun Aung, President, Union of Burma Chamber of Commerce
Mr. H.S.B. Nariman, President, Indian Chamber of Commerce
Mr. G.S. Nicoll, President, Burma Chamber of Commerce
Mr. Nelson Price, Standard-Vacuum Oil Company
Mr. R.C. Leach, General Manager, Burma Corporation
Mr. R.S. Carey, General Manager, Burma Oil Company

In addition to these, many Burmese active in education, public health, and industry were interviewed.

Fulbright Representatives

Dr. Frederick Dickinson
Mr. Winslow L. Christian
Dr. Paul F. Creasy
Dr. Louis E. Alley
Dr. J.R. King

Other Americans

Dr. Gustaf A. Sword, American Baptist Mission

5. As in other posts visited, a large percentage of time was spent in working-level conferences with appropriately designated representatives of the Government of Burma, in inspecting industrial plants, communications facilities, hospitals, schools, rice mills, etc., in an attempt to study first-hand actual conditions in the country. The Mission, while in Burma, continued the policy followed in countries previously visited of seeking information from Americans resident in Burma and from informed private citizens who possessed specialized information of interest to the Mission. The Embassy at Rangoon arranged a series of seven working luncheons attended by appropriate members of the Mission at which Burmese officials and others interested in the problems being studied by the Mission were present. These luncheons served a particularly useful purpose in enabling members of the Mission to meet non-office-holding representatives of leading Burmese political parties, including certain of Burma's most influential political figures.

As in all posts visited, representatives from the United States diplomatic mission attended the various conferences and participated fully as working members on the different working groups set up.

6. A list of the most important documents submitted to the Mission by the Government of Burma is as follows:

a) *Agriculture, Forestry and Related Subjects*
    (1) Note on American Technical Assistance Proposed in Relation to Agricultural Department.
    (2) Civil Veterinary Department memorandum of March 16, 1950, on Proposal for Technical Assistance of Economic Development.
    (3) Irrigation Department memorandum of March 16, 1950, on Proposed Visit of an American Agricultural Mission to Rangoon.
    (4) Memorandum of March 8, 1950, from Chief Conservator of Forests on Proposed Visit of an American Agricultural Mission to Rangoon.
    (5) Memorandum of March 15, 1950, from State Agricultural Marketing Board on Proposed Visit of an American Agricultural Mission to Rangoon.
    (6) Conclusion of the above memorandum, dated March 22, 1950.
    (7) Note on Timber Extension, dated March 9, 1950.
    (8) Letter of March 22, 1950, from the Office of the Collector of Salt Revenue.
    (9) Communication on Training in Sawmill Engineering, March 7, 1950.

b) *Industry, Mines, and Communications*
    (1) Requirements of the Ministry of Industry and Mines.
    (2) Note of the Mining Adviser on Possible Production of Coal from Burma.
    (3) Requirements of the Inland Water Transport Board.
    (4) Report on a Preliminary Reconnaissance of the Bowgata River, 1947 (Hydro-Electric Survey Board).
    (5) Report of the Hydro-Electric Survey Engineer on the Survey of Bowgata Project (1948-49).
    (6) Report on a Preliminary Reconnaissance of the Saingdin Falls, April 1948, Hydro-Electric Development.
    (7) Young and Buck, Inc. Mobilization Report on the Steel Plant Project; two reports dated March 14, 1949, and April 1, 1949, respectively.
    (8) Chart, Rangoon River and approaches.
    (9) Letter of April 1, 1950, from Commissioners for the Port of Rangoon.
    (10) List of Requirements of the Government Electricity Supply Department, April 1, 1950.
    (11) Rangoon Cotton Requirements for the Government Cotton Spinning and Weaving Factory.
    (12) New Airport Scheme, Mingaladon.

(13) Note of March 30, 1950, from Ministry of Industry and Mines, transmitting three documents of Electricity Supply.

(14) Document of March 31, 1950, from Ministry of Transport Communications, with enclosures on:

    (*a*) Immediate needs at the Inland Water Transport Board

    (*b*) Burma Railways

    (*c*) Assistance sought from Griffin Mission by Commissioners of Port of Rangoon

    (*d*) Immediate needs of the Telecommunications Department.

(15) National Planning Board Report on Preliminary Plan for the Mineral Industries.

c) *Public Health (Documents filed with U.S. Public Health Service only)*

    (1) Problems Affecting Health and Medical Services.

    (2) Medical College, Rangoon.

    (3) Pasteur Institute.

    (4) Rangoon General Hospital.

    (5) Harcourt-Butler Institute.

d) *Education*

    (1) Scientific apparatus and chemicals for State Post-Primary Schools.

    (2) List of apparatus and chemicals required for General Science Demonstration class at Post-Primary Schools.

    (3) List of apparatus and chemicals required for:

        (*a*) Matriculation Physics

        (*b*) Matriculation Chemistry

        (*c*) Matriculation Zoology and Botany

        (*d*) Post-Primary School General Science

    (4) Emergency Civil Engineering Classes, G.T.I., Primary.

    (5) Application for Help from the Griffin Mission, University of Rangoon, Faculties of Science and Engineering.

    (6) Provision for Physical Education and Games Equipment and Materials, together with separate lists for Primary and Post-Primary Schools.

    (7) Introduction of Woodwork and Carpentry into the Curriculum of Schools in Burma.

    (8) Mass Education Council, Burma.

e) *General and Miscellaneous*

    (1) Note Forwarding a copy of Burma-Japan Trade Agreement.

    (2) Budget 1949-50, The Honorable Finance Minister's Speech.

    (3) Abstract of Revenues and Expenditures.

    (4) Two Year Plan of Economic Development for Burma (Rangoon 1948).

Beginning of American Aid to Burma

Hla Maung

The Economic Background

Burma emerged from World War II with a shattered economy. A country rich by Asian standards, she had been a source of profitable investment for the British and Indian entrepreneurs who owned much of her productive facilities, a large share of her infrastructure and business and trade operations, almost all her factories, mines, oil wells and refineries and timber production. But she lay devastated when the British forces reoccupied Burma early in 1945. So also social facilities such as school buildings and hospitals. The colorful dresses worn by both men and women had given way to heavy, sack-like lower garments called "longyis" and equally drab upper garments called "aingyis." Even the golden spires of her pagodas which somehow survived, and which combined with the natural charm and gaiety of the people gave the country her unique picturesqueness, could not relieve the heavy atmosphere of gloom. The effects of war devastation left their mark everywhere.

The extent of the damage to Burma's economy caused by the War can be judged by two simple facts. Once the largest exporter of rice in the world—accounting for two-fifths of the world's export trade in that commodity and reaching a total of 3,500,000 tons a year after the Great Depression—Burma produced in 1945-46 only an estimated 2,701,000 long tons of paddy as against a normal crop of over 7,000,000 tons.[1] Her exports of petroleum and its products in 1938-39 were valued at over US$ 45.5 millions (at the exchange rate of Rs. 3.3 to one dollar),[2] and she supplied 52 percent of undivided India's requirements of these commodities.[3] At the end of the War, not only had Burma lost the Indian market but she had to import these essential commodities for domestic use, because all the wells and the main refinery were "denied" to the enemy when the British withdrew in 1942. In modern statistical terms, her gross national product (GNP) in 1949-50 (the period of the Griffin Mission's visit to Burma) was only 58 percent of the prewar year 1938-39 at constant prices[4]—evidence of the ravages caused by the insurrections during 1948 and 1949, and particularly the obstacles they placed on the path to economic recovery. The figure had recovered to 74 percent of 1938-39 by 1947-48, but

---

U Hla Maung was Secretary, Ministry of Finance and Revenue, Government of Burma, at the time of the Mission's visit.

fell off in 1948-49 to 67 percent and then fell further to 58 percent in the following year.

The Political Background

The political picture was also gloomy and uncertain, but with one ray of hope. Unlike prewar Burma with a multiplicity of political groups and factions, the Anti-Fascist Peoples' Freedom League (AFPFL) emerged as a strong and united political force with a charismatic personality—General Aung San, described by the Griffin Mission as Burma's George Washington—as its leader. Organized as a resistance group against the Japanese and under their very nose, it joined up with the British forces when they re-entered Burma in 1945 and gave them considerable help by harassing the retreating Japanese forces and killing thousands of them. The major military victories were of course won by the British Eighth Army and it was they who had smashed the Japanese military might in Burma and forced them to withdraw. But the help provided by an internal resistance movement was of no mean dimension.

But the attitude of the British towards the Burmese had not changed. The British Government of prewar Burma was now seated at Simla in India, and was headed by Sir Reginald Dorman-Smith as Governor. Their attitude towards the Burmese who had "collaborated" with the Japanese was one of toughness. They not only planned to return to Burma and run it as in prewar days, but the civilian (and military) officers serving in the military administration (Civil Affairs Service (Burma)) urged that Aung San be tried as a war criminal.[5] But the attitude of Admiral Lord Louis Mountbatten, the Supreme Commander of the Allied forces in Southeast Asia, was entirely different. He was not only determined to pursue "Great Britain's traditional policy of leniency and conciliation," but made it clear that his word must prevail in all policy decisions to be taken in Southeast Asia.[6] He encouraged contacts and cooperation between Aung San and his field commanders. Aung San had an unsatisfactory meeting with General Slim, Commander-in-Chief of the British forces in Burma, in May, 1945, and when Lord Mountbatten received the account of this meeting he asked Sir Reginald Dorman-Smith to agree to Aung San being informed that his resistance party would be considered for inclusion in the Governor's Council when it was reformed. But Dorman—Smith "telegraphed that he could not for a moment contemplate giving an undertaking to consider this."[7] Mountbatten however insisted on his policy of leniency and in June 1945, after a meeting in Delhi presided over by him, recognition was accorded to the Burma National Army as the "Patriotic Burmese Forces" (PBF). Mountbatten issued a directive in regard to the policy to be followed towards Burmans which read in part: "The guiding principle which I am determined shall be observed is that no person shall suffer on account of political opinions honestly held, whether now or in the past, even if these may have been anti-British."[8] And finally, only the single-minded action of Mountbatten led to the virtual recognition of the

Anti-Fascist Organization (AFO)—the earlier designation of the AFPFL—as the genuine representatives of postwar popular opinion in Burma.

Aung San was aware of these differences, and how the personal attitude of one person alone gave hope of fair treatment for Burma. A personal accord was established between him and the Supreme Commander and his close associates, but he saw no reason for optimism that this attitude of sympathy would persevere after the civilian government returned to Burma and took over control; and still less that the British would enable the Burmese to gain the political freedom for which he had originally joined with the Japanese and later revolted against them. The distrust became deeper when in May, 1945, the British Government issued an ultra-conservative statement of policy, embodying interim arrangements hardly acceptable to Burma's new leaders and a vague promise of full self-government within the Commonwealth but with the Shan States and other hill areas remaining "subject to a special regime under the Governor, until such time as the inhabitants signify their desire for some suitable form of association of their territories with Burma proper."[9]

When therefore the PBF was disbanded in agreement with Mountbatten and about 4,700 of its members ultimately registered for regular enlistment in the British Army, some 3,500 did not follow suit. Aung San himself refused the offer of an appointment in the new regular army with the rank of Brigadier. He chose to stay on in politics, and to prepare for further resistance if the British Government refused to grant independence to Burma. He therefore organized the members of the PBF who did not enter the regular army into the nucleus for a private army known as the People's Volunteer Organization (PVO). It had district formations throughout the country, and operated under a central headquarters controlled by Aung San.[10] This organization began to cache away large stores of arms and ammunition to meet future contingencies.

The distrust of British intentions deepened when Sir Reginald Dorman-Smith returned to Burma as the head of the civil government in October 1945, met representatives of the AFPFL and other parties and made certain proposals for the formation of a new Executive Council. He offered the AFPFL seven seats out of eleven on the Council, but Aung San rejected the proposal mainly because the Governor stipulated that *he* would choose his AFPFL councillors on their merits, while Aung San demanded the acceptance of a slate automatically and certain portfolios for his men.[11] The Governor then appointed the Council without AFPFL representation.

Aung San then concentrated on building up the PVO for armed resistance. The Socialists, one of the constituent elements of the AFPFL, built up the All-Burma Peasants' Organization (ABPO). The AFPFL drew heavy support from the labor movement—one of the strongest Unions (The Trade Union Congress of Burma) being affiliated with it through the Socialists. Even the civil servants organized themselves into the Joint Committee of Service Organizations and the AFPFL exercised great influence on it. Demands for high wages, etc., grew and it looked as if there would be another bloody revolution in Burma. But a dramatic change in British politics prevented disaster. The Labor Party came into power in Great Britain and took a more liberal attitude. Sir Reginald Dorman-Smith was replaced as Governor, no doubt under Mountbatten's advice, by Sir Hubert Rance—a trusted lieutenant of Lord Mountbatten's and formerly Chief of the Civil Affairs Service (Burma). But the momentum of discontent continued, and widespread strikes and other disorders broke out soon after his arrival. He reacted immediately and brought Aung San into the Executive Council within less than a month. He no doubt acted in the confidence that Aung San would bring the upheaval under control. His confidence was justified, for the General Strike was called off a week later. But he must also have come with instructions from the Labor Government—and advice from his former chief Lord Mountbatten—to enlist Aung San's full support as soon as he could. He therefore reconstituted his Executive Council and gave Aung San all the authority he asked for. Though designated as Vice-Chairman for purely constitutional reasons, Aung San became virtually a Prime Minister.[12]

Then followed direct negotiations with the British Government in London for independence, culminating in what came to be known as the Attlee-Aung San Agreement in January, 1947. It recognized Aung San's Cabinet as an interim government with the same status as a Dominion Government, provided for elections within four months to set up a Constituent Assembly, agreed on the early unification of the Frontier Areas with the Government of Burma and promised large scale British loans. Aung San returned to Burma in triumph, declaring Burma would gain full independence within one year. He concentrated first on enlisting the support of the frontier area people for creating a united Burma, through what came to be known as the Panlong Conference. He won both their warm friendship and agreement after difficult negotiations. All the minority groups (except the Karens) agreed to enter into immediate cooperation with the interim government. This was undoubtedly one of Aung San's major achievements, proof of his statesmanship and of the fact that a genuine bond could be forged between the vast majority of the hill peoples—always kept separate from the Burmese under the British—and the Burmese of the mainland. The agreement included the section of the Karens who lived in a separate area of theirs, the Karenni State, and could thus form a state of their own within the Federation—unlike the vast majority of the other Karens who lived dispersed and mixed with the Burmese population.

He then concentrated on convening elections for a Constituent Assembly and drawing up a Constitution for independent Burma so that Burma would become formally and legally independent within the year that he envisaged. But before its work was completed he lay dead with six of his closest and most influential Cabinet colleagues from a rain of bullets from an assassin's Sten gun—conspired by a political rival, U Saw, who later was tried for the murder, found guilty and hanged. Aung San's mantle then fell on U Nu's shoulders, his close colleague in the AFPFL. U Nu completed final negotiations with the British for Burma's independence and the country started on its path of freedom outside the British Commonwealth on 4 January 1948.

I have described the above sequence of events in some detail as a setting for

Burma's attitude to international politics, and to explain her deep distrust of past colonial powers, which naturally was the major factor in Burma's appraisal of their interests in Southeast Asia. These events help explain the reasons for Burma's determination to stay completely free from the influence of all such powers—to the extent of refusing to stay within the Commonwealth, even though it offered certain advantages. They also put in deeper focus her policy of strict neutrality as between all power groups, more so than many other neutral countries.

Developments since Independence

But Burma was not to enjoy her independence in peace or full unity, take advantage of her new status to rebuild her economy, or make full use of her potential and take a long step forward to economic growth. She was plagued with a series of insurgencies almost as soon as she won her independence. In fact, the Red Flag Communists under Thakin Soe took up arms against the Government even when Aung San was alive, but the White Flag Communists under Thakin Than Tun—the more powerful group—only went into opposition when Aung San expelled the Communists from the AFPFL and deprived Than Tun of the key post of Secretary General of the Party. He refused to let them occupy any position of power which would later enable them to take over control of the country. He believed in socialism, but wanted nothing to do with communism. He wanted to build Burma as a democratic state, devoted to the welfare of the common man, but not at the sacrifice of fundamental human freedoms. The first two years of independence were the most critical, when there were seven insurgent groups fighting against the government[13]—the two most powerful being the Communists and the Karens. The situation was so serious during these two years that at one time the Karen insurgents occupied an area a mere five miles from Rangoon and the Government had little or no control over the country except in a few cities.

But the Government and the Army fought on valiantly. Neither U Nu the Prime Minister nor General Ne Win the Commander-in-Chief gave way to despair. They carried on the struggle until by 1950 the country turned the corner, regained control over most of the land and restored communications both by rail and by internal waterways. They were frequently disrupted by small bands of insurgents, but the situation was entirely different from two years ago. Thus, the *Foreign Commerce Weekly* quoted a dispatch from the U.S. Embassy in Rangoon under dateline May 10, 1950 as follows:

Continued military success of the Government's armies and resultant weakening in the strength of the insurgent forces have injected a note of optimism into the economic picture in Burma. . . . The Government reoccupied Toungoo, and the Rangoon-Mandalay trunk road was reopened. . . . On April 27, the Government announced resumption of rail service between Rangoon and Toungoo.[14]

And the Special Correspondent of the *London Times* reported from Rangoon under dateline July 10, 1950:

When Thakin Nu, Prime Minister of Burma, launched his programme of "peace within one year" on July 19 last—the second anniversary of the assassination of the national hero, Aung San—few observers thought the programme could be carried out. Yet within a year the country has broken the backs of two major rebellions—Communist and Karen—and the Government has done much to strengthen the national morale and create the conviction that the country is over the worst of its internal troubles.[15]

And this was echoed by an editorial in the *London Times* of 12 July, 1950, under the title: "Better News from Burma."

Thus, when the Griffin Mission visited Burma from March 23 to April 4, 1950, the Government felt the worst of our internal troubles were over and that it was ready to go ahead with an accelerated program of economic, social and moral reconstruction and development.

The International Outlook

When Burma embarked on her independence, the international outlook by and large did not look too gloomy or discouraging. Our suspicions towards British intentions continued, as indicated above, after the conclusion of the War, but were largely dissipated by Mountbatten's personal attitude and the policies of the Labor Government. Burma's attitude toward other imperial powers was one of indifference. France she believed would not survive long as an imperial power, and the same would be true of Holland. Burmans knew little of Africa, and they were not very suspicious of imperialist intentions of Communist countries. But, despite the changed situation after the War, Burma felt that her survival as an independent country, wedged as she is between two huge land masses with overflowing populations, lay in the Charter of the United Nations; that in fact that organization offered the best guarantee against aggression to all the smaller and weaker nations of the world. This faith persisted despite the power struggles within that body between the United States and the Soviet Union, of which she was a front row observer, having become a member of the United Nations.

As regards Burma's appraisal of the part that the United States would play in world politics—in particular, whether she would attempt to replace the nations of Europe as an imperialist power in the East—there were two attitudes. The extreme left wing parties in Burma—which were strong but had little influence in the Government—firmly believed that she would. The others—including the Government leaders—did not think so. There was general acceptance of the fact that there would be a power struggle between the United States and the Soviet Union, both globally and within the United Nations, but this did not worry Burmans too much. They thought such a struggle natural, and the best line for them to follow was to stay out of it. The United States' attitude toward communism as such—as distinct from that towards Communist powers—was viewed in Burma both sympathetically—for many were passionately against the Communist doctrine—and with some measure of amusement, insofar as it influenced United States willingness to give aid to others in order to combat communism. The joke then current all over Western Europe, that all you needed to get substantial aid from the United States was a handful of active Communists, was repeated everywhere. But fear and suspicion for Burma's own safety because of the Communist menace she faced internally, and the belief amongst many that the inspiration for one section of the Communists—the Red Flags under Thakin Soe—came from the Calcutta meeting of 1948[16] and therefore from international communism, was strong. This fear was reinforced by the fact that H.N. Ghoshal—an Indian Communist—acted as the principal theorist in the other and more powerful Communist faction—the White Flags under Thakin Than Tun.[17]

Then came the successful culmination of the Communist revolution in China, which ousted the Chiang Kai-Shek Government from the Chinese mainland. Burma had no love for the Nationalist Government, and her socialist beliefs and general sympathy towards the Communist countries and their peoples gave no cause for suspicion that China under Communist leadership would become an imperialist menace. She established diplomatic relations quickly—being the first country outside the Communist bloc to do so. She concentrated not only on establishing close and friendly relations but also on settling the outstanding problem of her long land frontier with that country—which the British before the war had failed to do.

The negotiations that followed gave Burma her first taste of how difficult her task would be of maintaining friendly relations with Communist China without sacrifices on her part. The demands for a settlement on the part of China were tough, and there were two views amongst the Burmese leaders. The story is told in full detail by Dorothy Woodman in her *The Making of Burma*.[18] The details are irrelevant for our purposes—except insofar as they reflect Burma's anticipation as to what the future Chinese attitude would be when her interests were at stake, no matter in what sphere.

Talks started immediately after the end of World War II—when the Nationalist Chinese Government was still in power—continued when the Communist regime took over at the end of 1949 and did not conclude till October 1960, still leaving many in Burma dissatisfied and even angry. U Nu's hope of reaching an easy settlement between two friendly neighbors did not materialize. Even Jawarharlal Nehru's attempt in 1956—at the request of U Ba Swe, the then Prime Minister of Burma—to induce the Chinese Government to soften its demands produced no result. He expressed the hope in a message to Premier Chou En-lai that "this small matter of Burma-China frontier" would be settled soon, adding the plea that "Burma is relatively a small country; on the either side of Burma are these big countries China and India, and Burma naturally feels a little apprehensive of both these countries." Nehru, however, confined himself to suggesting that "perhaps he [Chou] might be good enough to invite U Nu who was not at that time Prime Minister and discuss it with him."[19]

U Nu was invited, following Nehru's suggestion. But tough bargaining went on, and the issue was not settled until October 1960—after China got involved in the much bigger dispute with India—and Burma acceded to China's demand that three small areas on the northeast border be "ceded" to her, against much opposition. Burma's decision was thus forced on her; situated as she was geographically, she had no alternative. While accepting Communist China as a friend, she realized she had to be watchful—in particular of China's future intentions.

Attitude Towards Economic Reconstruction and Foreign Aid

As soon as Aung San and his close associates assured themselves that independence for Burma was only a matter of time, they turned to problems of economic reconstruction and development. As regards the role of foreign capital, Aung San declared as early as 27 February 1947 that:

Burma will need foreign capital for fast economic growth, and we must welcome it. We shall accept foreign capital provided it will work under proper controls and not exploit as in the past. Foreign capital should reap fair rewards, and we would on our part benefit from the employment it gives to our peoples, and the growth of the economy.[20]

And on 6 June 1947, less than two months after the General Elections to the Constituent Assembly, he convened a conference of political leaders, administrators and technicians to draft plans for the reconstruction of Burma and its future development. It eventually resulted in the first development plan for Burma—called the Two-Year Plan, published in April 1948—but he was not destined to live long enough to see and guide this first attempt at Burma's reconstruction and development on a planned and coordinated basis.

As regards finance, Burma relied mainly on Great Britain and her promise of substantial loans, which she not only fulfilled—extending financial assistance in the form of loans amounting to over £70 millions by 1952—but eventually surpassed by agreeing to write them off altogether. As regards technical personnel, Burma did not extend the trust she acquired in Britain's political intentions to the British civil servants and technicians who had served in pre-war Burma, as she believed they would not change their colonial attitude. She turned to the United Nations and to the USA, and believed the latter could supply not only technicians who would work genuinely for the interest of Burma but was the only country under the immediate postwar conditions which could supply the plant and machinery for reconstruction and new projects. Thus, machinery for setting up the first new project in Burma after independence—the

Government Cotton Spinning and Weaving Factory—and the services of consulting engineers to plan and design it were obtained in the United States, with funds acquired from British sources. The only exception was the 200 looms installed in the factory, which were purchased in Japan on the advice of consultants. Burma further believed that American technology was the most advanced at the time—Europe herself only just recovering from the effects of the War with the assistance of the United States' imaginative Marshall Plan. And the methods and approaches of the T.V.A. had a great attraction for socialist Burma.

Economic Progress after Independence

But nothing much could be done during the first two years of independence, due to the insurrections by Communists and Karens. The Two-Year Plan itself was formulated at meetings held during nights amidst continual curfew, and when the machinery for the Spinning Mill was delivered by late 1949 as scheduled, it had to be stored in the Rangoon docks for over a year as the site on which the factory was to be built lay within two miles of the intensive fighting with the Karen insurgents who occupied the town of Insein. But Prime Minister U Nu's keen interest in economic planning and development continued unabated, and he directed that an American firm similar to that which assisted Iran in drawing up her Eight-Year Plan should be sought to help Burma with her planning and reconstruction.[21] His major concentration, however, was on defeating the insurgents and restoring order throughout the country, without which no economic reconstruction and development could take place. Even the morale of the people began to deteriorate, and this caused tremendous anguish and concern to U Nu.

The Hope Brought by the Griffin Mission

When, as already described, Burma turned the corner in her fight against insurgency by early 1950, and the Griffin Mission arrived with offers of aid for reconstruction and development, it was welcomed with open arms. Burma did not care as to what the political motivations were behind the despatch of the Mission. We knew what they were, for Ambassador-at-large Dr. Philip C. Jessup had just visited Burma and explained the United States point of view. We were confident we could use the economic aid it offered for accelerating reconstruction and social and economic development, provided the United States did not expect us to share in her political motivations and—even more emphatically—provided that military aid was not combined with the economic assistance. This positive feeling ran right through—from the attitude towards the Mission when it arrived, the negotiations which followed for the basic agreement in regard to economic aid, and later when a joint Burmese-American committee for administering the aid was set up. But the unusual understanding and sympathy shown by the Mission—reinforced by the attitude of Ambassador David M. Key and his able aides—made us feel more sure of ourselves that we could benefit from the aid offered without getting embroiled in American policies and her actions in the international political field, and that in particular we could do so consistently with maintaining close relations with Communist China. We were also confident that this was also the mood in the country, though the left wing was less optimistic than moderates like U Nu, that there would not be possible repercussions. When therefore the Mission wished to hold discussions with groups and personalities outside the Government, we raised no objections and provided them with full facilities.

Appraisal of Burma's Political and
Economic Situation

There was little difference between the appraisal of the above situation by the Griffin Mission and the Government, though we were not sure whether the Mission quite accepted the fact that we had turned the corner in regard to the insurgency. We knew—as the Griffin Mission did—that the economy lay devastated and needed urgent reconstruction and development, and we were pleased by the offer of assistance covering every sphere of social and economic activity; and particularly by the suggestion of the Mission's leader that we allocate approximately $2 million for engaging the services of consulting firms in the fields of economics, engineering and mining, as it echoed U Nu's earlier desire for obtaining such services on a direct-hire basis. But while we believed that the Mission appreciated the magnitude of the task before us, we were doubtful whether the response in terms of the amount of aid that would be offered would be commensurate with this appreciation. In fact, informal inquiries made directly in Washington revealed that the aid contemplated for Korea alone would be the same as that for Burma and several other countries combined, and that therefore Burma's share would be extremely modest. This was later confirmed by the fact that though the Griffin Mission proposed "a program of technical and economic aid estimated to cost $12,228,000 for the 15 months ending June 30, 1951,"[22] the United States Government informed the Burmese Government on an inquiry by the latter that it contemplated a program on a free grant basis of approximately $8 to 10 million by June 30, 1951. The total aid for the period 1950 to 1953 in fact amounted to only $19.7 million.[23] The principal reason for the lag was no doubt the time it takes for any aid program to gather momentum. Moreover, by the time the program in Burma went into full working gear (1953) it was terminated at Burma's request for political reasons, to be discussed below.

There was also doubt on the part of the Burmese leaders as to whether the Griffin Mission shared their extreme anxiety that moral rehabilitation was as important as economic reconstruction, that everything possible should be done not to disillusion the young rebels who were returning to the legal fold in large numbers and that they must be found useful employment, which of course meant large financial resources. The visit of the Griffin Mission was therefore immediately followed up by a direct request from the Foreign Minister of Burma on behalf of the Government to Ambassador Jessup for a loan of $50 million. This was reported by the *New York Times* correspondent C.L. Sulzberger under dateline May 2, 1950, from Rangoon.[24] He had an interview with the Foreign Minister himself, who emphasized the urgent need for moral rehabilitation of the youth of Burma through education, and the greater need of raising "the standard of health, culture and education to make people receptive to the true ideas of democracy" than "material rehabilitation such as the construction of housing" in order to wean the younger generation away from the path of violence. Negotiations were followed up actively in Washington, through personal interviews with Dr. Jessup himself and other leading officials in the State Department, the Export-Import Bank, etc. The State Department expressed great sympathy for the objectives, but felt it more practicable to extend the assistance requested through the "substantial" aid funds already decided on and which were to be administered by the ECA, because a straight loan would require congressional sanction and involve delay. Nothing came of it, and the aid actually given through the ECA remained modest in scale and covered this aspect only through the aid of $238,218 to the Burma Translation Society.

Burma has no preference as between aid on a project by project basis and a global amount of "program aid" unspecified as to projects. We knew we were not ready to accept a large sum as loan or aid and utilize it effectively, since we did not have either the organization, the expertise, or the operational personnel to plan and execute projects covering the economy as a whole on a planned and coordinated basis. The aid offered by the ECA on the basis mainly of rehabilitation projects to be formulated by the government—some independently, others in cooperation with United States technical and economic experts—was therefore not only acceptable to us but actually welcomed; provided only that there was no attempt at imposing anything on us or suggesting projects which would distort and prejudice our socialist policies, embodied in section 23 of the Constitution of the Union of Burma and under the Directive Principles of State Policy. At the same time, we felt that certain major aspects of reconstruction—such as rehabilitating the morale of our youth and finding them useful employment, education of the masses and bringing modern knowledge within the reach of the common people through an intensive program of translation into Burmese of large categories of literature in this field—could only be organized, guided, and implemented by the Burmese themselves. It would require large financial resources—which we did not possess—and therefore large-scale loans (or grants) on a global basis. Hence the approach to the United States Government through Ambassador Jessup. We were thus in need of both kinds of aid, and would have welcomed both.

Negotiations for Aid Agreement

The agreement in regard to aid was decided on in principle in discussions with the Griffin Mission, but had to be formalized by an Economic Cooperation Agreement. Negotiations were conducted mainly in Rangoon through the Foreign Office, but also in Washington with the State Department, as the author was there at the time. The principal technical problem so far as Burma was concerned arose from the fact that the proposed Agreement followed in some important respects the pattern of the agreements concluded with the European countries for the Marshall Plan programs—particularly the creation of a Counterpart Fund into which each country receiving ECA aid was required to deposit a sum in local currency equivalent to the dollar aid. This raised no difficulties in Europe, for the machinery and supplies—especially food—that her countries needed most would otherwise have to be bought with dollars which they did not have. They therefore welcomed the idea of securing such machinery and supplies by payment through local currency. Burma's position was different. She had a restrictive currency system, under which all issues of local currency above a sum equivalent to just over $20 millions had to be backed 100 percent by sterling. Large deposits into the Counterpart Fund would therefore have eaten into our foreign exchange reserves—small as they were—and restricted severely their utilization directly by the Government for rehabilitation and development purposes. Neither was Burma ready at the time to break away from the restrictive currency system; that came only in 1952 when the Central Bank was reorganized and the foreign exchange backing reduced to 25 percent of the total amount of currency issued by the Government. The problem was ultimately solved by an agreement that the requirement in regard to deposits into the Counterpart Fund would be operated with flexibility so as not to embarrass the Government's budgetary position. During the actual administration of aid from 1950 to 1953, this agreement was scrupulously honored and no difficulties ever arose in practice—as proved by the fact that out of a total aid of $19.7 million during the above period, the Burmese Government's contribution out of its own funds amounted to only $2.7 million.[25]

The other problem—small but touchy—arose out of the provision that money from the Counterpart Fund could also be used for the administrative expenses of the Special Technical and Economic Mission (STEM), the United States counterpart agency in Burma for the administration of aid funds. The Burmese Government was apprehensive that such expenditures would be substantial and create unfavorable reactions if the impression was created that STEM officials were spending Burmese funds lavishly on such items as American cars (identified in the minds of the common people as luxurious), houses provided with American-type household equipment (also considered luxurious), etc. These fears were set at rest by the assurance that such items of expenditure would be extremely small—approximately 2 percent of the deposits or less—and every effort would be made to prevent an impression of living luxuriously amongst people who were poor, just recovering from the devastation caused by war and insurgency, and whom the American experts and administrators had come to help.

The draft agreement proposed by the United States Government was scrutinized closely by the Burmese Government from the political point of view—whether it would embarrass her in any way in regard to her relations with other countries, or put any obstacles in the way of any of her activities inside the country consistent with her political and economic policies and attitudes. Two examples will illustrate the point. Firstly, when the draft agreement proposed by the United States Government contained a provision to the effect that "the Government of the Union of Burma will use its best endeavours to assure efficient and practical use *of all resources available* and to assure that the commodities and services obtained under this Agreement are used for purposes consistent therewith [italics mine]" it immediately raised the question in our minds whether the United States Government would attempt to have a say as to how we would utilize our *total* resources and thus attempt to influence our overall programs and policies. It was explained to us that though the term "all resources" may appear to be very wide, it was inserted in the Agreement as a general stipulation to satisfy the U.S. Congress. It was emphasized that there was no desire on the part of the United States to probe into or sit in judgment on the way Burma made use of her own resources, and that settled the issue. Similarly also in respect to the provision in the draft Agreement that the Government of Burma would use its best endeavors "to promote the economic development of the Union of Burma on a sound basis and to achieve such objectives as may be agreed upon by the two governments." The same apprehensions rose in our minds, but we were again assured that it was another general stipulation in order to satisfy the U.S. Congress; that no interference was contemplated. In fact, the phrase "sound basis" would include State socialism.

The same problem rose again later when the American Government at the time of the renewal of the ECA Agreement in 1952 inquired whether the Government of Burma would be willing to make a re-affirmation in an Exchange of Letters to the effect that "the Government of the Union of Burma are firmly committed to promoting international understanding and goodwill and in maintaining world peace and to cooperate in eliminating causes of international tension." Harmless though the wording was, and fully in line with our own international policies, the suggested clause was examined closely from the point of whether it would affect our freedom to act independently in any way. The word "cooperate" received particular attention. Finally, we suggested that this particular phrase should read: "cooperate within the framework of the United Nations Charter." This was agreed to, and the problem was solved.[a]

The above example relates to a period after the original Aid Agreement was concluded, and anticipates some of the later developments—with which I shall deal later. I refer to it in this context mainly to illustrate Burma's sensitivity to

[a]*Editor's note*: Although this paragraph refers to "renewal" of the ECA agreement, what actually happened was that the new U.S. aid legislation (the Mutual Security Act of 1951) required a new agreement. As the author indicates, this took some time to work out. Because aid could not continue without the new agreement, aid to Burma was actually suspended for several weeks in early 1952 while an agreed phraseology was being worked out.

the political implications of an economic aid agreement with the United States, and how a delicate issue was solved by mutual understanding of the political sensitivities and the particular conditions prevailing in each country.

The Final Agreement

All issues being thus finally settled, although the interests of the United States and Burma—and even the objectives of offering and receiving aid—were not always the same, the first Economic Co-operation Agreement with Burma was signed on 13 September 1950.

The Griffin Mission Approach

We were impressed by the uncommon perspicacity of the Griffin Mission—and those who continued the negotiations for an Agreement after it left—in analyzing the situation in Burma, by the elements they picked out as most important for reaching a rapport and by the indications they gave as to what factors they would emphasize in order to establish such rapport. These were of course embodied in clear and unambiguous terms in the Mission's Report to the State Department in Report No. 3 of May 1950 which refers to Burma. We did not know at the time what their actual observations and recommendations were, for the document was classified; but now that it has been declassified, it is remarkable how close we were in our interpretation of the realistic and sympathetic attitude of the Mission despite the many areas of possible misunderstanding of the implications of each other's political motivations.

The above is clear from the observations of the editor of this volume in the preliminary chapters. The very first sentence of the Preface recognizes that the Griffin Mission was sent out "with a frankly political purpose," in reaction to the "Communist defeat of Chiang Kai-Shek's forces on the Chinese mainland." The other sections also recognize that the interest of the United States lay in bolstering the economic strength of the peoples of that area in order to retard the expansion of Communist influence in Southeast Asia—that the United States would have to attempt to maintain a kind of military balance. This was clear both from the visit of Ambassador Jessup which preceded the Mission, and the inclusion of two Defense Department officers on the Mission when it visited Indochina, Malaya, Singapore, and Burma—the countries considered to be most directly threatened. But our attitude to the Communist regime in China was different from that of the United States; and our interest lay in cultivating the closest possible relations with them, if not from a naive belief that she would not end up with expansionist aims (and some top leaders believed she would) but from the realization that no power on earth could save Burma if Communist China wanted to expand southwards, because of her long land frontier with us; and that the only result of "provoking" China would be another devastation equal in severity to, if not more than, what we had already suffered from World War II. As indicated earlier in this chapter, this lay at the very basis of our relations with Communist China. We did not of course care to put the position in such bland terms to foreign missions and visitors, but the Griffin Mission got the message quickly. This fact is clearly proved by the following two extracts:

1. The Mission's Report on Burma states at page 189, under Section VIII, "Factors Limiting Amount, Kind, or Speed of Economic and Technical Aid":

... [they] are strongly opposed to making any commitment, or accepting any aid that implies any commitment, to line up with the Western powers in an anti-Communist camp. It may, for this reason, be necessary to avoid United States aid to certain projects that, desirable as they may be on economic grounds, may be interpreted as involving an anti-Communist motive. An example of such a project would be aid in the repair and development of airports in Burma which might be misinterpreted as potential U.S. air bases.

2. The editor of this volume further amplifies the point by the following statement at page 11 in Chapter 1:

In Indochina (where the Viet Minh were battling the French and Bao Dai's government, and where there was already a functioning United States military advisory group) and in Singapore and Malaya (where a separate Communist-led revolt was in full swing) there were important military factors to consider in planning possible aid projects, and the military representatives participated in discussing these. In Burma, it became apparent that their contribution was over-balanced by the suspicions their presence engendered in the host government, and Mr. Griffin cabled the Department of State requesting termination of their participation in the Mission. They left the Mission in the middle of its visit to Burma.

*Recommendations Concerning Administration of
Aid and Operational Attitudes*

The sensitivity of the Griffin Mission to Burma's political susceptibilities is reflected even in its recommendations regarding the organization for field administration and arrangements for operations, and the attitudes of the experts and technicians supplied under the aid program. Thus it states at page 192 of its Report on Burma:

The sensitivity of Burmans to the idea that political considerations might be involved in economic or technical aid programs should be taken into account in deciding the form of the organization set up in Burma to administer these programs.

And while the Mission recognized that there will have to be "a single U.S. aid representative to negotiate project agreements, discuss general aid policies with the government and with the U.S. diplomatic mission, provide general supervision and evaluation of aid personnel and programs, and carry certain administrative responsibilities . . . this official should be a Coordinator of Economic Cooperation Activities (CECA) . . . not a *Chief of Economic Mission* [italics mine]." This particular recommendation was not however accepted; the U.S. aid program was headed by a Chief of Mission, and it worked satisfactorily. The recommendation that "it would be desirable to set up a joint body with the Government of Burma to set policies for or actually direct certain aid activities, if this could be done without suggesting undesirable U.S. control" was accepted by both Governments. The program was administered jointly by a Burmese body called the Burma Economic Aid Committee (BEAC) consisting of all the principal Secretaries to the Government whose Departments would most need the aid available—Agriculture, Transport and Communications, Education, etc.—with the author, in his capacity as Finance Secretary, as Chairman, and STEM; the author taking the chair at all meetings. This joint operation also worked smoothly and without major disagreements on any point.

The recommendations made by the Griffin Mission in regard to the operational methods and approaches of the experts and technicians supplied under the program not only took full account of Burmese political and administrative susceptibilities, but anticipated many of the principles evolved by the United Nations and its specialized Agencies as regards the operational methods and approaches of their experts many years later through experience of the operation of the world's most wide-spread program of technical assistance. It is a measure of how quick the Mission was in grasping the essentials for the success of a program which was not only novel but involved many changes and adaptations in traditional attitudes.

The Mission's recommendation that technical assistance alone would get nowhere, and must be combined with adequate supplies of equipment and machinery in order to produce an impact and visible results, was also one of its best proposals. The United Nations learned this lesson and applied it effectively to its technical assistance programs only when the Special Fund was set up in 1959—nearly ten years after the initiation of its original program. A main reason was of course the quite inadequate financial resources it could muster at the start, and the urgent needs and requests of governments for purely technical advice and assistance covering a wide range of activities in every country.

The Working of the Program in Burma, 1950-53

Though the scope of this book carries the working of the ECA program through the first year in countries where they were initiated following the recommendations of the Griffin Mission, I have chosen to cover the years 1950 to 1953 for two principal reasons. Firstly, the program in Burma was terminated in 1953 due to reasons I shall describe later, so that this period constitutes one complete phase of ECA operations in Burma. Secondly, the program gathered momentum, and many outstanding issues of policies, programs, approaches, and techniques took a year to crystallize, so that actual operations (with a few exceptions) did not start in earnest until the end of the first year. This coverage will thus give a more realistic picture of the effort as a whole than concentrating on the first year alone.

In a short chapter, covering a vital and widespread program of policies and operations with ramifications spreading into several important spheres not only of Burmese-American relationships but also of the techniques and attitudes of mind relating to what is now universally recognized as a vital instrument of assistance to the development of underdeveloped countries, one can deal meaningfully with only the high spots. In Burma, for example, the three-year program, small though it was in terms of dollars spent, covered almost every field of reconstruction and development, ranging from $38,469 for one project to over $4 million for the rehabilitation of the Port of Rangoon—Burma's main outlet to the world—and two or three other smaller but important outports. Another project—Economic Planning and General Engineering Services—cost approximately $2 million in foreign exchange alone, and an almost equal sum in local currency during a period of two years. It was as I have said a unique experiment in the world of economic planning and implementation, for it brought together for the first time two consulting firms in the engineering and mining fields and one in the field of economics, working as a team. A program of this range and variety would require a book in itself if fully dealt with, even though the period covered was short.

Perhaps the first question of an overall nature that comes to one's mind—looking backwards after nearly twenty years of intensive effort by both bi-lateral and multi-lateral agencies and the wide experience that has accumulated in the process—is whether better results would have been achieved if the available funds were concentrated in a very limited area or spread over almost every sphere of activity in the field of reconstruction and development. The answer depends in my view largely on the conditions of each country, the urgency of needs in each sphere or spheres, the administrative and technical manpower available locally to work together with the U.S. experts and technicians and—above all—the objectives of the aid offered in relation to each country. So far as Burma was concerned, our appetite was so insatiable—following the extensive demands for reconstruction in almost every sphere of social, economic, and educational activity and the extremely urgent but unorthodox need for the moral rehabilitation of youth by weaning them away from the path of violence to one of peace and useful employment after we had turned the corner in insurgent activity—that we had to make a choice. The funds necessary for both were just not there. So the decision to apply the available funds in order to restore the prewar facilities as soon as possible was in my view the best for Burma. The average cost of each project was only a few hundred thousand dollars, but five—the rehabilitation of ports; agriculture and related activities; the provision of engineering; and economic services, both advisory and operational; public health and education—ranged in dollar costs from just over $1 million to $4 million.[26] The danger in spreading available funds thinly over a large area and concentrating on reconstruction of war-damaged facilities lay in restoring the economy on the old, prewar basis and failure to take advantage of modern technology. This was amply protected against in Burma, not only through the three consulting firms but also through many individual experts who brought new knowledge and experience, and some of whom at least had an impact. Perhaps our one failure was in not choosing a single project, supported by highly qualified technicians and new and modern machinery, which would have produced a visible impact within a relatively short period. The attempt we made was a failure. We realized the importance of choosing a single project which would have an immediate and visible impact, but in view of the long delivery dates quoted for new machinery in those days we decided to purchase a second-hand dredge that was immediately available in Japan, and were advised by our experts that though very old it could be repaired to do an effective job—under proper supervision. The port of Akyab [now Sittwe] in Arakan on the west coast of Burma had been badly silted up due to lack of regular dredging during the war, and we felt that if this dredge—which later was named the *Irrawaddy*—could clean up the port quickly and restore it to its prewar position of an important port, second only to Rangoon (like the ports of Bassein and Moulmein), the immediate visible impact we hoped for would be achieved and it would be a practical demonstration of the usefulness of the contribution the ECA program could make to Burma. So the dredge was purchased, but unfortunately the repairs were so badly done and the supervision so casual and poor, that when it arrived in Burma and was put to work at the Akyab port, it broke down constantly and never operated for more than a few hours at a time, and then only sporadically. Being a very old dredge, its sight also had an extremely unfortunate effect psychologically on the people of Akyab, who expected to see an example of modern American technology in the form of a shining new dredge. The *Irrawaddy* not only became an eye-sore but a joke, and gave the ECA program a bad start psychologically. We bought a new dredge from Germany later and used it in Rangoon—this time efficiently and without being an eye-sore. But the bad taste given by the *Irrawaddy* lingered; its adverse effects were never eliminated—being the first piece of large machinery delivered under the ECA program—and it was played up fully by a critical press.

The second highlight was the combination of expert advice with substantial supplies of plant and machinery, which I have dealt with already and will not repeat.

The third highlight was the cooperative and close understanding between the Burmese directing organ—BEAC—and the United States agency STEM, which smoothed over innumerable difficulties by informal discussions and other unobtrusive means. The atmosphere of understanding, cooperation, and cordiality could not have been closer.

The fourth highlight—with which also I have dealt with in some detail—is the keen perceptiveness of both the Griffin Mission and those responsible for subsequent negotiations and adjustments. Without it, and the many concessions made by each side to the political susceptibilities of the other party, there might have been no ECA program in Burma.

The last highlight was a failure—the failure to win the full cooperation of the public and particularly the press. Frankly, we did not discover a way of combining American ideas and approaches to publicity for the program with Burmese approaches and ideas and thus of ensuring favorable reception. So far as the local press was concerned, an unfortunate incident made them hostile from the beginning. Immediately after the program was initiated, they requested funds for setting up a Press Institute, the money to be spent mainly on a building and a small amount for equipment and literature. This was turned down by the Burmese Government after careful consideration at the highest levels, on the grounds firstly that the bulk of the expenditure (i.e., for the building) would have to be in local currency, the difficulties in respect of which I have already described in detail; and secondly that it was not a reconstruction or development project in its true sense. Perhaps we were wrong, and did not attach sufficient importance to its psychological impact on an important element in a democratic society, namely a free press, but we just did not have the funds, and the demands for physical, moral and educational rehabilitation were overwhelming. We could not meet even a large part of its local currency requirements, given our financial and budgetary position and the restrictive currency system. As a result many members of the press developed and maintained an attitude highly critical of the whole aid program and seemed to emphasize its failings while overlooking its successes and its promise.

The End of the First Phase, 1950-1953

The aid program initiated in Burma following the Griffin Mission recommendations came abruptly to an end on 30 June 1953, at the request of the Government of Burma. It was a deep disappointment to both sides, for as I have said the Burmans had accepted the American sincerity of purpose in giving aid without strings and recognized their superiority of technology. The start was not easy, as is apparent from the course of negotiations I have described. But a rapport had been established. We had begun to understand each other's approach and the reasons for certain positions taken. The program itself had gathered momentum, and goods and services had begun to flow through the pipeline.

It was the first time that the two countries had drawn together in economic cooperation. The United States of America was a dreamland to most Burmans before World War II. We shared many common ideals and many common human characteristics—an openness of heart and lack of formality in personal dealings not the least amongst them—but our contacts with that far-away land were few. It was Herbert Hoover who as a young Engineer/Manager had restored the Bawdwin lead and silver mines of Burma to a predominant position as a world producer in the 1920's; and it was the tough, practical minded American drillers who provided the core of the oil industry in Burma and helped establish its relatively important position as an exporter of petroleum and its products. Though contacts were few, we were thus not entirely strangers to American technical and managerial skills. And when after World War II all other developed and industrialized countries were struggling for their own survival, it was the United States alone which provided Burma and other underdeveloped countries with the hope of rapid economic recovery and growth, and bringing modern technology within their reach. So it was with optimism that we welcomed the Griffin Mission, and its leader and members proved themselves to be a perfect team of Ambassadors and harbingers of hope through their understanding, perspicacity and quick grasp of Burmese susceptibilities.

So when the end came in 1953, it was a disappointment for more reasons than one. The frustration was all the greater, for the reason for termination was entirely political. Burma's action was a reaction against what she considered to be American support of the Kuomintang troops that were retreating from China after their defeat by the Communists and about 12,000 of whom under General Li Mi remained on Burmese territory in defiance of the Burmese Government. Burma pleaded with the United States to apply pressure on Formosa to withdraw the troops, but got no satisfaction. We believed—and those in authority, particularly the Army, knew—that the Central Intelligence Agency (CIA) was actively supporting them. The Government decided that she could not both accept economic aid from the United States and tolerate her direct support of a foreign armed group operating within her territory and gave notice of termination of the ECA program with effect from 30 June 1953.

That the Burmans had their facts right is amply evident from the voluminous evidence Burma produced at the United Nations. She took what came to be known officially as the KMT question to the eighth session of the General Assembly held in September 1953. Her mood of frustration and of despair that the question would not be solved in that forum is clear from the eloquent and admirably restrained tone of the speeches of the leader of her Delegation, U Myint Thein. The tragedy of the situation was enhanced by the fact that the CIA was acting on its own authority—only the Secretary of State John Foster Dulles outside that authority having been apprised of the CIA activity. Knowledge of the project was so closely held within the CIA that it even escaped the notice of Robert Amory, the deputy director of intelligence.

The Burmese mood of frustration with kind but meaningless words of sympathy was described picturesquely but with sadness by U Myint Thein at the meeting of the First Committee of the United Nations General Assembly held on 5 November 1953, when he concluded one of his speeches by expressing "deep appreciation for the words of kindness showered on him by the Committee. One way of killing a cat was by smothering it with cream. He hoped that he and the Burmese item would be spared that fate."[27]

The full story of the tragedy, resulting from the fact that the CIA was acting as a government within the government without even the knowledge of the State Department (except the Secretary of State) and from the State Department in consequence keeping the United States Ambassadors abroad not only ignorant of the facts but actually giving them false assurances and thus landing them in many awkward situations, was revealed subsequently by two American journalists, David Wise and Thomas B. Ross, in their book *The Invisible Government*.[28] The following account of the Burma case is taken from that book.

When William J. Sebald was appointed as Ambassador to Burma in 1952, he knew of the KMT situation in Burma and the dangers it held. On his way to Burma via Washington, he demanded assurances from his superiors that the CIA was not supporting the Chinese Nationalist troops in Burma. He was told emphatically that the United States was in no way involved. So was Chester Bowles, Ambassador to India, who conveyed the same assurances to Jawarharlal Nehru and who in turn publicly stated that, on Bowles' word, he had convinced himself that the United States were not supporting the Nationalist guerrillas.

But the Burmans—especially the Army—were not to be deceived, for they had concrete proof of CIA support. Ambassador Sebald on his part dutifully conveyed the State Department's assurances to the Burmese Government, while at the same time regularly warning Washington that the troops threatened Burma's very existence as a parliamentary democracy which was friendly to the West. All he got in reply was repeated assurance from the State Department that the United States was not involved.

How embarrassing the situation was for Ambassador Sebald, and how great the potential threat to U.S.-Burma relations, can be gauged from the following incident described in *The Invisible Government*.[29]

General Ne Win, who as Chief of Staff of the Burmese Army was leading the battle against the guerrillas, arrived at a diplomatic function fresh from a meeting with his field commanders. He confronted Ambassador Sebald and angrily demanded action against the Nationalist troops. When Sebald started to launch into his standard disclaimer of United States involvement, the General cut him short. "Mr. Ambassador," he asserted firmly, "I have it cold. If I were you, I'd just keep quiet."

So the tremendous good will that the Griffin Mission built up in Burma was not only cut short abruptly, almost as soon as its physical expressions began to manifest themselves, but the friendship of Burma towards the United States, her faith in democracy and even in the United Nations when great power interests were involved, was threatened by the power of a "government within the government" in the American system.

Epilogue

The epilogue was, however, happier. W. Averell Harriman, the Assistant Secretary of State for the Far East, under the new Kennedy Administration, reversed the Dulles policy with President Kennedy's full backing. He directed that Taipeh be firmly impressed with the fact that such ventures as the KMT guerrilla activities in Burma would no longer be tolerated by the United States. The Nationalist Chinese quickly announced on March 5, 1961, that they would do their utmost to evacuate the remaining guerrillas. But it had little effect on Burmese suspicions about United States policy, no doubt because of the dilly-dallying that had gone on for years and also because the announcement came after the Burmese Army had on its own driven into Thailand and Laos, by January 1961, the 4,000 or so of the Nationalist guerrillas who remained deployed in Burma despite repeated assurances of withdrawal. And these 4,000 were the best of the KMT troops who remained on Burmese soil.

The epilogue, I said, was happier, because the success of the Burmese Army against the guerrillas and the confidence it acquired in its own strength did not entirely disrupt Burmese-American relations, either economic or political. Economic aid to Burma was resumed in 1956.[30]

This aid however took the form largely of long-term loans, at low interest rates, repayable in either kyats or dollars, and P.L. 480 sales of American surplus commodities. It lasted till 1963 after which no new dollar aid or surplus commodity sales have been requested by the Government of Burma. The total commitment during this period amounted to over $70 million.

New York, October 7, 1968

10 Needs for United States Economic and Technical Aid in Thailand [1950]

Summary

1. Thailand is a constitutional monarchy, although in practice the present government operates in an authoritarian manner. The present political situation appears stable under the regime of Premier Phibun, which came to power in November 1947. Thailand's most obvious danger comes from the possibility of Communist control by way of the large and powerful Chinese minority. There is a well-organized Chinese Communist party in Thailand and a small covert Thai Communist party. Special areas of potential trouble are the northeast provinces adjoining areas of Indochina controlled by the Vietminh, and the southern provinces, inhabited by 700,000 Malay-Moslems. Control of Thailand's large rice surplus would be a great asset to the Communist Government of China; and the Thais, if they felt themselves alone, might come to terms with the Communists (Section I).

2. In 1949 Thailand exported 1.2 million tons of rice, a factor of great significance to the food-deficit countries of Asia. Other exports included tin, rubber, and teak. The resources in large areas of Thailand are underdeveloped. To develop these, Thailand needs technical assistance and capital equipment. Thailand's finances are in good condition (Sections II and III).

3. Nearly 90 percent of the population is engaged in agriculture. Thailand's agricultural policy, therefore, seeks to improve rice production and increase its export. In the public-health field, there is need for more medical facilities and for additional trained personnel. The educational system in Thailand lacks trained teachers, equipment, and operating funds. The illiteracy rate is estimated at about 50 percent. Thailand lacks the trained administrative personnel to bring its government and economic activities up to modern standards (Section IV).

4. Because of its central position in Southeast Asia, Bangkok is the location of a number of regional offices of U.N. agencies. Thailand has been the object of a number of U.N. studies and specialized missions (Section V).

5. The U.S. Government has provided technical assistance to Thailand in several fields (Section VI).

6. It is recommended that a technical and economic aid program to Thailand be

Report No. 4 of the United States Economic Survey Mission to Southeast Asia, prepared during and following the Mission's visit to Bangkok, April 4-12, 1950; and first printed in Washington, May, 1950.

223

provided, amounting to $11,420,000 (Section VII). This would cover aid in the following categories:

Agriculture	$2,830,000
Public Health	3,065,000
Education	993,000
Industry, Transport and Communications	4,532,000

7. Limitations on the amount or speed of aid include the lack of trained technicians and officials in Thailand, and the language barrier (Section VIII).
8. With respect to the proposed program, there is less economic urgency in Thailand than political urgency. As a country that has come out solidly for the West, Thailand needs prompt evidence that its partnership is valued (Section IX).
9. The Government is rather firmly supported by its people. It should gain strength, of course, from aid-program publicity. Because of the pro-Western sentiment in Thailand, emphasis can be placed on the U.S. role (Section X).
10. Aid projects should be covered by detailed agreements. A small economic mission attached to the American Embassy should coordinate and supervise U.S. aid activities, although U.S. technicians made available to the Thailand Government should be directly responsible to that Government's appropriate departments. The establishment of a joint policy-determining body to consider objectives of the program and its operation may be desirable at some future stage (Section XI).

I. Summary of Political Conditions

Thailand is a constitutional monarchy operating in the form of a democratic parliamentary regime largely patterned after that of Great Britain. This fundamental system was established in 1932 by means of a coup d'état sponsored by a group of young military officers plus a group of young, Western-educated, democratic politicians. Since 1932, the course of Thai political history can be fairly described in terms of the ups and downs of these two cliques, which split shortly after the coup d'état. The leader of the military group is the present Premier, Field Marshal Phibun Songgram. Leaders of other political groups are Nai Pridi Phanomyong, who become Premier after leading the wartime pro-allied resistance movement, and Khuang Aphaiwong. Through all these changes, the fundamental parliamentary form based on a constitutional monarchy has never been abandoned, although in practice the present government operates in an authoritarian manner.

The present regime, which assumed power following a coup d'état in November 1947, has been under the direct leadership of Premier Phibun since April 1948. A new constitution drawn up by a constituent assembly and approved by Parliament incorporates the necessary framework of a democratically controlled parliamentary government, except for the provision for an appointed upper house. Basic civil liberties are guaranteed. In June 1949, Premier Phibun's Government resigned in compliance with the requirement of the new constitution and submitted itself to a general parliamentary debate which culminated in a two-to-one vote of confidence for the Government.

Following the accession to power of the present Government, there has been a period of control over opposing political groups. However, this policy has on occasion been modified in attempts to mollify the opposition.

There are two principal active or potential Thai opposition political groups. (1) The conservative Democrats, a loyal opposition strongly represented in Parliament and inclined to support the Monarchy and landed interests, are anti-Communist and pro-Western. (2) The supporters of Pridi Phanomyong, consisting of some liberals, a few Socialists, some opportunists and some members of the wartime pro-American underground, are predominantly non-Communist and not hostile to the United States. However, this group is the one which the Communists are most likely to approach. It is at present weak. The Government appears firmly situated, and neither of the two opposition parties is likely seriously to threaten the Government in the near future. The Government has made some efforts, partly successful, to incorporate certain elements from these rival groups in order to broaden the base of its support, and, when possible, the Government probably would not be averse to forming a coalition in which the military clique retained effective control.

Thailand's most obvious danger comes from the large and economically powerful Chinese minority, numbering some 3,000,000. In addition to controlling an important segment of the economy, these Chinese tend to support whatever government is in power in China and are susceptible to pressure through families and business associations in China now dominated by the Chinese Communists. The Government of Thailand is thus faced with a most serious problem by reason of the size, strength, influence and susceptibility to Communist pressure, of 3,000,000 Chinese residents.

There is a well-organized Chinese Communist party in Thailand, the hard core of which consists of several thousand members. In addition there are known to be many thousands of Chinese Communist sympathizers. Chinese Communist activities in Thailand are devoted (1) to welding all Chinese laborers into a strong, disciplined unit which could be used to paralyze the rice-milling and other industries, as well as the country's internal and export trade; (2) to increasing the flow of propaganda, largely directed against the United States, through the medium of controlled Chinese newspapers, pamphlets, and other publications indoctrinating the Chinese Communists and through control of Chinese schools indoctrinating children to make them effective instruments for Communist activities; (3) to extorting funds from the Chinese community as is now being done through the sale of Chinese Communist Government Victory Bonds; (4) to gaining control of the Chinese Chamber of Commerce (which has been successfully achieved) and other Chinese associations; and (5) to winning over the Chinese community by means of blandishments and intimidations. In all these activities, Chinese Communists, assisted by Soviet agents attached to the U.S.S.R. Legation at Bangkok, are having substantial success. The objective, namely, to gain political and economic control of Thailand with its foodstuffs and other raw materials, is plain to see—as is the general strategy.

There has been established a small covert Thai Communist Party, principally controlled by Chinese Communists. Within recent months the Chinese Communists in Thailand have also given particular attention to winning over the Thai people. The Thai are not naturally susceptible to communism per se, for traditional and religious reasons, and are inclined to be antagonistic to the Chinese. However, the propaganda being fed to the Thai people through the medium of several Communist-controlled Thai newspapers is not without its appeal, since it urges acquiescence to communism as the easiest course of action. There are some Thai who, although not Communist, are, because of their desire for peace and because of their lack of understanding of Communist tactics and discipline, susceptible to appeals resembling the Popular Front technique. In the event of Communist control of Thailand, some of these people would probably be included in the Communist government of Thailand.

A much lesser but potentially important threat lies in the minority of approximately 50,000 Vietnamese in the northeast provinces, nearly all of whom support the Communist-controlled Vietminh (which is engaged in revolution in Indochina) not so much because of ideological conviction but because of a desire to support a nationalistic effort to evict the French from Indochina.

Another important area of unrest is in the Thai southern provinces, where approximately 700,000 Malay-Moslems reside. These Moslems have certain genuine grievances against the Government in Bangkok, and there is known to be some sentiment for regional autonomy. These facts, coupled with the juxtaposition of the southern provinces to Malaya,[a] afford ground for serious concern about this area.

There is also the great temptation presented to Communist China to obtain control of the largest exportable rice surplus currently being produced in Southeast Asia. This surplus may well be a compelling factor in Communist strategy in view of famine conditions in China. It should also be remembered that an effort to obtain this rice in order to save the lives of millions of Chinese would have strong kinship and political appeal to the Chinese minority in Thailand, most of whom have relatives in China.

Moreover, not without reason, many Thai officials refuse to accept the view that the Communists will ignore Thailand until after the subjugation of either Burma or Indochina or both. They reason that the Communists might endeavor to take Thailand first to obtain its rice and split Southeast Asia in the process.

Under the impact of the factors above, if they resulted in rapid deterioration of conditions, the danger might arise that the Thai, feeling themselves alone and believing a Communist victory to be inevitable, might decide that wisdom is the

---

[a]Where extensive revolutionary activity was then being carried on under the leadership of Communists of Chinese extraction and loyalties (see Chapter 7—Ed.)

better part of valor and attempt to come to terms with the Communists on superficially desirable terms. There is a precedent for such behavior in the Thai record during World War II. Thailand's success in maintaining her independence amidst colonial imperialism has been based in part on a clever policy of playing rivals against each other and making final decisions on the basis of an estimate of who is likely to win. If the Thai believe that Western (and particularly American) protestations of sympathy and support are not to be backed up by aid, they may begin to consider and explore possibilities of a truce or accommodation with the Communists. The fact that such an accommodation would not be genuinely in Thailand's interest is irrelevant. Substantial American aid now would certainly lessen such a possibility, particularly if coupled with aid to the present friendly Governments of Indochina and Burma. However, it should be emphasized that, in spite of the uncertainties facing them, the determination of the Government to defend its independence is indicated by the overt measures already taken and by its open self-alignment with the West (as seen in recognizing Bao Dai).

The absence of Western colonialism in Thailand has resulted in the absence of the extreme anti-Western passions which inflame much of the Far East, thus making it much easier for the Thais to cooperate with the United States politically than it is for some other governments. Thus, economic aid to Thailand can be a relatively simple, politically clear-cut project, involving no contradictory foreign policies and involving no complicated relations with a metropolitan or former colonial power.

Finally, our encouragement of Thailand is in accord with our general foreign policy, because Thailand is an independent, stable, and progressive country, which sincerely desires to align itself with anti-Communist nations.

II. Summary of Economic Conditions

Among the nations of Southeast Asia, Thailand occupies at present a unique position. Economically underdeveloped and underpopulated, yet with a comparatively stable government and an economy oriented toward the West, basic conditions are unusually favorable for the effective improvement of production, standards of living, and foreign trade.

The basis of the economy of Thailand is agriculture, with rice as the most important crop both domestically and in foreign trade. Despite increased domestic consumption resulting from population growth, Thailand exported 1.2 million tons of rice in 1949, largely to other Asiatic countries. Other major exports include tin, rubber, and teak. Opportunities also exist for the increased production and export of many products, including tapioca, shellacs, vegetable oils, hides and skins, and certain drugs. In return, Thailand imports all her required capital goods and large quantities of fuel and manufactured consumer goods—petroleum products, textiles, electrical products, kitchenware, and similar items.

The maintenance and increase of Thailand's exportable agricultural surpluses are of major importance to maintain political stability in Asiatic countries dependent on food imports. At the same time, increased agricultural and mineral exports offer the most immediate opportunity to Thailand to pay for an increase in the inflow of capital and consumer goods urgently needed for the further development of her economy and the increase of living standards.

At present, resources in large areas of the country are under-utilized due to lack of transportation and power. Existing facilities were in many cases severely damaged during the Japanese occupation and have not been fully restored. The damage to capital equipment and the inadequate amount of electric power also seriously handicap attempts to increase the domestic production of light consumer goods, which would reduce foreign currency requirements and make more effective the utilization of local resources and labor. Malaria and other epidemic diseases sharply reduce the effectiveness of labor in major agricultural areas. Similarly, inadequate basic education and vocational training limit both the immediate effectiveness and the ambition of a large segment of the population. All of these conditions can be improved, some of them dramatically, by the assistance of U.S. technicians working cooperatively with the Thai Government.

The Government of Thailand has recognized its need for technical assistance to improve economic planning, operations and development, and earnestly desires assistance. A number of U.S. and U.N. technical missions have visited Thailand at the request of the Government to advise on various economic and financial problems. The Government has, at its own expense, provided considerable aid to Thai students for technical training abroad. From our conversations with the National Economic Council, established by the Thai Government to plan a long-range program of rehabilitation and economic development, it appears clear that U.S. technical advisers would be welcomed and would have an immediate economic effect, both within Thailand and in increasing the flow of Thai exports to other critical Asiatic areas.

In addition to technical assistance, Thailand needs capital equipment in the fields of irrigation, transportation, electric power, communications, and light industry. Such equipment can be installed and used most effectively under the planning and direction of U.S. technicians. The capacity of the country to purchase or finance capital equipment in the immediate future is limited. Whereas in 1948 and 1949 the Thai Government had a surplus of dollar funds, that surplus was due primarily to ECA dollar purchases of large quantities of rice for China and Korea. These purchases have stopped. Although estimates vary, all agree that in 1950 Thailand dollar earnings will not permit her to pay for or to finance the volume of capital goods and services urgently needed for speedy rehabilitation and development; however, by borrowing and possibly by use of some part of her more than $200 million of gold and foreign-exchange holdings (see next section), Thailand may be able to obtain a substantial amount of capital equipment. The United Kingdom and Japan can supply some capital goods, but these alternative sources of supply are limited, both in quality and particularly in terms of slow delivery schedules.

In summary, this Mission wishes to re-emphasize that Thailand possesses both the resources and the internal stability to utilize aid effectively and that the resultant increase in production will both afford a strong underpinning to a free and friendly government in the critical heart of Southeast Asia and make possible an important flow of food and raw materials wherewith to strengthen Japan, India, Ceylon, Malaya, and the Philippines. The political problem posed by the drive of Communist imperialism in Asia is immediate, and only immediate aid can be politically effective. It is for this reason that we recommend most strongly the initiation of the following program of technical and material assistance within 4 months.

III. Summary of Financial Conditions

For the fiscal year 1950, the Thai annual budget estimates provide for an expenditure of 1,949,366,000 baht,[b] to be met from current revenues, an increase of some 20 percent above similar estimates for 1949. In addition, the 1950 budget provides for emergency capital expenditures of 521 million baht to be met from Treasury reserves or loans, an amount almost identical with that provided in the 1949 budget. The latter category includes appropriations for such undertakings as the following: establishment of new industries (gunny-bag, paper, weaving, distillery), improvement of civil aviation facilities, rehabilitation of transportation, new irrigation works, highway construction, electric power rehabilitation, special aids to agriculture.

During the past year, the volume of notes in circulation has remained stable, with no substantial increase between January and October 1949. During the same period, however, the reserve position of the Bank of Thailand has been further improved by an increase in gold holdings from 769 million baht in January 1949 to 976 million in October 1949, and a similar increase in foreign exchange holdings from 770 million baht to 1,086 million baht. As of mid-April 1950, the Bank of Thailand held gold valued at 1,477 million baht ($118 millions), of which $42 millions was earmarked gold held in Japan but released by SCAP. At the present moment, the Bank of Thailand has a reserve of more than 80 percent gold and foreign exchange against currency in circulation.

The Bank of Thailand presently holds government securities valued at 370 million baht as a part of its currency reserve, a reduction or more than 50 percent in the past 12 months. An additional 139 million baht in government securities is held by the Bank against government deposits of 441 million baht.

During the 12-months' period October 1948–October 1949, the internal floating debt of Thailand, comprised of Treasury bonds and bills, was reduced from 555 million baht to 456 million baht.

---

[b]$156,000,000 at the official rate of 12.5 baht to $1 U.S. For many transactions, the legal free market rate of about 22 baht to $1 U.S. is applicable.

The foreign-currency debt of the Government of Thailand is small and has been reduced during the last fiscal year. Total outstanding sterling loans as of October 31, 1949, amounted to £1,636,550, a reduction of some £350,000 from the previous year. During the same 12-months' period, an outstanding rupee credit of Rs. 45,727,332 was entirely repaid, and outstanding dollar credits were reduced by nearly $500,000 to an outstanding total of $5,733,644 (of which some $4,000,000 is expected to be established as a Fulbright fund). Thus the total external debt requiring foreign-exchange servicing amounts at present to little more than $10 million (and the Fulbright fund, when established, will not require foreign-exchange servicing). The World Bank has at present under consideration a sizable dollar credit to Thailand for the improvement of transportation and port facilities and expansion of irrigation and electric-power facilities.

From the foregoing it is apparent that Thai finances are in good condition. The baht is stable both domestically and in foreign trade; currency reserves against note issue are unusually high; and at current rates of expenditure, revenues bear a reasonable relation to expenditures. Budgetary flexibility is, however, not great for the meeting of extraordinary expenditures out of increased revenue. By far the greatest portion of revenues is from indirect taxes, primarily on imports and exports, and almost the entire government supply of foreign exchange arises from its control over the export of rice, tin, and rubber.

IV. Urgent Economic Problems

A. Agriculture

1. General. The economy of Thailand is dominated by her agriculture which, in turn, is largely dependent upon one crop—rice. Nearly 90 percent of the population of 18 million is engaged in agriculture (mostly rice farming) and fishing. Rice occupies over 90 percent of the total crop land and accounts for well over half of the value of Thailand's exports. Other agricultural crops are rubber, cotton, tobacco, copra, fruit, and vegetables, of which rubber is the only important export crop. Teak is also exported.

Although the most obvious feature of Thailand's agricultural policy concerns the improvement of rice production and its export, the welfare of the farmer also commands the sincere attention of the Government. Previous and present measures for the aid of the farmer have dealt chiefly with the construction of irrigation systems for the farmers' use and with Government-sponsored cooperatives for the extension of credit, for the procurement of production aids, and for cooperative marketing. The irrigation systems are stabilizing natural conditions of water supply and have resulted in increased stability of rice production. The cooperative program has not been generally successful in reaching a large part of the population, in spite of Government subsidies, but the Government is determined to extend and perfect it.

Improvement in agricultural conditions requires strengthening and coordination of existing educational research and extension institutions. They are the only media through which the cooperatives of the country have a chance of becoming effective. Simultaneous and coordinated programs for the testing and adoption of improved practices, tools, and plant and animal materials, the retraining of agricultural officers and the training of new agricultural personnel for public service, the extension of technical and other assistance to farm operators and the eventual development of a comprehensive system of rural education will help the farmers to understand and respect Government policies. These steps are necessary to prepare the rural citizen for the responsibilities of land ownership and for financial support by the Government. He will be capable of participating in the formation and operation of socio-economic institutions such as credit, consumer, and producer cooperatives to raise his own level of living; and to bring about greater social, economic, and political stability within his community and his country.

The Thai Government's policy of aiding the citizen and giving him a greater stake in the national economy is sincere. Its programs to accomplish this have been faltering and in many respects misguided. The effectiveness of its rehabilitation is limited by insufficient experience at the top, by inadequately trained public servants at all levels, and by the present shortage of certain equipment and materials needed to spark urgent economic programs, which will make possible the initiation and development of desirable social and technical reforms. This emergency requires both material and technical aid.

2. Criteria for Selection of Emergency Agricultural Projects.

a) *Stimulation of direct benefits to producers and handlers of agricultural commodities.* Immediate economic assistance should concentrate on projects which will permit early improvement in the national economy, bring early economic return to the largest possible number of individual farmers, and generate confidence among producers and handlers of agricultural commodities in the objectives of the national agricultural programs and in the governmental personnel administering them.

b) *Improvement of administrative level of competence.* Professional training and experience in agriculture in Thailand has been more academic than practical. The agricultural production and processing in the country is greatly limited by the lack of competent public servants capable of planning and guiding agricultural improvement. Emergency assistance programs should be designed to increase as rapidly as possible the competence of national technicians at all levels from the administrator and professional to the village worker.

c) *Organization of public services.* The administration of public services is very diffuse. The activities of civil departments of the ministry are uncoordinated. There is also little coordination between education, investigation, and extension. The emergency aid projects should be selected to promote the organization of national public services into coordinated institutions which will have within them the factors of growth and increasing prestige.

d) *Relationship of agricultural development to industrial, health, educational, and transport projects.* The agricultural programs must not only be coordinated within themselves (i.e. research, education, and extension coordinated with agricultural production and marketing) but also must be related to other services such as health and education and to economic programs in such fields as transport and industry.

B. Current and Long-Term Health Problems

The physical plant and equipment for health services of Thailand were not subjected to destruction and looting such as occurred in Burma and Indonesia. Prewar buildings and apparatus are still largely intact. The one medical school continued to function throughout the war, although on a much reduced scale.

In Thailand before the war there was no extensive public-health program. The health services were confined, for the most part, to the operation of a system of small government hospitals and public-health centers throughout the country, staffed by poorly-paid and undertrained routine personnel. The medical training centers in existence produced enough doctors and nurses to fill vacancies in the government service, but the better qualified graduates were absorbed by private or mission hospitals. The Government of Thailand wants to establish a preventive program and extend the present minimum-medical-care facilities. But there is a lack of trained, experienced people to organize, train, and direct a team of public-health workers, and there is no equipment or apparatus with which to get under way rapidly. The principal health and medical officials of the Government are experienced and well-trained—many from American schools— but their number is limited, and they lack experienced supporting and field staff.

There are an estimated 1,000 doctors with modern training in Thailand, 400 of whom are in Bangkok, while there are approximately 34,000 practitioners of indigenous medicine (drug and herb arts). For purposes of civil administration, the country is composed of divisions, provinces, and districts. The district is the basic unit for the administration of public-health services. Each of the 500 districts has an average population of about 36,000. Only 10 districts have a public-health physician; only 2 have more than 1 physician. All other districts are staffed by sanitary inspectors and midwives. The sanitary inspectors are responsible for reporting and controlling communicable diseases, dressing minor injuries, dispensing and selling simple remedies, registering births and deaths, and conducting all sanitary inspections. Both sanitary inspectors and second-class midwives have only slightly better than the equivalent of an elementary education in the United States, plus a one-year training course which undertakes to survey the entire subjects of human anatomy and personal hygiene.

In Thai general hospitals, there are 85 to 100 physicians and 100 trained nurses for 2,575 beds, excluding the mental and leper hospitals and mission hospitals. All such hospitals average only about 50 beds each. The general hospitals are likewise staffed with sanitary inspectors with additional training (called second-class doctors), second-class midwives, and a variety of semi-skilled workers.

Thailand now does not have an established public-health program, sufficiently trained personnel, or necessary equipment and apparatus with which to inaugurate a good program of preventive services. Hence, whatever material assistance in the medical and health fields the United States provides to Thailand must be provided in association with American technical advisers.

In the area of health and medical affairs, there is no foreseeable limit to the amount of assistance that Thailand needs and wants. Many of its public-health and medical officers trained in the United States during the past 15 years have a great deal of confidence and respect for the United State institutions and desire to model the program for their country on United States practice and experience.

C. Education[c]

The educational system in Thailand is starving from lack of trained teachers, of materials and equipment, and of funds. At the same time, there is need for guidance in organizing and developing educational programs and using modern educational techniques. Discussions with Thai education officials indicated a keen desire for advice and help in coping with the admittedly tremendous problem they have to solve.

The illiteracy rate is high—69.9 percent of those over 10 years of age—in spite of the fact that elementary education between the ages of 7 and 11 has been compulsory and free since 1921. Beyond the elementary schools, the volume of formal education is small; the total enrollment in recognized public and private schools at all other levels totals less than 250,000. Only 34,000 are enrolled in adult education classes and 13,000 in vocational classes, despite the low level of literacy and the critical need for more highly skilled workers.

Throughout the educational system, equipment is inadequate both in quality and in quantity. In the engineering and science laboratories at Chulalongkorn University, for example, 500 students are reported to be using facilities designed for 100.

The teacher shortage requires that heavy reliance be placed on part-time instructors, drawn from other occupations. Full-time instructors have excessively heavy schedules. In the universities, the individual teaching loads often reach 30 hours a week. Many elementary school teachers also conduct adult education classes in the evenings. Salaries for elementary school teachers average about $15

---

[c]The figures quoted are based on data submitted as authoritative by the Ministry of Education and on the report of the UNESCO Consultative Educational Mission to Thailand (Feb. 10-Mar. 3, 1949). The statistics are questionable. It is believed they are adequate, however, for reaching general conclusions as to shortages and needs in the field of education.

a month, a level below that of the average unskilled worker. Living costs have increased 14 times in the decade ending in 1948, while teachers' salaries have increased only about 8 times.

If a larger proportion of the national budget were devoted to education, some alleviation of the shortages in both personnel and facilities would be possible. Expenditures for education in 1948 amounted to 5 percent of the total national budget. Approximately the same percentage applies currently in fiscal year 1950. This is in contrast to the Philippines, for example, where from 5 to 6 times as large a portion of the budget is devoted to education.

Guided by the belief that it would be unrealistic to assume that there would be any appreciable immediate increase in funds allotted, the Mission, therefore, concentrated in consultation with Thai officials on developing aid proposals which might strengthen the limited programs now being carried on. Proposals whose effectiveness would be largely dependent upon substantially increased expenditures by the Thai Government were discarded.

The administration of the educational system is highly centralized; the Ministry of Education directs and controls all institutions of learning. Textbooks are subject to approval by the Department of General Education. Uniform systems of examinations and curricula are prescribed by the Ministry. Educational institutions are under regional supervision. Thus, the aid proposed by the Mission might be effectively administered through these established provincial channels.

In February and March 1949, a study by a UNESCO mission in Thailand resulted in broad recommendations for the general reorganization and development of the educational system over a 10 to 15 year period. It was also proposed that another educational mission be appointed to work out the detailed implementation of these recommendations. Such a mission is now under consideration by the Thai Government.

After careful review, the Mission determined that its proposals did not conflict with or duplicate those of UNESCO. The UNESCO activities are on a long-range planning basis and involve no projects requiring immediate action. At the same time, the Mission's proposals appear to strike at many specific educational needs listed by the UNESCO group whose later actions might thereby be strengthened and facilitated.

D. Industry, Transport, Communications

Owing to the illness of one of the members of the Mission, this section is still in preparation. When completed, it will be duplicated separately.[d]

---

[d]This supplement was never prepared, but a number of specific projects in these fields were planned and carried out. [Ed.]

E. Management Training

In order to bring its governmental and economic activities up to modern standards, Thailand will have to develop an educated, effective middle class from which administrative and technical personnel can be selected for training for the most responsible positions. It is this pool of potential governmental and managerial talent that is lacking today. The Thai Government has recognized the need and the fact that competition from the Chinese obstructs the development of Thai personnel. Many laws have been passed to limit Chinese commercial activities and to encourage Thais to enter business. So far, however, the effort has failed, because the Chinese usually circumvent or flout the law, while the Thais themselves seem to have little taste for trade.

Thailand would find it easier to solve this problem with outside assistance. Other countries could help by establishing internships for Thai businessmen and government administrators and by providing managerial talent for Thai-owned business concerns in Thailand.

F. Long-Term Technical Aid Needed

1. Statistics. In addition to the general statistician requested from the United Nations (see Section V), there is need for expert advice in two major fields of activity of the Ministry of Commerce: 1) price indexes and cost-of-living indexes (with emphasis on sampling techniques) and 2) business and trade statistics. It is probable that two experts should be provided for assistance in these quite different fields. Each expert would organize the collection and analysis of the necessary statistics and train two or three Thais to carry on the work. Grants are also needed to pay for the statistical training in the United States of four Thais, two of whom are already in the United States.

There is also need in the Ministry of the Interior for a Thai statistician to be trained in the United States in census taking, the registration of cattle, and election registrations.

2. Patent and Copyright Law. Thailand has no adequate laws protecting patents and copyrights, and desires to develop such laws, especially to the extent required to implement commitments that might be made in a modernized treaty of friendship, commerce and navigation. To this end, the Ministry of Commerce would like to send a mature Thai lawyer abroad to study the nature and administration of patent and copyright law in the United States and other countries.

3. Price Control, Stockpiling, and Rationing. In view of Thailand's unsatisfactory experience with price control and rationing during and after the last war, the Department of Trade Control of the Ministry of Commerce would like to send a mature official abroad to study measures taken and kinds of administration found effective in other countries, particularly in the United States, Canada, and the United Kingdom. Some improvement in the present system could then be anticipated and plans laid for a fuller development before the need again arises.

4. Taxation. Design of the tax system and administration of tax collection are two areas where much improvement is considered by Thai officials to be needed. The Revenue Department of the Ministry of Finance would therefore like to have the advice of an expert on taxation (possibly through the United Nations) to advise on overhauling the whole Thai system of taxation and would also like to send three senior officials abroad to study tax collection and administration in the United States, in Hawaii, and in other countries where tax problems similar to those in Thailand have been successfully handled.

5. Social Welfare Administration and Social Work. The Thai Ministry of the Interior desires to have expert advice on social welfare administration and social work, including the administration of public welfare institutions, social security laws and administration, and social case work. In addition to consulting an expert in this broad field, the Ministry would like to send two senior officials abroad, one for study of social welfare administration, and one for study of social work. It is possible that the U.N. Division of Social Activities might be particularly interested in providing technical assistance in these fields.

6. Labor Problems. The Thai Ministry of the Interior would like to send one senior official abroad to study protective labor legislation, labor unionism, and government participation in labor relations. This is very similar to the training furnished by the ILO, which might be prepared to grant the needed fellowship.

7. County and Municipal Government and Administration. The Thai Ministry of the Interior wishes expert advice in the field of county and municipal government administration and their relationships to state government; and would like to send a senior official abroad to study this general subject.

8. Public Works Administration. The Thai Ministry of the Interior wishes to send a senior official to the United States to study certain aspects of public works administration, particularly the building and repair of roads and streets, airports, schools and other public buildings, parks and playgrounds, water and sewage systems (especially in Florida and New Orleans), sanitation and conservation works, rural electrification, street railways and motor bus systems.

V. Aid Being Received or Planned From Sources Other Than the United States

Because of its central position in Southeast Asia and its relatively stable political situation, Thailand has been chosen as the location for a number of the regional offices of the United Nations and the specialized agencies. ECAFE (Economic Commission for Asia and the Far East) has its headquarters in Bangkok, as do the U.N. representative of the Division of Social Activities for the Far East, the UNICEF Far Eastern Mission, and the FAO regional office. Although these are strictly regional offices, their location in Bangkok means that it is especially convenient for Thai officials to consult them, and Thailand therefore gets full benefit from their activities, although these have not yet been very extensive.

Thailand has been the object of a number of U.N. or specialized agency missions in the past several years, including an FAO mission on agriculture and forestry, an FAO mission on fisheries, a UNESCO mission on educational needs, an International Monetary Fund mission, and an International Bank mission. Moreover, Thailand has received the following technical assistance from various U.N. organizations:

FAO–Equipment for rinderpest vaccine factory and veterinarian for temporary assistance in 1948; and an expert on fish breeding practices (1948). FAO specialists on fertilizers and on farm mechanization problems have also been made available.

UNESCO–Expert to advise on fundamental education and one or two fellowships for study abroad. UNESCO is operating two pilot literacy projects, and has set aside money to cover an educational mission to follow up and develop in detail the recommendations of the 1949 UNESCO Mission. Thailand has requested UNESCO to provide technical assistance in teacher training and science teaching, to include 10 experts, a number of fellowships, books, and equipment, and the establishment of a Field Science Cooperative Office in Bangkok.

UNICEF/WHO–Allocation by UNICEF of $152,600 for malaria control demonstrations (by WHO team now in the field) and for fellowships, the latter administered by WHO. Expenditure has so far been approved by UNICEF of $31,000 for supplies and of $24,100 for 7 one-year fellowships. Thailand has requested a joint WHO/FAO technical assistance program to improve food production and health standards in malarial areas in the province of Chieng-Mai, to begin in September 1950, to cost a total of $2,836,000 for its entire duration of 5 years and 4 months, and to consist of certain equipment and supplies in addition to 8 experts for a survey period of 4 months in 1950 (1950 cost: $336,000) and 44 experts for operations in each of the 5 following years ($500,000 per year).

Thailand has also requested a WHO/UNICEF technical assistance project concerned with treponematosis, with emphasis on yaws and congenital syphilis, to begin as soon as personnel can be appointed, to cost $143,370 (of which Thailand would contribute $71,370 and UNICEF $72,000), and to consist of 3 foreign experts, auxiliary personnel, and certain supplies and equipment.

United Nations–Two fellowships for study abroad (one, railroad traffic control in Belgium; one, statistical techniques in the U.S.). The U.N. statistical office is now trying to obtain a statistical expert for Thailand as requested.

Five fellowships in social welfare services have been allocated to Thailand for 1950.

The International Bank is currently considering the Thai request for a loan of about $30 million to make possible railroad rehabilitation and the development of irrigation and hydroelectric power projects.

The Commonwealth Plan of aid to Southeast Asia is likely to provide for some technical or other aid to Thailand, but not a great deal.

The United Kingdom helped greatly in the rehabilitation of Thai railroads in 1945 to 1947 by assigning railway units (about 300 men) of the British Armed Forces to reconstruction work at no cost to the Thai Government.

There is also a British financial adviser to the Thai Government, paid by the latter.

A number of private religious missions provide educational and medical services in Thailand.

VI. Aid Being Received or Planned
From United States Sources

The U.S. Government has provided the following technical assistance to Thailand:

Two monetary experts from the Treasury Department, to advise on establishment of postwar exchange rate (1946).
Three economic geologists from U.S. Geological Survey, to make preliminary survey of Thailand's mineral resources (1949–50).
An adviser in air-route traffic control provided by the Civil Aeronautics Administration.
One tin expert from the Reconstruction Finance Corporation to expedite postwar tin exports (1946–1950).
Special training in the United States for 30 Thai engineers by the U.S. Bureau of Reclamation and Irrigation (1947).
One scholarship in the United States, under State Department program (1947–48).

Smith-Mundt funds in the amount of $48,034 have been allocated for fiscal 1950 to cover:

Two agricultural experts from U.S. Department of Agriculture to advise on rice culture and animal husbandry (1950).
One expert to advise on harbor development (funds allocated for 1950).
Two trainees, in agriculture and fisheries (funds allocated for 1950).

The United States granted Thailand a $10 million surplus property credit, under which it secured about $6 million worth of needed material. A Fulbright agreement is now under negotiation to use about $4 million of this debt for the baht expenses of exchange students and professors. Some $200,000 of the Fulbright fund would be earmarked for use during the first year.

In addition, Thailand has received technical assistance from private American organizations, as follows:

Pan American Airways provided personnel to operate airport facilities at Bangkok airport and trained Thai staff. This service was provided free of charge in order to assure adequate airport maintenance and operation (1946–1947).

Aeronautical Radio of Thailand, a company financed by the airlines using Bangkok airport, employs an American manager and other foreign employees to maintain airport communications and training (continuing).

North American Aviation Company provided an expert to assist the Royal Thai Air Force in setting up their assembly system at the aeronautical work shop (1949).

The International General Electric Company provided two hydro-electric engineers to advise on a site for a proposed hydroelectric project (based on earlier surveys by the Danish firm, Christiani and Nielson). This advice was free, in return for certain commitments in placing orders for electrical equipment if Thailand received a loan for the project.

The Anaconda Copper and Newmont Company provided a mining engineer and geologist to survey certain areas for mineral resources in 1946–48. They were not employed or paid by the Thai Government, but the company agreed to make their findings available to other American firms.

The Thai Government itself employs an American economic adviser and an American commercial adviser and has also recently employed (and now wants to find for employment) an American political adviser. Two American lawyers were also apparently engaged (in 1948–49) to present Thailand's claim to gold impounded in Tokyo (now released to Thailand).

Many private American groups, mostly religious, provide educational and medical services in Thailand, and at least 6 groups offer up to 16 scholarships in all for Thais to study in America. At the end of 1949, there were nearly 300 Thai students in the United States, mostly financed by the Thai Government.

VII. Recommendations for Emergency Assistance

A. *Agriculture*

(1) Irrigation		$ 1,530,000
(2) Land reclamation		200,000
(3) Insect and rodent control		150,000
(4) Rice improvement		90,000
(5) Rubber, silk, tapioca, etc.		105,000
(6) Fisheries (cost included in project #7)		
(7) National Agricultural Center		580,000
(8) In-service training of Thai technicians in the U.S.		175,000
	Total	$ 2,830,000

B. Public Health

(1) Malaria control		$ 1,200,000
(2) Demonstration & training teams		1,300,000
(3) Assistance to professional schools		420,000
(4) U.S. consultants and advisers		145,000
	Total	$ 3,065,000

C. Education

(1) Vocational training		$ 235,000
(2) Elementary schools		170,000
(3) Adult education		25,000
(4) Universities		175,000
(5) Athletics		45,000
(6) Books and periodicals		75,000
(7) Technical pamphlets and translations		145,000
(8) Audio-visual aids		73,000
(9) English Language training		50,000
	Total	$ 993,000

D. Industry, Transport and Communications

D. Industry, Transport and Communications		$ 4,532,000
	Total	$ 4,532,000
	Grand Total	$11,420,000

A. Agriculture

1. Irrigation (2 positions and equipment; total cost $1,530,000). Thai irrigation systems consist of low-level canals, which are used for transportation in addition to providing water for flooding of lands, and are quite different from U.S. systems, which use high-line canals for distribution of water and surfaced roads for transportation. The result of Thai methods is generally adequate but, in hundreds of areas affecting many thousands of farmers, crops are uncertain because of low-water levels. This is being slowly corrected by major installations of water control works. In the meantime, motor-driven low-lift dragon-bone pumps are being sold at cost by the Irrigation Department to individual farmers. Medium-lift pumps (4-6 meters and 4" to 6" discharge) are badly needed in the Central Plain.

From a political standpoint, irrigation assistance is particularly needed in the northeast provinces because of social unrest caused chiefly by depressed economic conditions. By increasing the very poor yields in this area, irrigation would not only raise the standard of living of the farmers there (with resulting political benefit) but would also increase Thailand's exportable surplus of rice. The streams in the area have low-water levels, and high-lift pumps (10 meters lift) are required.

The pumps would be sold for local currency to individual farmers and to farm cooperatives. They would provide immediate material evidence to the farmers that the government is promoting programs specifically designed for their welfare.

The pumps, especially the larger high-lift type, would provide a material incentive for the more rapid development of the farm cooperative movement and the growth of extension services.

Personnel (Estimated cost $30,000). The Irrigation Department is well-staffed and well-administered and has adequate shop and transport equipment as well as a store of parts and materials to meet normal needs. They can make excellent use of pumping and other equipment provided. Two agricultural engineers with experience on small irrigation projects are recommended to maintain a check on the methods of disposal and the end use of equipment provided.

Equipment (Estimated Cost: $1,500,000)

2-to-4-meter lift kerosene motor driven Centrifugal pumps:
  250—4" discharge
  250—6" discharge
10-meter lift Diesel motor Centrifugal pumps:
  50—6" discharge
  50—8" discharge
  20—10" discharge
  10—12" discharge
5 sets of tractor and ditcher for excavating ditches of:
  2-4 feet bottom width, 2-5 feet depth and
  6-15 feet top width

2. Land Reclamation and Colonization (3 Positions and equipment; total cost $200,000). This project is designed to relieve an aggravating economic and political situation. Large tracts of land in single ownership and formerly farmed to rice by tenants are now abandoned and grown over with coarse grass and shrubs. Much of this land is in the Central Plain, where the only significant land tenure problems exist. This project is also proposed as a practical means of giving stimulation and orientation to policies of the Government to improve the lot of the producer by (1) purchase of land from the landlord, (2) fitting it for production by mechanical means, (3) organizing farmer cooperatives, and (4) colonizing the land by sale to owner operators. Throughout Southeast Asia there are forces at work which will eventually compel a change from the traditional hand methods of paddy culture to more modern machine methods. The farmer and his wife, and more particularly the farmer's son and daughter, are losing interest in the drudgery of transplant paddy culture. There is a shortage of agricultural labor. Mechanization will come or production will decline. Competent guidance is needed to investigate the possibilities and limitations of mechanization and to direct its growth.

The Thai Government proposes to purchase three tracts of about 800 acres each for reclamation by plowing and fitting for irrigation and planting by machinery and for colonization.

The land reclamation projects would be on the Central Plain within a 25-mile radius of the National Agricultural Center at Bangken. They would provide much needed action projects for investigating the possibilities and limitations of mechanical cultivation; provide training of machinery operators and maintenance personnel; provide experience in the desirable revision of irrigation practices, rate of seeding, and harvesting; and give experience in the organization and operation of farm producer and marketing cooperatives.

The technical personnel supplied from the United States, as well as national personnel, would be available during the non-cropping season for the training of personnel and agricultural engineering investigations at the National Agricultural Center in Bangken.

Personnel (Estimated cost: $40,000)
Agricultural Engineer	1
Trainer in Operation	1
Trainer in Maintenance	1

Equipment (Estimated cost: $160,000). The Mechanical Equipment Co., Ltd. of Bangkok has had some experience in Thailand in the mechanization of rice cultivation. Upon request they submitted a list of equipment which they consider adequate for the fitting and cultivation of one unit of 800 to 1000 acres of rice. The mechanization of three units of land is recommended.

3. Insect and Rodent Control—Milled Rice (2 positions and equipment; total cost $150,000). Storage losses in milled rice are difficult to estimate but are generally considered to be significantly large. Losses are primarily produced by rodents and storage insects and result from inadequate storage structures, unsanitary storage, and lack of knowledge of control measures and materials.

There are more than 600 rice mills in Thailand under private ownership and operation, each of which has several warehouses for milled rice. The warehouses are of many types of construction but for the most part are not designed for insect control nor for prevention of loss due to rodent damage. There are eight large rice mills owned and operated by farmer cooperatives. It is proposed that an entomologist and storage engineer be assigned to the National Agricultural Center at Bangken. They would conduct a survey of the storage facilities in the country and institute insect and rodent control measures. In addition to their work on commercial storage they would be available at the National Agricultural Center for research and instruction activities.

Personnel (Estimated cost: $30,000)
 Entomologist   1
 Storage Engineer   1

Materials and Equipment (Estimated cost: $120,000)
 List of equipment has been duplicated separately.

4. Rice Improvement (2 positions and equipment; total cost $90,000). Improvement in paddy and improvement of rice production in Thailand. A project for paddy improvement by mass selection followed by breeding is just getting under way. Although there are approximately 600 rice mills in the country, there is no mill where tests can be made of the milling quality of paddy.

Improvement in rice milling requires the installation of additional equipment in the present rice mills as well as the adjustment and repair of existing equipment. Significant improvement will also come gradually if training is given in rice-milling technology to present mill operators. It is proposed that a small pilot mill be installed at Bangken to run milling tests on rice varieties developed in the crop improvement program, to test and demonstrate modern milling machinery, and to train men in milling practices.

Personnel (Estimated cost: $30,000)
 Crop Improvement   1 (Dr. Love)
 Milling Technologist   1

 Pilot mill, to be located at National Agricultural Center (Estimated cost: $60,000). Capacity 1200 to 1500 lbs. paddy/hr. (Southern Construction & Mill Supply Co., Houston, 2, Texas.)

5. Rubber, Silk, Tapioca, Sticklac, and other Complementary Crops (5 positions and equipment: Total Cost $105,000). Production of complementary crops is significant and capable of being expanded. These provide a direct source of dollar exchange.

U.S. agriculturists acquainted with Thailand, Thai agriculturists, and U.S. businessmen engaged in export believe that there is great opportunity for the further development of complementary crops. The most important of these crops at the present time are rubber, cassave, pepper, stick-lac, and silk. There are undoubtedly others, including pepper and spice, which are capable of further development. The Thai agricultural technicians have concentrated primarily on rice and given little attention to crops of a complementary nature. Cassava and rubber are now produced primarily by small farmers or peasants. Lac and silk not only offer opportunities for the grower but also opportunities for the rapid development of small industries. All occur in districts in which it is especially important to provide additional activities and income.

Personnel (Estimated cost: $75,000)

Rubber Production & Processing	2
Processing of Cassava	1
Silkworm Culture & Distribution	1
Lac Production	1

Equipment (Estimated cost: $30,000)
Laboratory and transport.

6. Fisheries (2 positions, charged to Project 7). Fish products are of great importance in the Thai diet. They provide the principal source of animal protein. Inland fish culture in ponds and streams has become a part of the rural culture. Marine fishing on the other hand is relatively underdeveloped. There are at present no technicians in Thailand capable of designing and conducting projects for its development.

The mission was presented with a proposed marine fishery project involving more than a million dollars of capital outlay. It is believed that this project has been studied by the FAO and recently reported upon. The proposed fishery experts would work at the National Agricultural Center to improve investigation and instruction in fish culture, and would assist the Thai government in the development and appraisal of projects proposed for the investigation of the possibilities of marine fishing.

7. National Agricultural Center (14 positions and equipment; total cost $580,000). Thai agricultural officials plan to consolidate current uncoordinated public services in agriculture into a National Agricultural Center with headquarters in Bangken. The National Agricultural Center will have a single director under the Minister of Agriculture; its programs will be reviewed by the Joint Commission for Economic Development; projects within the program may be proposed by the Joint Commission for Economic Development, by the various departments of the Ministry, or by the staff of the Center; its projects will be developed with the advice of a board composed of representatives of the various Departments of the Ministry and chaired by the Director of the Center.

The Center will have responsibility in three technical fields, investigation, education and training, and extension. These fields will include responsibility for analysis and advice on agricultural problems. The Center will not be responsible for action projects in economic development. Action projects will be carried out by the regularly constituted agencies of the Thai Government.

Personnel of the Center may be called upon for analysis and advice on problems in their subject matter fields. Where necessary their services may be required for the prosecution of action projects.

Investigation. Research projects for the development of improved plant and animal materials and for improved fertilization, cultivation, processing, storage and marketing practices, etc., will be conducted by Center personnel at Bangken and in other parts of Thailand under the guidance of Center technicians. These same technicians will also participate in education and training, extension, and analysis and advisory functions.

Education and Training. The Center will conduct the Agricultural University and provide special training courses for extension workers, officials of agricultural cooperatives, machinery operators and machinery repairmen, etc.

Extension. Present rural agricultural agents will be brought into the Agricultural Extension Service and will function in the field as staff members of the National Agricultural Center. Their cooperation with farmers, farm cooperatives, irrigation districts, and other producer and marketing organizations will be directed from the Center by the Assistant Director for extension. All rural extension workers will be brought to the Center as soon as possible for intensive training in extension methods and materials and will be brought back annually or oftener for refresher courses. These intensive courses will be supplemented by regional conferences on problems within the national agricultural program as they relate to specific regions.

Estimates. Estimated dollar costs are for 15 months for personnel, including salary, allowances, and travel; and for materials and equipment:

Investigation and Education and Training

Personnel (12)		$165,000
Research Administrator	1	
Education Administrator	1	
English teachers	2	
Animal Husbandry	1	
Poultry Husbandry	1	
Crop Improvement	1	
Upland Crop	1	
Soil & Fertilizers	1	
Cooperatives	1	
Agricultural Engineer		
Machinery Operation	Charged to Project #2	
Machinery Maintenance		
Fishery Experts	2	(Note also Project #6)
	12	
Equipment & Materials		$325,000
Extension		
Personnel (2)		$ 30,000
Extension Organization and Administration	1	
Information Aids	1	
Equipment & Materials		
(Including 20 pick-ups)		$ 60,000
	Total	$580,000

8. In-service training of 35 Thai Technicians in the U.S. (Estimated cost: $175,000). The sending of Thai technicians to the United States for in-service training is of great importance to all emergency activities in the field of agriculture. It is the only practicable way to increase competence of Thai personnel in certain fields. In many other fields it is the most rapid manner in which this can be accomplished.

Practical work-training of Thai personnel in the United States in the application of science and technology to agriculture will stimulate pride of profession in the agricultural services of Thailand. This work training will extend horizons of endeavor and will reveal opportunities for the improvement of Thai agriculture which are not now imagined by their professional personnel.

Work-training is important to all fields of activity, including education, investigation, action projects, agricultural extension, and the organization and operation of farm cooperatives. It will have an immediate effect on the rate of improvement in public services and in the long run may well be the most important activity which United States technical cooperation can provide. The Mission was provided with a large number of requests for training in many fields; after extensive consultation the number recommended for the first year is 35. The fields have been selected and the Thai officials have individuals in mind for each of the training grants. Although the proposed fields and candidates seem to be well justified, it is quite likely that both of these will change somewhat with time. A list of the presently proposed fields for training grants follows:

Trainee grants requested by The Ministry of Agriculture of Thailand:

Departments	Requirements	Trainees
1. Agriculture	Soil and fertilizer	1
2. Agriculture	Pest-infestation	1
3. Fisheries	Fish distribution	1
4. Livestocks	Pathologist	1
5. Livestocks	Bacteriologist	1
6. Irrigation	Small irrigation development	1
7. Agriculture	Mechanization	1
8. Fisheries	Gear technology	1
9. Livestocks	Poultry and swine husbandry	1
10. Irrigation	General engineering	2
11. Cooperatives	Cooperative marketing (producers)	1
12. Forestry	Forest management	1
13. University	Educational administration	1
14. Fisheries	Brackish water fish culture	1
15. Livestocks	Animal husbandry	1
16. Irrigation	Geologist	1
17. Cooperatives	Cooperative marketing (consumers)	1

Departments	Requirements	Trainees
18. University	Research	1
19. Fisheries	Inland fish culture	1
20. Livestocks	Animal nutrition	1
21. University	Poultry husbandry	1
22. Agriculture	Extension services	1
23. Livestocks	Parasitologist	1
24. University	Swine husbandry and dairy sciences	1
25. Livestocks	Animal products	1
26. Forestry	Silvicultural research	1
27. University	Upland crops	1
28. University	Agricultural engineering	1
29. Forestry	Wood preservation	1
30. University	Pathologist and entomologist	1
31. Forestry	Forest botany	1
32. University	English subjects	2
33. University	Agricultural chemistry	1
	Total	35

Emergency Cooperation in Agriculture:
Recapitulation

No.	Project	Positions	Personnel	Material	Total
			Cost		
1	Irrigation (Pumps)	2	$ 30,000	$1,500,000	$1,530,000
2	Reclamation & Colonization	3	40,000	160,000	200,000
3	Insect & Rodent Control	2	30,000	120,000	150,000
4	Rice Improvement	2	30,000	60,000	90,000
5	Complementary Crops	5	75,000	30,000	105,000
6	Fisheries	2			
7	National Agricultural Center	12	195,000	385,000	580,000
8	Trainees (35)			175,000	175,000
		28	$400,000	$2,430,000	$2,830,000

B. Health

Thai health officials submitted to the Mission a series of 10 to 12 project requests for consideration. The projects were moderate in scope, addressed to some of the most important needs, calculated to have a reasonably immediate impact on the people, and prepared in relation to the kinds of technical aid which is being sought from the United Nations and its specialized agencies.

1. **Malaria control–$1,200,000.** Each year there are in Thailand an average of 50,000 reported malaria deaths–one-fifth of the deaths from all causes–and it is estimated that there are at least 3,000,000 cases of illness from malaria each year. Actually, as reporting is incomplete, the figure is probably much larger. Malaria is found in every part of the country, but its incidence is not uniform. The northern section of the country, around Chieng-Mai, for example, is particularly fertile and contains some of the best land in the entire country; it is also the most highly malarial section of the country.

Each of the particularly malarial areas in the north, in the center, and in the southern peninsula could support additional population up to at least three times the number of people now living in these areas were it not for malaria and other diseases. In the Province of Sara-Buri, for example, the government has set aside 3,321 square kilometers for colonization. Only 23,000 people now cultivate 212 square kilometers of this land, which is estimated to be capable of supporting nearly 100,000. In 1945-47, an average of 10,000 malaria cases each year received treatment at the Malaria Field Station. The known spleen rate among children is over 75 percent.

A World Health Organization 5-man malaria control team in the Serapee district near Chieng-Mai is spraying and draining 100 square kilometers (36,000 people). This project began in July 1949 and was scheduled for two years. The Thai Government has also requested a joint FAO/WHO technical assistance program to improve food production and health standards in malarial areas in the province of Chieng-Mai (see Section IV). WHO is paying the salaries and travel expenses of the team at present in the field; UNICEF is providing DDT, trucks, bicycles, and laboratory equipment to the value of $31,000 and has approved $24,100 for 7 one-year fellowships. The Thai Government is making an almost equal contribution in housing, subsistence for the team, the cost of local labor, and 30 sanitary inspectors for field work.

The Thai Government requested assistance from the United States in extending these malaria control activities in three other sections of the country–extension of the present hyperendemic area in the north, a new center in the Sara Buri Province, and one in the southern peninsula which would also include filariasis control. In this southern peninsular district, populated by approximately 2,000,000 people, surveys have shown that between 31 and 50 percent of the school children have micro-filaria in the bloodstream without any outward signs of elephantiasis.

Assistance from the United States is also requested for the equipping of a

Malaria Institute in Chieng-Mai. The Thai Government will complete the building of laboratory facilities and quarters for the staff. The United States is asked to provide the basic laboratory equipment for routine work and for limited research by entomologists and parasitologists. The routine laboratory and research work is necessary not only to facilitate control measures and further study but also to serve as a training center for Thai malariologists, sanitary inspectors, and native control teams.

Because the Thai Government does not now have sufficient trained staff to organize and operate this Institute for the beginning period, the United States is asked to provide the necessary professional staff and supervisors during the time that Thai scholars are obtaining training in the United States. Assistance from the United States is requested in the form of fellowships for an average of three Thai trainees per year for a five-year period in various aspects of malaria control work.

The estimated cost for a 15-month period ending June 30, 1951 for these malaria projects is $1,200,000, and they are recommended on the understanding that as many control teams will be trained and put into the field as the Thai Government can afford to support with local staff and expenses.

2. Demonstration and Training Teams in Field—$1,300,000. Because of lack of sufficient trained personnel and of the necessary equipment and supplies, there has been only a limited program for bringing health and medical services directly to the Thai people. Most of the available professional personnel are taken up by the central government planning and the staffing of the government hospitals. It is now proposed to put as many mobile public-health teams on the road as there are personnel available, jointly staffed by American and Thai doctors and nurses, to bring both preventive and curative services to Thai people in smaller communities, and for training native medical and nursing staff as rapidly as possible.

The request to the United States is for *a*) sufficient American staff with full equipment to organize and operate five mobile teams for maternal and child health services, personal hygiene and nutrition, school health services, and for general public health and sanitation work and *b*) for sufficient equipment and supplies to launch three native teams who are now available and who will need only intensive short term training.

The Thai Government also requested one or two American teams with full equipment to organize and operate a medical and dental program of health services for school children in Bangkok and to train Thai personnel.

The Thai Government also requested one complete tuberculosis control unit with full equipment for diagnosis and treatment of tuberculosis and for training additional Thai physicians and nurses in this work.

Fellowships for the training of Thai physicians and nurses in maternal and child health, nutrition, venereal disease, general public health, sanitation, tuberculosis, and school health services to the number of an estimated average of 15 for one year each are also recommended.

The estimated total cost of these mobile units and the related fellowships for 15 months ending June 30, 1951, is $1,300,000 and is recommended on the understanding that the number of teams to be organized and set to work will be limited only by the availability of Thai staff for training purposes.

3. Assistance to Professional Training Schools—$420,000. Because a large number of the teachers in the professional schools and many Thai government health officials previously studied in the United States, there is a natural desire to want to adapt their professional schools to those in the United States. All schools—medicine, dentistry, nursing—suffer from an over-emphasis on lectures and an underdevelopment of practical laboratory experience and the study of specimens and reference books. Part of this imbalance results from lack of equipment and apparatus and both museum and library materials, but it is also caused by a shortage of trained teachers. The need for additional teachers exists in both schools of Medicine (Siriraj and Chulalongkorn), and the schools of dentistry, pharmacy, public health, and veterinary medicine.

United States assistance in equipment and training of professional teachers would be a partial renewal of a program started 20 years ago by the Rockefeller Foundation, when 10 American physicians and nurses taught full time in the Siriraj Hospital.

The Thai Government requested that American professors be brought to these schools for teaching and that selected members of their own professional staff be sent to the United States for further training. The 5-year development program of these schools envisions a total of 20 American professors coming to Thailand for an average of 2 years each and between 12 and 15 Thai scholars and trainees per year coming to the United States for an average of 1 year each.

The estimated total cost of these recommendations is $420,000 for 15 months ending June 30, 1951, for 8 American professors (average $20,000 each) and for 12 trainees (average $5,000) plus an estimated $200,000 in books, apparatus, equipment, and teaching aids.

4. U.S. Consultants and Advisers on Special Problems—$145,000. The Government of Thailand requested advisers in the following fields:

1. Organization and administration of public health services
2. Environmental sanitation
3. Cholera control
4. Plague control
5. Leprosy control

The Government of Thailand, anxious to establish and push forward rapidly a broad program in public health and curative medicine along modern progressive lines, requested that the United States send an experienced public health officer to make a complete survey and recommendations on the present health organization and administration. This will require a man with experience in both preventive and curative medicine, who is prepared to spend not less than 6 months in visiting a variety of health centers and hospitals. There is evidence that a carefully thought-out set of recommendations would be accepted. Because these recommendations will be important to all other health projects recommended for Thailand, this adviser should be sent forward at the earliest possible date. He should also bear in mind and make recommendations on the staging of other projects.

Because there is no program in environmental sanitation at this time, the Government of Thailand requested that the United States make available an experienced sanitary engineer to make a survey of the rural sanitation needs and to organize a long-term program for the improvement of sanitation in small towns and villages. (Urban sanitation is a responsibility of the Ministry of Interior, not Public Health.) Because plague and cholera have broken out periodically in epidemic proportions in Thailand, the Thai Government asked that an American adviser spend not less than six months in reviewing their laboratory facilities and procedures and their various control measures and give advice on how they might be improved.

The Government of Thailand recognizes that, although leprosy is no longer an important problem in the United States, there are an estimated 80,000 cases in Thailand. The Government desires the advice of an adviser, from the United States or some other country, to examine and evaluate the present leprosy control and treatment measures.

The Government of Thailand also requested fellowships for 15 trainees to study these several specialities (above) in the United States or elsewhere for a 1-year period.

The estimated cost of these advisory and training services for 15 months ending June 30, 1951, is $145,000. They are recommended.

C. Education

1. **Vocational Training—$235,000.** There are in Thailand 190 public and 80 private vocational schools with an enrollment of about 13,000. Increasing emphasis is being given to vocational training by the Government as a means of meeting the country's growing need for skilled workers. The budget for this training has been increased substantially in recent years—from 8.5 million baht in 1948 to 11.9 million baht in 1950. Aid in developing vocational training has first precedence, according to the Ministry of Education, over its other education assistance requests.

One of the most serious concerns of the Ministry is its present inability to provide a sufficiently high level of vocational training. Except for eight or nine secondary schools, all are on the elementary level. The Putumwan Engineering School in Bangkok, for example, is the only engineering school in the country on the secondary or pre-college level. Training available in most of these schools is inadequate to qualify candidates for jobs in private enterprise. Teachers, equipment, and guidance are needed and have been requested.

In response to these specific requests, it is recommended that a vocational education adviser be made available to the Department of Vocational Education to assist in organizing the training program, to revise the curricula, and to develop the work in the schools and workshops; that four candidates be selected for further training in the United States as teachers in vocational fields (engineering, woodwork, dress-making, and commerce); and that equipment and materials required to meet the most urgent needs of the program be provided, selected if possible in consultation with the training adviser assigned to the Department, and be distributed throughout the country.

Estimate:

1 technician	$ 10,000
4 trainees	$ 25,000
Equipment	$200,000
Total	$235,000

2. Elementary Schools—$170,000. Only 41 percent of Thailand's educational budget is for support of the elementary schools. Yet in these schools are 2.6 million of the country's 2.8 million total of students enrolled in all educational institutions. The free education provided by the Government to children between the ages of 7 and 11 thus amounts to less than one dollar per child per year. This should speak for itself as to the quantity and quality of equipment and materials, textbooks, and teaching staff that is available.

Further evidence of the acute shortages faced in the field of elementary education and of the quality of training being given is that only 14 percent of the 73 thousand teachers have a teaching certificate of any sort.

The elementary school system consists of 18,564 schools. Also, there are 26 training schools for elementary teachers. Assistance for these, both in equipment and advisory personnel, has been requested by the government.

To assist the Government in attacking this problem, it is recommended that one educational expert be assigned to the Ministry of Education to work particularly with the teacher-training schools in introducing modern teaching methods and that, at the same time, training in the United States be provided to five Thai teachers for study in this same field.

It is believed much can be accomplished by improving the content and format of existing textbooks. One technician is recommended to work with the Ministry on this problem and on the development of other teaching materials, while related training will be given in the United States to one trainee.

The equipment needs of the schools are very great. However, because of the very magnitude of these needs and the admitted lack of personnel sufficiently trained to make effective use of the equipment that might be provided, it is believed initial assistance should be limited. It is recommended that each of the 26 training schools and the 100 largest (over 20,000 enrollment) elementary schools be stocked with sets of demonstration and training equipment which have been requested for them by the Ministry. This equipment would not be used in the 100 schools alone but would be available for circulation among other schools in the area. (Estimates are based on equipment lists for rehabilitation of war-devastated schools prepared by the U.S. Office of Education and come to about $1,250 and $780 respectively for each kind of school, including shipping costs.)

Estimate:

2 technicians	$ 30,000
6 trainees	$ 30,000
Equipment	$110,000
Total	$170,000

3. Adult Education—$25,000. The low literacy rate (31.1%) among persons over 10 years of age has been of continuing concern to the Government. Although the primary interests of the Ministry of Education are in assuring literacy and vocational skills among the younger groups, with consequent emphasis upon those phases of the education program, there is an active though small program of adult education. Classes are being carried on in different parts of the Kingdom in some 500 schools, all but 13 of which are located in the provinces. The 34,000 enrolled students are about half fully illiterate and half semi-literate. Classes are conducted in the evenings, in almost all cases by the regular day-time public school teachers. To develop the program, there are 186 directors of adult education in the provinces, whose job is to disseminate information about the classes and to attract persons to enroll. Dr. Frank C. Laubach of the Committee on World Literacy and Christian Literature of New York worked with the Government in early 1949, helping them to establish a nationwide literacy campaign. Also, literacy projects are being conducted in Bangken and Korat by UNESCO.

It is recommended that an expert in organization and operation of adult education programs, as requested by the Ministry, be provided to assist in further development of their program, and that two trainees be brought to the United States for study in extension and adult education methods.

Estimate:

1 technician	$15,000
2 trainees	$10,000
Total	$25,000

4. Universities—$175,000. There are at present five chartered universities, all in Bangkok. These are Chulalongkorn University, the University of Moral and Political Science, the University of Fine Arts, the University of Agriculture, and the Medical University. Assistance to the latter two has been provided for in the sections on agriculture and health.

The largest of these schools are Chulalongkorn, with an enrollment of about 2,200, and the University of Moral and Political Science, with an enrollment of about 4,000 plus some 16,000 extension (correspondence) students. Chulalong-korn suffers particularly from lack of equipment in its engineering laboratory, and both schools suffer from lack of trained permanent faculty. It is recommended that six teachers (in the fields of geology, mining and metallurgy, engineering, and business and accounting) be brought to these schools from the U.S. to strengthen their staffs, pending availability of more Thai graduates in those particular fields which can make important contribution to economic development.

One trainee to be sent to the United States on vocational guidance techniques is recommended for the University of Moral and Political Science. No trained personnel in this field are now available to that university.

In view of the technical assistance in mineral investigations now being given the Thai Government by the United States, and the great mineral potential of the country, it is thought important that assistance be given in making training facilities in that field available. At present, the University completely lacks equipment for such training. Necessary equipment for such a laboratory is recommended.

It is recommended also that an English teacher from the United States be added to the staff of each of these two universities. Much of the reference materials required by the advanced students is available only in English, yet they lack the familiarity with the language necessary to make most effective use of those materials. This is a serious shortcoming, emphasized by education officials, faculty, and students themselves.

Estimate:

8 teachers	$120,000
1 trainee	5,000
Equipment	50,000
Total	$175,000

5. Athletics—$45,000. The Mission believes that any encouragement that can be given to development of physical education in Thailand is extremely valuable, as a means for both physical and psychological strengthening of the youth of the country, providing them with a constructive outlet for their energies during their leisure time, and tending to create a better balance in an educational routine that now suffers from over-bookishness.

Aside from the regular school system, an important field for encouraging athletics is the Boy Scout Movement, which gained great popularity before the war, was dormant for some time, and now is undergoing a strong revival. This also is true of a similar girls' movement, under auspices of the Junior Red Cross organization.

Although there is under the Ministry of Education a Physical Education Department, no requests were made for assistance in physical education, nor was any interest expressed when the possibility was brought up by the Mission in its discussions. The dominant interest of the Ministry was obviously in the traditional academic and vocational lines of education.

It is recommended that one physical education instructor be provided, and two trainees to be sent to the United States, together with funds for making available a limited amount of athletic equipment in Thailand. If the Ministry of Education should show increased interest in this field, the assistance might be channeled through it. Otherwise, arrangements should be made for providing this aid through USIS.

Estimate:

1 instructor	$15,000
2 trainees	10,000
Equipment	20,000
Total	$45,000

6. Books and Periodicals–$75,000. Technical books and periodicals in English are seriously lacking in Thailand, as they are in all the other Southeast Asian countries. There is a strong demand for such books for those who are studying or who are doing active work in their specialized fields. Adding to the effect of these shortages is the fact that few if any trained librarians exist, so that those few volumes which are on the library shelves are often difficult if not impossible to locate and use.

At the University of Moral and Political Science, for example, the library is at present managed on a part-time basis by one of the political science instructors, who studied in the United States but has had no library experience and must devote his main effort to his teaching responsibilities. He is doing the best he can, but that is no solution. There is no cataloging system; the books are simply recorded in sequence as they come in, and the few thousand volumes in the library are totally inadequate to meet needs even if they were well organized. This is the situation in a university with an enrollment of some 4,000 regular and 16,000 extension students!

It is recommended that a U.S. librarian be brought to Thailand to work with the Ministry of Education in organizing the existing libraries, particularly in the universities. This librarian should also be responsible for teaching a regular course in library science to a selected group of persons who are already engaged in or planning to enter library work. This might include personnel from each of the university libraries, from each of the special departmental libraries of the government, from the national library, from the public libraries, and from the school libraries under the Department of Education. It is estimated that six months training would be sufficient to qualify these persons to do a minimum job of effective organization and management of their own libraries, after which the U.S. librarian would be available to advise and assist. Two of the most capable of this group should be sent to the United States for further training in library science.

It is recommended that U.S. books and periodicals be presented to existing libraries where there is evidence that they are needed and can be put to good use. Distribution should be through USIS, in consultation with the Ministry of Education and the U.S. librarian assigned to assist that Ministry.

Collections of books and limited numbers of subscriptions to periodicals might be given to the special libraries of the various government departments (irrigation, education, fisheries, police, public welfare, etc.; provision for agricultural and medical libraries has been made separately under those sections of this report), to the public libraries throughout the country, to each of the universities, and to the vocational, teacher training, and secondary schools. A limiting factor in the distribution of these books is the ability to read English. This factor has been taken into account in estimating the quantities of books and the number of libraries which could effectively be helped at this time.

Estimate:

1 librarian	$15,000
2 trainees	10,000
Books and periodicals	50,000
Total	$75,000

7. Technical Pamphlets and Translations—$145,000. There is continuous and heavy demand for technical materials published in the United States, as a result of an insatiable desire on the part of the Thais to know how things are done in the United States. The publications of the U.S. Government Printing Office, prepared by the various technical agencies of our Government, are now being made available in limited quantities through USIS. This nowhere begins to meet the demand. Yet these, and similar type pamphlets published by U.S. private organizations, serve as an effective and inexpensive way for disseminating technical information among large numbers of people. It is the belief of the Mission that this can be an important factor in supplementing and back-stopping the work done by the U.S. technicians in their specialized fields, and in reaching large numbers of people throughout the entire country.

It is proposed that funds be provided for the purchase and free distribution of these publications in English, to the extent that an English reading audience exists; and that selected pamphlets in all fields be edited as necessary and translated for distribution among the non-English reading population. To the greatest extent possible, translating and publishing facilities in Thailand should be utilized.[e] Adequate facilities are believed to be available. It is recommended that distribution of these materials be made through USIS, in consultation with the various Ministries or private organizations which might be concerned.

Estimate:

$145,000 ($20,000 for English publications, plus 50 pamphlets in editions of 50,000 each at $2,500 per pamphlet).

8. Audio-Visual Aids—$73,000. Audio-visual aids are proposed here as an additional means for strengthening the projects recommended above, and

---

[e]The above two paragraphs parallel, almost word for word, the similar recommendations for Burma, on pages 184-185. [Ed.]

indirectly for contributing to the training aspects of all those activities proposed by the Mission which involve the interchange of know-how.

USIS is currently working with the Irrigation Department on construction of a pontoon barge to house a mobile information unit, to travel the waterways, equipped with library, radio, phonograph and records, moving picture and film slide equipment, and a public address system. It is recommended that funds be provided to equip this unit fully (the construction cost of which is being borne by the Thai government), and that funds also be provided for full construction of two other such units to be operated by USIS or possibly by the Ministry of Education. This would provide one unit for operation in the extensive canal systems in each of the central, north and northeast plain regions.

Funds also are recommended to provide films, film slides, and projectors to each of the governmental departments for use by them in the field, to certain of the training schools and to other educational institutions. To assist in the development of training film materials in this country, one U.S. technician is recommended to work with the Ministry of Education, and one trainee to study the use and development of audio-visual aids in the United States.

Estimate:

1 technician	$15,000
1 trainee	5,000
Mobile units	35,000
Films & Projectors	18,000
Total	$73,000

9. English Language Instruction—$50,000. There is in Thailand a widespread interest in learning English. It is proposed that funds be made available to existing institutions in Thailand, particularly those of the American missionary groups, to enable them to broaden their English language instruction work and to enable them to obtain the added staff and equipment necessary to conduct courses of instruction in English. This instruction, not necessarily connected with existing academic courses, would be aimed at the broad class of the population who might be reached through night schools or through mass education projects. It is recommended that this program be handled through the USIS, which itself might also directly undertake the conduct of such courses.

D. Industry, Transport, Communications—$4,532,000

Detailed information on recommendations for these fields is not yet available owing to the illness of one of the members of the Mission. When recommendations have been prepared in detail, they will be duplicated separately. Total cost of projects recommended is estimated to be $4,532,000.[f]

---

[f]See footnote d, above.

VIII. Limitations on Amount, Speed or Kind of Aid to Thailand

Like other countries in Southeast Asia, Thailand has only a limited number of officials, experts, and advanced students who are well enough trained and who know enough English so that they can profit fully from association with American experts in Thailand, or from training or graduate fellowships in the United States. This shortage is less marked in Thailand than in Indochina, Indonesia, and even Burma, but it still constitutes an important limitation on the scale of U.S. (or U.N.) technical assistance activities.

The Thai Government's own finances are quite sound (except for the necessity of financing rice exports to Japan while waiting for repayment in the form of capital goods) and inflationary forces are fairly well under control. It is therefore feasible for the Government to provide the local currency needed for development projects or other economic aid projects, and the inflationary impact of such projects as are currently planned is not likely to be large enough to be of concern.

Probably the most serious limiting factor for such programs is the shortage of Thai managerial and technical personnel competent to carry them on. So much of Thailand's business is run by Chinese, and the tradition that government and business require quite different capabilities is so strong, that the training of a Thai managerial class for Thailand's hoped-for future development projects may turn out to be a very serious problem. Until steps are taken to develop a Thai middle class, from which future managers and technicians can be drawn, the speed of Thai economic development will be held down.

There are only a very few areas (the extreme north, a few bandit-ridden localities, and the southern provinces far down the Malay Peninsula) where foreign technicians could not safely work on projects of economic development or improved social services.

IX. Considerations in Providing Aid to Thailand

Thailand in the past has shown skill in accommodating the principal political powers in the Far East, favoring now one and then another. Currently, the Thai Government has been underscoring its strong pro-Western declarations by such actions as recognizing Bao Dai and publicizing its intention to attend the Sydney conference. If we are to sustain the present line of Thai orientation, prompt concrete evidence of our appreciation of its partnership should be produced. The speed and nature of U.S. economic and technical aid should be planned with this in mind. There is hardly any important economic urgency in Thailand. There is a political urgency. A quick gesture calculated to impress Government leaders and the people—particularly the educated elite in Bangkok—may produce much more desirable political results than a long-range economic project, too difficult to publicize, which may increase our vulnerability to charges of ulterior U.S. interest, such as the sale of surplus equipment, etc.

Thailand is genuinely interested in the United Nations and its specialized agencies (and certainly flattered that several regional offices are located in Bangkok). It is therefore of particular importance that any U.S. aid programs be coordinated with, and not compete with, assistance that is being supplied, or can be supplied, through agencies affiliated with the United Nations.

Finally, some Thai requests for aid are likely to be on the impractical side. Imagination gets little self-criticism in Bangkok, especially if someone else is paying the bill. It will not hurt relations, in fact it will help them, if assistance projects are tactfully screened and if ideas are guided into the most useful channels.

X. Public Information Activities Related to U.S. Aid Program

As national traditions and the experience gained by uninterrupted independence provide a strong stabilizing force in Thailand, there is not the same need to build up faith in the Government that exists in Burma, Indochina and Indonesia. The Government has pretty firm support from the people. Helping it do a good job, and publicizing the job it does, will of course strengthen it and help prevent the development of potential sources of social unrest. Provision should therefore be made for adequate support of U.S. aid programs by public information activities.

On the other hand, the relative strength of the Government and the relative weakness of anti-Western sentiment in Thailand mean that more emphasis can appropriately be placed than elsewhere in Southeast Asia on publicizing the United States role in technical and economic aid activities. The United States can take the credit without damaging the government in power. In this way, the possibility of an opportunistic switch by Thai leaders will be reduced, for the United States will become widely known as a friend of Thailand, and one not to be lightly discarded.

XI. Field Organization for Administration of Economic Aid Programs in Thailand

All aid projects should be covered by detailed agreements negotiated in advance, in which the functions and responsibilities of the American technicians involved would be clearly defined. The load of administrative work in the field entailed by this program would therefore primarily be:

1. Negotiating detailed project agreements (and their renewal) covering each kind of aid activity, and discussing general questions concerning the program which are raised by the Foreign Minister with the U.S. diplomatic mission.
2. Representing the U.S. Government on any joint policy-determining board of any joint commissions that may be set up.

3. Liaison with private U.S. groups employed by the Thai Government under contracts financed by United States.
4. Liaison with United Nations or other non-U.S. agencies supplying economic or technical aid to Thailand.
5. Distribution of U.S.-supplied commodities or equipment not consigned directly for use by an agency of the Thai Government, and end-use inspection and reports on all U.S. supplied commodities or equipment.
6. Determination of U.S. recommendations on use of local counterpart funds available for use in connection with the program.
7. Processing trainees selected by groups made responsible under each project agreement.
8. Continuing inspection, general supervision, and appraisal of success of various programs and performance of individual technicians, and taking steps to improve their functioning, where considered necessary, by renegotiating project agreements, having personnel shifted or replaced, recommending changes in program of aid supplies or equipment, etc. This function includes terminating programs that do not appear to be contributing fully to mutually agreed objectives, or to U.S. political objectives.
9. Providing administrative services for U.S. technicians in the field (payroll, housing assistance, employment of alien personnel, office space and services, travel, etc.).

These functions indicate the need for a small economic mission attached to the American Embassy, to comprise two or three top personnel capable of general direction of the mission, a somewhat larger number of mature technicians who, with the top personnel, would perform functions 1, 2, 3, 4, 6, and 8; an accounting, distributing, and reporting group to perform function 5; and administrative personnel (perhaps merged with those of the Embassy in a Joint Administrative Staff) to perform function 9. Function 7 could and probably should be performed by expanding the USIS staff that will presumably soon be carrying out this same function for persons exchanged under the Fulbright Act and the Smith-Mundt Act.

The group performing the above functions, other than 7, should be headed by a single Coordinator of Economic Cooperation Activities (CECA). It is the view of the present U.S. Ambassador to Thailand that present political and economic conditions are both so delicate and so inter-related in Thailand that there should be the closest working together of the diplomatic mission and the economic aid mission. For this reason, it is recommended that CECA be made directly responsible to the Chief of the U.S. diplomatic mission in Thailand. This would insure integration of all U.S. economic and technical aid activities, under whatever law (including where applicable ECA, Section 303 of MAP, Smith-Mundt, Fulbright, and Point Four) and would also insure conformity of all economic and technical aid activities with U.S. political policy in the area.

The question of establishing a joint policy-determining body to consider over-all objectives and means of aiding economic development in Thailand was not discussed with government officials, although it is believed that such a joint body may be desirable at some future stage.

Moreover, it may be advisable to establish joint commissions in specialized fields (such as rural health service or farm tool distribution), to take title to certain equipment and perhaps distribute certain commodities and handle the proceeds from them. One or more representatives of CECA should sit on each such joint body or commission.

U.S. technicians made available to the Thai Government should be responsible to the appropriate Thai Government department or bureau, or to a Joint U.S.-Thailand commission, for carrying out the tasks agreed in the applicable project agreement. Direction of their work while in the country should therefore come from these authorities. Technical backstopping and advice would, of course, be available to them from the Departments or organizations in the United States of which they were employees. General supervision and appraisal of their performance on these agreed tasks should be the responsibility of CECA and his staff, who should have authority to recall them if their performance was unsatisfactory on either technical or personal grounds.

Appendix

1. The Mission arrived in Bangkok at noon on April 4 and remained in Thailand until 6:30 a.m. April 12.
2. During the visit of the Mission to Thailand it was composed of the following persons:

Department of State:

   The Honorable R. Allen Griffin, Chief of Mission, with the personal rank of Minister
   Samuel P. Hayes, Jr., Deputy Chief of Mission and Adviser
   Henry Tarring, Jr., J.G. White Engineering Company, Consultant to the Department of State, Adviser
   Walter Walkinshaw, Adviser
   William McAfee, Adviser
   Eleanor L. Koontz, Secretary
   Mary Randolph, Secretary

Department of Agriculture:

   Ross E. Moore, Adviser
   Paul V. Kepner (April 7-16), Adviser
   Albert H. Moseman (April 7-16), Adviser

Public Health Service:

Howard M. Kline, Adviser

3. Members of the Mission participated in the following formal conferences during the visit in Thailand:

a) Preliminary Discussions with Embassy officials, April 4, 3:00 p.m.
b) Conference with Minister of Agriculture, April 5, 8:30 a.m.
c) Conference with Minister of Foreign Affairs, April 5, 10:00 a.m.
d) Conference with Prime Minister, April 5, 2:00 p.m.
e) Discussion with American Businessmen, April 6, 10:00 a.m.
f) Conference with Working Committee on Technical Assistance of National Economic Council, April 6, 2:30 p.m.
g) Conference with Minister of Commerce, April 7, 9:00 a.m.
h) Conference with Minister of Education, April 7, 9:45 a.m.
i) Conference with Minister of Communications, April 7, 11:30 a.m.
j) Conference with Minister of Industry, April 7, 2:30 p.m.
k) Conference with Minister of Public Health, April 8, 9:30 a.m.
l) Conference with Dr. Johnson, U.S. Geological Survey, April 10, 9:30 a.m.
m) Conference with National Planning Representatives, April 10
n) Conference with FAO Representatives, April 10
o) Conference with ECAFE Representatives, April 11, 9:00 a.m.
p) Final Coordinating Conference with Embassy Officials, April 11, 11:00 a.m.
q) Discussion with Student Leaders, April 11, 2:30 p.m.

4. A list of certain of the persons consulted during the visit of the Mission in Thailand in addition to the Cabinet Ministers indicated previously follows, not necessarily in order of rank within specific groups:

American Embassy

Ambassador Edwin F. Stanton
John Stone
Graham Quate
Alcott Deming
Burr Smith
William Anderson

Thai Government Representatives

Field Marshal P. Philbun Songgram, President of the Council
Phra Chuang Kaset Silpakarn, Minister of Agriculture

Nai Fuen Suphanasan, Assistant Minister of Agriculture
General Luang Mangkorn Prom Yothi, Minister of Interior
Nai Liang Chayakan, Assistant Minister of Interior
General Phra Boriphan Yutthakit, Minister of Commerce
General H.E. Phya Thepatsadin, Minister of Communication
Nai Pathom Pothikaeo, Assistant Minister of Communication
Nai Sawat Piemphongsan, Assistant Minister of Finance
Nai Worakan Bancha, Minister of Foreign Affairs
Phra Manuphan Wimolsat, Minister of Justice
H.E. Phya Borirak Wetchakan, Minister of Public Health
Colonel Nom Ketunut, Assistant Minister of Public Health
Major General Sawat Sawastikiat, Minister of Education
M.L. Det Sanitwong, Governor of the Bank of Thailand and Member of the
    National Economic Council Board
Dr. Luang Phayung Wetchasat, Director-General of the Public Health Dept.
M.C. Sithiyakorn Worawan, Director-General, Department of Industrial
    Works
Nai Insee Chandrastitya, Director-General of the Agriculture Department
Nai Thanat Khoman, Acting Director of the Economic Affairs Department,
    Ministry of Foreign Affairs
Nai Sunthorn Hongsladarom, Acting Secretary-General of the National
    Economic Council
Nai Sawai Habanananda, Ministry of Communication
M.L. Manich Chumsai, Ministry of Education
Nai Sommai Hoontrakun, Head of Research Division, Bank of Thailand
Nai Puey Ungphakorn, Ministry of Finance
Dr. Joseph W. Gould, Economic Adviser to the Prime Minister's Office
Mr. James T. Scott, Adviser to the Ministry of Commerce
Luang Thara Direk, Chief Engineer, Irrigation Department
Luang Suwan Wajok Kasikit, Rector, Agriculture College
Nai Porn Srichamorn, Director, Government Power Station
Phra Suwaphan Phithayakarn, Director-General, Transport Department
Nai Sanit Tunggamani, Post and Telegraph Department
Dr. Chu Sitachitt, Public Health Department
Dr. Sawat Daengsawang, Public Health Department
Dr. Nit Wetchawisit, Public Health Department
Dr. L. Chalerm Phrommat, Public Health Department
Dr. L. Phinphak Phityaphaet, Public Health Department
Nai Yong Chutima, Public Health Department
Nai Naga Devahastin
Nai Rachan Karnchanawanich, Department of Mines
Pra Norarat Chamnong, Under-Secretary of Commerce
Luang Thavil Sethaphanit, Director-General of Foreign Trade Department
Dr. Vebul Thamavit, Secretary-General, University of Moral and Political
    Sciences

Luang Sawat Sarasatphut, Director-General, Department of Education
Dr. Thal Nelanidhi, Faculty of Sciences, Chulalongkorn University
Khun Witthayawut, Chief of Technical Division, Vocational Education Dept.
Phra Charoen, Faculty of Engineering, Chulalongkorn University
Nai Charoen Chenakun, Dean, Faculty of Engineering, Chulalongkorn University
Khun Prasert Suphanat, Dean, Faculty of Economics, University of Moral and Political Sciences
Prasert Pakumanon, Faculty of Political Science, University of Moral and Political Sciences

U.S. Businessmen—among others, the following:

Willis Bird, exporter-importer, Representative of American President Lines
E.L. McClure, International Harvester
Richard Fisher, Pan American World Airways
Walter Lacount, Bank of America
Alexander MacDonald, Bangkok Post
Gordon Lowry, Getz Brothers
Gordon Brown, Girdeaux Company

Other Americans

Dr. Robert L. Pendleton, Professor of Tropical Soils and Agriculture, The Johns Hopkins University, In Thailand for Department of Agriculture
Dr. Harry H. Love, Department of Agriculture
Dr. Ritz, Seventh Day Adventist Mission
Dr. Johnson, Geological Survey

ECAFE Representatives

Mr. P.S. Lokanathan
Mr. Norman Gould
Mr. Giletti
Mr. Gilpin

FAO Representatives

Mr. William Cummings
Mr. Charles Coltman
Mr. Huberman

5. The Thai Government submitted the following documents dealing with requests for assistance:

A. A coordinated lists of experts and trainees needed in various fields of activity and of aid requested with appendixes presenting detailed information on the type and amount of assistance needed. These appendixes are listed herewith, the numbers given to them by the Thai Government being shown in parentheses.

Agriculture, Fisheries

1. Department of Fisheries, Memorandum on Technical and Economic Assistance (A-1)
2. Department of Agriculture, Memorandum on Technical and Economic Assistance (A-2)
3. Memorandum on Requests in the Line of Forestry (A-3)
4. Royal Irrigation Department Memorandum on Technical and Economic Assistance (A-4)
5. Department of Livestock Development, Memorandum on Technical and Economic Assistance (A-4)
6. Department of Cooperatives, Memorandum on Technical and Economic Assistance (A-5)
7. Department of Kasetsart University (Agriculture), Memorandum on Technical and Economic Assistance (A-6)
8. Addenda setting forth order in which the Ministry of Agriculture requested Technical and Economic Assistance.
9. Series of Appendixes dealing with: transportation needs of agricultural technicians; commercial fertilizers; stored rice infestation; emergency assistance for fisheries; emergency assistance for livestock.

Industry, Communications, Commerce

1. Memorandum on Rail Transport (B-1)
2. Brief outline of Present Situation of Telecommunications in Thailand (B-2) (together with charts)
3. Highway Project (B-3)
4. Experts and Trainees for Civil Aviation (B-3)
5. Memorandum on the Bar at mouth of river. (B-3) (charts showing general plan-Bangkok Harbor furnished separately.)
6. Request for Assistance under Point Four, including services of an expert statistician for Department of Commercial Intelligence and opportunity for Department's members to study abroad. (C-1)

7. Expert Assistance required under Point Four for Export Trade Promotion (C-2)
8. Request for Point Four Assistance for Department of Trade Control (C-3)

Education

1. Projects for Technical Assistance-Request of the Ministry of Education (with which were included lists of desired materials (D-1)

General

1. Ministry of Interior Memorandum on Point Four Program on Technical Assistance in 1950 (E-1)
2. Revenue Department Point Four Report and Tobacco Monopoly Point Four Request (F-1)

Public Health

1. Department of Public Health Memorandum on Point Four Aid (G-6)
2. Department of Public Health Memorandum on Nutrition (G-6)
3. Requests for Malaria and Filariasis Control (G-7)
4. Infectious Diseases Project (G-8)
5. Maternity and Child Welfare (G-9)
6. Assistance Needed for Tuberculosis Control.

B. The Thai Government submitted these additional documents on Industry, Communications, Commerce (Documents are numbered in sequence with those in previous section on Industry, etc.):

9. Statistics, Memoranda, and Documents submitted to the World Bank Mission, a comprehensive file of information on many phases of Thailand's economy.
10. Siam Money Act 2461
11. Factories Act BE2482
12. Law on Organization of Railways and Highways
13. Preparation for Enactment of Patent and Copyright Laws
14. Requests of Department of Industrial Works
15. Training in General Analytical Works
16. The Needs of the Department of Science
17. Present Activity, Future Plans – for Department of Industrial Promotion
18. Need of Technical Assistance – Division of Factory Control
19. Outline of Tentative Thailand Government Program for Communication, Commerce, Industry

20. Plan for the Establishment of a Pilot Plant for Tin Smelting and Production of Tin Foil
21. Technical Assistance in Metallurgical Industry
22. Royal State Railways of Thailand, Rehabilitation and Improvement, Project 1949
23. Table of General Statistics on Railroads
24. Immediate Technical Assistance Required of the Royal Department on Mines
25. Project for Two New Sugar Factories
26. Scheme for the Development of a General Textile Mill
27. Proposal for a New Slaughter House
28. A Project to Build a New 50-ton Paper Mill
29. Project for a Modern Tannery
30. List of Machinery Tools Required for Makasan Workshops
31. Technical Assistance in Mining
32. Training Schemes in Collaboration with Point Four Thai Geological Survey

C. The Thai Government submitted the following additional documents on Educational Problems (Documents are numbered in sequence with those in previous section on Education):

2. Report of the Education Sub-committee (which tentatively revised previously stated priorities)
3. Program of Vocational Education Improvement
4. Booklet on Literacy campaign
5. Vocational Education Statistics, Ministry of Education
6. Summary — Education in Siam; Ministry of Education
7. Report of the Consultative Educational Mission to Thailand (UNESCO), Feb-Mar., 1949
8. Proposals for a Follow up-Educational Mission to Thailand (UNESCO)
9. Geography of Siam — with Chapter on Education
10. Calendar — University of Moral and Political Sciences

D. The Thai Government submitted these additional documents on Public Health which are numbered in sequence with those in previous section on Public Health (These documents are on file in U.S. Public Health Service only):

7. School Dental Project
8. Venereal Diseases

11 Needs for United States Economic and Technical Aid in Indonesia [1950]

Summary

1. The Republic of the United States of Indonesia (RUSI) is a federation of states, operating under a provisional constitution. After the RUSI had achieved independence in December 1949, the leaders of its most important state, the Indonesian Republic, began a campaign, which is still continuing, for the creation of a centralized unitary state as contrasted with the present federal system (Section I, A.).

2. The internal threat from Communism exists primarily in relation to the Chinese Community, the left- wing fringe of the labor unions, the Indonesian Communist Party and elements of the Indonesian press (Section I, B.).

3. The RUSI has pursued a foreign policy of caution not unmixed with suspicion, giving evidence of its desire to remain aloof from the current world struggle. A critical point of friction in Netherlands-Indonesian relations is likely to be the RUSI claim to western New Guinea (Section I, C.).

4. The prewar economy of Indonesia was based on export of raw materials, the proceeds from which paid for imported consumer goods. Its present production of export commodities is one-half the prewar volume, and agricultural output generally is down. Inflationary pressures in Indonesia remain strong, and the government at present has a huge public debt. During 1949 the trade deficit of the area amounted to 105 million guilders (Section I, D and E.).

5. As a country of some 75 million people, producing important raw materials and strategically located, Indonesia has great importance for the United States (Section II).

6. Outstanding problems today are inflation and the lack of a trained government staff large enough for the country's needs. More than 70 percent of the Indonesians are engaged in agriculture, which provides not only the nation's food but more than 50 percent of its exports. There is need for technical training of Indonesians in this field. Needs in the health services are primarily for technical personnel and for the short-term replacement of equipment and facilities destroyed during recent years. The Government has had inadequate facilities and funds to improve educational opportunities,

Report No. 5 of the United States Economic Survey Mission to Southeast Asia, prepared during and following the Mission's visits to Djakarta, Bogor, and Bandung, April 12-22, 1950; and first printed in Washington, May, 1950.

269

and 90 percent of the Indonesians are illiterate. There is need for industrial development to meet consumer demands and to provide work for the rising number of unemployed (Section III).

7. Dutch economic interests are still important, and the Dutch Government feels a continued responsibility for the success of the new State. Commonwealth Nations are also interested in the area, and a limited amount of U.N. assistance has been received (Section IV).

8. In 1948 and 1949 the ECA provided $104 million of aid, and in February 1950, the Export-Import Bank authorized the extension of credits up to $100 million. A Fulbright Agreement is currently being negotiated (Section V).

9. A program of technical and economic aid is proposed, estimated to cost $14,445,000 for the 15 months ending June 30, 1951 (Section VI). This would cover aid in the following categories:

Agriculture, Fisheries, Forests	$7,005,000
Public Health and Medicine	4,500,000
Education	1,365,000
Transportation, Power and Industry	1,250,000
Newsprint	325,000

10. There are limitations on the amount of an aid program and the speed with which it can be developed. The shortage of trained officials limits Indonesia's ability to utilize outside aid. There is some question as to the extent to which Dutch advisers can or will continue to serve. The time and efforts of Indonesian officials are currently taken up in handling political and military problems resulting from the formation of the new Republic, and in the various internal struggles for power. There also remains the security question, which limits the extent of aid operations in certain sections of the country. A final and most significant limitation springs from the budgetary situation of the Government (Section VII).

11. American aid should be dissociated from the influence of Dutch personnel. Special attention should be given to avoiding any appearance of ulterior United States interest, and projects of particular interest to the leaders in Jogjakarta should be stressed (Section VIII).

12. Public information support for the aid program should strengthen the popularity of the Government and demonstrate United States interest in the area (Section IX).

13. All aid projects should be covered by detailed agreements between the Governments. A small economic mission should be attached to the United States Embassy to supervise aid projects and to handle the administrative work in the field. It may be advisable to establish joint commissions in specialized fields to distribute certain commodities and supervise some programs (Section X).

I. The Current Situation

A. *Political–Internal*

The Republic of the United States of Indonesia (RUSI) is operating on the basis of a provisional constitution. The President of RUSI is Sukarno and the Prime Minister, Dr. Mohammad Hatta. As independence leaders of long standing and great prominence, they are most capable of commanding support both in the government and among the populace. The Cabinet is made up of technicians and representatives of the leading parties. Its composition also takes into account the need for balance between the former Federalists and the representatives of the Indonesian Republic.

Divergence between Federalists and Republicans has been and remains a lively issue. In the areas which the Dutch controlled, and in areas they reconquered from the Indonesian Republic during their two police actions, the Dutch set up autonomous states or *negaras*. After the Republic of the United States of Indonesia had, on December 27, 1949, achieved its independence, the leaders of the Indonesian Republic (the State which had provided the energy and manpower in the struggle for freedom) began a campaign for the reincorporation of the negaras within the Republic and thus, for the extension of the authority of the Republic throughout Indonesia. Although the RUSI provisional constitution provides in a general way that the future composition of Indonesia be determined through an orderly electoral procedure, the RUSI Government has generally stood idly by and let the Republic pursue its campaign. The main reason has been that RUSI leaders, a majority of the RUSI Cabinet, and many members appointed to the RUSI Parliament are former Republicans and have been active in the Republican cause.

As of the middle of April, all states (negaras) have either been incorporated or are in the process of being incorporated into the Republic, with the exception of East Sumatra and the extensive island areas of East Indonesia. In the latter area, armed resistance has been offered by members of the former Royal Netherlands-Indonesian Army (KNIL) (Koninklijk Nederlandsch-Indonesisch Leger), Indonesian troops who had served under Dutch command, and who had fought against the Indonesian independence forces in the two Dutch police actions. Some of these troops, most of whom are East Indonesians, would resent the incursion of Javanese troops who now comprise the bulk of the RUSI Army. In addition, many East Indonesian leaders reject the claim of the Republic to be the dominating national force.

The Republican leaders at Jogjakarta and their following in the Indonesian Republic are still a radical and revolutionary group inspired with the aim of achieving complete independence from Dutch traditions. As a part of their drive for independence, they advocate a fairly extreme socialist economy. Their particular influence extends as well to East Java but diminishes somewhat in West Java and Sumatra.

The RUSI Government has declared its intention to settle peacefully the relationship between the Republic and the two member states still remaining outside it. This goal will be sought in forthcoming conferences, and RUSI has announced that preparatory studies are being hastened with a view to determining the national state structure under a new and permanent constitution. Whatever charges may be made against the precipitate endeavors of the Republic at aggrandizement, it is highly probable that the movement it started will result fairly shortly in the creation of a strong, centralized national state. The influence of the Republic within the future state remains to be determined; however, the leading Cabinet members and administrators in the RUSI Government at present, although a majority are Republicans, are moderates who can be counted upon to exercise a restraining force both politically and economically. Some concessions may be made to the Republicans in the form of the proposed new constitution.

B. Special Problems

1. Communism. The internal threat from communism exists primarily in relation to the Chinese community, in the extreme left-wing fringe in the labor unions and Indonesian press, and in the coastal areas susceptible to easy Communist penetration from the mainland. Up until now the Chinese minority of nearly two million has been relatively inactive but, after the eventual establishment of relations with Communist China, it may be expected that Communist organizers will make some headway among the Chinese community through nationalistic appeals, blackmail, family pressures, and offers of business opportunities. Large sections of the Indonesian press are dominated by left wing radicals, some undoubtedly Communists, who consistently support the cause of Russia and Communist China. Labor organization, which had never been allowed to evolve under Dutch rule, is in a fairly chaotic state. Communists have undoubtedly penetrated several local groups and dominate SOBSI, an association of labor unions which passes as a central federation but which in reality exercises little control. Except for Medan, which is open to Communist influence from Malaya, Communist organization has been intermittent and inefficient and has been frustrated to some extent by factionalism between the Comintern Communists and the Tan Malaka National Communists.

The major political party in Indonesia, the Masjumi, is becoming increasingly Islamic in character and would seem impervious to Communist doctrine. (Except for Bali, Indonesia is predominantly Moslem.) The most important Indonesian leaders are quite aware of the internal threat of communism and have dealt promptly and vigorously with overt Communist attempts to seize power.

2. Armed Forces. Reorganization of the national army is a difficult problem. With the achievement of independence RUSI assumed control over the Tentara Nasional Indonesia (TNI), the army of the Republic, which comprised many guerrillas and irregulars. With the TNI and local forces taken over from the negaras, the present army numbers between 175,000 and 200,000. It is the Government's aim to establish the national army of RUSI, Tentara Republik Indonesia Serikat (TRIS), with some 100,000 troops. In the meantime, however, employment must be found for the demobilized young people and irregulars belonging to the old TNI, many of whom are undisciplined. In accordance with the Hague Agreement, the bulk of the Royal Netherlands Indonesian Army (KNIL) numbering about 50,000 are also to be incorporated in TRIS. Although most of the men in KNIL are reported to be willing to join TRIS, despite their recent battles with the Republic, many of the officers are Dutch and Eurasians and are still subject to irresponsible Dutch influences bent on sabotaging the new RUSI state. Exploiting the racial and cultural differences between East Indonesia, where most of KNIL originated, and Java, which supplied most of the men in TNI, certain dissident elements in KNIL have engaged in plots to maintain the independence of East Indonesia as a separate state. Brief armed conflicts have occurred in Makassar and Ambon. The highest Dutch and Indonesian authorities are striving to work out amicably the assimilation of the KNIL with TRIS, but the problem is a most difficult one and will remain so for quite some time.

The eventual training and organization of the new national army is another pressing question. The bulk of the forces now in East Java were Japanese trained, while the tradition of the army in West Java is primarily Dutch. An academy for coordinated training has been set up and it is hoped to bring about uniformity within a year. Another defect of the national army is its lack of supply and pay services. Many of the troops have been paid only sporadically and accordingly have been tempted to live off the land. The Dutch Military Mission of 800 members shortly to be created will assist in both the formation of adequate services and training of the army along Western lines.

3. Labor. The organization of responsible and orderly labor groups is another pressing problem. Throughout all of Indonesia there have been a number of recurrent wildcat strikes. While some of these have been of Communist inspiration, the cause, in most cases, has been the low wages paid labor under the former Dutch regime, wages now acknowledged to be inadequate in terms of present greatly inflated prices. Many of the strikes, however, have been of an irresponsible nature and have continued even after wage demands have been met. Because of their lack of training, Indonesians have been generally excluded from skilled trades, professions and higher administrative positions. Furthermore, no attempt was made by the Dutch to train Indonesians in these categories. This factor constitutes another element of labor unrest. The origin and character of the strikes, which in many instances have severely damaged national interests, points to the need for the development of a responsible employer-labor relationship.

C. Foreign Policy

Since the achievement of independence, the Indonesian Government has pursued a foreign policy of caution, not unmixed with suspicion. It gives evidence of desiring to remain aloof from the current world ideological struggle, at least until the administration has had time to put its house in order and feel its way in world affairs. Accordingly the Nehru policy of political neutrality has found some appeal in responsible circles. RUSI has taken steps to establish relations with Soviet Russia and Communist China with a view to normalizing, as it hopes, its contacts with the principal powers. The responsible leaders consider their country so defenseless as to be unable to participate in any military strategic bloc at present. They do not believe Communist China can become an international military power for several years. Nevertheless, they are apprehensive of the threat of communism in Asia, and hope in the meantime to participate in developing some kind of solidarity among the non-Communist countries of Southeast Asia. In its present form, this idea exists only in vague outline and is conditioned by certain reservations concerning the stability of the Philippines and the suitability of association with such countries as South Korea. Because of an earlier affinity with some of the nationalist Indochinese leaders now with Ho Chi-minh, the RUSI leaders view Bao Dai with dark suspicion as a puppet of the French. For the present, internal problems are the cause of chief concern and, in view of the troubled world situation, with which it as yet has had so little experience, the RUSI Government considers that for the immediate future the safest course is to adopt a middle position.

Conferences of the Netherlands-Indonesian Union are regarded by the Indonesians as a useful vehicle for the settlement of certain problems left outstanding by the Hague Agreement, but as yet there has been little popular appreciation in Indonesia of the purposes of the Union. Both RUSI and the Netherlands Government strongly persist in their claims to Netherlands New Guinea and, although a mixed commission has been set up to submit a report by July 1, the New Guinea issue is likely to become a critical point of friction in Netherlands-Indonesian relations.

D. Economic Situation

The economy of Indonesia is characterized by a dual form of production in which the big, mostly foreign-held plantations operate side by side with the small native holdings. The large properties produce in quantity the three leading exports of this area, namely, petroleum, tin, and rubber. The small native land holdings produce for the most part the staples of the Indonesian diet of rice and sundry vegetables, as well as a significant portion of Indonesian export crops. In 1940 the small native farm produced 47 percent of the rubber, 55 percent of the tapioca, 79 percent of the kapok, 88 percent of the copra, and 97 percent of the pepper exported.

Compared with neighboring Asiatic countries, the standard of living in Indonesia is relatively tolerable, even though quite inadequate by Western standards. The great fertility of the volcanic soils of Java permit it to support a very dense population (960 persons per square mile on Java and Madura in 1941, with some districts running as high as 2,200 persons per square mile), although at a considerably lower living standard than obtains in most of the other islands of the archipelago. It is estimated that, in 1940, 273 pounds of cereal, 421 pounds of root crops, and 18 pounds of nuts and pulses were available for consumption per person in Java. The prewar average annual consumption of textiles in Indonesia was 11 meters per person.

Besides a rich soil and climate favorable to agriculture, Indonesia has substantial fish and forest resources, and important mineral deposits (oil and tin). Agricultural, forest, and mineral resources have been effectively exploited and have been able to compete successfully in world markets by combining native manpower and competence with Western (primarily Dutch) capital, technical research, and management.

The prewar economy of Indonesia was based on the export of raw materials, the proceeds from which were used to cover the cost of imported consumer goods (200,000 to 300,000 tons of rice a year, except in 1941, when production equaled consumption, and large quantities of textiles), in addition to capital equipment, the service on foreign capital, and personal remittances to the Netherlands. In 1940, the value of exports amounted to $512 million and imports $244 million. Eighteen percent of the external trade of Indonesia before the war was with Holland, but Holland was by far the greatest beneficiary of the payments for invisible imports indicated by this commodity export surplus. In 1939, the amount of foreign capital invested in business enterprises was estimated at about $1,150 million, of which about 75 percent was Dutch, 13.5 percent British, 2.5 percent American, and a substantial percent Chinese. In addition, Indies government bonds valued at approximately $800 million were held abroad (and required servicing), practically all by the Dutch.

Despite Indonesia's great potential wealth in natural and human resources, after 8 years of war and revolution its production of export commodities is only one-half of the prewar volume, and output of foodstuffs ranges from 10 to 20 percent below that of prewar production. The country's lack of self-sufficiency in rice has caused a substantial drain on meager foreign exchange resources. Its transport system and public utilities are barely adequate for the present low level of production and trade. Essential to revival in agricultural production is large-scale rehabilitation of plant and equipment of western-type estates.

The final $40 million of ECA aid made available in 1949 has been expended chiefly for textiles and rice, which are now arriving. A Netherlands credit of 200 million guilders has also been made available. Even this assistance will not be enough, and Indonesia is seeking credits to cover the import of additional consumer goods, in view of the anticipated 1950 balance of payments deficit of approximately 500 million guilders. The Export-Import Bank authorization for a $100 million loan is expected to be reserved for capital projects only, and

Indonesia's gold reserves of about $180 million are reported to be needed to help support the value of its currency.

The expectation, for some months prior to the transfer of sovereignty and for several months afterwards, that drastic monetary reforms were imminent (see below, Section E, Financial Situation) induced large scale hoarding of export commodities and speculative price rises. During the first part of March 1950 export products held in anticipation of currency devaluation totaled at least $100 million in value. The movement of these still enormous holdings into export trade was deterred by the fact that the domestic price level for most of these commodities remains above that prevailing in world markets, and by apprehension that further monetary changes of a far-reaching nature (and hence great speculative profits) might be in prospect.

Imbalance in domestic and foreign prices and the unattractiveness of the official rate of exchange for exports has stimulated abnormally large smuggling—estimated to amount to as much as 250 million guilders in 1950. Preliminary official figures for the first half of April 1950, however, indicate that legitimate exports have regained the January level after declining in February to a low point in March.

E. Financial Situation

1. Inflation. Inflationary pressures in Indonesia remain strong. Retail prices of important foodstuffs rose during the last half of 1949 by 25 percent in Djakarta; by 35 percent in Surabaya. By February 1950, there had been further rises of 3 percent in Bandung, but a decline of 13 percent in Surabaya. To some extent, these price rises reflected the seasonal increase of rice prices in December, January, and February. While they did not quite restore prices to their early 1949 levels, when the effects of the second police action were still felt strongly, they indicated the underlying instability of the price situation. The volume of domestic output for home consumption, plus the volume of imports, is less than prewar, and falls far short of absorbing—at unchanged prices—the money income available to an enlarged postwar population. The stores are full of goods, but mostly luxury items, not the types and grades most effective as incentive goods. Lack of incentive means inadequate production, which in turn feeds the inflation. Public finances are sharply out of balance, and in 1949 the deficit of the United States of Indonesia bordered on 1.5 billion guilders. This was about 45 percent of the total 1949 expenditures of the government of RUSI, and represented nearly one-third of the total money supply on December 31, 1949. (Moreover, the budget deficit is expected to increase sharply in 1950.) This deficit was met partly by foreign financing, involving no immediate increase in the money supply; by borrowing 200 million guilders from the Bank of Java; and by an additional government note issue of 100 million guilders; thus increasing the currency in circulation by approximately 300 million guilders (after an expansion of 400 million guilders in 1949). Even the currency reform of March 1950, reducing the total money supply by somewhat less than one-half (see below, paragraph 5) does not appear to have brought effective demand down into balance with the supply of goods.

2. Public Debt. From the Netherlands Indies Government the new nation on December 27, 1949, inherited a huge debt of about 4.2 billion guilders, approximately one-third of which was externally held. This debt remained even after the pre-independence debt of 6.2 billion guilders had been reduced by 2.0 billion guilders in accordance with the Round Table Agreement.

Prior to independence, the public debt had risen to about 6.2 billion guilders. Of this total 2.5 billion guilders was internal debt and 3.7 billion guilders constituted external debt. The internal debt (expressed throughout in guilders) consisted chiefly of (a) advances by the Java Bank (950 million), (b) government notes (NICA currency, 950 million), and (c) treasury bonds (550 million). The major categories of the external debt were (a) bonded debt (871 million), (b) foreign-exchange and foreign-credit accounts (1,358 million), (c) account current with treasurer (927 million), (d) Netherlands account (356 million). If unbalanced budgets continue, which now seems likely for some time, the public debt will continue to increase.

3. Balance of Payments. The trade deficit in 1949 amounted to 105 million guilders, with exports valued at 1,040 million guilders and imports valued at 1,145 million guilders (excluding exports and imports of the oil companies, totaling 688 million guilders, whose transactions are not yet subject to the foreign exchange regulations, in view of the heavy rehabilitation expenses they have had to bear). Net payments for invisibles were heavy, about 500 million guilders, mostly to the Netherlands for profits, interest, dividends, and pensions.

The unstable price situation is not susceptible of correction by rationing and price control measures alone, as demonstrated by developments over the past 4 years, and the monetary and financial actions which the Government took in March 1950 were designed as supplementary measures to help bring the price situation under control.

4. New Exchange System. Under the new foreign-exchange system adopted in March 1950, receipts from abroad must be sold to authorized banks at an exchange rate of U.S. $1 to 3.80 guilders, the rate officially established by the Foreign Exchange Institute; and, in addition, the seller receives a certificate (or certificate credit) from the buying bank, denominated in guilders, equal to 50 percent of the official guilder value of the foreign-exchange receipts.

A market has been created for these certificates by requiring their presentation to authorized banks for the purchase of foreign exchange, together with the usual foreign-exchange permit and, as the case warrants, an import license; at the same time, the Foreign Exchange Institute has fixed the price of the certificates by offering to sell them at 200 percent of their face value. The intensity of the demand for foreign exchange insures that the Institute will not have to buy the certificates at this price in order to maintain the desired value.

As a result, sellers of foreign exchange obtain a rate of U.S. $1 to 7.60 guilders (3.80 directly in guilder, plus 3.80 by selling the 50 percent certificate at twice its guilder face value). Purchasers of foreign exchange must pay 11.40 guilders for U.S. $1, for they must pay (a) 200 percent of the face value of the certificates needed and (b) 100 percent of the value of the exchange permit at the official rate. The two rates are not applicable to certain classes of transaction. Firms which combine exporting and importing functions are not required to sell their certificates, and may use them to purchase foreign exchange. Such firms obtain an "export" rate of U.S. $1 to 5.70 guilders, but, on the other hand, they obtain an "import" rate of U.S. $1 to 7.60 guilders. Capital transfers to Indonesia which constitute desirable investment activity, as defined by the Foreign Exchange Institute, receive certificates equal to 100 percent of their official guilder value, or a rate of U.S. $1 to 11.40 guilders. Other classes of transactions with preferred status include imports of rice, flour, textiles, and a few other items; remittances by foreigners in Indonesia in private and official employment; exports originating with small farmers, who are offered extra inducements to discourage hoarding and smuggling to Singapore; and costs, including foreign fees and commissions, incurred in connection with exports.

By the introduction of this system the government hopes to increase its revenues and stimulate exports. Authorized banks are required to transfer to the government the difference between their guilder receipts and payments arising out of the operation of the system, excluding, of course, normal banking commissions and charges. The government estimates that, by obtaining the differential between the "export" rate and the "import" rate, it will increase revenues by 500 million guilders in 1950.

It is hoped that, in response to the inducement of higher guilder prices, exports will rise enough to increase foreign-exchange earnings. This would enable an expansion of imports, and, on the basis of higher guilder values for both exports and imports, the government expects its revenues from export and import duties and taxation to increase during 1950 by 800 million guilders. On the other hand, if continued deficit financing and consumer shortages—both absolutely and relative to the volume of money—result in further price increases, the export inducement features of the new exchange system may be nullified.

The government's objectives include the stimulation of exports and the increase of imports. A healthier economy with more stable prices would help achieve these objectives as well as contribute to political stability. As part of its over-all attack on these problems, the government, on March 19, took action to effect a sharp reduction in the money supply.

5. Reduction of Money Supply and Compulsory Loan. From March 19, 1950, all currency in circulation—except for notes issued by the Republic of Indonesia—in denominations of 5 guilders and above was required to be split in half. The left halves became legal tender for 50 percent of the face value imprinted thereon, and between March 22 and April 16 they were to be exchanged for new RUSI notes at public agencies and banks. Their legal-tender quality ceased on April 9.

The right halves, no longer legal tender, are usable for the purchase of 40-year government bonds, to be issued at a later date, which will carry an interest rate of 3 percent. These halves will be usable at 50 percent of the face value imprinted thereon. It is not clear to what extent buyers will have a choice between marketable and savings bonds.

At the same time, banks were instructed to transfer 50 percent of their deposits, with some exceptions, to "Subscription Account 3 Percent Government Loans."

Republic of Indonesia currency ceased to be legal tender on May 1, and was to be exchanged for new banknotes at varying rates, depending on the locality where the currency was held.

As a result of the above program, the money supply was reduced by somewhat less than half.

6. Financial Prospects. Indonesia's financial situation in the coming months is dependent in part upon the extent to which the reduction of the money supply will act as a deflationary force. It is also to a great degree dependent upon the success of foreign-exchange measures in increasing exports and decreasing smuggling. The possible resulting increase in imports, together with any forthcoming United States aid, should go a long way toward reducing inflationary pressures arising from absolute shortages of rehabilitation and consumption goods.

A portion of the currency in circulation (10 percent) is in denominations of 2½ guilders and less, and this portion was not subject to the monetary regulations of March 19. Furthermore, in anticipation of the government's action, and with some foreknowledge thereof, deposit balances were widely distributed among the banks prior to March 19 and "cloaks" were used—in order to come under the proviso, insofar as possible, that bank balances below 400 guilders and the first 200 guilders of bank balances between 400 and 1,000 guilders were exempt from the regulations of March 19. There are 21 banks in Indonesia with many branches and agencies and also innumerable types of banking institutions which accept deposits, with the result that widespread distribution of balances was not a difficult undertaking. At the same time, prior to March 19, the banks were drained of their currency holdings in denominations of 2½ guilders and less.

Insofar as entrepreneurial activities are concerned, an attempt will be taken to maintain the scale of activities by borrowing. Undoubtedly, the ability of the banks to extend credit has been impaired temporarily, owing to the loss of assets (50 percent reduction in cash held) and to their need for more guilder funds to finance foreign payments (as a result of higher exchange rates). But this will be offset to some degree by non-bank borrowing and, if need be, by the sale of assets by persons or firms who would have preferred to borrow. An economy in the use of funds will probably be practiced through the holding of smaller cash balances, which will increase the velocity of circulation, with the result that the existing money supply will be called upon to do more work than would otherwise be the case—at possibly higher interest rates. In this connection, the right halves of the old currency are being sold at substantial discounts, and thus constitute additional liquid assets in general circulation.

The money-supply reduction program has not completely succeeded in removing the distrust of the currency which has existed for some time. This distrust continues to induce hoarding, and in particular, persuades exporters to accumulate stocks, notwithstanding higher guilder prices for exports. At the same time, importers are still reluctant to part with stocks.

The new exchange-rate structure is inflationary in character and may, unless foreign-exchange resources (hence imports) are increased at a fairly rapid rate, counteract such deflationary effects as are caused by reducing the money supply. Prices of imports have already risen. In fact, the price control office, effective April 1, advised importers that they could triple the price of their floor stocks, except of workers' rationed textiles, wheat flour, petroleum products, and newsprint. These higher prices may offset somewhat the effects on the importers of freezing half their cash balances and of the lower sales volume that may result from the reduction in the money supply. On the other hand, importers' profit margins on all imported goods were to be reduced to an average of 25 percent, effective May 1, 1950.

Basic to all problems besetting the new government is the difficult budgetary situation. Expenditures in 1950 are estimated at about 4.5 billion guilders, with one-third to be devoted to the army. The government wants to demobilize the army but at the same time is acutely aware of the need for providing employment for guerrilla veterans and the dangers involved in not doing so. In the absence of acceptable job opportunities for the army, government outlays on this account are likely to continue at high levels. In addition, the government lacks experience; moreover, inefficiency and possibly corruption will probably cause expenditures for regular governmental services to rise.

Tax and other revenues, prior to the monetary and financial measures taken in March, were estimated at 1.5 billion guilders. To this sum the government now adds 800 million guilders from customs duties and taxes, at existing rates applied to higher import and export values, and 500 million guilders from the differential rates of exchange. Although the government seems to have decided to liquidate its debt to the Bank of Java with the "proceeds" of the compulsory loan, it may be forced to defer repayment in order to finance the budgetary deficit. Over the first three months of 1950 the government's debt to the Bank of Java increased by one-third, from 1.2 billion guilders to 1.6 billion guilders.

7. Conclusion. In view of the strength of inflationary pressures in Indonesia, any aid programs undertaken should be designed to make the maximum contribution to economic production and to political stability, and the minimum contribution to inflation. Aid supplies imported in connection with the program should be sold in order to obtain local currency needed for particular projects. Release, for use in connection with such programs, of the ECA counterpart fund now available, amounting to some 350 million guilders, should be scheduled in such a way that it results in the minimum contribution to inflationary pressure. It should therefore be allocated predominantly to projects that promptly increase the availability of consumer goods (by expanding their production or distribution),[a] and its release to different projects should be timed in such a way that inflationary expenditures are so far as possible counterbalanced by deflationary additional flows of goods to consumers.

It should be noted that nothing can be done with the counterpart fund that could not be done by using regularly budgeted governmental funds. The only reasons for using the counterpart fund at all are (1) projects can be selected with regard to strictly economic considerations, and thus concentrate on those with the minimal inflationary effects; (2) U.S. participation may help carry out these projects more effectively and economically than would otherwise be the case; and (3) the U.S. gets some credit for aiding these projects.

II. Importance of Indonesia

Indonesia is an archipelago lying between the Southeast Asia Mainland and Australia, comprising some 2,000 islands (of which Sumatra, Java, Celebes, Borneo, and New Guinea are important land masses), and extending over a distance of 3,000 miles. With the Malayan Peninsula it forms what is often called the Malay Barrier between the Indian and Pacific Oceans, dominating the gateways between the two. Most sea traffic between these two oceans passes through the Malacca Straits. If that should be closed, most sea traffic would flow through the Sunda Straits between Java and Sumatra. If both of these straits were closed, shipping would take far longer and be much more expensive between the Indian and Pacific Oceans. As an area in which great ocean highways meet, therefore, Indonesia and Malaya together are comparable to the Caribbean or Mediterranean Seas.

Economically, Indonesia is important as a major producer of commodities needed for the commercial economy of the United States and other countries, as well as strategic commodities needed for stockpiling. In 1939, Indonesia accounted for the following shares of total world exports: pepper, 85%; kapok, 72%; rubber, 37%; agave, 33%; copra products, 27%; oil palm products, 19%; sugar, 11%; and coffee, 4%. During the same year, it accounted for the following share of total world production, most of which was also exported: cinchona bark, 91%; tin, 17%; petroleum, 3%.

Rehabilitation of production and resumption of export of many of these commodities will help Europe, and particularly the Netherlands, achieve a viable economy, for these raw materials will help supply European needs without requiring dollar payments by Europe, and the exports to the United States will earn dollars that may again, as in the past, flow to Europe in payment for goods and services bought from Europe. Indonesia is already an excellent export

---

[a]Examples of such projects are seed farms and fish hatcheries, both of which give increased return within a year, and roads that open up areas producing food or other surpluses.

market for American goods and bears promise also of becoming again an important area for American investment. The prewar value of American investments was estimated to total about $85 million.

As a great country, strategically located, with perhaps 75,000,000 people, producing important raw materials potentially contributing to a reestablishment of triangular world trade and hence to the success of ERP, Indonesia has great importance for the United States. It has a special political importance, also, as a former colonial area that has achieved independence without bitterness (though with some suspicion) toward the West. If Indonesia finds that cooperation with the West can be mutually advantageous and if it is able to reestablish a healthy economy internally and externally (which is highly improbable without Western help), it can become one of the bastions of the free world, in an area where such potential bastions are notably lacking. Its sympathies certainly do not lie with communism, which was vigorously suppressed when the Communists became openly militant. Although nominally searching for a "middle" position, Indonesia will inevitably be pulled toward the West by the individualism of its people as well as by its economic interests, if its own internal economic and political problems can be solved. To have Indonesia as a full political and economic partner in a free world would be of prime importance to the United States and to other like-minded nations. It would also be an example of great influence on the other countries of Southeast Asia, some of which feel the need of closer points of support than the United States or the British Commonwealth can furnish.

III. Dominant Immediate Economic and Political Problems in Indonesia

A. General

The most pressing economic and political problems in Indonesia are so fundamental in origin and so pervasive in influence that real solutions are beyond the capacity of a foreign government that is not asked (and does not desire to be asked) to take either the political or the financial responsibility needed for their solution. There are, however, certain steps that a foreign government may properly take in aiding the Indonesian government to overcome its difficulties. Outstanding today are the two following problems:

1. Inflation and the three major sources that feed it:
   a) Excessive government expenditures, through deficit spending for a swollen army and state bureaucracy;
   b) Inadequate production for home consumption and for sale abroad to pay for essential imports—especially textiles and hand tools;
   c) Lack of confidence in Indonesian currency and a somewhat unrealistic exchange rate, resulting in the hoarding of both home consumption and export goods, and smuggling of the latter.

2. Rebuilding of government staff and social services, now adversely affected by:
   a) Wartime deterioration and destruction;
   b) Departure of many Dutch administrative and technical personnel;
   c) Desire to discourage the use of the Dutch language and lessen dependence on a single Western nation.

There is also, of course, the long-run problem of increasing production to balance population increase and, if possible, run ahead of it, so that standards of living can be improved.

Certain of these problems are spelled out in greater detail in the following pages.

B. Agriculture

More than 70 percent of the Indonesians with recognizable occupations are engaged in agriculture. They not only provide the nation's food intake but also produce more than 50 percent of her exports. Undoubtedly this group also provides more than 70 percent of the nation's annual baby crop, more than 70 percent of the young people who go into industry, transport, and other service, and more than its share of the young men who enter the army and guerrilla units.

The nation has great problems which it would like agriculture to solve. The Government officials describe these as economic problems, such as greater production of food to provide an increased and more nutritious diet, and greater production of export products required to pay for import necessities.

The producers of food, fiber, fish, and forest products do not concern themselves with national economic problems. In fact they are not aware of them. The rural Indonesian has strongly felt desires and is keenly aware of the extent to which they are or are not satisfied. Many of his tools are in disrepair. He seeks new ones to ease his toil. Peasants in many areas, seeing how fertilizers increase yield, want to obtain them. The fishermen and their families, totaling about 5 million, are concerned that produce from the soil be available in adequate supply at reasonable cost and that forest products be sufficient to meet their housing and boat-building needs. The tillers of the soil, on the other hand, require a diet richer in animal protein; their present protein needs are supplied primarily from fish. According to a survey made by FAO in 1946, the animal protein intake in Indonesia is the lowest of any country in the world—about 4 grams per day per person.

The chief dissatisfaction of the Indonesian farmer, fisherman, and forester is not with the production resulting from his labor. Western science applied by the Dutch has resulted in the development of high yielding crops. Agricultural, forestry, and fishery research in Indonesia are the most developed in Asia, and a system of public services effectively carries the work of the technical institutions on production problems down to the village. The producer's influence on his income, however, ends in the field, the forest, and at the beach. He is not satisfied with the return he receives for his surplus production.

Marketing and credit are largely in the hands of the Chinese money lender, merchant, and miller, while the import and export business is controlled by Europeans—primarily Dutch.

Indonesian agriculture is characterized by small units which produce primarily for subsistence. Only their surpluses enter national and international trade, and these are produced first to pay taxes, to secure essential tools of production, and finally to exchange for their few other necessities. Beyond these the farmer produces a surplus only to the extent that he can exchange it for commodities which he considers worthy of the additional labor.

A problem of first magnitude for Indonesia is to restore and then to increase production for both internal consumption and for export. The national leaders attribute the slump in production to the physical destruction resulting from the war and the postwar revolution, as well as to general unrest in the country. Though these may be primary causative factors, surplus production in agriculture rises with incentive and shrinks or vanishes if the surplus products cannot be exchanged for goods or services considered commensurate with the additional labor required to produce the surplus.

Program Consideration. An emergency program in agriculture should include aid in the development of Indonesia's technical resources, marketing and credit, health and education, supply of consumer goods, and light industry.

Technical Resources. Before the war, all of the top-level posts and most of the immediately subordinate posts in agriculture were occupied by Dutch administrators, technicians, and teachers. These comprised more than 600 agriculturists. This number has been reduced to 408 at the present time and is expected to be reduced to 228 during 1951. The Indonesians have developed some of the best technical institutions in Asia, and their work in tropical agriculture is known and respected throughout the world. But very few Indonesian agriculturalists have been trained in Holland. Training for Indonesians in Java has been at the agricultural high-school level and at what they call the medium-school level. Not until after the war was a curriculum in agricultural science adopted. The curriculum consists of a five-year college course and is now in its second year.

The expansion of its technical resources is of prime importance for maintenance of agricultural efficiency in the archipelago and for diversification and expansion of its agricultural production. The Government of Indonesia has not been able to work out a contract with terms of reference and perquisites which are attractive to additional Dutch technicians. Many, if not the majority, of the Dutch technicians and administrators now in advisory positions are not equipped either by attitude or desire to work for maximum progress in Indonesian agriculture. They have a nostalgia for the days when the Dutch held the leading positions, responsibility, and authority. The attitude toward the Dutch of the Indonesians who are now in the administrative positions is also not conducive to the best development of technical services. The Indonesians do not know how far to trust the Dutch. They have but recently gained their authority and position. They are cognizant of their technical limitations but are unwilling to accept objectively the advice of the Dutch advisers who were formerly their chiefs. Whether the Dutch and the Indonesians will be able to achieve the necessary psychological adjustment to permit objective work under the new arrangement is certainly debatable.

Although the relationship between the Dutch and the Indonesians is not one of mutual confidence nor conducive to the best development, it is certainly not probable that foreign advisers from the United States could replace them to a major extent. Leading Indonesian officials would like to have advisers from the United States but it is unlikely that U.S. technicians could work in Indonesia without developing friction between themselves and the Dutch or between themselves and the Indonesians.

The most important short-run objective of a U.S. agricultural aid program should be (a) to retain the qualified and loyal Dutch technicians, if possible, but to stand ready to replace them gradually with technicians from other Western powers, primarily the United States; and (b) to increase the competence of Indonesian technicians as rapidly as possible by giving them work experience in the United States.

In the long run, an increased rate of effort will be needed in the training of Indonesian technicians at all levels in Indonesia, and there will be need for the gradual training of a larger number of Indonesian technicians abroad. This will undoubtedly require American professors in the College of Agriculture and American scientists and technicians in Indonesia's research, extension, marketing, and credit institutions, probably working in association with both Dutch and Indonesian personnel.

Marketing and Credit. The educational, investigational, and other special institutions in the field of agriculture have been dedicated to research, teaching, and extension in the field of agricultural production. Nothing has been done in the field of marketing or credit. The producers of crops, forest products, and fish feel that they are fairly well-equipped in the production of their commodities but are greatly dissatisfied with the returns they receive for their labors. There has been a rather unique symbiosis in the economy of Indonesia. The Dutch have conducted the import and export business. The Indonesians are the producers of raw commodities. The Chinese handle all of the marketing including the collection of rice and other agricultural products from the small producer, the milling and processing of the crop, and its distribution to the consumer. Conversely, the Chinese is the agent for the distribution of consumer goods which the producer requires in exchange for his labor.

It was impossible during the time available to secure data as to the price spread between the prices of what the producer has to sell and those of the goods he needs to buy. One gets the impression, however, from officials, farmers, fishermen, and others, that disparity between these two elements is very great. Certainly there is dissatisfaction with the present situation.

Production credit is also in the hands of the Chinese merchant. Here, again, it was impossible to get accurate data as to credit terms, but the general claim is that interest rates are high, bordering on usury.

It is of the greatest importance that technical assistance be given in the field of credit and marketing, including instruction in the educational institutions, investigation of the marketing and credit systems that exist, and technical assistance in the development of marketing and credit institutions. Ultimately it is believed that the extension personnel will require training to equip them to advise on the organization of marketing and credit cooperatives at the village level.

Long-range agricultural development will require both increased primary education of the village youth in order that the producer may participate in marketing and credit cooperatives, and education of government personnel at all levels from the agricultural high school to the agricultural university. Emergency action should include the bringing of selected Indonesian agricultural officers to the United States to study the operation of our marketing and credit cooperatives.

Health and Education. Public services in health and education have been concentrated primarily in the cities. Although this subject is dealt with in another portion of the report, it is important that mention be made of the significance of health and education to the stability of agricultural communities and to the efficiency of agricultural production and marketing. A start has been made to give some experienced rural school teachers in-service training in agriculture by the extension personnel. It is important that this work be increased and intensified. It is of the greatest importance that fundamental education be made available to increasing numbers of village youth. Adult education of rural people should also be undertaken.

Consumer Goods. This section includes discussion of small tools of production as well as consumer goods, primarily textiles and the utensils required for rural living.

The agricultural, fish, and forest commodities are produced with elementary mechanical aids such as hoes, axes, knives, simple plows, fishing nets, small fishing craft, and so forth. These production goods have generally been imported since Indonesia has specialized as a producer of raw materials. There was no importation of hand tools during the war years. A short visit to the rural areas will reveal that the present tools are worn almost to the point of dilapidation. The farmers' efficiency is greatly reduced by these worn-out tools, and the labor required for production is greatly increased. However, the primary cause for the greatly reduced production of agricultural, forestry, and fishery products is probably the reduced incentive resulting from the inadequate supply of the things that the producer desires and needs.

The long-term objective should include detailed studies of the producer's requirements and the development of light industries to furnish these requirements where comparative advantage exists.

The emergency objective should be the prompt supply of small hand tools and other incentive goods, primarily textiles.

Industry. The Indonesian economy has been closely integrated with the economy of Holland. The Indonesian has been a supplier of raw materials, producing his own essential food requirements, and importing most of his other essentials from Holland. As a result, the typical Indonesian today is a field worker and a transporter of his surplus production to ports of embarkation. Such an economy results in overpopulation in the rural areas, inefficient use of the labor supply, and insufficient incentives for production. It is of the greatest importance that industry be developed in the towns and cities to make better use of the manpower available. Proper industrialization will result in more efficient and increased agricultural production, lower the population pressure on the land, supply the rural producer with simple tools of production, and permit a greater supply of incentive goods and a higher level of living.

Industry is treated in another section of this report. It seems desirable, however, that the importance of indigenous light industry to the efficiency of agricultural production and distribution and to the level of living of rural peoples be cited in this agricultural section.

C. Health

The assistance in the field of health services needed in Indonesia at this time consists primarily of technical personnel and the short-term replacement of equipment and facilities which were either lost or severely damaged during the war, the occupation, and subsequent "police actions." The exact nature of long-term assistance to Indonesia is not foreseeable at this time because it will be conditioned by, first, the rate at which Dutch technicians depart and the willingness of Indonesia to request and use other foreign technicians in their place; secondly, the rate at which the RUSI determines to extend health services; and, thirdly, the rapidity with which native Indonesians can be trained to take over new responsibilities. These rates of expansion are now rather sharply limited by the fact that the public health service was decentralized in 1935-36 to the state and localities, by the shortage of both local and central tax revenues, and by the shortage of trained personnel at all levels.

Need for Technical Experience and Personnel. The technical staff and "know-how" in Indonesia has been provided by the Dutch in all departments for three and a half centuries. Now that the Dutch are leaving, voluntarily and involuntarily, the whole atmosphere in the Dutch Colony is largely one of defeatism and of disparagement toward the capacity of Indonesians to run effectively their own government. This attitude of disaffection on the part of the Dutch in general is not characteristic of those in the field of health and medicine, but the latter are naturally affected by the spirit and outlook of their associates in other fields. In the realm of health the Dutch have been primarily research men, medical school professors, and directors of the principal divisions of the Ministry of Health, and, as such, have enjoyed a relative isolation from the political turmoil of the last 10 years (i.e. they were not as directly or immediately involved as Dutch officials in military, police, or economic departments). Nevertheless, a number of the laboratory directors, research men, and some hospital and public health men serving in the field are now leaving or planning to leave in the near future.

The immediate issues involving technical health personnel in Indonesia are, therefore:

1. Whether the Indonesians have the capacity to maintain and direct the existing system of laboratories, hospitals, health clinics, research centers, etc., without advice and guidance from some outside source. This is essentially a question of technical competence or capacity and cannot be decided within a short time. Much depends on how many of the Dutch personnel remain and conscientiously work, how rapidly the Government follows its declared long-term policy of putting Indonesians in all important posts, and whether the Government seeks technical aid from other sources.
2. Whether the Indonesians now have or can recruit sufficient technical personnel to fill the positions vacated by the Dutch and by Indonesians promoted to more important positions for which they were not previously eligible.
3. Whether Indonesians can organize and staff the new health and medical programs which they plan to start and which are above and beyond the programs previously known there—new hospitals, mass vaccination, mass malaria control, etc.

Apart from the question of the technical capacity of the Indonesians in the future, it seems perfectly clear that at this time they do not have the necessary staff to fill Dutch vacancies, staff programs to prewar levels, and extend additional necessary services.

Any program to meet these needs is complicated by the cautious hesitancy of the Government, so recently liberated from technical domination by the Dutch, to seek assistance from another foreign power. Moreover, since the orientation of Indonesians has been almost exclusively European, primarily Dutch, they have had no substantial experience with American assistance, even though they have general respect for American scientific work. Hence, any American technical assistance will have to take into account the fact that though the needs are very great, Indonesians are cautious and do not know us well.

It may be concluded that the short-term needs in Indonesia are for technicians and equipment in selected fields as requested by the Government, geared to the volume of needs and to the establishment of confidence in American advice. The long-term need clearly is for the training of Indonesians in sufficient number and in the appropriate specialties to be able to staff their own programs adequately.

D. Education

In the field of education the RUSI faces enormous problems. Before the war the administration spent comparatively little money on education, with the result that the population is still approximately 90 percent illiterate, one of the world's highest rates of illiteracy. In 1930, of the various racial groups in Indonesia, 75 percent of the Europeans, 29 percent of the Chinese, and 6.4 percent of the Indonesians were literate. The war and subsequent turbulence in Indonesia destroyed many essential facilities and interrupted educational processes. Even now many school buildings are still being used by the Army. Thus educational opportunities are poorer today than in prewar years, though the number of pupils in elementary schools has increased.

In 1939, approximately 2,300,000 pupils were attending elementary schools and slightly over 50,000 went on to intermediate schools. In the same year 777 students, of whom less than one-third were Indonesians, were graduated from secondary schools. Facilities for college education were even more limited.

Formerly, intermediate and higher education was conducted principally in the Dutch language. At the primary level a reaction has taken place against the use of Dutch, and, in certain areas of the Republic, the teaching of Dutch is being abolished. The Government has already proclaimed English to be the second language of instruction, in addition to the vernacular. However, the schools where instruction was or is in Dutch still possess far greater facilities than the former Indonesian language schools. At the present time, therefore, a considerable dislocation in teaching is taking place, though much of the higher teaching is still carried out in Dutch because of the availability of Dutch teachers and text books. Until a sufficient number of teachers are trained who can give instruction in Indonesian and until the necessary Indonesian text books are prepared, the facilities for carrying out the Government's desire will severely limit its ability to make the transfer to instruction in the vernacular. With respect to this, a difficulty presents itself in the fact that the Indonesian written language is still in a formative state. A committee has been set up to establish standard technical terms.

As a result of the dearth of facilities, the Government has been unable to institute free and compulsory education. Even in the primary schools payment is required, and this precludes the education of the children of many low-income families. Thus education is limited largely to the families of those in Government positions and to the very small Indonesian middle class.

Education is a long-term problem but one in which immediate assistance can be of immense benefit. As in other countries visited in Southeast Asia, adequate funds are not available to pay for the needed educational program. Thus with funds, equipment, and supplies short, the new Government is having the greatest difficulty in making a start on its education program. Any amount of material or technical support that can be received from the outside world will be readily usable. The Indonesians regard the education problem as one of the most serious they face and one which serves as a bottleneck to further progress in producing indigenous leadership and qualified administrators and technicians.

A booklet, "A New System of Education for Indonesia," published in February of 1948, outlines the educational system which is projected, with its emphasis on a single primary system of education, and opportunities for various types of vocational training opening up at the conclusion of the first six years, in addition to opportunities for secondary school courses.

E. Industry, Transportation, and Communications

The need for the development of an industrial economy in Indonesia arises from two major factors. First, there is an urgent need for the production of consumer goods, and, second, Indonesia is rapidly developing a major unemployment problem which must be relieved by employment elsewhere than on the land.

The economy of Indonesia is primarily based on agricultural production. To increase this production it is necessary to give the farmer an incentive to produce more than is needed for the immediate requirements of his family. This incentive can be given only by making available to him goods that he desires. At present these goods are not available in sufficient quantity to create this incentive, and foreign exchange is not available in sufficient amount to import these consumer goods. On the contrary, foreign exchange must be used to meet the deficit in food production. Production of consumer goods locally for home consumption will help meet this demand, and surplus production for export will help provide the foreign exchange needed to purchase raw materials, when necessary, for those industries whose products are for home consumption.

The employment of people for agricultural production is far in excess of that needed to assure economic use of the land. This is particularly true in Java. The anticipated disbanding of part of the army will further aggravate the unemployment problem. The Indonesians contemplate a large migration of the population from Java to Sumatra. As a very long-term objective this may well help balance the employment and land situation, but it will contribute little to meeting the need for consumer goods. The creation of small industries capable of expansion will both meet the need for consumer goods and furnish gainful employment.

Communications present a third grave problem in the economy of Indonesia. Large tonnages of agricultural products must be carried from the farm to the main centers of population and to the seaports for export. This is accomplished by coastal ships, by railway, and by motor transport. Present facilities are meeting the current demand, but production is now at a low ebb, and with increased production transportation facilities may prove insufficient. This may involve the extension and improvement of harbor facilities; the increasing of tonnage in coastal ships; the extension of rail lines and the increase in motive power and rolling stock; the extension of highways and the increase in trucking capacity. In some cases it may involve the expansion of air facilities. These problems, all of which must be met, require planning, coordination, and execution.

F. Commodities

Indonesian production, both for domestic consumption and for export, is well below prewar levels. As the country consequently has lacked adequate proceeds from export sales, the government has had to put very strict limitations on imports. To some extent this has involved a vicious circle, for the shortage of imported textiles has resulted in reduced incentives to produce the export commodities needed to build up foreign exchange receipts. Of top priority in breaking out of this circle is assistance in purchasing textiles abroad, and additional newsprint to make possible better information activities in explaining the situation to the general public.

G. Public Administration

The lack of trained and experienced personnel in technical and administrative posts in the government services of the RUSI constitutes a formidable barrier to effective government and to full utilization of resources for economic development, and is a major limitation on the amount of technical assistance that can be absorbed by Indonesia. The country achieved independence before adequate preparation of the necessary personnel had been made. The Dutch did not develop enough technical and administrative personnel among the resident population for the responsible positions in government, and the withdrawal of Dutch personnel from these positions will inevitably result in a great deterioration in the quality and effectiveness of governmental administration.

There is a very thin layer of highly trained and competent personnel, a fairly large group of personnel trained at the lower levels, and a big gap in between. Very few functionaries speak English, and these few are mainly in the top brackets of government. There are, consequently, not many governmental personnel who can spare the additional time required to work with foreign technicians who might be available as advisers or co-workers, and still less who know English and would therefore be able to work with American or Commonwealth personnel who did not know Indonesian. Moreover, there are relatively few civil servants who are at the same time adequately prepared in language and professional training to profit fully from advanced training in the United States or other foreign countries and able to be spared from their present tasks. Most of them are now terribly overworked, and if they left for training abroad, they could not be replaced.

The great need for training of present and additional governmental personnel in these countries, coupled with the shortage of people who might be effectively trained abroad, argues strongly for the setting up of training programs in public administration in Indonesia itself as one of the most essential and potentially most fruitful kinds of technical cooperation.

IV. Aid Now Being Received or Planned from Sources other than the United States

Dutch economic interests in Indonesia are still very important. Moreover, the Dutch Government feels a keen and continuing responsibility for the successful maturation of the newly born state, whose people have so long been a Dutch responsibility. Consequently, the Dutch Government has brought pressure on the many Dutch civil servants in Indonesia to remain there and help the new government get under way. Although Indonesia pays the salaries of these Dutch technicians and advisers, many now remaining would have left without this Dutch pressure, and this must therefore fairly be counted as a form of "technical assistance." Certainly, it much reduces the amount of technical assistance that Indonesia would otherwise have to seek from Western countries to carry on its government and to maintain its educational, medical and other services, and its scientific and technical research.

Some fellowships are provided for Indonesians to study tropical agriculture in the Netherlands, at the secondary school level (Agricultural College at Deventer, and the Agricultural Training School at Boskoop) and at the university level (Agricultural University at Wageningen). Moreover, the Rotterdam chapter of "Nederland Helpt Indonesia" allotted in 1949 some 350,000 guilders for equipment for 7 vocational schools to be located in East Indonesia. Immediately after the war in 1945, the Netherlands provided a credit in guilders equivalent to approximately $500 million to finance the then Netherlands-Indies deficit on invisible account with the Netherlands. The Netherlands 1950 credit of 200 million guilders and the 1949 action of the Netherlands in scaling down by two billion guilders the external debt of Indonesia both have been, of course, of great economic assistance. The local press in Indonesia has reported that Swiss banks will grant Indonesia a credit of 50 million Swiss francs (about $12 million) for the purchase of machinery in Switzerland, and that Indonesia has asked the French Government for a loan of some 15 billion francs (about $43 million) with which to buy railway rails, locomotives and cars, as well as other machinery and chemicals. Indonesian officials, however, deny these reports, stating that nothing has so far materialized along these lines.

New Zealand has proffered "technical assistance" to Indonesia and established two fellowships for Indonesian students. This is perhaps the forerunner of considerably more aid from Commonwealth countries. At the Sydney Conference to be held late in May, the first steps are expected to be taken to put into effect the "Spender Plan" of Commonwealth aid to Southeast Asia.[b] It is reported that Australia, in connection with this plan, intends to concentrate on Indonesia what aid (technical and other) it can afford for this general area.

In August 1949, the United Nations International Children's Emergency Fund (UNICEF) approved $34,000 for nine fellowships in health and education

---

[b]This plan, now called the "Colombo Plan", was adopted at a meeting of Commonwealth countries in Colombo, Ceylon, in October, 1950 [Ed.].

to be administered by WHO (two of these fellowships were granted to students already abroad; they have now completed their studies in malaria control and have returned to Indonesia). UNICEF also approved the use of $74,000 for child-feeding, using milk constituted from dry whole milk, partly reinforced by cod-liver oil and ascorbic acid.

Total UNICEF allocations (as distinct from approved expenditures) for Indonesia were reported in February 1950 to be $1,221,100, most of which was expected to be used for child-feeding.

Indonesia has requested the World Health Organization (WHO) and UNICEF to provide technical assistance in a joint treponematosis project with main emphasis on yaws control combined with prevention of congenital syphilis. This program would begin as soon as personnel could be appointed; would last 2 years (initially); would involve three foreign experts, 26 local technical experts and auxiliary personnel, and supplies and equipment; and would cost an estimated $365,363, of which Indonesia would contribute $43,730 and UNICEF $321,633.

V. Aid Now Being Received or Planned from United States Sources

In 1948, the ECA provided $64 million for aid to Indonesia, of which $15 million was in the form of loan funds. In 1949, between the signing of the Hague Agreement on November 2 and its coming into effect on December 27, ECA provided another $40 million in grants. These funds were used primarily to purchase rice and textiles, which are now arriving.

In February 1950, the Export-Import Bank announced that it had authorized extension of credits up to $100 million to Indonesia to be made available as individual projects were developed by RUSI and approved by the Bank. No individual projects have been submitted as yet for approval, but it is planned to ask for credits for development of food production, automotive transportation, roadbuilding and repairs, railroad rehabilitation, inter-island air transport, coastal shipping, harbor reconstruction, water power and irrigation, industry, and rehabilitation of estate agriculture.

The U.S. Army Department carried out an aerial mapping project in the Eastern Archipelago during 1948 and 1949, of great value for the geological and geodetic services of Indonesia. The Director of the Geological Survey expressed interest in having this carried out for other parts of Indonesia as well, although as yet no official proposal for this has been received.

There is currently under negotiation with Indonesia a Fulbright agreement to cover the disposition of the approximately $3 million worth of Indonesian guilders received for surplus property sold to the country. When the agreement is signed, these funds will be available for many kinds of technical assistance activities.

Several private religious groups operate missions in Indonesia and provide medical and educational services there.

The Standard Vacuum Corporation has been training Indonesians at the Sungei Gerong plant at Palembang since January 1948. There are 72 classes for 1,100 employees. Courses include English (the most popular, with 424 students), typing (157), literacy (100), nursing, basic supervision, auto driving, welding, pipe fitting, diesel operation, surveying, arithmetic, shorthand, and food handling.

VI. Recommendations for Emergency Aid

It would not only be inappropriate, but would also be going far beyond what has been requested, for the United States to attempt to solve the inflation in Indonesia by, for example, maintaining a specified level of consumer goods imports through balance-of-payments aid or attempting to solve the government personnel problem by providing a large corps of trained civil servants. There are however, a number of less sweeping but potentially very helpful measures that have been requested by the Indonesian Government and that could appropriately be taken by the United States. These are described in detail below.

Summary of Program Recommendations

A. Agriculture, Fisheries, Forests

In-service trainees to the U.S.	$ 100,000	
Equipment for Agricultural Stations, etc.	250,000	
Provision of small tools	1,125,000	
Fishing equipment	3,430,000	
Rehabilitation of forest production	2,100,000	
		$7,005,000

B. Public Health and Medicine

Hospital equipment	200,000	
Out-patient clinics	610,000	
Malaria control	1,800,000	
Drugs, instruments	1,000,000	
Books, laboratory equipment	375,000	
Dental services	200,000	
Hygiene and sanitation education	175,000	
Other projects	90,000	
Trainees to the U.S.	50,000	
		$4,500,000

C. *Education*

Materials for general and vocational schools	$400,000	
Laboratory materials	115,000	
Equipment and teacher, Faculty of Sciences, Bandung	80,000	
Books requested by University of Indonesia	200,000	
Allocation of funds for teacher training schools	100,000	
50 Indonesian students to U.S.	200,000	
English language program	250,000	
		1,365,000

D. *Transportation, Power, Industry*

Contract between RUSI and U.S. Engineering firm	1,250,000

E. *Commodities*[c]

Newsprint	325,000

F. *Training in Public Administration*

(U.N. activity)		....
	Total	$14,445,000

A. *Agriculture*

1. In-service trainees to the United States (20)–$100,000. A professional hierarchy has been maintained in Indonesia for many generations, made up of various categories of professional men on the basis of their academic preparation. Top-level men were those with full academic and graduate training. In a lower category were those with undergraduate college education only. A still lower category comprised those trained in Holland for the subprofessional fields, specifically for work in the Colonies. Most of the above personnel were Dutch nationals. The highest category of Indonesians comprised those who had

---

[c]In addition to which it is recommended that a grant of $11 million be made to cover processing costs of raw cotton if a CCC credit to finance purchase of $22.5 million of raw cotton can be obtained.

subprofessional training in what are called the medium schools of agriculture. A lower category included those trained in agricultural high-schools; farther down the scale were village youths with 6 years of primary school and 1 year of farm school or extension work. There has been little or no advancement of persons from one category to the other. At the present time, there is a fairly large number of Indonesian nationals with medium-school education and with several years of quite excellent experience. These are the men on whom Indonesian agriculture must place its primary dependence until such time as graduates start coming out of their agricultural colleges and gain sufficient experience to carry on their work. Indonesian agricultural officials are very interested in having medium school graduates accepted in the United States for practical work experience in professional fields such as forestry, soil conservation, extension, and work with credit and marketing cooperatives; it is recommended that 20 such trainees be selected and sent to the United States for a year's work experience.

2. Equipment for agricultural stations, libraries, agricultural schools, and a veterinarian laboratory for foot and mouth disease—$250,000. There are agricultural schools for the training of village boys in extension work in all of the agricultural districts. These schools are very short of equipment, primarily of slide and projection equipment and visual aids. It is recommended that equipment and supplies be provided for such schools, to an estimated value of $66,000.

The Veterinarian Institute at Bogor was established in 1908. Now under construction is a building for work on foot and mouth disease. The Institute not only carries out the diagnostic work on all types of animal diseases in Indonesia, but also has a trained force of field men including veterinarians in the major agricultural districts and subprofessional veterinarians in the various municipalities. According to the latest statistics, about 50,000 animals are attacked yearly by foot and mouth disease. It is recommended that Indonesian veterinarians be brought to the United States and Mexico to study the campaign to eliminate foot and mouth disease being carried on in Mexico as well as the production of serum and vaccines. In addition, it is recommended that technical equipment to the value of $50,000 be provided for the foot and mouth disease laboratory.

Indonesia maintains 6 medium agricultural schools with entrance requirements and course work similar to the non-degree curricula in our State agricultural colleges. These schools were, for the most part, utilized as hospitals or concentration camps during the war and, as a result, lost much of their equipment. It is recommended that equipment be provided for 6 medium agricultural schools to the value of $90,000.

The general agricultural experiment station at Bogor has done some of the best investigational work on agricultural production problems in tropical agriculture. The Ministry of Agriculture submitted requests totaling nearly $200,000 for technical equipment for this institution. It will probably deserve considerable support under Point Four. As an emergency matter, it is recommended that $44,000 be provided for the purchase of technical journals; for equipment for the Botanical Institute (the building for which is about 90 percent completed); and for some laboratory equipment for inland fisheries.

3. Provision of small tools: hoes, axes, plows, choppers, nails–$1,125,000. The importation of small tools, including hoes, plows, axes, sprayers, nails, etc., and their distribution to the user, is carried on under normal conditions by private trade. In the postwar period, these private channels were difficult to reestablish, primarily because of licensing control, the lack of foreign exchange, and the necessity for importing other goods. In addition to this, large areas were cut off from supply sources during military and "police" actions, and now have very great and urgent need for hand tools. In addition to this need, the Government's program for demobilizing soldiers and, after a period of training, guiding them into productive enterprise places an additional demand on tool supplies.

More than 60 percent of Indonesia's rubber production comes from small holders. Experience and research have shown that the best procedure is for the small holder to work up latex into unsmoked sheets, leaving the finishing for export to be done in regional smokehouses. The small rubber holder needs coagulation pans and rubber-mangling machines. These have not been available in sufficient supply because of the shortage of foreign exchange.

Small kerosene motor-powered centrifugal pumps have been used to a limited extent in Indonesia to provide supplemental irrigation. The provision of additional pumps through sale to farmers at reasonable prices and credit terms would provide incentives to production, giving proof to the farmer that the Government was mindful of his interests, and it would be an initial step in the mechanization of agriculture. It is recommended that the following sums be provided for the purchase of small tools and supplies to be sold to private users and thus generate a local currency counterpart fund:

Type of Tool or Supply	Number	Value
Hoes	300,000	$375,000
Plows	10,000	100,000
Knives	50,000	25,000
Axes	20,000	25,000
Knapsacks	500	5,000
Nails	100tons	25,000
(for locally produced weeders)		
Carbon Steel	100tons	30,000
Rubber rolls	6,000sets	180,000
Aluminum coagulation pans	400,000	260,000
Low lift motor-driven centrifugal pumps	150	100,000

4. Fishing Equipment—$3,430,000. Fish provide the major protein in the Indonesian diet. The consumption of fish has always been low—under 7 kilograms per person per year before the war and 3 kilograms at the present time. This decrease is due primarily to shortage of fishing materials, especially in Java; lack of fishing boats, especially small motorized boats, in the whole of the Archipelago; and the lack of small craft for transport. The shortage of fish is not only detrimental to the Indonesian diet but is an important factor contributing to inflation and to unrest in the area. It is recommended that, as an emergency matter, about 900 tons of yarns, lines, and twines be provided. The Indonesian estimate, to be further checked, is 2 million dollars.

Fishing on the north coast of Java and Sumatra with small, 35-foot motorized fishing boats of the Japanese type was successfully introduced before the war. At the present time, however, fishing is carried on with small sailing boats each of which bring in a yearly average of 12 tons of fresh fish as against 50 tons with motorized boats. Both the sail and the motorized fishing boats have been greatly reduced from prewar supply. It is recommended that a contract be made with Japan to deliver 60 small fishing boats complete with 15-horsepower, semi-diesel motors and that funds be allocated to provide an additional 100 motors to be installed in hulls built in Indonesia. For 60 motor boats complete, and for 100 additional motors: $600,000.

In many fishing areas, mainly located in the smaller islands, production could be increased considerably if fishermen were assured that the product could be well-preserved and regularly transported. This would require a fleet of ten carriers of 50 to 100 ton capacity for the transport of dried and smoked fish: $320,000.

Insulated small carriers also are required for the rapid transport of fresh fish from out-of-the-way and distant fishing ports to ports near the consumption centers. In addition, these carriers would make it possible for small sailing vessels to remain at sea during several consecutive days. For 10 carriers of 20-ton capacity and 10 carriers of 10-ton capacity: $320,000.

Inadequate land transport limits the distribution of fish to inland areas and thereby reduces the total catch. It is recommended that 80 truck pick-up and jeep chassis be supplied under emergency funds. Bodies, some insulated, could be constructed in Indonesia with counterpart funds. Total: $190,000.

5. Rehabilitation of Forest Production—$2,100,000. The rehabilitation of Indonesia's forests and the restoration of sustained production of forest products is a principal key to sparking rapid economic development in the Archipelago. Provisions for adequate housing, for shipping and fishing, and for the occupation of present unemployed and of men to be released from the armed services, depend, to a considerable extent, on an increased and assured supply of forest products. The lack of adequate supplies of forest products, probably more than any one thing, limits the widest range of economic activity.

The early restoration of forest production will require primarily the provision of small tools such as hand saws, skidding chains, steel cable, rigging sets, etc. In addition, there will be required certain heavier equipment including tractors, motor cranes, winches, etc. as well as equipment—axles and wheels and housings—for the push-cart forest railroad. It is recommended that such tools and equipment, to a total value of $2,100,000, be provided.

B. Health and Medicine

1. Hospital equipment—$200,000. Out of roughly 60,000 hospital beds in Indonesia (primarily in Java) before the war, 45,000 beds were privately owned and operated; approximately 10,000 were operated by local bodies and self-governing states; and only 5,000 beds belonged to the Central Government. All hospitals were under a single management and control (military) during the war and revolutionary period, but in 1948 private hospitals were returned to their owners, and only 20,000 beds are at the present time in publicly supported hospitals, local and federal.

Although during the wars only a few hospital buildings were damaged, nearly all equipment in public and private institutions was either pillaged or damaged, much of it beyond repair. For example, at the close of World War II only one X-ray unit for 70 million people was in working order. The Dutch and the Indonesians together have repaired and replaced a considerable amount of this equipment, but the very slow schedule of deliveries from European manufacturers and the shortage of dollars for purchases in U.S. markets have kept hospitals still far below prewar standards. At the present time, the pressure for hospital care is so great, especially in the population centers (Djakarta, Jogjakarta, and Surabaya) which grew very rapidly during the war, that only an estimated 60 percent of those seeking hospital care can be admitted.

The Central Government has no accurate figures on the hospitalization or demand for hospitalization in the self-governing States and in locally operated hospitals. Indeed, it is not known whether many of them are still standing or in operation. Additional hospitals have been planned and a few—both central and local—are now under construction. But there remains a very considerable shortage of equipment for established hospitals, and a need for additional equipment for new hospitals or extensions which are now under construction. The short-term needs of Indonesia for hospital equipment alone have been estimated in the millions. It is recommended that $200,000 be provided immediately for the replacement of essential equipment in selected public hospitals outside Djakarta, on condition that U.S. advisers review the needs and advise on the specifications to be ordered.

2. Policlinics—$610,000. Before the war an estimated 1,700 policlinics—out-patient clinics, some of which were also equipped with simple 20-bed hospitals—were in operation in Java alone. Only about half these policlinics were open daily and attended by nurses or partly trained male helpers. The most important ones were visited daily by a physician; others were visited once or twice a week by a medical person. The hospital beds attached to these clinics were used by midwives once or twice a week to advise mothers on prenatal and infant care.

During and since the wars, the clinics have been closed and the buildings wrecked or occupied as houses. The poorly paid semi-skilled staff have for the most part shifted to other work. As an immediate measure of reconstruction the Dutch Red Cross organized and sent (paid for by RUSI) 14 mobile clinic teams of an average of 10 persons each for a 3-year period, 1946-49. These clinic teams saw as many as 15,000 patients per week in the more populous areas, but their work has now stopped and they have returned to Holland.

The urgent need at present, therefore, is to organize and equip mobile teams in order to continue and extend these direct health services to the people on a regular basis. Although the present view (Dutch) is that these mobile teams are only a temporary substitute until fixed clinics can be reorganized and reopened, it is both the experience of Indonesia with the mobile Dutch Red Cross teams and the longer American experience that mobile teams will become an established part of the health and medical program in preference to fixed clinics. The Ministry of Health estimated that their immediate need is for 80 mobile teams fully equipped in order to provide two such teams for each residency. (A residency is a civil government subdivision which on Java serves about 3 million people, and somewhat fewer on Sumatra and the other islands.)

It is recommended that immediate aid in meeting these short-term needs for clinic services be provided in the form of two mobile units fully equipped and staffed by one U.S. physician and one U.S. nurse each for training Indonesian personnel in American methods and in the use of American equipment. It is also recommended that 40 mobile units fully equipped—composed of two vehicles each—be provided for release to native personnel after short-term periods of training. Some units should be barge-mounted in order to serve riparian and seacoast dwellers in outlying islands, whereas the majority for use on Java and Sumatra should be wheel-mounted. The estimated cost of these 42 units, together with the necessary personnel for one year is $610,000.

3. Malaria control—$1,800,000. Virtually the entire island of Java and great areas of Sumatra and the other islands are highly malarial, especially along the seacoast and in the low foothills. Between 30 percent and 40 percent of the population of Java have attacks of malaria annually, and in many localities the known spleen index rate runs between 90 percent and 100 percent. Sanitation work, such as sluices, dikes, and drains, in the larger towns fell into disrepair by neglect during the wars, but many have been rehabilitated by local labor in the last 2 or 3 years. Practically nothing was done before the wars to prevent or control malaria in the rural areas. In endemic and hyperendemic areas only patients who were able to come to hospitals or clinics received treatment. In epidemic areas quinine was distributed on a mass basis to reduce mortality.

At the present time there are three small field laboratories (Djakarta, Surabaya, Macassar) which are equipped for routine malaria work. Eight professional people work in these laboratories with little or no supporting staff and insufficient materials for a real malaria campaign.

As visualized by the Government of Indonesia, the principal needs for malaria control at this time are staff and equipment for a malaria training center to train a number of local workers, further experiments with house spraying, and a supply of DDT and spraying apparatus to get a limited control program started in a small area. There are no plans at the present time for extensive spraying of breeding places because of the opposition of the Ministry of Agriculture and Fisheries and because of the unwillingness of farmers to permit field spraying.

American malariologists already have a huge fund of knowledge about mosquito control, but the species and habits of the Indonesian malaria vectors (sundicus and aconitus), and the tropical weather and living conditions, including bamboo houses and walls, will require some adjustment of established U.S. practice.

It is recommended that 20 American professional malaria control workers be sent to Indonesia to assist in the training of the Indonesian staff, in laboratory work incident to field control, in organization of field teams and instruction of foremen of spraying teams, and in the evaluation of the efficiency of this work. It is recommended that $1,800,000 be provided to permit the spraying of the homes of from five to eight million persons with DDT twice yearly, together with the necessary supplies and equipment and the expenses of the American staff. This will make a substantial inroad upon the incidence of the disease and will also meet one of the principal short-term needs of the Government of Indonesia. The long-term needs consist principally of the training of Indonesian malariologists and entomologists in the use of mass control measures.

4. Drugs, medical supplies, and instruments–$1,000,000. Practically the entire supply of drugs, medical supplies, and instruments was cleaned out of the hospitals and clinics during the war and the period of insurrection which followed. Because of the slowness of delivery by European manufacturers and dollar-exchange difficulties, the Government has found it difficult to get an adequate supply of the drugs and instruments which are needed in quantity, and expensive drugs and instruments are virtually unobtainable. The commonest drugs and instruments include aspirin, the sulfas, penicillin, chloroquin, vitamins, etc., and forceps, knives, needles, scissors, sutures, etc.

It is recommended that $1,000,000 be provided to meet the short-term needs of the health centers and hospitals in Indonesia for drugs in common use (for distribution through public pharmaceutical depots); and for medical supplies and instruments in general use in the same hospitals and health centers, on condition that U.S. personnel participate in the distribution of these items. It should be understood, however, that this is wholly a temporary measure and that no long-term supply assistance of this kind is planned.

5. Books, laboratory equipment, and apparatus–$375,000. As in other war and revolution-torn countries, these supporting materials were confiscated, destroyed, or exhausted. For example, the Eykman Institute, which is engaged in routine bacteriological, serological, and chemical tests and examinations for hospitals, health centers, and private physicians in and around Djakarta, and in tests of foodstuffs and cosmetics as required by law, is operating at something like 50 percent of its normal efficiency. Similarly, the two Institutes Pasteur (one in Bandung and the other in Jogjakarta) which are engaged in the preparation, manufacture, distribution, testing, and research on vaccines and sera and on routine work for hospitals, public health laboratories, and private physicians in and near the immediate vicinity of their locations, have not suffered any special damage to their capital equipment but they have lost a good deal of their operating apparatus and supplies. The University of Indonesia faculties in chemistry, medicine, dentistry, hygienics and bacteriology are also in urgent need of additional supplies of equipment.

It is recommended that $375,000 be provided to meet the short-term needs of all these institutions for library and laboratory materials on condition that U.S. personnel participate in the selection and distribution of these items. At the same time it should be understood that this is a one-time emergency grant and that there is envisioned no long-term supply assistance of this character.

6. Dental Services. Prior to the war there were no public dental services of any kind but, because of the accumulated backlog of dental needs during the years of war and revolution, the Government commandeered and pooled all dentists and dental equipment and made free dental treatment available to everyone. All 95 dentists and 150 dental technicians and nurses were put into this pool. More recently, as new dental equipment became available, the Government has permitted dentists to resign and to resume private practice. Now, only 37 dentists remain in the government service, but the dental school in Surabaya is again in full operation and will shortly begin to graduate additional numbers of dentists. The present program of the government is to continue public dental services for adults only for emergency treatment, and to concentrate on juvenile or school dentistry and on dental hygiene education and propaganda.

The Government of Indonesia requested 16 mobile, fully equipped units, each to be staffed by one trained native dentist and one or more native dental nurses or assistants (*mantri-gigis*).

Because it is doubtful that the Government could put this number of units into full operation, it is recommended that only six fully equipped mobile dental units be made available at this time, together with one full team of U.S. dental personnel (one dentist and two dental hygienists) for training native personnel in the operation of mobile clinics and one U.S. team (one dentist and one dental hygienist) for teaching in the school for dental nurses and "mantris." It is estimated that the cost of this recommendation for a one-year period would be $200,000. The long-term needs of Indonesia for dental services can best be met by the training of native dentists, by native dental faculty and by in-service training under the advice of U.S. personnel.

7. Hygiene and Sanitation Education. A rural hygiene demonstration unit and a training school for village house visitors was established in mid-Java in 1932.

House visitors, though poorly paid and not very well educated, were employed in considerable number to give instruction and advice on personal hygiene and home sanitation to school children, villagers in their homes, indigenous midwives, village heads and priests, and to village clerks on birth and death reporting. The importance of these house visitors lies in the fact that they were the continuous and direct contact between the official health department and the people and local officials.

The demonstration unit and the school have been closed, the equipment lost, and the personnel gone elsewhere as a result of the war. The Government of Indonesia places a high priority on the reestablishment of this rural center and school at an early date and intends to open a complementary center for urban sanitation and hygiene education. For the reopening of the rural center and school the needs include full equipment and supplies for the making and showing of films, posters, charts, slides, exhibitions, leaflets, bulletins, etc.—all known devices of individual and mass propaganda—and includes also the printing of birth and death certificates. The short-term needs, therefore, can best be met by the allocation of an estimated $175,000 for one year but should be made available only on condition that one American health educator advise on the assembly and use of the equipment. Aid for the longer term plan for establishment of an urban center should not be given until more is known about the effectiveness and success of the rural center.

8. Other Projects—$90,000. The Government of Indonesia presented to the Mission a variety of other requests on which no specific recommendation is made at this time, either because of inadequate evidence of the emergency character of the needs or because of the uncertainty of the technical capacity of Indonesians to organize and staff such projects at this time.[d] No doubt is expressed that the people of Indonesia need such additional special services and programs, but the evaluation of how and when they ought to be undertaken must await a more detailed local study. Among the services which the Government of Indonesia desires either to inaugurate or to strengthen substantially, and in which they desire U.S. assistance, either technical or material, are:

a) A nation-wide blood transfusion service with the necessary equipment and supplies, plus one or more U.S. biochemists to organize and direct both the gathering of blood and the preparation of plasma and of blood derivatives and substitutes.

b) Reestablishment and reequipment of ship and airport quarantine services, including one or more quarantine officers to plan the service and give advice on the use of special equipment.

---

[d]Note also the Indonesian request for a WHO/UNICEF project to control yaws and congenital syphilis, described in Section IV.

c) Tuberculosis control, including U.S. experts on the organization of such services and the production of BCG vaccines.

d) Leprosy control and research including several physician advisers.

e) Water chemist for advice on water purification and standards.

f) Nutrition program including dietary research and propaganda.

g) Smallpox and plague control, including especially care and ambulances for the transport of staff, live vaccines, and patients.

The extent to which the United States might appropriately give material assistance in these areas can and will be more satisfactorily evaluated by the U.S. technicians whose advisory services are sought in connection with each of these programs. Accordingly, it is recommended that the U.S. personnel requested (items *a* to *g*) should be made available at an early date and their recommendations on equipment and materials needed should be accepted as the basis for further consideration. The estimated cost of a minimum of 6 technicians (possibly as many as 10) is $90,000 for one year.

9. Indonesian Trainees to Study in the United States–$50,000. The needs of Indonesian technicians for further training are much greater than 10 trainees per year, but the number of places which can be effectively filled is limited by the fact that the adequacy of the scientific background of Indonesian trainees for formal education in the U.S. is unknown and by the fact that very many Indonesians do not use English readily. Hence, it is recommended for the present that not more than 10 Indonesian trainees per year be brought to the United States for study, at an estimated cost of $50,000 per year.

C. Education

The requests of the RUSI for assistance in educational work and the Mission's recommendations for U.S. assistance in this field are discussed in the paragraphs which follow.

1. Materials for General, Vocational and Technical Training in Primary and Secondary Schools–$400,000. According to figures received from the Government, there are 21,500 primary schools in Indonesia, with a total of 3,000,000 pupils. It is the hope of the Government to expand the primary school system until 15 million pupils are in attendance. In the meantime supplies are inadequate to meet the most rudimentary pupil needs in the great majority of the existing schools, and the provision of certain equipment for primary and vocational primary schools was a priority request of the Government.

Members of the Mission who visited primary schools outside Djakarta had an opportunity to observe first-hand the lack of adequate pupil-use equipment. The schools in which instruction had been in Dutch were much better equipped than those in which instruction had been in Indonesian. In the latter, pupil-use items were limited to a few copybooks per schoolroom and perhaps one-third to one-half enough copies of a very limited number of text booklets, so limited that they could not be left in the hands of the pupils after class. In these schools also there was a lack of group instruction equipment such as blackboards, charts, and the like. The provision by the United States of certain of the materials requested, such as copybooks, pencils, tracing-paper, slates, etc., for primary schools would place in the hands of pupils and teachers equipment which otherwise will not be provided in the foreseeable future, and would represent assistance not only to the pupils, but to a new Government striving to improve its school system as an indication of its interest in the welfare of the people.

Included in the requests received from the Government was a request for technical-training equipment for vocational primary schools. There are 689 such schools giving technical training courses to a total of 52,500 pupils. The items requested include scissors, hammers, hand-saws, screw-drivers, etc. It was not possible for any member of the Mission to visit a primary school where vocational training was in progress. In higher level technical and vocational schools visited, both teacher and student activity appeared well directed. In view of the fact that the majority of the pupils do not go beyond primary school it is believed that the teaching of rudimentary vocational courses is especially desirable, and the Mission favors the provision of a portion of the requested materials.

Members of the Mission who visited secondary-school-level technical training and domestic science schools were impressed with the quality of the training offered and the interest shown by the students. The Standard-Vacuum Company has established a vocational-training school of its own at Palembang, and Americans familiar with its work spoke most highly of the ability of the Indonesians to learn certain skills quickly. It is believed that a portion of the $400,000 recommended above should be used to expand the facilities for technical and domestic science type training on the secondary-school level.

2. Laboratory Materials and Chemicals for High School Science Courses, and One Exchange Teacher—$115,000. All the countries of Southeast Asia which requested help for their schools displayed marked interest in training in the sciences. One of the requests received from the Government of Indonesia was for equipment, including certain chemicals, for high school science courses. The cost of such equipment has made it impossible for the Government to replace stocks depleted or destroyed during and since the war. It is believed that this request should be favorably considered and that the funds allotted should be spent over a period of time as it becomes evident to those administering the assistance projects that previous purchases of such equipment are being put to good use. It is believed that one science educator, not necessarily from the United States, should be provided in connection with this phase of the program to advise the recipient schools on proper use of the equipment and to maintain a check on its use.

3. Equipment for Laboratories for General Physics, General Biology, Pharmacy, Chemistry, for Faculty of Science, Bandung, and Two U.S. Professors–$80,000. The Faculty of Science, Bandung, part of the University of Indonesia, was founded in 1947 and is the only faculty of science in Indonesia. At present it is seeking to develop adequate laboratory facilities, since it now has only limited facilities made available by the Faculty of Engineering, Bandung. It is also attempting to enlarge its staff to meet the increasing demands of Indonesian students for scientific training. As indicated previously in this report, the number of Indonesians receiving a college education has been very small, and there have been no facilities within Indonesia for training of the type offered by this faculty. Heretofore those desiring such training had to go abroad to obtain it. The Department of Education estimates that in August of this year at least 200 freshmen will seek to obtain instruction under the Faculty of Science, Bandung. In the opinion of the Mission the laboratory equipment requested for this faculty could be immediately and effectively used. It was proposed that up to 6 U.S. professors be provided to assist the present teaching staff of approximately 20. It is recommended that 2 science professors be selected to teach in Chemistry or Physics. Though the number of students reached through this branch of the University will not be large, it is the opinion of the Mission that the assistance proposed would be justified, both for its contribution to a limited field of education, and for its impact on a small but influential segment of the student population.

4. Books Specifically Requested by Faculties of the University of Indonesia–$20,000. The books requested are for the Faculty of Law and Social Sciences, Djakarta; the Faculty of Medicine, Surabaya; the Institute for Physical Education, Bandung; and the Faculty of Arts and Letters, Djakarta. Though the number of students who can use English as a medium of instruction is limited, it has been designated as the second language, and Indonesians are seeking through the use of it to broaden the educational materials available to them. It is recommended that the above sum be allotted to finance purchases of the books desired.

5. Assistance in Translation and Printing of Texts–$200,000. No written request for this kind of aid was received from the Government, but Indonesians accompanying members of the Mission on inspections of schools in the Djakarta area indicated that United States assistance in this field would be most welcome.

As indicated previously in this section on Education, there is throughout the school system a great lack of equipment of all types. The new Government is finding it difficult to maintain present levels of equipment and has no prospect of financial support for its proposed expansion of the public school system. One of the greatest deficiencies is that of adequate texts which, in the primary and secondary schools in Indonesia, are often paper-bound 30-50 page booklets. In many schools there are only a few texts available for each class, and they have to be used sparingly and in common.

The schools in which instruction was in Dutch were in general much better equipped than were the schools where teaching was in Indonesian (Malay). The Government is now attempting to have certain of the Dutch language texts translated into Indonesian as one of the steps to increase the materials available in Indonesian schools. The chief obstacles to satisfactory progress in this program are a lack of funds to pay translators, and a lack of paper and printing equipment. It is believed that the sum proposed for the work would enable a significant start to be made on this project through speeding up the translation of certain texts and making possible increased printing of these and other appropriate materials. It is conceivable that part of the funds might be used for importing printing equipment which could turn out the type of simple paper texts now in use. The Mission was informed that presses in Indonesia have a backlog of many months work, that in the past most of the printing of texts was done in Holland; and that there is no possibility of present printing facilities in Indonesia meeting the increasing demand for printing of texts.

6. Allocations of Funds to meet Dollar Costs of Increasing the Equipment and Books and Expanding the Facilities of Schools which Train Teachers for Primary, Technical, and Domestic Science Schools—$100,000. As in all areas of the world where the schools have inadequate financial backing, the lack of trained teachers seriously handicaps efforts of the Government to improve educational conditions. The success of the Government's plan to expand and improve primary schools will depend on increased financial support for schools and an expanded teacher-training program. The Government is aware of the need for expansion of its teacher-training schools on as high a standard as possible. While in Djakarta, members of the Mission visited a domestic science and a primary-teacher training school, though the latter was not in session when visited. In each case the supply of equipment was much greater than that in the regular schools. The domestic science school, which was in session, seemed to be performing a successful task of teaching subject matter adjusted to the needs of Indonesians. It was easy to understand why many more students than can be accepted apply for admission both to the teacher-training classes and to the pupil-level classes. In the one advanced secondary-level technical school visited in Djakarta, teaching carpentry, blacksmithing, electrical work, automatic repair, and the use of modern machines, instruction appeared to be of a high caliber and student work was kept to a high standard. Members of the mission were informed that graduates of the domestic science school and the technical training school had no difficulty finding jobs; that the demand for such trained personnel exceeded the present supply, as does the demand for trained primary school teachers. It is believed this proposed allocation of funds should be made to assist the Government in its efforts to maintain and expand its teacher-training institutions of the above-mentioned types.

7. Study of 50 Indonesian Graduate Students in the United States in Agriculture, Medicine, Engineering Education, Business, and Public Administration, etc.—$200,000. Comparatively few Indonesians have studied abroad, and the majority of those who did so in the past went to Holland. It is estimated that there were never more than 200 Indonesians studying in Holland in any one year. The number of Indonesian graduate students studying abroad was limited by the small number who completed college-level work in Indonesia and by financial considerations. Though both restrictions still obtain, there is a genuine interest on the part of the Indonesian students in going abroad and a desire, now that Indonesia is independent, to pursue education in countries other than Holland, with particular interest in the possibility of going to the United States. The expense of graduate work in the United States is, however, prohibitive for most Indonesians. It is believed that funds allocated to cover certain dollar costs of graduate courses would be an investment both in the professional training of Indonesians and in improving understanding between two countries which have had comparatively little contact with each other.

8. English Language Program (Including 15 Instructors)–$250,000. It is estimated that not more than 400,000 Indonesians had at any one time learned Dutch. Dutch scholars themselves frequently published serious scientific articles in English because of the wider field of readership gained thereby. In view of the comparatively small number of Indonesians having a vested interest in the continuation of Dutch as a medium of communication, it is not surprising that, as previously noted, English has been selected as the second language of instruction in the RUSI. Though there appears to be a genuine and widespread interest in learning English, the facilities for doing so are poor. It is believed that a program designed to provide better facilities for the study of English should comprise two parts: (a) the provision of books, printed materials, teaching aides necessary to get publications in English into the hands of many Indonesians–$100,000 and (b) the provision of teachers of English for teacher training institutions for the University, and for public classes to be carried on in major centers of population under the direction of the USIS–$150,000.

In connection with the provision of printed materials, a study should be made of present methods and materials used in teaching English in the schools of Indonesia. As a result of this study, appropriate printed materials on various levels could be made available through the school system, together with recommendations on teaching methods. Publications should also be made available for those not in the schools, as experience in other countries has revealed a considerable interest in the study of English among adults. It is this group which is likely to appreciate most having printed materials available.

The real impact will have to be imparted to the program by persons especially selected to teach English either as supervisors of English teaching in the school system, as teachers in higher centers of learning, or as persons responsible for the mass program to be handled under the direction of the USIS. It is estimated that 15 such persons should be selected. Though certain of these should be Americans, not all need be (or probably could be, since few Americans know the language of Indonesia, and there is no present way of estimating the number of those who would be available for such work). Some of the teachers should work through established educational institutions; the rest through USIS courses in English to be open to the public. To give this part of the program wide impact it is proposed that English teaching be carried on in a number of centers of population throughout Indonesia.

D. *Transportation, Power, Industry*

1. Transportation. The Indonesians presented to the Mission projects covering harbor extension, construction of new harbors, shipping-safety aids, new shipping tonnage, harbor dredging, extension of rail lines, extension and repair of railway-repair facilities, new rail motive power, new rail rolling stock, new highway construction, new trucks, buses, automobiles and motorcycles, new automotive repair facilities, spare parts for automotive equipment, airfield extension, air pilot-training schools, air-communications systems, new aircraft, new telephone, telegraph, and radio systems. Some of these projects are to be presented for loans to the Export-Import Bank and others for loans from other sources. The justification for these projects is based almost entirely on the prewar situation, that is, there were a given number of trucks, locomotives, railway freight cars, etc., before the war; therefore, they need so many today. The Government has not supplied such needed information as the amount of tonnage offered the railroad for movement each day and the percentages thereof they are able to handle, the turn-around time on railway freight cars, and the availability of locomotives. They have given figures on the increase of passenger traffic in 1949 over 1940. The passenger traffic has not been analyzed, however, as to the cause of the increase. For example, it is not known whether the large number of unemployed are moving around the country in search of employment, a situation which would be of a temporary nature, or whether the increase in passenger traffic has been caused by more stable factors and is likely to continue. It would certainly be unwise to purchase rolling stock to accommodate a mass movement of unemployed, if traffic would return to a lower level with the return to normal conditions throughout the country.

Indonesian officials requested additional warehouse facilities at the Port of Djakarta, but upon inspection it was found that the existing warehouses were used only to approximately 30 percent of capacity. This condition is explained by the use of the continental method of operation of the harbor. Dock and warehouse facilities are leased to the various shipping companies, in this case the Dutch companies, and only two docks out of a total of nineteen are available for all other shipping. When the great majority of shipping was conducted by the Dutch companies, this system worked very well, but with the increased shipping by non-Dutch companies the two dock spaces and their warehouse facilities are not adequate. This is true even though many of the docks in the harbor are unoccupied and their warehouses are practically empty. The problem is whether added facilities should be provided or whether a means can be devised to permit non-Dutch ships to use existing Dutch-controlled facilities.

2. Power. In the development of an industrial economy the supply of electric energy is of primary importance. To determine the most economical means of power development extensive studies are necessary. The projects presented by the Indonesians in most cases are suggestions for small diesel additions to existing power plants and the construction of additional hydroelectric facilities. Plans were not sufficiently developed nor was there enough time to permit an adequate study of these proposed projects. Indications are, however, that, while the need for power extension exists, these projects do not adequately meet the need. In discussions with the power generating officials it was indicated that little firm power would be added by the hydro development proposed, but they principally would add secondary power. In many industries, particularly chemical industries, firm power is necessary to make their establishment economically sound.

Therefore, prior to any large expenditure for power development, a coordinated study of power demand with relation to industrial expansion should be made. This study should develop not only the anticipated size of the demand but also the characteristics of the demand to assure proper development thereof.

3. Industry. Planning for industrial development in Indonesia is still in a formative stage. It is planned, however, that development should be directed to supply the basic requirements of the people, food, clothing, and housing. Industries under consideration include fertilizer plants, farm implement plants, cement factories, textile mills, saw mills, paper factories, and rubber-remilling plants. These plants and perhaps many others using indigenous raw materials could and should be developed. However, prior to entering into such a program, studies should and must be made to determine size, location, raw material supply, power demand, communication facilities, and economics of installation. These studies have not been adequately developed nor is personnel available in Indonesia for their direction.

4. Dutch Advisers. While Dutch advisers are technically adequately trained, they have not been able in most cases to adjust themselves to present-day conditions in Indonesia. Most are awaiting the first opportunity to return to Holland and are doing as little as possible in the interim. Whether consciously or subconsciously many of their recommendations are more to the interest of Holland than to the interest of Indonesia.

They are outspoken in their conviction that the Indonesians cannot administer the country, and Indonesians are apprehensive of taking their advice. It is felt, therefore, that the Dutch advisers should be supplemented, at the earliest possible date, by high level advisers to the Indonesians who can direct the efforts of Dutch technicians into the proper channels.

5. Recommendation—$1,250,000. It is recommended that a contract be consummated between the Indonesian Government and a top-level American engineering firm to furnish executive technical advisers to the Indonesian

Government for the planning, coordination, and execution of the projects mentioned above and to advise in the current operation of existing facilities to assure that maximum benefits are derived therefrom. Activities of advisers should not be restricted to fields specifically mentioned above, but the contract should be sufficiently flexible to permit additions to and contractions of the staff as need therefore becomes evident. This contract should be financed by the United States Government, U.S. dollar costs to be provided by appropriation and local currency costs to be from counterpart funds.

E. Commodities–$325,000

In view of the scarcity of newsprint in Indonesia, it is recommended that 2,500 tons be provided, at a cost of $325,000. Sale of this newsprint will create counterpart funds.

(It was evident that there was an urgent need for textiles, and the Mission, in its telegraphic report, recommended that a loan to cover $22.5 million worth of U.S. raw cotton be extended to the RUSI, if possible as a CCC credit, as had been previously recommended by the Ambassador. The Mission further recommended that a grant be made to cover processing costs, for which no estimate was then available. The best current available estimate is that processing costs amount to approximately 50 percent of the cost of the raw cotton.)

F. Training in Public Administration

In all the fields of governmental activity mentioned above, and in other fields as well, a major barrier to self-help by the Indonesians is their lack not only of technicians but also of experienced and competent administrative personnel.

The Mission discussed this subject with top governmental officials in Indonesia and concluded that training programs in public administration were of very great potential importance. The Mission felt, however, that, if the United States itself were to set up training programs of this sort as part of its bilateral technical-assistance program, suspicion might arise that the curriculum would be unduly influenced by the private-capitalist economic philosophy or the cold-war political urgency characterizing present day United States thinking. As the people of Indonesia are already suspicious of Western (including U.S.) economic and political objectives in this area, the effectiveness of a training program of this sort might be considerably reduced if the training were identified solely with the United States. For this reason, the Mission suggested to Prime Minister Hatta and Minister Djuanda that a request might be made to UNESCO (it subsequently developed that the proper U.N. agency would be the United Nations itself, which is setting up an Institute of Public Administration) for the establishment of training programs in Indonesia in the field of public administration.

An adequate training program in this field might include not only a full-time and rather formal curriculum in public administration but also intensive two-or three-month training institutes, and part-time afternoon or evening courses which could be taken by government civil servants. There should also, of course, be in-service training abroad for such civil servants or potential civil servants as could be spared.

In view of experience in the United States where business and public administration are often taught in the same institution, and in view of the great shortage of non-Chinese businessmen throughout Indonesia, it is believed that consideration should be given to extending the coverage of such training programs as are established to include business administration as well as public administration.

VII. Limitations on Amount, Kind, or Speed of Aid Program

Before the war, the Dutch reserved most of the better civil service positions for themselves. They trained few Indonesian deputies and appointed few to posts at the higher levels. In 1938, for example, only one executive department of the central Government had an Indonesian as director. One large city in Java, Bandung, had an Indonesian mayor. Practically none of the teaching staff at the University were Indonesians.

In the Central Government in 1938, there were 14,395 Europeans, about half of whom were recruited from the Netherlands, and most of the rest, Eurasians; 58,041 Indonesians; and 918 Chinese; and others. The following breakdown by level of position gives a more complete picture, however:

Percentage Distribution by Race of Civil Servants in
Central Government of Netherlands East Indies
October 1, 1938

Race	Lower Personnel %	Lower Intermediate %	Purely Intermediate %	Higher Personnel %	Total %
Europeans	1	33	58	92	20
Indonesians	99	64	40	7	79
Chinese, etc.	0	3	2	1	1

Source: Lennox A. Mills and Associates, "The New World of Southeast Asia," University of Minnesota Press, Minneapolis, 1949, pp. 90-91.

Although the Indonesians gained some administrative experience during the Japanese occupation and while fighting the Dutch, the administration of the latter period was primarily military in character. With the achievement of independence, RUSI accordingly found itself with very few qualified Indonesian officials and civil servants.

This shortage of trained officials and civil servants will very seriously limit Indonesia's economic recovery and development and its ability to utilize effectively either financial or technical aid. Most of the projects proposed for Export-Import Bank financing require trained managerial and technical personnel, equally as much as they require new equipment. The equipment will be wasted without the personnel. If personnel are diverted to these new projects from others, the latter will function less efficiently: Indonesia can build up its plant only at a rate somewhat slower than it builds up its trained personnel, for it has a deficit, not a surplus, of the latter.

Similarly, foreign technical-assistance programs will generally require the participation of Indonesian technicians to work alongside, and eventually to replace, temporary foreign technicians (whether U.S., U.N., or other). The absorptive capacity for foreign technicians will, therefore, also be limited by the availability of Indonesian technicians.

The answer would seem to be to begin by training Indonesian technicians. This means a much slower economic development, of course. It also faces its own limitations.

In the first place, there are relatively few technicians who are well enough trained and know enough of a foreign language (except Dutch) to profit from study abroad. Those who are qualified cannot be spared from their present jobs for further training. There are even, in fact, relatively few semi-trained technicians who can be spared from their jobs for further training. Night schools offer one possible solution, but one that means a long hard grind.

In the second place, the schools are not graduating nearly enough Indonesians to supply the number of students who should be studying at technical schools. Technical personnel form a pyramid, and the base is too small in Indonesia to support as large numbers as are needed on the upper levels.

Finally, the nationalistic revolt against the use of the Dutch language in the schools and its replacement by the unformed and inconsistent Indonesian national tongue (based on Malay) will certainly be a major barrier to technical training. Technical books are not available in Indonesian; foreign teachers will be slow to learn the vernacular; and the language itself is inadequate to express the precise and complex concepts of modern science and technology. Because Dutch is unpopular and Indonesian inadequate (and useless as a channel of international communication), some consideration is being given to making English the second major language. Many science courses already use English texts simply because they are the best. Too few natives know English yet, however, to enable it to be used generally in education and technology.

All of these factors will impede the formation of a trained body of Indonesians able to replace the departing Dutch and to take on the technical responsibilities of further economic development.

There are even barriers to the effective use in Indonesia of the remaining Dutch civil servants and to the effectiveness of aid programs in which Dutch technicians will be called upon to participate. As a result of the Hague Agreement, Indonesia was obliged to take over the bulk of Netherlands civil servants from the former Netherlands East Indies Government. This has proved to be a mixed blessing. Many of the Dutch have resented their demotion from executive posts to posts of an advisory nature, while the Indonesians have been jealous of the much higher salaries that continue to be paid their Dutch colleagues. A certain number of Dutch officials were involved in the "Westerling affair," and the Indonesians, furthermore, suspect that many Dutch civil servants are primarily engaged in protecting Dutch national interests. It may be anticipated that some of the Dutch will be less than enthusiastic about American programs of aid, especially technical aid, and may find ways to sabotage such programs.

The new exchange regulations, which render difficult the remittance of salaries and pensions, will undoubtedly result in the departure of many Dutch advisers and civil servants. Consideration has been given to ways of supplementing the salaries paid these Dutch by giving them U.S. aid dollars to cover their remittance needs, but difficulties of selection of desirable Dutch, as well as possible undesirable Indonesian reactions, suggest that this may be impractical. As American salaries are far above Dutch salaries, consideration has also been given to replacing the Dutch with German or Chinese technicians (the latter from among refugees from Communist China), paying their transportation from dollar grant funds. This is one possible solution that needs further study.

The Indonesians realize their inadequacy to deal with complicated modern problems of administration and technology and will have to depend upon Dutch technical assistance for some time to come. Accordingly, they will probably find ways and means of keeping those Dutch colleagues whom they trust and who are useful to the Government. The Dutch technical assistance that continues is likely to be on a greatly reduced scale, and the efficiency of government, education, medicine, research, etc., will suffer accordingly.

The top Indonesian officials are energetic and up to now there has been little evidence of corruption in the government administration. In its reaction to the West, Indonesian thinking is colored, however, to a large degree by the country's unfortunate experience, particularly in recent times, as a Dutch colony. Accordingly, there is some inclination to view Western influence and intervention with a certain amount of suspicion. This is likely to lessen the effectiveness of American technical aid, at least until these suspicions are overcome. However, since their economy is dependent upon Western markets and methods, most Indonesians realize that they have an interest in maintaining close relations with the Western countries, provided no element of subservience or exploitation is involved.

At the top level, however, Indonesian officials are currently so deeply involved in personal jockeying for positions; in political problems resulting from the drive for power conducted by the Republic of Indonesia; and in the military problems of amalgamation of KNIL and TNI into TRIS, with demobilization of 100,000 soldiers projected, that they have little time for economic problems. This itself will seriously limit the effectiveness of measures to control inflation and encourage economic development.

Although the Central Government is meeting overt challenges to its authority quite successfully (e.g., the "Westerling" and "Makassar" affairs), there remain certain elements affecting the public security that would make unwise the operation of technical aid projects in some areas. The two states remaining outside the Indonesian Republic, East Sumatra and East Indonesia (which includes Celebes, Bali and Borneo, as well as a great many smaller islands) oppose the extension of Central Government influence, and technical teams in those areas, while probably welcome on their own account, might be opposed as representing the Central Government, or might be caught in the midst of civil conflict. On Java and Sumatra the major cities appear safe enough, but even on these islands there are rural areas where potential or open rebellion exists. In West Java the Darul Islam forces still make sporadic raids, in East Java some Communists and other dissidents are active; and in Sumatra there is much labor unrest and, at present, an epidemic of serious strikes. One of the serious threats to law and order is actually the Indonesian Army (TNI) itself. Men in uniform exact tribute in various communities, and a kind of personal banditry obtains. Demobilized soldiers, both now and in the future, are an even more serious threat, for they are not at all inclined to turn in their arms and take up peaceful, but dull, pursuits. Moreover, the active smuggling trade in Sumatra and Riow may eventuate in police activities uncongenial to technical assistance operations. Lack of security thus still limits somewhat the extension of aid to Indonesia.

Finally, the difficult budgetary situation of the Government, already burdened by a large annual deficit, will be a barrier to development projects or technical aid projects that require any financial contribution at all from the Indonesian Government, or even the participation of personnel in technical government bureaus (already greatly understaffed). Utilization of ECA counterpart funds, or counterpart funds derived from new supplies, may obviate the need for governmental financial contribution; but it must be recognized that participation by governmental personnel will be likely to slow up, not speed up, operations, as these personnel are already overworked.

VIII. Considerations Affecting Aid Administration

Although the Indonesian leaders still lean on many of their Dutch advisers and recognize the great value of Dutch technicians who really have the interests of the country at heart, it is apparent that they want to be able to get technical assistance and advice from other sources too. This reflects their natural desire to pursue an independent course, as well as their doubts about the disinterested nature of some of the advice they have been receiving.

For this reason, American aid should, so far as possible, be dissociated from the influence of Dutch personnel. Plans and project agreements should be worked out directly with Indonesians. Training programs and research projects should be carried on in fields or in localities where they involve few, if any, Dutch advisers. The Indonesians have difficulty making their own decisions, and the Dutch tend to jump in and suggest the proper decision for them; far better to let the Indonesians make some mistakes and acquire self-confidence through joint participation with non-Dutch technicians. Proposals to finance Dutch technicians through U.N. or U.S. technical assistance programs should probably be rejected, in order to give the Indonesians a wider range of sources of advice, providing them with alternative advisers who would keep each other on their toes, and making it difficult for any ulterior motives to influence advice without being quite apparent.

The Indonesian suspicion of the motives of the Dutch has a tendency to generalize itself into a suspicion of the motives of all Western countries. For this reason, a special effort should be made to get the U.N. and its specialized agencies to undertake as many operating technical programs as they can carry on effectively. This would bring into play technical skills from many countries and would provide a source of advice that should be as objective as any could be.

Even in strictly U.S.-aided programs, special attention should be given to avoiding any appearance of ulterior interest. In some cases, this may even mean refusing aid to a particular project, just because such aid could easily be misinterpreted. (Misinterpretations will undoubtedly easily arise anyway and will certainly be made by Communists, and probably even by some of the enthusiastic nationalists in the country.)

Moreover, the extent of control exercised by the United States in any joint activities should be minimized for the same reason. The Indonesians will resent what appears to be, at the best, a continuing paternalism and at the worst a self-interested domination. Some loss in efficiency would be a small price to pay for avoidance of this source of friction.

As Jogjakarta is the center of the most potent political force in the country, special attention should be given to projects that will be of particular interest to the leaders of the Republic there and that bring in the personnel of the technical government departments there as participants in joint operations.

In view of the thinness of the technically trained layer of Indonesians in all government departments, a special effort should be made to find semigovernmental or private organizations that would provide Indonesian participation in joint technical cooperation activities. In such cases detailed project agreements would be made with the Government, specifying the activities, areas, and other elements involved in the joint endeavor. This would bring into play a much wider range of Indonesian technical personnel.

While personal security and governmental authority remain somewhat uncertain, emphasis should be given to those activities likely to strengthen the Government's efforts directly. Projects likely to help in this way include improved food production, importation of consumer goods (especially textiles), supply of drugs, medical equipment and health services, improved transportation and radio communications, and provision of small farm tools.

IX. Public Information Support for the Program

The aims of U.S. economic aid to Indonesia are really four:

1. To help relieve inflationary pressures;
2. To aid rehabilitation and development of social services, agriculture, industry and transportation;
3. To strengthen the popularity of government leaders who are already anti-Communist and at least tolerant toward Western interests and ideals;
4. To demonstrate U.S. interest in the welfare of Indonesia, to counter both the possible pull of communism and the already apparent suspicion of the West.

In a country as large and as economically disrupted as Indonesia, the United States can do only a little toward the first two aims without expending much more money than seems feasible. Even if the money were available, certain limitations inherent in the situation would prevent its rapid expenditure, as pointed out in Section VIII, above.

On the other hand, effective public information support for U.S. aid activities can create, even with the relatively small expenditures that are feasible, an important impact on the latter two aims. An expanded United States Information Service program in Indonesia should be one of the first activities undertaken, in order to describe among other things the objectives and forms of U.S. aid, the process of joint planning of aid, the plans agreed upon, the beginning of operations, their progress, and their results. In a country such as Indonesia, where relatively little money can be spent quickly (except by taking over a balance-of-payments responsibility or the responsibility for providing social services on a large scale), the cost of the public relations program needed may appear to be disproportionate to the actual cost of the aid furnished. Where there is an important political objective, however, as in this case, such expenditures are clearly justifiable in terms of the political advantage derived for the funds expended.

This is especially important where exaggerated hopes have already been aroused. Many Indonesians had naively thought that independence would bring them quickly an easier life and a higher standard of living. Now that this has not happened, there will be a tendency to expect that "American aid" will achieve for them what independence failed to achieve. The problem of gently deflating these hopes without losing friends is a big one, and deserves adequate financial support.

X. Field Organization for Administration of Economic Aid Programs in Indonesia

The recommendations made for economic and technical aid to Indonesia stress the provision of key commodities and equipment and the training of technicians in the United States. Because there are many highly competent Dutch technicians already in Indonesia, some of them the best in the world, and because there are comparatively few Indonesian technicians to work with additional American technicians in the field, only relatively few U.S. technicians are proposed, except in connection with particular projects for which U.S. equipment and supplies would be provided.

All aid projects should be covered by detailed agreements negotiated in advance, in which the functions and responsibilities of the American technicians involved would be clearly defined. Therefore, the load of administrative work in the field entailed by this program would primarily be:

1. Negotiating detailed project agreements (and their renewal) covering each kind of aid activity, and discussing general questions concerning the program which are raised by the Foreign Minister with the U.S. diplomatic mission;
2. Representing the U.S. Government on any joint policy-determining board or any joint commissions that may be set up;
3. Liaison with private U.S. groups employed by the Indonesian Government under contracts financed by the United States;
4. Liaison with U.N. or other non-U.S. agencies supplying economic or technical aid to Indonesia;
5. Distribution of U.S.-supplied commodities or equipment not consigned directly to an agency of the Indonesian Government, and end-use inspection and reports on all U.S.-supplied commodities or equipment;
6. Determination of U.S. recommendations on utilization of local counterpart funds available for use in connection with the program;
7. Processing trainees selected by groups made responsible under each project agreement;
8. Continuing inspection, general supervision, and appraisal of success of various programs and performance of individual technicians, and taking steps to improve their functioning, where considered necessary, by renegotiating project agreements, having personnel shifted or replaced, recommending changes in program of aid supplies or equipment, etc. This function includes terminating programs that do not appear to be contributing fully to mutually agreed objectives, or to U.S. political objectives;
9. Providing administrative services for U.S. technicians in the field (payroll, housing assistance, employment of alien personnel, office space and services, travel, etc.);

These functions indicate the need for a small economic mission attached to the American Embassy, to comprise two or three top personnel capable of general direction of the Mission; a somewhat larger number of mature technicians who, with the top personnel, would perform functions 1, 2, 3, 4, 6, and 8; an accounting, distribution, and reporting group to perform function 5; and administrative personnel (perhaps merged with those of the Embassy in a Joint Administrative Staff) to perform function 9. Function 7 could and probably should be performed by expanding the USIS staff that will presumably soon be carrying out this same function for persons exchanged under the Fulbright Act and the Smith-Mundt Act.

The group performing the above functions, other than 7, should be headed by a single Coordinator of Economic Cooperation Activities (CECA). It is the view of the present U.S. Ambassador to Indonesia that present political and economic conditions are both so delicate and so interrelated in Indonesia that there should be the closest working together of the diplomatic mission and the economic aid mission. For this reason, it is recommended that CECA be made directly responsible to the chief of the U.S. diplomatic mission in Indonesia. This would insure integration of all U.S. economic and technical aid activities, under whatever law (including ECA, section 303 of MDAP, Smith-Mundt, Fulbright, and Point Four) and would also insure conformity of all economic and technical aid activities with U.S. political policy in the area.

The question of establishing a joint policy-determining body to consider over-all objectives and means of aiding economic development in Indonesia was not discussed with government officials, partly because objective and competent advice of this sort would presumably be available from the private engineering group whose contract with the Indonesian Government it was recommended that the United States finance (see Section VI, D5 above), and partly because of anticipated touchiness of Indonesian leaders about any arrangement that might be interpreted as re-establishing some measure of foreign control (see Section VIII above). Certain reforms, such as those undertaken by the JCRR in China, would not be necessary in Indonesia, where they are already in progress and require only additional aid. Land tenure reform efforts in Indonesia by outsiders would almost certainly be opposed at this time; agriculture extension work is well developed, as is rural medical service (both lack adequate funds, personnel and equipment); and a good deal of work in education at the literacy level is already being carried on. It is likely that the audio-visual techniques used by the JCRR could be adapted with benefit to Indonesian conditions, but this could be done by attaching advisers (with some funds) to existing government services.

On the other hand, it may be advisable to establish joint commissions in specialized fields (such as rural health service, or farm tool distribution), to take title to certain equipment and perhaps distribute certain commodities and handle the proceeds thereof. One or more representatives of CECA should sit on each such joint commission.

U.S. technicians made available to the Indonesian Government should be responsible to the appropriate Indonesian Government department or bureau, or to a Joint U.S.-Indonesian commission, for carrying out the tasks agreed in the applicable project agreement. Direction of their work while in the country should come therefore from these authorities. Technical backstopping and advice would, of course, be available to them from the departments or organizations in the United States from which they were assigned. General supervision and appraisal of their performance on these agreed tasks should be the responsibility of CECA and his staff, who should have authority to recall them should their performance prove unsatisfactory on either technical or personal grounds.

Appendix

1. The Mission arrived in Djakarta at 2:30 p.m., April 12 and remained in Indonesia until 4:00 a.m., April 22, 1950.
2. During the visit of the Mission to Indonesia it was comprised of the following persons:

Department of State

> The Honorable R. Allen Griffin, Chief of Mission, with the personal rank of Minister
> Samuel P. Hayes, Jr., Deputy Chief of Mission and Adviser
> Henry Tarring, Jr., J.G. White Engineering Co., Consultant to the Department of State, Adviser
> William McAfee, Adviser
> Eleanor L. Koontz, Secretary
> Mary D. Randolph, Secretary

Department of Agriculture

> Ross E. Moore, Adviser

Department of Treasury

> Alexander Lipsman, (April 12-April 20), Adviser

Public Health Service

> Howard M. Kline, Adviser

3. Members of the Mission, during the visit to Indonesia, participated in the following formal conferences:

a) Orientation Conference with the American Ambassador, April 12.
b) Conference with IR. Sukarno, President of the Republic of the United States of Indonesia, April 13.
c) Conference with Dr. Mohammed Hatta, Premier of the Republic of the United States of Indonesia, April 13.
d) Conference with Dr. Herling Laoh, Minister of Communications, Power and Public Works; and Dr. Raden Djuanda, Minister of Economic Affairs, April 13.

e) Joint Conference with representatives of various ministries of the Government of the R.U.S.I., April 14. This was followed by conferences of the following groups:
   (1) Working Group on Agriculture
   (2) Working Group on Transport, Industry and Mining
   (3) Working Group on Public Health
   (4) Working Group on Education
   (5) Working Group on Finance
   (6) Working Group on Point Four

f) Conference with representatives of the Faculty of Sciences, University of Indonesia, Bandung, April 15.
g) Conference with representatives of the Faculty of Technical Sciences, University of Indonesia, Bandung, April 15.
h) Conference with the Premier toward end of the Mission's visit.
i) Numerous working level conferences between appropriate United States and Indonesian representatives.

4. The following is a partial list of the persons consulted during the visit of the Mission to Indonesia (names within groups are not necessarily in order of rank):

American Embassy

   The Honorable H. Merle Cochran, Ambassador
   Jacob D. Beam, Counselor of Embassy
   Arthur J. Campbell
   Joseph W. Wander Laan
   Duncan Campbell
   Robert W. Rinden
   Charles T. Gross
   Francis J. Galbraith
   N. Paul Neilson
   Gilbert L. Newbold

Officials of the Republic of the United States of Indonesia

   H.E. President Sukarno
   H.E. Dr. Mohd Hatta, Premier and Minister for Foreign Affairs
   H.E. Anak Agung Gde Agung, Minister for Internal Affairs
   H.E. Dr. Sjafruddin Prawiranegara, Minister of Finance
   H.H. Sultan Hamengku Buwono IX, Minister of Defense
   H.E. Dr. Raden Djuanda, Minister of Welfare

H.E. Dr. Herling Laoh, Minister of Communications, Power and Public Works
H.E. Dr. Johannes Leimena, Minister for Health
H.E. Dr. Supomo, Minister for Justice
H.E. Dr. Abu Hanifah, Minister for Education
H.E. Dr. Wilopo, Minister for Labor
Dr. Saubari, Sec. Gen., Ministry of Finance
Dr. Teko Sumodiwirjo, Sec. Gen., Ministry of Welfare
Dr. Sutoto, Sec. Gen., Ministry of Communications, Power and Public Works
Dr. Sumitro Reksodiputro, Sec. Gen., Ministry of Education
Dr. Surono, Sec. Gen., Ministry of Health
Dr. Sutikno, Sec. Gen., Ministry of Labor Affairs
Dr. Icksan, Sec. Gen., Ministry of Foreign Affairs
Dr. Darmawan Mangunkusumo, Director Gen., Industry, Mining and Trade
Dr. Hermen Kartowisastro, Director Gen., Agriculture and Fisheries
Dr. Abdul Karim, Director of the State Bank
Mr. E.T. Kuiper, Vice-Chairman, Institute for Foreign Exchange
Dr. Sudjono, Chief, Pol. Dept. of the Ministry of Foreign Affairs
Dr. Surachman Tjokroadisurjo, President Curator of the Indonesian Universities
Dr. E.A. Kreikan, Official of the Ministry of Education
IR. Indratjahja, Official of the Ministry of Communications, Power and Public Works
Dr. J. van der Ploeg, Advisor Gen. for Agriculture and Fisheries
Dr. W. ten Hove, Dr. J.P. van Aartsen, Bureau for Agro-Economic and Agro-Political Studies
Dr. Susilo, Chief, Service of Forestry
Dr. J. Fokkinga, Adviser, Service of Forestry
Dr. Kaslan A. Tohir, Chief, Service of General Agriculture
Dr. J.H.L. Joosten, Chief, Agricultural Extension Service
Dr. C. van der Giessen, Adviser, Gen. Research Station for Agriculture
Dr. J. van der Vecht, Chief, Institute for Plant Diseases
Dr. F. Wawo Runtu, Chief, Civil Veterinary Service
Dr. R. Sutisno, Chief, Gen. Inst. for Livestock Breeding
Dr. K.N. Reuter, Representative, Service of Sea Fisheries
Dr. Kusnoto, Director, Royal Botanical Gardens
Dr. J. van Slooten, Adviser, Royal Botanical Gardens
Dr. van Raalte, Chief, Botanical Laboratory (Treub Laboratory)
Dr. C. van Steenis, Editor of "Flora Malesiana."
Dr. M.A.A.M. Wirtz, Adviser to Provincial Agricultural Extension Service for Western Java at Bandung
Prof. Dr. C.J. Jaski, Dean of Faculty for Veterinary Science, University of Indonesia, Bogor
Prof. Dr. H.J. de Boer, Dean of Faculty for Agriculture, Univ. of Indonesia, Bogor

Dr. M. van Bottenburg, Sub-Chief, Service of Forestry
Mr. Suradibrata, Director, Industrial Department
Dr. W. van Warmelo, Adviser, Industrial Department
Dr. G.J.H. Davis, Staff Officer, Industrial Dept.
Dr. H.J. van Oorschot, Officer, Industrial Department
Dr. Saroso, Director, Trade Department
Dr. Ismail Thajeb, Chief, Central Import Office
Dr. P. Creutzberg, Staff Officer for Econ. Affairs
Mr. J. Ph. Andel, Staff Officer for Press and Pub. Relations
Jhr. Dr. E.R.D. Elias, Officer for Economic Affairs
Dr. D. Groenweld, Director Economic Planning Dept.
Dr. C. van Der Straaton, Officer in Planning Department
Mrs. E.F. Sluimen, Secretary in Planning Department
Mr. Akkersdijk, Ministry of Economic Affairs
Dr. Leeman, Dean, Faculty of Science, Univ. of Indonesia, Bandung
Dr. Posthumus, Dean, Faculty Technical Sciences, University of Indonesia, Bandung
Dr. Broersma, Prof. of Mathematics, University of Indonesia
Mr. Sundaro, Inspector of Primary Schools
Mr. H.P. Berlage, Meteorological and Geographical Service
Mr. P.C. Binkhorst, Railways
Mr. N. Guldenaar, Harbors
Mr. Ament, Civil Aviation
Mr. Meesters, Department of Public Works

Netherlands Officials

Dr. H. Hirschfeld, High Commissioner
Mr. Swaan
Mr. O. Hong Djie, Telecommunications

5. The following documents were submitted to the Mission during its visit to Indonesia:

General

1. History and Political Structure of Indonesia—March 4, 1950.
2. The Economic Structure of Indonesia (Transmitted with letter of April 12 from Dr. Djuanda.).
3. Brief Outline of Development Projects (Transmitted with letter of April 12 from Dr. Djuanda.).
4. Schematic Surveys of the Organization of the Ministries of: Internal Affairs; Traffic; Economic Affairs; Health; Finance (Administration); and Foreign Affairs (Provisional Organization).

5. Memorandum of April 13—Extract from a letter from the Head of the Ceramic Institute of Bandung.
6. Economic and Financial Survey of Indonesia, April 2, 1948.
7. Letter of April 19, 1950 from Dr. Djuanda to Mr. Griffin enclosing the following studies:

a) Proposal concerning the needs of the agricultural sector;
b) Requirements in the fields of agriculture, fisheries and forestry;
c) Project for the acceleration of the restoration of the productive capacity of the economy of Indonesia;
d) Table—Industrial Department.

8. Some Proposals on the Point Four Program.
9. Memorandum of March 29, 1950—Vacancies at Scientific Institutes.
10. Memorandum of March 29—Study Abroad.
11. Memorandum of March 29—Scientific Apparatus for the Laboratory for Testing Materials.
12. Memorandum of March 28—Scientific Apparatus for the Laboratory for the Investigation of the Sea, at Pasar Ikan, Djakarta.

Agriculture

1. Export-Import Bank Projects—Development of Foodstuffs.
2. Export-Import Bank Projects—Estate agriculture.
3. Memorandum March 31, 1950—Reforestation.

Industry, Communications

1. Memorandum, February 1, 1950 from Dr. Djuanda covering Export-Import projects.
2. Export-Import Bank Projects—Automotive Transportation.
3. Export-Import Bank Projects—Road Building Equipment for Repairs and Rehabilitation of Present Network and Eventual Construction of New Hard-Surface Roads.
4. Export-Import Bank Project—Railways.
5. Export-Import Project—Inter-Island Air Transport Project.
6. Export-Import Bank Project—Shipping.
7. Export-Import Bank Project—Harbors.
8. Export-Import Bank Project—Industrialization Projects.
9. Export-Import Bank Project—Development Project for the Western Part of Java.
10. Export-Import Bank Project—Electric Power Supply and Irrigation.
    a) Export-Import Bank Project—Telecommunications Equipment.

b) Export-Import Bank Project—Memorandum concerning the estimate of the motor vehicles required for the year, 1950.

11. Ministry of Communications, Power and Public Works Emergency Project, Harbors.
12. A Federal Development Project for the Western Part of Java prepared by Prof. Dr. IR W.J. Von Blommestein.
13. Scientific Apparatus for the Laboratory for Testing Materials, March 29, 1950.
14. Description of the Observatory—J. Voute.
15. Letter of April 21, 1950 from Dr. Hatta to Mr. Griffin on Public Works and Transportation.
16. Mining Department of Indonesia—Geological Survey—Note for Mr. Hayes and Mr. Tarring.
17. EximBank Project—Four year proposal (in Dutch) No. PH 212.
18. Building Program of Central Reconstruction Foundation.
19. Want-list of tools and equipment for road-rehabilitation in Indonesia.
20. Want-list of Bridge-Deck Beams, etc., for Public Works in Indonesia.
21. Proposals from Division of Irrigation and Sanitation with regard to technical aid and assistance.
22. Ministry of Communications, Power and Public Works—Civil Aviation.
23. Ministry of Communications, Power and Public Works—Motor Transport.
24. Commission for the Rehabilitation of the D.K.A.
25. Ministry of Communications, Power and Public Works; Memorandum of Department of Shipping.
26. Emergency Plan Rehabilitation Railways.
27. Ministry of Communications, Power and Public Works, Emergency Transport Program.
28. Meteorological and Geophysical Service—Memorandum for ECA-Commission—April 18, 1950.

Public Health

1. Memorandum April 11—Short Survey—The Ministry of Health.

Documents on the following subjects were also submitted. These documents are on file with the U.S. Public Health Service only.

2. Hygiene Education
3. Chemicals for bacteriology
4. Smallpox Institute and Pasteur Institute
5. Eykman Institute
6. Blood transfusion service
7. Tuberculosis
8. Dental service

9. Anti-leprosy activities
10. Sanitary engineering
11. Nutrition
12. Malaria control
13. Hospitals
14. Pharmaceutical service
15. Quarantine service

Education

1. Outline of Activity and Composition of the Ministry of Education, Instruction and Culture of the USI.
2. Memorandum from Ministry of Education, Instruction and Culture on the Education System in Indonesia and the Organization of the Federal University. Attached as annexes were the following documents indicating educational needs of Indonesia:

a) Instruments Needed by the Various Faculties of the University (Filed with U.S. Public Health Service)
b) Chemicals Needed by the Various Faculties (Filed with U.S. Public Health Service)
c) Books Needed by the Faculties of the University of Indonesia
d) Materials Wanted for Primary Schools
e) Materials for High Schools

3. Facts on University of Indonesia and its Needs.
4. Memorandum—Number of Students at University of Indonesia—April 1950.
5. Figures on Faculty of Science, University of Indonesia.
6. A New System of Education for Indonesia.
7. Letter of April 15, 1950, on the Fulbright Act.
8. During the visit to Indonesia the Mission took a two-day trip to Bandung, stopping at Bogor en route for visits to the General Agriculture Experiment Station, the Botanical Gardens, and the Veterinary Institute. In Bandung other visits were made to the various faculties of the University of Indonesia located there, to the Lembang Observatory, and to a Hydroelectric Plant. This trip afforded an excellent opportunity to view a cross section of Java, to observe agricultural methods and health conditions, and to visit schools outside the Djakarta area.

Abbreviations and Glossary of Terms

Act for International Development. The legislation authorizing President Truman's "Point Four Program"; Title IV of the Foreign Economic Assistance Act of 1950, Public Law 535, 81st Congress, 2d Session, June 5, 1950.

AFPFL. The Anti-Fascist People's Freedom League, the dominant political party in Burma in 1950.

Bao Dai. Formerly the Emperor of Annam, recognized by France as the Chief of State of Vietnam in the March 8, 1949 agreements in which, among other provisions, Annam, Tonkin and Cochinchina were unified as an "associated state within the French Union."

Bell Mission. U.S. Economic Survey Mission sent to the Philippines in July, 1950, headed by Daniel W. Bell, former Undersecretary of the Treasury.

CIA. Central Intelligence Agency of the United States, the principal government agency engaged in espionage, analysis of intelligence, and covert operations abroad.

Colombo Plan. A cooperative plan for technical and financial assistance to the countries of South and Southeast Asia in which member nations of the British Commonwealth (and now other nations) provide assistance bilaterally to various countries and coordinate their aid programming through a central secretariat in Colombo, Ceylon. Originally proposed by Australian Foreign Minister Percy Spender, the plan was agreed upon on May 17, 1950, at a Commonwealth Conference in Sydney, Australia, and was established at a conference held in October at Colombo.

Commonwealth Aid Plan. Also referred to as the Spender Plan. Early name for the Colombo Plan, which see above.

China Aid Act. The 1948 legislation authorizing a major program of economic aid to China; Title IV of the Foreign Assistance Act of 1948, Public Law 472, 80th Congress, 2d Session, April 3, 1948.

Dacoits, dacoitry. Bandits, banditry (Burma).

ECA. Economic Cooperation Administration, the U.S. agency authorized by the Economic Cooperation Act of 1948 to administer the European Recovery Program (Marshall Plan) and also economic assistance to China and Korea.

Economic Cooperation Act of 1948. The legislation authorizing the European Recovery Program (Marshall Plan); Title I of the Foreign Assistance Act of 1948, Public Law 472, 80th Congress, 2d Session, April 3, 1948.

ERP. European Recovery Program (Marshall Plan).

European Recovery Program. The program of U.S. economic aid to Western Europe (and dependent overseas territories) carried on in 1948-1952; often referred to as the Marshall Plan, after Secretary of State George C. Marshall, who first proposed the program in a speech at Harvard University in June, 1947.

European Productivity Program. A program of technical assistance to European industry, designed to help raise industrial productivity there by acquainting Europeans with the technological advances made in the United States, much of which had occurred during World War II.

Fulbright Program. A program of international educational exchange proposed by Senator J. William Fulbright and authorized by Public Law 584 (79th Congress, 2d Session, August 1, 1946), under which local currencies paid by foreign governments for surplus American military supplies left in their countries at the end of World War II could be used to finance educational exchanges. Subsequently Fulbright grants (in local currencies) were supplemented by dollar grants authorized by the Smith-Mundt Act or by Point Four.

Godowns. Warehouses.

Griffin Mission. U.S. Economic Survey Mission to Southeast Asia, which during March and April, 1950, visited Indochina, Malaya and Singapore, Burma, Thailand and Indonesia and recommended the initiation of U.S. technical and economic assistance to those countries.

JCRR. Joint Commission on Rural Reconstruction, a Chinese-American joint body that administered cooperative programs of agricultural reform and development in mainland China in 1948 and 1949 and thereafter on Formosa. U.S. participation was specifically authorized by the China Aid Act of 1948, and its work was made possible by economic aid from the United States.

Joint Commission on Rural Reconstruction. See JCRR.

March 8 Agreements. A series of agreements between France and Bao Dai (for Vietnam), Cambodia and Laos, under which the three Indochinese States were recognized as "associated states within the French Union" with full internal sovereignty and limited diplomatic representation. See "The Current Political Situation" section of Report No. 1, pages 63-64.

MAAG. Military Assistance Advisory Group. The military aid missions set up in most countries receiving military aid under MDAP and later under MSP.

Marshall Plan. See European Recovery Program, above.

MDAA. Mutual Defense Assistance Act of 1949. The legislation authorizing military assistance primarily to NATO allies, but also authorizing in Section 303 that $75,000,000 be used in the "general area" of China. Public Law 329, 81st Congress, 1st Session, October 6, 1949.

MDAP. Mutual Defense Assistance Program. The military assistance program authorized by the Mutual Defense Assistance Act of 1949 (See MDAA).

Melby Mission. U.S. Military Survey Mission sent to Southeast Asia in July, 1950, shortly after the outbreak of the Korean War. It was a joint mission, under the direction of John Melby, of the State Department, Major General Graves Erskine, of the Department of Defense, and Glenn Craig, of the Economic Cooperation Administration.

Military Assistance Advisory Group. See MAAG.

MSA. Mutual Security Agency, the agency which succeeded ECA on January 1, 1952, as the administering agency for economic and technical aid to ERP countries and their dependent overseas territories, to Formosa and to Southeast Asia (and later to Korea).

MSP. Mutual Security Program. The total program of military, technical and economic aid authorized by the Mutual Security Act of 1951 (Public Law 165, 82nd Congress, 1st Session, October 10, 1951). The Act established a Director for Mutual Security, who was responsible for coordinating and supervising the military aid program carried on by the Department of Defense, and the technical and economic aid programs carried on by the Technical Cooperation Administration (within the Department of State) and the Mutual Security Agency (successor to the Economic Cooperation Administration).

Mutual Defense Assistance Program. See MDAP.

Mutual Security Program. See MSP.

NATO. North Atlantic Treaty Organization, the military alliance of the United States, Canada, and 10 Western European nations, established under the

North Atlantic Treaty, which was signed on April 4 and came into force on August 24, 1949.

OEEC. Organization for European Economic Cooperation. The organization of nations participating in the European Recovery Program through which they reviewed each other's economic and fiscal policies and developed coordinated estimates of needs for economic aid.

Point Four. U.S. program of international technical cooperation for economic and social development, authorized by the Act for International Development (June 5, 1950). First proposed by President Truman in his inaugural address of January 20, 1949.

POL. Petroleum, oil, lubricants.

Public Law 165. Mutual Security Act of 1951. See MSP, above.

Public Law 329. Mutual Defense Assistance Act of 1949. See MDAA, above.

Public Law 402. U.S. Information and Educational Exchange Act of 1948. See Smith-Mundt Act, below.

Public Law 472. Foreign Assistance Act of 1948. Title I was the Economic Cooperation Act of 1948; Title IV was the China Aid Act of 1948.

Public Law 535. Foreign Economic Assistance Act of 1950. Title II was the China Area Aid Act of 1950; Title IV was the Act for International Development.

RI. Republic of Indonesia. The unitary state that on August 17, 1950, succeeded the federated Republic of the United States of Indonesia. See RUSI.

RUSI. Republic of the United States of Indonesia, the federated state established by the Hague agreement between the Netherlands and Indonesia, whereby Indonesian independence within the Netherlands-Indonesian Union was achieved on December 27, 1949.

SAMB. State Agricultural Marketing Board in Burma.

SCAP. Supreme Commander of Allied Forces in the Pacific. The designation in 1950 for General MacArthur's headquarters in Japan.

Smith-Mundt Act. United States Information and Educational Exchange Act of 1948 (Public Law 402, 80th Congress, 2d Session, January 27, 1948).

Authorized a program of educational exchange that replaced and broadened the Fulbright Program (which see) but the term "Fulbright grant" continued in popular usage.

SOBSI. The central federation of labor unions in Indonesia.

Spender Plan. See Colombo Plan, above.

STEM. Special Technical and Economic Mission established by the United States in each country in Southeast Asia where it carried on a program of technical and economic aid.

Sydney Conference. See Colombo Plan, above.

TCA. Technical Cooperation Administration, the organization established by and within the Department of State in 1950 to administer the Point Four Program of technical assistance to underdeveloped nations, under the Act for International Development.

Technical Cooperation Administration. See TCA, above.

UMNO. United Malays National Organization, the dominant political organization in Malaya in 1950.

UNICEF. United Nations International Children's Emergency Fund, now the United Nations Children's Fund. A specialized agency of the United Nations which, with governmental and private funds, provides clothing, diet supplements (e.g., dried milk), and medical and health supplies for the relief and care of children in low income countries.

United States Information Service. See USIS, below.

USIS. United States Information Service, the overseas staff of the United States Information Agency, responsible for most public information, public relations and educational and cultural relations activities (including Fulbright and Smith-Mundt exchange of persons programs) abroad. USIS personnel function as staff of the diplomatic missions.

Notes

Notes to Chapter 1

1. U.S. Congress, Senate Foreign Relations Committee, *Hearings on Extension of European Recovery—1950*, 81st Cong., 2d sess., 1950, p. 359.

Notes to Chapter 2

1. Cf. William L. Holland, ed., *Asian Nationalism and the West* (New York: Macmillan, 1953).

2. *Economic Survey of Burma* (Rangoon: Ministry of Finance, 1951). Also see U Tun Wai, "Burma," Chapter 1 in *Asian Economic Development*, ed. Cranley Onslow (New York: Praeger, 1965).

3. John Paul Meek, *The Government and Economic Development of Indonesia*, 1950–1954, Doctoral Dissertation Series, Publication No. 17,622 (Ann Arbor, Mich.: University Microfilms, 1956).

4. Charles Wolf, Jr., *Foreign Aid: Theory and Practice in Southeast Asia* (Princeton: Princeton University Press, 1960), p. 83.

Notes to Chapter 3

1. U.S., *Public Law 911*, 81 Cong., 2d sess., January 6, 1951.

2. *U.S. Foreign Assistance: Obligations and Commitments, July 1, 1945-June 30, 1960* (Washington, D.C.: International Cooperation Administration, March 31, 1961.)

Notes to Chapter 9

1. J. Russell Andrus, *Burmese Economic Life* (Stanford, California: Stanford University Press, 1948), p. 44.

2. *Ibid.*, Table 23, p. 164.

3. *Ibid.*, Table 18, p. 119.

4. *Economic Survey of Burma, 1951*, presented in Parliament by the Hon. Minister for Finance and Revenue—Table III, p. 3.

5. Hugh Tinker, *The Union of Burma*, fourth edition (London, New York: Oxford University Press, 1967), p. 17.

6. *Ibid.*, p. 16.

7. *Ibid.*, p. 16.

8. *Ibid.*, p. 16.

9. *Ibid.*, p. 18.

334

10. *Ibid.*, p. 17.

11. *Ibid.*, p. 19. But there is difference of view in respect of the number of seats offered. Tinker states that the League demanded eleven seats out of a council of fifteen but that the Governor offered seven. Maurice Collis states in his *Last and First in Burma* (Faber and Faber, London, 1956, p. 257) that it was the League which demanded seven seats out of eleven, that the Governor would have accepted the demand but that the British Government in London was opposed.

12. *Ibid.*,p. 21.

13. See the Griffin Mission Report on Burma, p. 154, above.

14. *The Foreign Commerce Weekly*, dated June 26, 1950.

15. *The London Times*, dated July 11, 1950.

16. Robert A. Scalapino, ed., *The Communist Revolution in Asia* (Englewood Cliffs, New Jersey: Prentice Hall, Inc., 1965), p. 295.

17. *Ibid.*, p. 295.

18. Dorothy Woodman, *The Making of Burma* (London: The Cresset Press, 1962), chapter XIX.

19. *Ibid.*, p. 527.

20. Maung Maung, ed. and comp., *Aung San of Burma*, (New Haven: Yale University Press, 1962), pp. 133-4.

21. Louis J. Walinsky, *Economic Development in Burma, 1951-1960* (New York: Twentieth Century Fund, 1962 p. 83.)

22. See the Griffin Mission Report on Burma, p. 151, above.

23. *United States Economic Cooperation Programs*, issued by the Agency for International Development, November 1967, p. 1.

24. *New York Times*, dated May 3, 1950.

25. *United States Economic Cooperation Programs*, issued by the A.I.D., November 1967, p. 1.

26. *Ibid.*, pp. 2-6.

27. *Summary Records of Meetings of the First Committee of the General Assembly*, 16 September to December 1953, forming part of the official Records of the General Assembly, Eighth Session.

28. David Wise and Thomas B. Ross, *The Invisible Government* (New York: Random House, Inc., 1964), chapter 7.

29. *Ibid.*, p. 131.

30. *United States Economic Cooperation Programs* issued by the A.I.D., November 1967, p. 13.

About the Contributors

Dinh Quang Chieu is a mechanical and electrical engineer, who received his professional degrees (ECP and ESE) from the University of Paris. He was an official of the Vietnamese Government at the time of the Griffin Mission's visit to Vietnam, and was consulted by the Mission at that time. From 1952 to 1957 he served the Vietnamese Government as Administrator of United States of America Aid to Vietnam. He is now a consulting engineer with the American Trading Company of Saigon.

Samuel P. Hayes is an economist and educator. He received his A.B. from Amherst College in 1931, and his Ph.D. from Yale University in 1934. He has taught at Mt. Holyoke College, Sarah Lawrence College and the University of Michigan, where he was also director of the Center for Research on Economic Development. He has served for ten years in the United States Government, mainly in the State Department and foreign aid agencies, in North Africa, Europe and Indonesia, as well as in Washington, D.C. He was deputy chief of the Griffin Mission and subsequently chief of the United States Special Economic and Technical Mission to Indonesia, and then Assistant Director of the Mutual Security Agency, in charge of Far East programs. He has been president of the Foreign Policy Association since 1962, and is the author of many articles on economics, statistics and foreign aid, as well as *An International Peace Corps* (Public Affairs Institute, 1961) and *Evaluating Development Projects* (UNESCO, 1966).

Hla Maung is a career government official, who received his B.A. from the University of Rangoon, and studied further at Oxford University. He joined the Indian Civil Service in 1935, serving in Burma. From 1948 to 1958, he was in the Burmese Civil Service, and was Secretary of the Ministry of Finance and Revenue at the time of the Griffin Mission's visit to Burma. In this capacity, he was a principal point of contact for the Mission, coordinating many of the Burmese reports and requests. As Secretary of the Ministry of National Planning until 1953, he had charge of all technical assistance activities in Burma. In 1955, he became Burmese Ambassador to Yugoslavia and Minister Plenipotentiary to Italy. In 1961, he joined the United Nations Development Program, and served as the UNDP Resident Representative first in Iraq and later in Libya. He is now retired and living in Rangoon. He is the author of *Development Administration in the Developing Countries* (in manuscript).

Léon Pignon earned his law degree from the French École Coloniale. Most of his career was spent in the French colonial administration, mainly in Indochina. He was High Commissioner in Indochina from 1948 to 1950 and held that position at the time of the Griffin Mission's visit there. He was the French delegate to the United Nations Trusteeship Council, 1950-1954; and Director of Political Affairs, Ministry of French Overseas Territories, 1954-1959. Since 1962, he has been Counsellor of State in the French Government.